ANDREY,

lappa_andrey@hotmail.com

Cell Phone:
(380)-044-203-88-01

www.yoga.com.ua/lappa

Andrew Lappa

YOGA

TRADITION OF UNIFICATION

To Lesly
from autor.
A. Lappa
22.05.2000

KYIV 2000

Russian text editor A. Kostenko
English translation A. Molotay
English text editor M. Pollard
Corrector A. McAllen
Book layout by V. Virich
Pictures by A. Lappa

K.: 2000 — 398 p.

ISBN 5-220-00214-7

Having an extremely modern spirit and content, this book represents Yoga in its truly traditional understanding — as the Pathway to Unification. According to its definition yoga must cover all spheres of a human being — spiritual, psychic and physical. Unfortunately, some aspects of this Tradition have not been sufficiently spread throughout the world. In particular, an enormous layer of dynamic practices, of which popular manuals, at most, contain a single set of Surya Namaskar, fell out of Hatha Yoga.

On the basis of the teaching of all the world-known masters of Yoga: Khrishnamacharya, Pattabhi Joice and B.K.S. Iyengar as well as his own many years of practical experience of yoga, Andrew Lappa intends to describe all yoga Vinyasas (motion and breathing exercises) as well as a number of out-of-the-way Yoga practices — in particular, the mysterious Dance of Shiva. But the results appeared to be something far and away bigger, i. e., complete classification of all possible elements of physical, breathing and psychic yoga exercises and a universal algorithm for compiling individual training programs therefrom. Thus going beyond a simple «book about Yoga» this profound work will be useful to all practitioners of Yoga and martial arts.

ISBN 5-220-00214-7

CONTENTS

Part IV

Part V

Part VI

ACKNOWLEDGEMENTS

Using the opportunity I would like to express hearty appreciation of the modern Keepers of the Tradition of Yoga: Pattabhi Joice and B.K.S. Iyengar, for inspiration and invisible spiritual support. Andrew Sidersky, for long-lasting productive exchange of experience and cooperation, as well as for precious advice in writing the text of this book. Ludmila Vandalovskaya, for long-lasting cooperation and spiritual support in developing the theory and practice of some aspects of training. Militaryman and mathematician Alexander Chunikhin, for assistance in developing the mathematical models serving as the basis for advanced techniques of the Dance of Shiva. Manual therapist, Oleg Tyborovsky, for cooperation in the process of perception and development of the safest training programs. And to all my students for vigorous participation in the search for and adjustment of the most effective Yoga technique algorithms. As well as to the publishing collective: Andrew Dikhtyar, Andrew Kostenko, Michel Pollard, Ann McAllen, and Vyacheslav Virich for their warm attitude and good-quality work in the preparation of the layout of this book.

FOREWORD

The publication of this book was preceded by long years of practical experience. My destiny was formed in such a way, that I have been travelling for a long time, since childhood. A year in Mongolia and China with my parents began a lifetime of travel. As a teenager I traveled almost the entire Soviet Union as a member of the Ukrainian national swim team. During my student years, I also explored numerous mountain regions of the former USSR: Carpathians, Crimea, Caucasus, Altai, Tan-Shan, Phanes, Khibines, Lake Baikal, Caspian, White and Black Seas and Sakhalin. On these journeys I visited datsans in Buryatia and mosques in Samarkand, Bouchara, Pherghana and mountainous Tajikistan.

While training in the Ukrainian national youth swim team I practiced Yoga, since the 8-th form of school, and for the period of fourteen years had mastered almost all of the Asanas in «Light on Yoga» by B.K.S. Iyengar even before my first trip to India. Since 1988 I started to work as a professional instructor of Yoga and as a reward for my active actions in spreading Yoga in Kiev eight years later India's Ambassador in Ukraine graced me with the opportunity to attend a free course at the Yoga Institute of B. K. S. Iyengar in Puna. So the way to India was opened for me, and later to Nepal and Tibet.

My first long trip in India I traveled the length and breadth of the country and visited nearly every ashram and spiritual place known in CIS literature. During this time I was fortunate to take a course not only with B. K. S. Iyengar, but also with K. Pattabhi Joice, currently the keeper of the Ashtanga-Vinyasa-Yoga tradition in Mysor. I practiced yoga with Yogacharya Rudra at Shivinada's Ashram in Rishikesh, I delved into many varieties of meditation at Rajneesh's Ashram in Puna, and felt the spirit of the Shri Arubindo commune in Auroville. I felt sense of love and magic I saw at Satya Sai Baba's ashram in Bhuttapati, and was the witness of war in Srinagar, Kashmir's capital. I joined everyday Buddhist prayers and rituals in various Ladakh and Nepalese monasteries. His Holiness the Dalai Lama blessed and granted me the «vinous rope» in his residence of Dharamsala. I was inspired by Hinduism's tantric traditions in the temples of Khajuraho, Konarak, Bhubaneswar and Puri. I experienced the reality of shocking rituals in Benares, and achieved the deepest peace in the «Cave of Vasistha» in the Himalayas. A succession of religious traditions in the cave temples of Ellora and Ajanta. I realized the sacral sense of the temple dances of Orissa and Tamil Nadu inspired me. I felt the freedom of the deserts and power of forts in Rajastan. I found many friends among spiritual fellows and professional teachers from India, Nepal, Tibet and Western countries and I also visited many other places, never known before in our country, that have saved a valuable spiritual legacy. But only recently, approaching my thirty-third year, have I understood that everything that I had been lucky enough to see in my life, and everything that had been acquired as practical and spiritual experience added up to only one mission. And then I understood why one day I left the bus at a lifeless mountain passage in «the heart of the Himalayas»...

* * *

The road from Nepal to Tibet, via the Chinese border, was a tremendous height, reaching from time to time 5 thousand meters over sea-level. Of course, compared to the surrounding peaks at about seven-eight thousand meters each, it was only slightly higher than the «bottom», but, in fact, it was almost at the same level with Elbrus, the highest point in the mountains of Caucasus.

After many hours of climbing along a serpentine mountain road, the bus finally reached the top of the passage. The driver stopped the car near a Tibetan yurt next to a canopy on dirty wooden posts serving as a temporary shelter from snow and rain, the place where travellers, moving between Nepal and Tibet could take a meal.

Surrounded by slushy, melting snow and cold damp fog, we were inside a frigid cloud lying on the mountain. Invisible mountain peaks towered on either side of us, but beyond fifty meters, the world was only grey.

Just like everyone else who had taken that bus, I went to have a meal at that Tibetan «restaurant». It was a present to meet a people on the way and, felt lucky not to be alone in this high, unconquerable mountain world.

Before reaching the shelter I felt that something was happening to me. It was so obvious that it suppressed the strong hunger and fatigue I had acquired during the exhausting bus ride on the serpentine mountain road.

I looked around as if trying to see the source that would explain the strange dominance I continuously felt. But the surroundings were absolutely normal: the fog, our bus at a distance, and travelers impatiently bustling around the yurt waiting for some hot meal.

Being experienced in mountaineering in the USSR, I had prepared myself by taking a light tent, a primus, and a kettle. But here, in the Himalayas, was the first time I had come across the situation where one could manage quite well without all these things. Almost everywhere in the mountains (up to 4.5 — 5 km high) there were human settlements, simple «guesthouses», small shops and restaurants. One could find a hot meal, and a cheap overnight stay. Then, in the morning leave there, backpack and engage any local boy as a porter to go higher into the mountains, reach glaciers and unassailable snow walls, where climbing would only be possible with special equipment, and return «home» to a cozy room on the same day.

In about an hour the driver returned to the bus and gave a sharp signal that echoed through the emptiness around us. This was an invitation to return back to the bus and go ahead.

But I had been wandering back and forth between the bus and the yurt during all the lunch-time, «scanning» the surrounding area in search for the «mysterious source».

The utmost watch by the strange way was combined with unusual weak will, my body felt as heavy as lead. And all my motives to do something, to go somewhere or to strive for something cleared away like a smoke. Simultaneously with seeing the surrounding objects with my eyes, I Saw immovable and clear structures, colour «grids».

Indifferent to what might happen, to whether I should stay on this road and wait for the next bus, even if it took in a week, and it might not have vacant seats...

I stopped on the very top of the passage and watched the turn of the road that hid the bus. A strong wind lashed my face with dusty water. And I felt myself on the top... The top of the passage was the upper point of the cavity between two giant peaks, which, although invisible, but could be «heard». All this «called up» some associations with my present place on this Planet...

Solid waves of the Power runs down through me from above. Disbelieving that all this was really happening to me, I stood with my feet wide to avoid falling as I felt myself becoming heavier and heavier.

Suddenly standing became absolutely impossible. I turned over my backpack, which was setting nearby, rested my back on it and closed my eyes. Instantly something started to change inside me, and I started to «take-off», rising above the body that rested on the backpack. «Floating» slightly from side to side I stabilized, hovering at about three meters above the body, and felt simply «petrified». After noticing some Essence somewhere in the space behind me, just «behind my back». Not with my eyes but with some wonderful Seeing I saw its beauty, which made my hair raise.

It was impossible to understand what it was: he, she or it. But its (?) broad face dangled in the air like a chimera above me for some more time, baring its long tusks, and staring with its sultry predatory eyes wide open. His (?) forehead was decorated with a wreath of beaded human skulls. Fear and real Death surrounded me. But she (?) seemed to be studying whether I was ready for something...

It was growing dark.

My senses slowly recovered. I looked around trying to establish my place and find a spot to stay overnight. Nepal and India rested somewhere in the valley far below.

I turned back and understood that this is the beginning of the Tibetan plateau.

This passage was not only the highest point between the two valleys, India and Tibet, it was like a Rubicon connecting two ancient spiritual cultures...

Only now I noticed how worn-out, wet, cold, and hungry I was. It showed myself unreasonable to test my health moreover by spending the night on a bed of snow in a strange place, and I headed towards the Tibetan yurt...

The morning was glorious. The clouds rose much higher and dispersed in some places opening a splendid blaze of snow-white peaks. The sun was beginning to burn and there were springs everywhere.

The area was absolutely lifeless, but clear and colorful. Water drained into the bed of a small river running from the north to east from the side of Tibetan plateau. A little bit lower, on the south-west, a lake formed, its blue mirror reflecting the snowy peak towering behind it...

Long posts stood along the crests of the nearest hills with a thin flagged thread stretched between them. Mortar-like stones stood on the other crests of hills.

Such signs were everywhere in the Himalayas and served as landmarks for spiritual pilgrims, directing them to the holy places of their pilgrimage.

I went up to the ridge and followed the signs. After about a two kilometer walk, I discovered a small «temple», if it could be so called at all, standing on the ridge of the hillside. (Such structures can be seen throughout the territory of Nepal, Tibet, India. They are designed for prayer or meditation for the pilgrims or the dwellers of the nearby villages, and are constructed in Places of Power. Their design represents a highly simplified form of a Hinduist, Buddhist or a Moslem temple, although a very small one, designed for one man.)

I approached it without expecting anything extraordinary. This was a Shivaist «temple». Inside the central whitewashed wall there was an ash-drawn «Om» sign, and a rusty combat trident stood in the corner. A small «Shiva-Lingam», and a terrible-looking whip, lay on the floor among ashes of burnt incense and dried flower-leaves.

I went inside, under the «temple's» dome, and felt a sudden powerful «electric» wave which pierced all of my body from top to bottom. So I rose up on my toes as if somebody had grabbed my hair and vigorously pulled it upwards.

It had been a long time, since I had become acquainted with a flow of such nature. Once in the Crimea (at peninsula Tarkhankut in the Black Sea), when I was 25 years old, and long before my trip to the Himalayas, the same flow had raised me above the ground during «the raising of Kundalini» while I was in the «Lotus» posture. That time I had stretched my arms downwards, hardly reaching the ground. I still disbelieve this myself, but my friends, who were not far from me, near the tent, saw that also. And they said it was a long period in the air rather than a jump of «transcendental meditational practice».

But now this flow operated while I stood upright. I Saw a giant cobra rising from «inside of me», somewhere from the solar plexus. Its body seemed to have the diameter of at least three meters and reaching dizzy heights up in the sky. Its head reached the skies and had a golden crown on top.

All this was accompanied by a terrible sound as if somebody simultaneously pressed all the keys of an organ; the sound was swelling like an avalanche.

I had two feelings: on the one hand I was overwhelmed by the demonstration of such power and splendor, on the other hand, however, there was fear of annoying this powerful Creature contemplating the Universe. My hair was standing on end...

«Awed», in a blessed «fever» for about two hours. When something was finished, and it completly transformed my consciousness. (This process has no something same with epilepsy. Even though it may occur on the spur of the moment, it may be interrupted at any time because it is always controlled by consciousness. Those people who deem such processes an illness or a «syndrome» are those who have never experienced similar spiritual experience personally).

When it was all over «The Picture of the World» radically changed, and I felt absolutely clear in the silence of peace.

The world was perceived globally as one whole thing. I felt an exact understanding of the sense of life... But life somewhere in the valleys seemed a stupid fuss and a delusion...

I walked for half a day following the signs, first along the ridge of the hill, then on the steep mountain slope which was rising higher and higher. Finally, I reached a passage behind which was a long canyon that entered a glacier between splendid snow peaks. These places were absolutely desolate although something made me be on the alert. I had a feeling that the stones around me were alive and moving...

I always travel alone so as to be able to avoid being distracted by companions and in order to contemplate all that surrounds me, staying tete-a-tete with the Infinite. This is risky but the risk can be overcome by believing in fate...

There was a stone mortar behind which I could not see another sign... I must have climbed rather high because I started to feel slight heart ar rhythmia, when my chest and head blood pressure increased. I dropped my backpack near the mortar, rested on it and took a nap...

I was awakened by a loud clap and a push. I looked around in dismay but saw nobody. I felt «the creeps». I looked around again and again but nothing changed, there was just snow and stones. I closed my eyes again, intending to take a little bit more rest, but «something inside me moved again and stretched my body», it forced me upright into Siddhasana, with my eyes closed...

First, I saw a bar of gold hanging motionlessly in «inner space». Then appeared «Vajra», currents of suspended lightning, descending from the splendid source somewhere above. Then Something appeared naked, looking like Buddha or Mahawir, it seemed to be cast of gold, had ideal proportions, but no sex features. It was sitting with one leg bent, like in Siddhasana, with the other hanging down. Its head was crowned by a unique gold headdress which vaguely resembled a helmet. One of its arm was hanging along its body and folded at the elbow to direct its palm at me. All fingers of the hand were slightly bent, except the forefinger, which was straight and directed upwards. With this mudra It both calmed me and suggested me to be attentive. Its other arm was smartly directed to the side, slightly bent at the elbow and palm turned to the sky with all of the fingers folded inward, except the forefinger, which pointed at something on the side. I was astonished to see that instead of eyes It had just two hollow openings that made it look like a robot... In a couple of minutes it suddenly disappeared.

I opened my eyes and looked at the place it had been pointing to. It was in the eastern direction. There, at the foot of a snow-covered peak, was a rock. I could not understand what the meaning of all this was, and what I should do further. It was the second half of the day and the sun was dropping. I seemed to have pulled my senses together, and when I imagined that no matter where I went or how I rushed now, I would be forced to spend the night somewhere on the same rocks, this made me feel somehow uncomfortable. But this «Fellow» intrigued me. And I at the same decided to go to the rock it had pointed to.

Having approached one side of the rock, I moved along keeping my eyes on it from time to time. After walking for about a hundred meters, I discovered a cleft that could not be seen at a distance. Stepping closer I saw some elaborate symbols or drawings carved in the stone on the walls near the entrance. After looking inside I understood that it was the entrance to a cave.

I was scared. My legs were trembling. And if it had not been for those drawings, I would have probably not dared to enter. But I thought that I would never forgive myself unless I satisfied my curiosity. I took a light out of my backpack and entered inside.

The cave was formed by a split of rock and, most likely, was once very deep. But about fifteen meters from the entrance, it appeared to be blocked by a blind wall. Possibly, to prevent uninvited guests like snakes and other creatures coming from the depths of the earth. Everything here bore traces of human presence. The walls and the ceiling were smoked. There was a fireplace in the middle of the cave, and the walls had torch openings. And near one of the walls was a bed made of flat stones.

It was hard to imagine that the place was habitable. Of course there were no problems with water, though this could not be said about food... I still cannot understand where the resident of the cave got his food because the area for many kilometers around was severe and lifeless, even in summer. In winter, when the temperature here falls to minus fifty degrees Celsius, it is absolutely inconceivable where he would have gotten something to burn and warm himself. (In general, Himalayan locals often use the dried dung of mountain yaks to make fire and cook food).

All this only concerned the life of the cave's host, but his creative activity astonished me immensely.

Through the soot on the walls there could be seen numerous strange drawings which slightly resembled Egyptian writings scratched on the stone. Different walls showed drawings of different types.

The western wall was covered with multiple «lines» which were composed of a great number of simple drawings of men in different postures. Some of them were so simplified that they were lacking some limbs, e. g., hands, legs, and head. Maybe this was for some reason unimportant for the artist. These «lines» of drawings were different in length and formed chaotically positioned vertical columns that also had different lengths. Besides the figures, there were stars with five, six and twelve rays with drawings of men on top.

The eastern wall also showed «lines» which consisted of simple drawings of hands and some strange variously positioned circles and loops resembling the infinity sign. There were four drawings in each «rows». These «rows» also formed vertical columns. There were two «lines» of such columns, and I counted eight «rows» in the columns with the drawings of hands. The number of such columns was also eight. But the columns composed of different circles and loops were also different. This wall also had some «swirling» symbols in the shape of swastikas with smooth wave-like twists. Each of them twisted first to one side, then to another. This swastikas consisted of four, eight, sixteen, thirty-two and sixty-four rays. The more rays they had, the less was their resemblance to a swastika, but more to the sun.

There were not so many drawings on the artificial blind wall, but they were touched with some inexplicable beauty. On the left, above the very cave's floor there were intricate «snakes» and unusual symbols. All of them were different. On the right, above the very cave's floor there were images of different gods and some inscriptions. And in the middle, between them, there were several «rows» of men in different postures. Over all of these a huge Yantra in the shape of concentric circles was depicted. Rays divided its margin into sectors with human drawings inside. Closer to the middle there was a circle with different «snakes» inside, in which march closer to the center there was a circle of godlike faces. And in the center there was a multi-ray double-sided swastika which looked like the sun. Unfortunately, since the wall was artificial, it seemed worn by time and many of the elements of the drawings on it had disappeared.

Enthralled with my discovery, I completely forgot about the time and noticed that it was dark outside only when the batteries of my light discharged and it started fading away. I had a couple of candles with me and lit one of them. It seemed strange that now I felt myself quite comfortable inside the cave. It was as cozy as home. There were neither mosquitoes nor bats, and I could hardly believe that I was «god knows where», far from people and civilization.

Having taken a bite of dried fruits and nuts, I decided not to burn the candle, and to go to bed early so that I could use its light in the morning in order to have a closer look at these walls. I laid my sleeping bag on the stone bed, blew out the candle and lied on my back. Only then did I notice that I was ill and probably had altitude sickness and a high temperature. Most likely it was due to the fact the I had climbed over three kilometers for three days without due acclimatization...

For some reason I did not want to sleep at all, and suddenly somebody pressed down on my shoulders. I jerked, trying to jump to my feet, but the hands of somebody firmly pressed my shoulders to the stone bed. I opened my eyes and peered into the darkness, but saw nothing. Suddenly «ultra-violet» light flashed somewhere behind me. I closed and reopened my eyes peering in the dark, but the light did not disappear. After that the silhouette of a man in a mantle and a high head-dress appeared at a distance just opposit of me. He approached smoothly as if he was flying in the air. His garment reflected the light with the «ultra-violet» shine. He stopped very close in front of me. The shape of his head-dress was extraordinary: high as an Egyptian's, but cut front to back at an angle, and not strictly oval but wavy in the front. It was decorated with shining patterns which resembled intertwined mandalas, in the middle of the hat was a violet crystal in the shape of a long water-drop turned upside down. It was totally impossible to tell the sex of the silhouette by the face. No hair showed from underneath the hat, as if he was bald. The face was pale-white but was «ultra-violet» due to the light. He showed proper and exquisite features. The same as his predecessor, he had two hollow openings instead of the eyes and the expression of his face was absolutely neutral. He affected me so strongly by his look, that my state was completely controlled and manipulated by him. He kept up my fear to prevent me from «jerking», at the same time did nothing bad to me.

Trying to understand him, I looked into his eyes and was drowned within them. From this moment on, I realised that we had an high rate information exchange, without any words and thoughts. He was likely to be reading all the content of my consciousness, at the same time sending extremely packed conceptual codes back. This lasted for only a few minutes. After that, he disappeared in the same smooth fashion and the light died away.

I cautiously moved. There were no hands on my shoulders. I jumped up and lit the candle. I walked around the cave and looked outside, there was nobody. I became scared and decided to leave the candle burning for the whole night. Sleeping was impossible, however. When the first candle burnt away, I lit another one and did not notice how I finally fell asleep...

The impact of this night's events is still felt in me, assisting to realise fundamental events and directing me in my life...

Despite high temperature and constant chill, I lived in the cave for two more days, until I ran out of all sources of light, including matches. During this time I copied everything that was possible to copy from the walls, and despite a strong desire to stay in this holy Place, my common sense pushed me to return to civilization in order to prevent the development of my illness.

On my way to the road, I understood that differences in drawings on opposite walls were in some way connected with their directions towards India and Tibet...

The next day a lorry going to Lhasa picked me up.

Materials from the drawings I found in the cave have become a part of this book...

INTRODUCTION

The time has come to step beyond only training methods and instructions, to the understanding of the True Goal and realization of technological essence of the Yoga Tradition.

In the last few years numerous sources on Yoga have been published, (these had previously been totally unavailable or very rare). But presently there is little knowledge available in print about the universal laws and phenomenas essential to the foundation of Yoga practices not depending on differences of practical styles. And this gap may be filled by this book.

People in modern society have lost the ability to trust in words. In order to take action they need to know a lot of about a specific goal and a means to accomplish it, and without this they find a lot of reasons to have doubts.

That's why I devoted this book to a generalization and systematization of accumulated experience, guide to help better perceive the world one is dealing with by following the Tradition of Yoga. While the karmic choice of how to use this knowledge in the future, and which schools and styles to follow, is left to the reader's Free Will.

Writing in any field always lags behind the temps of development and the true progress of the knowledge in that field, for new experience and perception come faster that one can write about them.

It is a common rule that upon the completion of a book that new practical experience and a deeper understanding of the book's content make its material seem hopelessly out-of-date. But, of course, not for the readers; this seems to be an ever-lasting story. This is precisely why I quite clearly understand that this book is only meant to summarize a particular stage of development, and that tomorrow's new experience may lead to new horizons of the truth, and then, possibly, I will have to criticize myself.

In this book I have tried to avoid the rewording of available information, and to write only about matters which have never been published in any special literature before, or to view well known aspects of Yoga practices with a new angle. Therefore, the greater part of this book's content is original and has never been published before.

This book uses the Sanskrit names of *Asanas, Pranayamas, Bandhas* and *Mudras* according to the terminology and technique of the authoritative book by B.K.S. Iyengar «Light on Yoga», since it is widely available and known to the majority of Yoga practitioners.

The book also includes chapters dealing with insufficiently investigated processes that I have encountered in the practice of yoga. I hope that the reader will be open-minded to these materials and introduce their own view to the development and complete perception of these issues.

The techniques of any exercises described in this book may give the impression that they are overcomplicated and not suitable for you. This is not really so. What you need to do is to get rid of maximalism and «not to try on yourself» the exercises of advanced leveles immediately. The perfect system can satisfy the demands of every person, from a feeble beginner to an advanced teacher. One only needs to correctly evaluate one's capabilities and true level of development, and remember that the progress depends only on you. It is unnecessary to compare your abilities with those of other Yoga practitioners. In exactly the same way you should not deem this system as not being suitable for you because your actual level of development is still not very high.

The publication of this book was preceded by many years of the search for knowledge, persistent practice and realization of laws serving the basis for the Tradition of Yoga. And I have been lucky to study the practices and techniques of different Yoga schools and styles. At the same time I have always resorted to Free Style in my practice, combining the knowledge I learned through study, the feeling of the Supreme Goal, and my own «findings» that incorporate the most effective elements of various styles.

The majority of experienced practitioners who have followed the Tradition of Yoga for a long time sooner or later come to the same place.

This book contains no basic techniques, and therefore one may have the impression that the material proposed here can hardly be used in practice. It is totally wrong to think that. In this book the reader will fine something better than simple techniques of exercises. It contains Universal Keys to the Knowledge of Yoga. These Universal Keys will allow the individual to design a training program and at the same time remain creatively free and independent. Among the basic set of exercises, the best one is the individual program developed especially for you.

The system represented herein suggests consciousness of the practitioner. It has been created for those who possess practical Yoga experience and Wisdom. It is for those capable of using the Knowledge, Seeing the Substance of Phenomena and Acting Consciously and Creatively.

Few practice this consciousness, but those who do are leaders.

The basis of this book is served by the Spirit of Unity which coveys the gist of the Yoga Tradition without trespassing on Your Freedom and life mission.

The information is like a traffic sign, but everyone must, using one's own karmic motivations, independently decide where and why to go.

Life is an ancient fairy tale. Like ancient travellers, everyone still faces the cross-road stone... What do I choose? Do I go straight... Turn to the right... Have a rest here... or turn back?

Part I

PATHWAY

TRUE PATHWAY AND MASTER

True Knowledge has no source other than the One. He is the True Master. But at the same time the Keepers of the Yoga Tradition from ancient times stress the importance of the worldly, human master. Worldly masters are the champions of the Power and Knowledge of the One. And sincerity and mutual confidence between the master and the student are absolutely necessary for the transfer of this Power and Knowledge. Only in this case differences in experience and in personal mission disappear, one demonstrates one's highest potential and only then may the Miracle of Initiation of the New Keeper of the Tradition occur.

The Master conveys the accumulated experience of numerous generations of Keepers whose deeds have enhanced the power of this Tradition, and this enables the student to avoid wasting time repeating previous and realized mistakes.

The True Tradition of Yoga has no specialized, copyrighted or patent-protected names. Simply Yoga. This ancient word implies an unconditional Unification with the Unbounded. The Yoga Pathway has personal directions for the different people. *The Ones Who Achieved* prefer to avoid using any names at all because they see the limitation of the Freedom even in this single word. They are not oriented towards concrete material expression, but towards abstract ideal preservation and the following of the Gist of Unification.

The True Pathway implies complete Freedom of Choice. It is for those who are capable of loving the only One Master and receiving his lessons in any form He creates.

NATURAL AND INVERTED FLOW

From the time of the «Big Bang», all forms of life have a direction. This direction is given once and a special Counter measures the duration of the life of all creatures.

All spiritual schools created their own principal positions with respect to how one should live, along this initially set direction or backwards, against its flow. Also, there are schools which accept both, depending on the situation.

Besides, any flow has explicit and implicit anti-flow. In this way, for example, the motion of electrons in semiconductors implies the counter motion of «vacancies».

The schools that insist on the supremacy of the **Natural course** of events bring the Higher Will to the foreground, which sets their direction and sense of life.

The schools oriented towards the **Anti-Force** declare their goal as the inversion of the natural course of events, i.e., motion against the linear time flow.

The schools which insist on the **Conscious Choice** of measures, depending on the Goal and situation, teach both, as well as what to apply and when.

A human being's life processes are *directed* in exactly the same way as any other creature's.

The secret of rejuvenation and obtaining extraordinary powers lies with the ability independently to control such directions, to hold in own hands Counter of Life and consciously to realize own mission (Dharma) in the life under the guidance of the Higher Sense of Being.

There are numerous physical and psychic power manipulations developed in Yoga, which are devised for the inversion of the direction of natural flows as well as for the leading of the first plan of the natural processes.

One of the typical means of inverting the flow of main powers is *Brachmacharya* (versatile control of senses) and the use of inverted postures in training. These postures result in different powers, which in a natural state act in the lower and upper centers, rush one to another and mix, manifesting themselves in a third quality. Likewise any manifested power in life may be reversed, be it an obtrusive appetite, sexual obsession or a negative thought pattern.

The stopping of thoughts and fluctuations in the consciousness removes the unnatural barrier between the body and the Spirit, and restores both the natural processes in the organism and the natural actions of a man.

WILL AND POWER OF SPIRIT

The will manifests itself when power is restrained and kept under control.

A human being has a life power concentration and distribution place. This is an extremely small zone within which all life energy of a human may be controlled. Numerous doors surround this zone. Each of these *doors* opens its own path, its own sector of directional thinking, feeling and action, which are necessarily followed by the reaction of the Infinite.

A «normal» man, as a rule, keeps this *door* wide open and freely exposed to the blows of the multi-direction winds of the outer Will, accumulating the Power. In the East, the attention of such a person can be compared to a cloud which moves from one door to another, taken by the winds of social opinion, prestige, advertisement, personal ambitions, weak points, habits and other «pests».

But where is attention - there is Power... There is your life and your money. And the one that controls your attention is the true Master. The Power is subject to his Will.

In this situation freedom is gained through conscious control of one's own *doors.* A true Master willfully decides where, when, and to what extent a *door* should be opened by controlling the capacity of the flow in the desired sector of action. His Will manifests itself only at the time the *door* is intentionally closed (with resignation) or opened for a precisely set width. His Power of Spirit keeps the *door* in a position that is not dependent upon external sensual influences.

Only by the saving of control over these *doors* can a Will be manifested and the Power of Spirit be increased. And if its potential becomes high, the open *door,* followed immediately by the *intention,* attracts the required result.

One may hardly believe in such effect, but this magical law operates with the same precision as the law of gravitation.

The greater the potential of Power of Spirit, the faster the required result will be achieved. Everyone who preserves the Power of Spirit and lives in the Spirit knows it from one's own experience.

The level of the true Freedom of the Spirit depends on the extent of one's modesty and resignation.

Only one mistake is possible, and that is an attempt to be humble for the achievement of a concrete tangible goal, as the Power cannot be deceived. And if one is making spiritual deeds with a secret plan to achieve a particular goal, this very goal will undermine spiritual development. But the Power of the One, being the incarnation of universal power ties and sees the real motivation. So it only gives what is already protected by a detached attitude. That which has already become absolutely indifferent. Only that attitude, in the absence of which one has resigned oneself for a long time.

The existence of the goal implies a *desire.* A strong *desire* is absolutely necessary for reaching the goal by general ways available for all people, but the same desire can become a problem in terms of magical realization.

YOGA AND MORALITY

Morality is the principal law on which human behavior is based. This is very important where this law comes from: either from outside or from inside.

Morality coming from outside points a man what to do and what not to do. But while diseases-weaknesses live in the human consciousness the demands and prohibitions will only feed them. Sooner or later «the dam will be destroyed» and the person will commit «a sin».

Individual morality originating from the inside is based on *love*, and can develop in the individual as a simple and natural state of pure consciousness. And it is obtained through the liberation from mental delusions, a balance of powers and the growing up of the Spirit.

The value of such morality is much higher than that, of the social morality dictated by an external authority.

If a man is not in possession of internal harmony and has unbalanced powers raging inside him, it is useless to teach him to love and be patient. He will go on manifesting aggression until the actual source of unbalanced aggression bursts inside him and while the compressed springs of unvented powers of delusions exist in his consciousness. Therefore, one should strive to exterminate the misleading powers of such spiritual disease through the balancing of the powers by using real stabilizing exercises for internal rather than external morality.

One should influence the source rather than the result. Therefore, actual development of true morality in the Tradition of Yoga gives preference to the purification and balance of consciousness. And the results of this practice will not be immediate, but these changes *actually* take place.

True morality cannot be imagined without love, the dynamic unification with the object of attraction. This may be a specific or abstract object. Accordingly, the state of love may be expressed in specific actions or in an abstract state. In the Tradition of Yoga the process of unification with the object is called *Samyama*. This is a continuous transition from *Dharana* (concentration of the rays of attention on the object) to *Dhiyana* (contemplation and fusion with the qualities of the object) and further to *Samadhi* (the ecstasy of complete identification with it).

Mastership does not entitle one to relax and «retire on one's laurels», because without continued practice downfall and degradation can follow even the highest of levels achieved. Without constant vigilance and balance new mental delusions may develop.

Each stage of practice demands conformity to the codes embedded in the complexity of the exercises. An Automatic Law monitors access to the power of each exercise by different stages of complexity and the capacity of powers involved.

The practitioner's state of consciousness and moral foundations determine his way of living: what and how he eats, how long and how he sleeps, what work he does, what stresses he endures, etc.. His way of life, consequently, determines the state of his body, senses and mind; and these qualities of the body, senses and mind are the main factors limiting his practice.

That is why, traditionally before starting to practice Yoga, students begin purification exercises and moral enhancement as a foundation for the complex transformations. Some may ignore this and start practicing only power aspects of Yoga, as the followers of some magic clans practice it, but the Power may not be mislead. Practice without this higher stage of consciousness is most likely to result in various traumas and karmic problems. Sooner or later Karmic Law forces such «deceivers» to either give up yoga practices due to the state of their health, or to respect the absolute necessity to balance consciousness and accept internal morality.

Asanas are the codes of the state of consciousness. And their physical elaboration is just a simple test to know the level of development and balance of one's consciousness. Practicing *Asanas, Viniasas and Pranayamas* is a desire to gain access to higher levels of being rather than simple physical training.

Neither circus, nor sport acrobatics constitute Yoga. These practices are purely physical and are not oriented to change the consciousness. Although, of course, an acrobat's physical background may readily serve as a basis for development of advance consciousness.

One should avoid a sport approach in elaborating *Asanas, Viniasas and Pranayamas.* Yoga is not a sport! Athletes can age quickly or develop diseases in middle age. But real Yogis do not have diseases and preserve good looks until an extremely old age. In Yoga greater priority is given to the feeling of personal limits rather than the complexity of exercises. Therefore, it is useless to compare the practice of one yogi with the practice of another one. Because their practice in principle is incomparable.

And it is also important to remember that a young body's strength and flexibility do not allow a person to claim oneself an advanced yogi. True Yoga presumes the recognition of higher planes of being, which only becomes possible with the progress and the growing up of the Spirit.

KEY TO MASTERSHIP

The Universal Algorithm for achieving individual mastership, which can be applied to any art, serves as the basis of the system proposed in this book.

Let us study it, taking the practice of Yoga exercises as an example.

A human body always has a circle of limitation, a potential limit of mobility, strength and endurance — «the Limit of the Marginal Circle». Within this circle is a «Subject Zone».

Usually, before starting to practice Yoga, a man has no clear realisation of where this Limit lies and what falls within his Subject Zone. But the Margin can be clearly detected rather soon after starting Yoga practice. In this event all suitable exercises form the «Subject Arsenal» of instrumental and technical abilities of the student.

Expansion of the Subject Arsenal can be achieved by two methods.

The first method consists of combining and developing new ties between separate components of the Subject Arsenal. According to this method all suitable exercises are divided into elementary components (particular positions of arms, legs, body, head and fragments of dynamical movements), and synthesized to create new exercises included in the Subject Arsenal.

The second method consists of the expansion of the Marginal Circle Limit through regular training and attempting to acquire previously absent qualities and functional abilities (for example, at the physical level: flexibility, static and dynamic strength, static and dynamic endurance, coordination and reaction). This allows the inclusion of new exercises to the Subject Arsenal. Then returning to the first method, the resulting elements are used to construct new exercises — by combining these elements between themselves or by simply using the elements of simpler exercises.

On one hand these methods allow the creation of new exercises, and on the other hand, they allow one to choose the most efficient ones among the suitable exercises. Developing the Subject Arsenal and the Subject Zone is directly connected with the improvement of control and the spreading of consciousness.

In this way the practice of Yoga may be applied to any art.

For example, for a scientist the Arsenal will be in the academic knowledge of the laws and the technical possibilities of experimental facilities used to obtain new knowledge. For a trader — in the assortment of goods in his store as well as in his technical abilities in attracting the attention of buyers to such goods (by using advertising tricks and various marketing «hooks»).

Expansion of the Subject Zone is connected with the expansion of consciousness, and its division into elementary components. Integration of these components into new combinations allows the perfection of this Zone. It unites all one's accumulated life experience, and leads efficiently to progress in the selected sphere of life.

This is the key to understanding the content of this book.

The practice of Yoga has two mutually supporting methods for advancement to perfection and true mastership. They are training under a specified program and spontaneous training.

The expansion of the Marginal Circle Limit and the enrichment of the Subject Arsenal (*Kriyas, Asanas, Vinyasas, Pranayamas, Mudras, Rasas*, and etc.) is achieved by attacking personal limits during the course of regular and multiple repetition of certain preset *over-the-limit* training exercises. The development of new links within the Subject Zone is achieved by the searching for, and mastering of new, previously unknown forms and algorithms of motions, as well as by using various combinations in spontaneous *heuristic* training.

Practically no one practices training under a prescribed program throughout his/her life, therefore, the second method naturally derives from the first one. An accumulation of practical experience performing predetermined complexes inevitably leads into new perceptions through spontaneous *gaps* and unexpected combinations with no rules, that spring from the senses rather than from the mind. Such *heuristic epiphanies* contain the Spirit of freedom, and should not be suppressed or restrained. But, one should be extremely attentive and cautious in attempting them, as the motion to the Non-Subject Zone is always ties with surprises.

METHOD OF PRACTICE

The method of mastering the yogi resource Arsenal is simple. It resembles learning the ABCs.

First one learns to write separate «letters», i.e., performing static forms, or *Asanas*.

Then, one masters syllables, where the letters are connected with a «tails». These are dynamic *ties* between *Asanas*, or *Vinyasas*.

After that one writes whole «words» — performing short dynamic *series*, i.e. *Vinyasas*, consisting of *Asanas*, with the movements serving as links between them, these are performed using the rhythm of breath. Such «words» have the *meaning of power*.

After this, one writes «sentences» by performing *complexes,* consisting of several *Asanas* and *Vinyasas.* Such «sentences» have an *extended meaning of power.* Usually these complexes are studied in the regime of dictation both under a master's guidance and independently, according to a prescribed program.

But when a student accumulates enough practical «language» experience, there appears the possibil ity to write «compositions» with a definite subject at the beginning and a free subject thereafter, i.e. one can independently construct training complexes, both achieving the goal and creatively expressing oneself.

Those who achieve this goal become masters in yoga, just if his/her yoga-«texts» resonates with the sound of Harmony and Beauty.

GOALS AND MEANS

An real ization of the *inner sub-spaces* in Yoga occurs when the form transforms into it's content, that is, when perception goes from the obvious into the hidden. When this happens physical, breathing, and other exercises are the only means to accumulate and strengthen the Power of Spirit.

A real ization of the *outer sub-spaces* occurs in the opposite direction, that is, from the content to its form and from the hidden to the obvious. In this case Power of Spirit is expressed in versatile external transformations of the forms with respect to it.

But real ization the ties between the *outer* and *inner sub-spaces* allows one to experience and make certain of the unity of Global Space.

It is essential to grasp once and for all that Yoga, through various physical forms is regarded as the means that allow one to achieve spiritual goals, i. e., to change one's state of consciousness. While spiritual ideals are solely defined as the means for transforming the material world. An emphasis on one of these two tendencies is accentuated solely as the means to achieve their equil ibrium and to embody the Harmony of Being.

This is the only context in which one can correctly interpret the content of this book.

Part II

FORM

ORGANIC FORMATION THEORY

ASANAS

All things manifested in this world have a form determined by the organizing Power and defined by their present state of consciousness. Every form has dual characteristics, which Yoga customarily divides into two groups: *Ha* (concentration, light, activity, presence) and *Tha* (relaxation, dark, passivity, absence).

Even living person has a form. And nobody can be free of the unconscious feeling of the dualism in the human form. But the state of unconsciousness and satisfaction with life depends on this feeling.

An *Asana* in Yoga is regarded as a shape taken consciously on that or other level of material organization. But in order to control different material forms, it is necessary first to study to realize the phenomena that occur at various levels of organization of matter. Everything in this world is woven from a «single material», and that is the principle similarity that, according to an ancient wisdom, allows us to, «know ourselves, and in turn, know the world»...

Any material form in the multidimensional world is arranged into several levels of organization. And a person can realize them by contemplating the form. But the ability to penetrate in this or that level of material organization depends on the sensitivity and experience of the contemplator.

Thus, the human form may be perceived at several levels, which are listed below.

The Organic form always contains two groups of qualitative heterogeneous structures. These are contracted muscles fixing the form of the body (*Ha*) and relaxed, stretched muscles (*Tha*).

When a yogi does an *Asana*, his inner consciousness allows him to feel differences in body temperature, the tone of his nervous system, and the direction of blood circulation and blood pressure. By following his breathing process he sees the biological rhythms of his body.

To develop organic form, in-depth «vertical» movement is necessary. The form looks static only from the outside, but inside, the practitioner always creates conditions for increasing the contrast between the *Ha*- and *Tha*-sectors. He does this by trying to «dive» as deeply into the form as possible and increase the stretch of muscles, tendons and bursas of the joints of the *Tha*-sectors, while at the same time drawing and contracting relevant groups of muscles and tendons of *Ha*-sectors.

The dynamic linkage of static *Asanas* between them directs the «horizontal» movement within the practitioner's inner flexibility limits.

The organic form is not only the totality of material elements which the human organism consists of, but also the totality of its «functional appendages» in the surrounding material world, from clothes and ball-point pens to computers and subordinated people.

The power form is expressed through the presence of signals (*Ha*) or their absence (*Tha*), as well as through the tension between *Ha* and *Tha*. Insignificantly weak signals are not a real *Tha*-absence of signals, but are expressed against the background of extremely strong signals within a limited range of perception. This range tunes itself to rough signals, since the danger is most likely to exist in the rough signals.

Understanding how the power form looks is simple if one takes its technical counterpart (i. e., a computer) and imagines only the electric current without the wires and chips inside it. Power *Asana* is a shining manifestation of power lines separated from the power flow channels (*Nadis*).

Development of a power body means the improvement of sensitivity and control of the signals, at the expense of spreading simultaneous perception with both weak and strong signals.

The psychic form (*Rasa*) of a man is like a psychic *Asana*. Each Rasa has its own power coloring and is connected with the complex manifestation of all the work of the power centers (Chakras).

The tension of the psychic field is psychic *Ha*, whereas its relaxation is psychic *Tha*.

Any electric current has a field and likewise the signals of the senses also have powerful psychic fields most powerful within the nerve plexus zones.

The development of psychic form demands the ability to transform one's psyche by expanding the range of accessible *Rasas* (psychic *Asanas*), and also the possibility to fix the slightest qualitative changes in them.

The mental form of a man is a «momentary cut-instant focus» of the dynamics of his thinking or fixations of images perceived by him simultaneously. Mental *Asana* is a form which is a result of multiple power and psychic functions which create a total picture out of the perception multiplicity.

Concentration on the rays of attention on the object or a process is the *Ha* of the mind, whereas the dissipation and distraction from particular objects or processes is the *Tha* of the mind.

The development of the images perceived by the body means the rising of the concentration level (*Ha*) of the rays of attention, and distinguishes extremely small elementary concentration points within images.

While developing the ability more and more to abstract from the different objects and processes, and perceive nothing in particular (*Tha*).

The spiritual form is the Power of the organizing will program distributing the life energy of a human being. The humbleness of life energy, or its conscious direction, demands the *Ha* of the Power of Will (manifestation of will) and the strengthening of the Personal Spirit. Whereas the dissipation of the life energy is the *Tha* of the Power of Will (lack of will), weakening the Personal Spirit.

Spiritual *Asana* represents the configuration of the «*Ha-Tha*-sectors», the organized Power of Will then distributes and directs the life energy to particular organs and structures of the mind, senses and body.

The development of a will-program means the strengthening of the Personal Power of Will and the increasing of the level of the life energy humbleness, exactness and dosage of its conscious direction, as well as the ability to distinguish the spiritual influences, the qualities of Powers standing behind them, and the ability to surrender oneself to the Higher Power.

The causal form is the array of Global Ties of the One, or a sum of everything that exists in the Universe. All karmic battles are fought here, and it is a champion of the grace and retribution of the One. *Ha* of the Global Ties means evolution and the act of the Creation. Whereas the *Tha* of the Global Ties means degradation and Destruction. Causal *Asana* is the «configuration of personal Fate at a given moment of the life».

Global Ties are subject to the One. And personal development with respect to these ties demands an realization of their operation and one's own Mission within the Plan of the One.

The absence of form, Formlessness is an Over-The-Limit Emptiness belonging to a space where perception of the Global Ties spreading in the Endlessness of the Universe dies out. All above-mentioned forms possess *Ha*-quality, i.e., the presence in the manifested Being. But Formlessness opposes them and possesses the *Tha* — quality - absence. And it does not mean comments by definition...

***

A human body may take various shapes, but the shapes are limited by the structure of the human body.

Any movable part of a human skeleton consists of two bones connected by one joint. This joint enables movement of the bones with respect to each other. If we place these two bones in some «neutral» position between marginal flexibility limits (Fig. 1a), and assume that the lower bone is fixed, then the upper bone will have 8 main directions for movement (Fig. 1b-i): a) neutral, b) bend forward, c) bend back, d) bend right, e) bend left, f) turn right, g) turn left, h) stretch, i) compress.

In addition, there is the possibility of 20 bi-directional combinations:

eight options of bends with turning, four of bends with compression, four of bends with stretching, two of turning with compression, two of turning with stretching.

And sixteen three-directional combinations also exist: eight options of bends with turning and stretching, and eight options of bends with turning and compression.

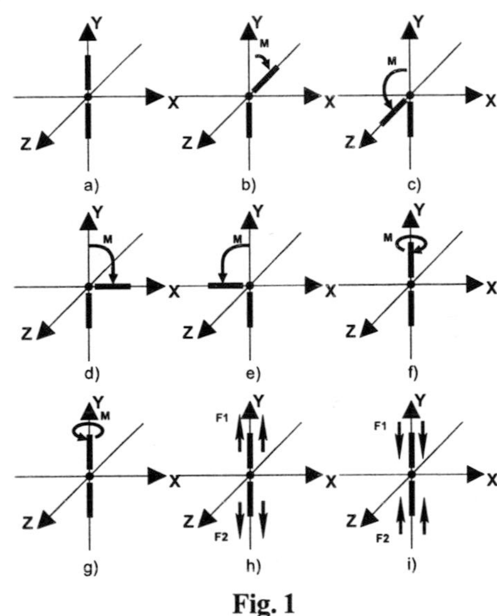

Fig. 1

The number of possible bodily forms depends on the depth of the bend, the turn, the stretch or compression, which depend on the level of contraction of the muscles that move the bones relative to the joint.

This shows that muscle tension may be changed within quite a wide range. Therefore, the number of possible intermediate positions within the limits of any bend, turn or stretch is very high. The number of possible forms of the body is conditional upon the number of joints.

It is well known that the human skeleton has over two hundred joints. In order to calculate the number of possible forms the body can take, it is necessary to know the *discretion level* in the operation of muscles. That means the minimum shift in the joint in which the smoothness of the change of the form is impossible and cannot be followed by the signal system. Movements beyond the *discretion level* cause the joint to pulsate.

Of course, this limit is different from one man to another, depending on sensitivity of his signal system. It can be altered with the advancement of sensitivity, so that awkward movements are substituted with smoothness and plasticity.

Sensitivity is developed through the purification of the perception channels and the development of attention, leading to an increase in the number of followed forms.

On the basis of the above, even without any precise mathematical calculations, we can estimate that the number of possible forms in any human's body is measured in hundreds of thousands.

This is the theory, but in reality human joints appear to be extremely different from the theoretical model, and have a great number of constraints that substantially reduce the number of possible bodily forms.

So, for example, **knee** and **elbow joints**, as well the «**knuckles**» of the **hand** and **feet** move in one plane. If we take a straight, relaxed arm or leg in a straight position, bending is only possible until the tissues of the forearm and the shoulder or the ankle and the thigh touch each other. The «back bend» against the straight line is almost impossible, and is seldom found, even in people born with hyper-flexible joints (not more than 15 per cent of the norm).

Side movements of the knee and elbow joints or the knuckles are almost impossible for a man. Even when individuals are capable of side movements, it is considered to be pathology, since when a joint moves in a «staggered» way, it is quickly worn out (like a worn out bearing in a car).

The structure of the **shoulders** and the **hip joints**, and the possible positions of these joints, are close to the theoretical model described above.

The **ankle** and the **wrist** function as something in between the knee and the thigh, and the elbow and the shoulder, respectively.

The **spine** is a sophisticated system of joints, which easily bends back and forth, but is «staggered» and ruined under deep transverse motions or turning. Moreover, it is connected with the ribs, decreasing the flexibility in the breast section.

The **breastbone** has a low mobility joint which changes its form only upon deep formation movements in the breast section.

The **lower jaw** is connected to the skull by a pair of joints, which provide mobility in both longitudinal and transverse directions and also allows circular motions in the horizontal plane around the vertical axis. But, it is almost impossible to turn it around the third (horizontal) axis.

The mobility of the **skull** bones is so small that it does not participate in the change of the body form.

In order to avoid injuries and reduce the wear of the joints, it is desirable to increase the free space and reduce the compression in the joints by longitudinal stretching, combined with any bending or turning of the joints.

Usually, longitudinal compression occurs naturally during strength exercises, where the weight of a part or the whole of the body is lifted. This is least desirable when doing exercises aimed at developing the ultimate flexibility of the joints.

Therefore, the first six mobility directions in the practice of Yoga are the main ones (Fig. 1б-ж). Whereas the last two, longitudinal stretching (Fig. 1щ) and compression (Fig. 1и), are secondary.

Theoretically, any form of the body has to be described by ninety different positions of its main elements, however in practice the anatomi cal restrictions in the knee and elbow joints limit the same to seventy-eight.

Fig. 2 (see p. 48 — 49) gives a universal formation scheme showing existing forms of the body, and ways of constructing new ones with regard to all elements of the body and the main directions of their mobility. In this scheme *Gherandasana* — «the posture of Wise *Gheranda*» is shown as an example.

With the help of this scheme any form of the body may be assigned a digital code, excluding the confusing array of the names given for this form in different schools of Yoga.

Using the whole range of all possible mobility directions depicted in the scheme (Fig. 2), one can separate any body form into elementary components, and recombine them to create a variety of new forms to include in training sets. Thus the practice may creatively be developed, remembering that the new body forms are the codes for the creation of ties in the psychic-energetical structure and in the body of the One. These new ties expand individual consciousness and «increase the level of generation and the power of the biocomputer».

THE SYSTEM OF EXPANDING AND BALANCING THE ARSENAL OF FORMS

In natural conditions, each fragment of the movement of any living crea ture (static form of the body – *Asana*) corresponds to a definite state of consciousness. And not only humans, but many other living beings on the Earth, can take different forms of the body, which correspond to particular states of consciousness, in order to fix and to transfer by this semantic codes (by their own appearance) this or that shape-intuitive information about their own state to those who watch them. For example, in the event of extreme danger, some insects pretend to be dead, and people, likewise being in an undesirable or dangerous situation, sometimes prefer to pretend that this situation does not exist. But people, unlike other creatures, in addition to being able to take forms, which are common for their natural behavior, are also capable of taking forms which are initially absent in nature at all.

The issues of natural behavior and morality are not the subjects of this section. The examples given only demonstrate the universal tie between the body form and the state of consciousness, as well as the practical possibility of controlling this dependence in life.

The tie of external form with internal state of consciousness, is two-sided. It is not only the body that reflects the consciousness, but, by changing the form of the body, relevant signal codes are translated into the con sciousness that transforms it. More over the possibility of controlling and ruling both the body forms and the consciousness state is simultaneously developed. In this case the controlling structures become a kind of «mediator» on the way of a direct tie between the body and the consciousness.

By accumulating practical experience in controlling and directing this code in one's own body and consciousness, a man develops the ability to «see through» to the real state of other people, irrespective of the psychical or physical masks used.

As a result the bones serve as special types of «antennaes», which perceive «subtle» information and at the same time they form these or those changes of torsion fields. Each joint acts as an energy center that controls energy flows and field tensions. And the increase in the mobility of joints, and the number of forms performed, facilitates both the purification of one's power channels and the expansion of one's conscious perception range.

The ultimate configuration of combined forms determines the number of logical ties within the «breadth» and «scope» of consciousness, as well as the intensity and capacity of the psychic-energetic structure and process. Therefore, Yoga uses various means to ever expand the arsenal of subordinate forms.

Looking at the human skeleton one can distinguish 15 main zones of joints where the control of energy flows occurs. These are the three pairs of leg joints (hips, knees and ankle joints), three pairs of arm joints (shoulders, elbows and wrists) and three spine sections (lumbar, dorsal and cervical). On the basis of the formation theory, each of these zones has six main directions of movements and changing of there form: forth and back bends, side bends, and side turns. Therefore, there are (15x6) 90 main directions of skeletal mobility («sectors»).

But among these 90 main directions, there are a number of technically similar skeleton mobility, the only difference being that they are performed asymmetrically on one leg or the other, or on one or the other side. The asymmetrical exercises performed by this or that leg, asymmetrical bends to the sides and twists, correspond to such technically equal form changes. These asymmetrical exercises are absolutely different in effect, which should be accounted for in practice, but their technique is absolutely similar, so the complete arsenal of skeleton mobility is reduced to 42 technically different directions as presented in Table 1.

№	Body part	Ele-ment, joint	Move-ment direction	Graphic example	Asana complexity levels			
					1	2	3	4
					Muscular	Tendon	Joint	Hollow
1	Spine	Loin	Bend forth	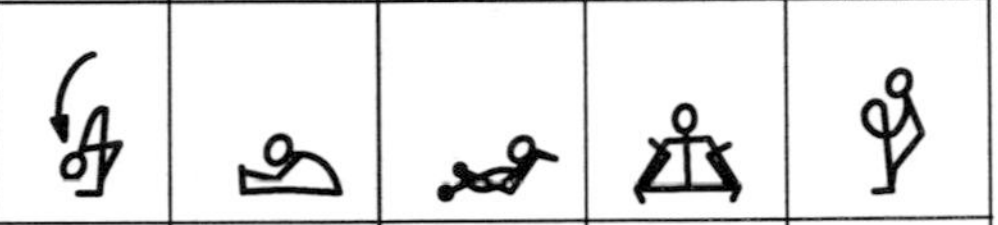				
2	Spine	Loin	Back arch					
3	Spine	Loin	Bend aside					
4	Spine	Loin	Rotation	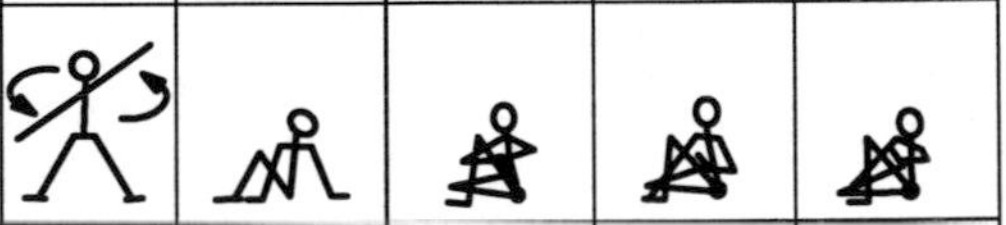				
5	Spine	Chest	Bend forth	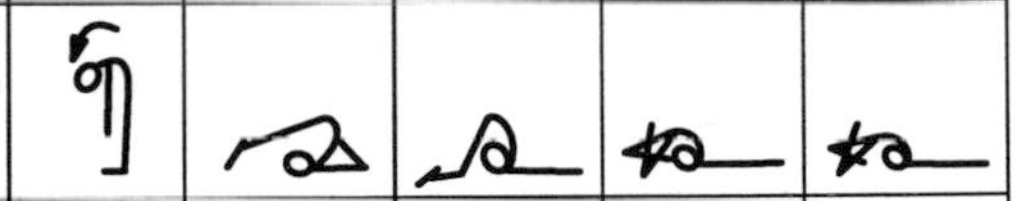				
6	Spine	Chest	Back arch					
7	Spine	Chest	Bend aside					
8	Spine	Chest	Rotation	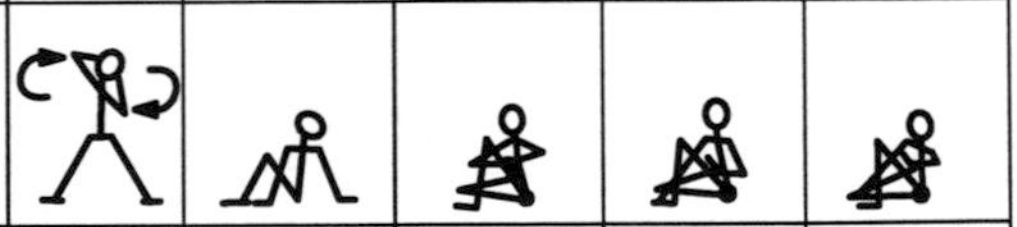				
9	Spine	Neck	Bend forth	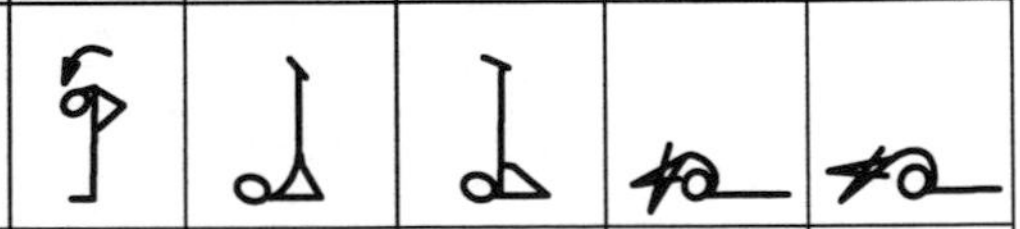				
10	Spine	Neck	Back arch	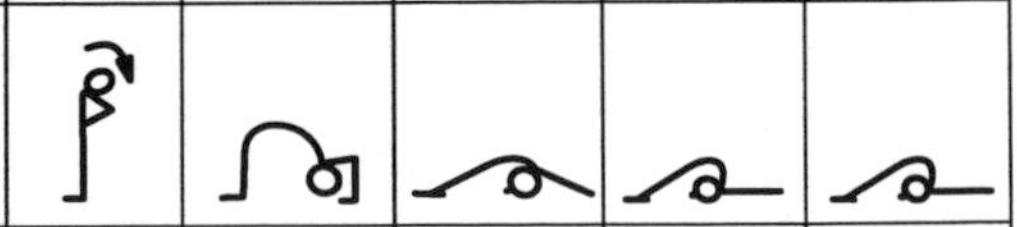				
11	Spine	Neck	Bend aside	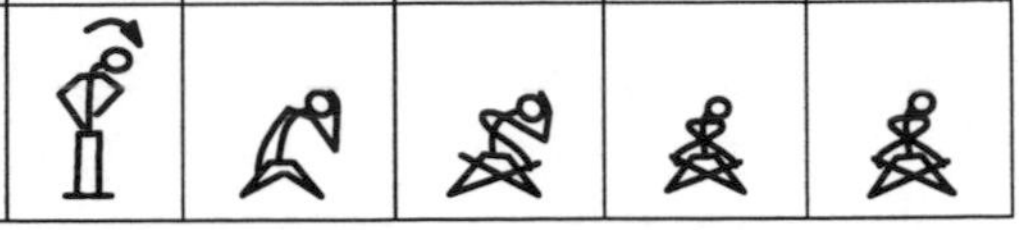				

№	Body part	Element, joint	Movement direction	Graphic example	Asana complexity levels			
					1	2	3	4
					Muscular	Tendon	Joint	Hollow
12	Spine	Neck	Rotation	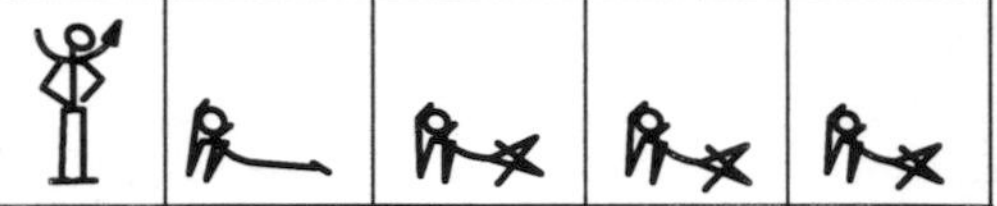				
13	Leg	Thigh	Longitudinal drawing forward	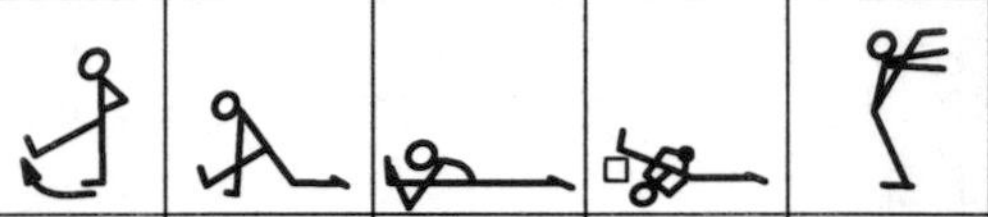				
14	Leg	Thigh	Longitudinal drawing backward	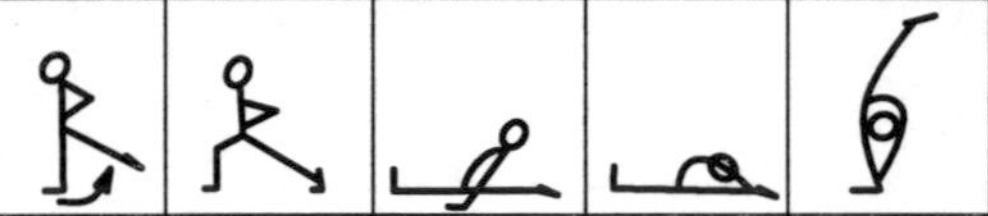				
15	Leg	Thigh	Transverse drawing outward	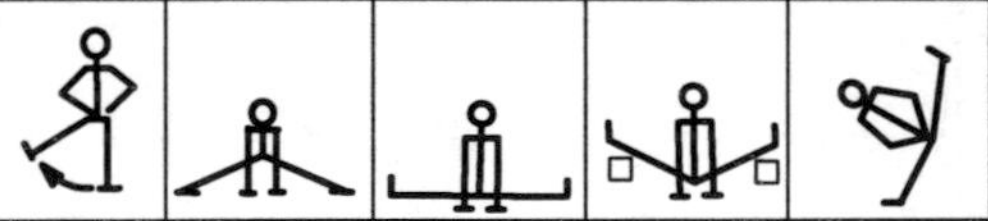				
16	Leg	Thigh	Drawing inward	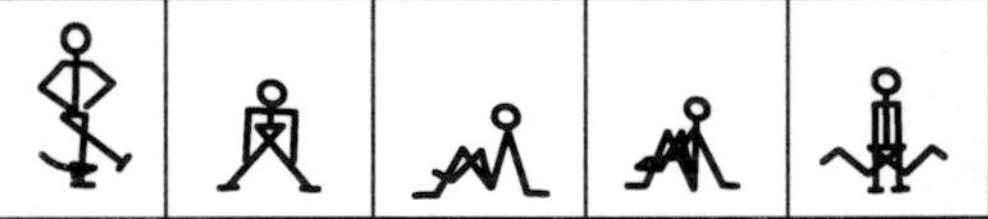				
17	Leg	Thigh	Outward rotation	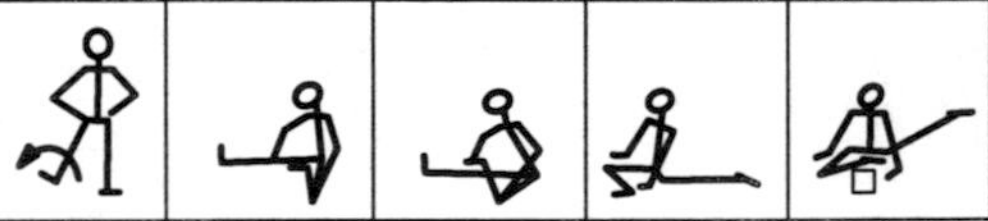				
18	Leg	Thigh	Inward rotation	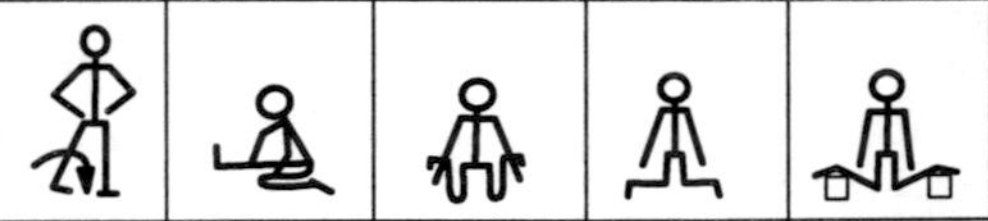				
19	Leg	Knee	Longitudinal unbending					
20	Leg	Knee	Bending outward					
21	Leg	Knee	Bending inward	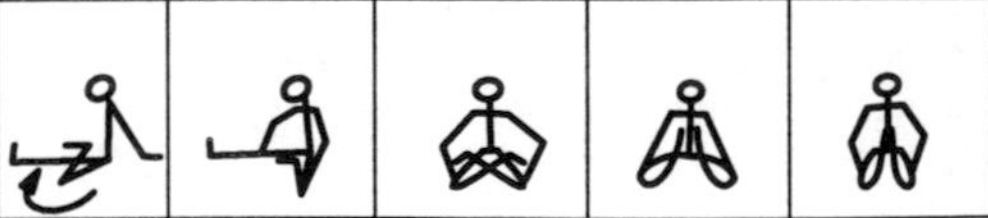				
22	Leg	Ankle joint	Longitudinal drawing forward	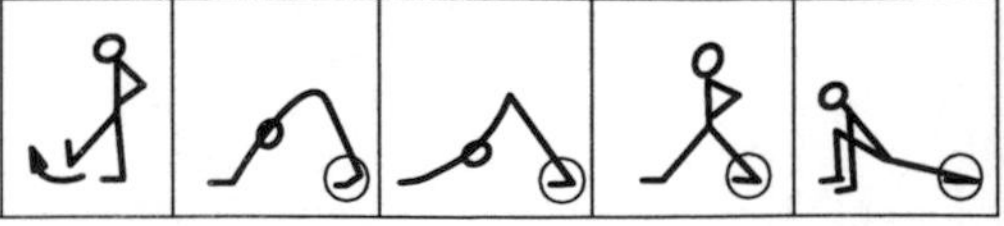				

№	Body part	Ele-ment, joint	Move-ment direction	Graphic example	Asana complexity levels			
					1	2	3	4
					Muscular	Tendon	Joint	Hollow
23	Leg	Ankle-joint	Longitudi-nal drawing backward					
24	Leg	Ankle-joint	Transverse drawing inward	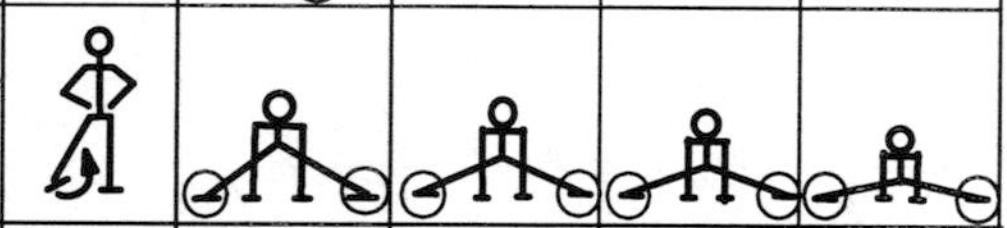				
25	Leg	Ankle-joint	Transverse drawing outward	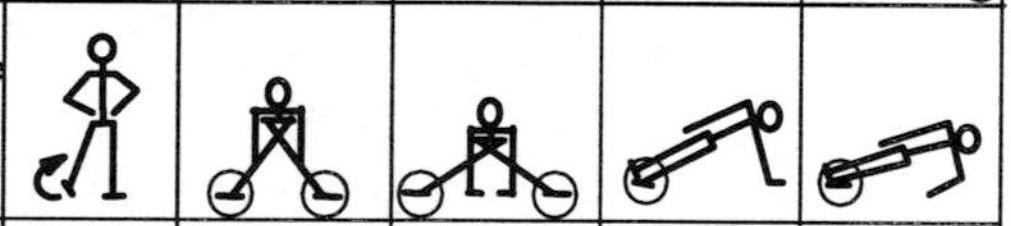				
26	Leg	Ankle-joint	Outward rotation					
27	Leg	Ankle-joint	Inward rotation	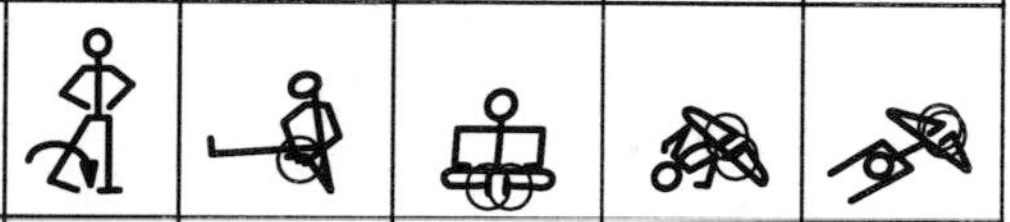				
28	Arm	Shoul-der	Longitudi-nal drawing up and back					
29	Arm	Shoul-der	Longitudi-nal drawing down and back	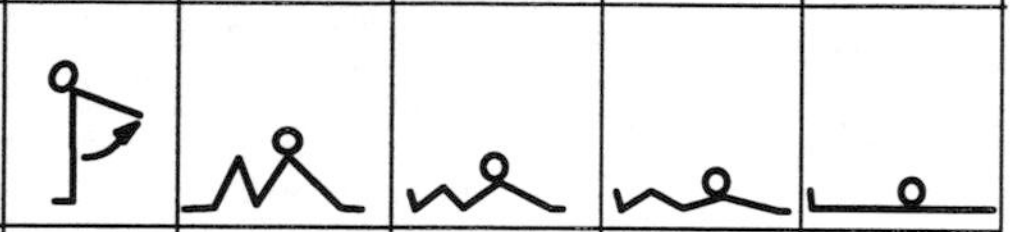				
30	Arm	Shoul-der	Transverse drawing outward and back					
31	Arm	Shoul-der	Transverse drawing inward and back	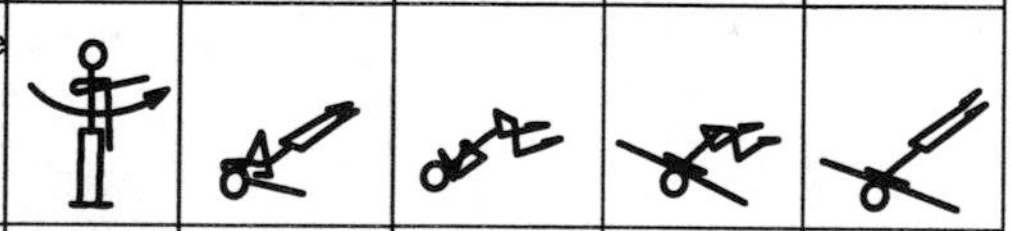				
32	Arm	Shoul-der	Outward rotation	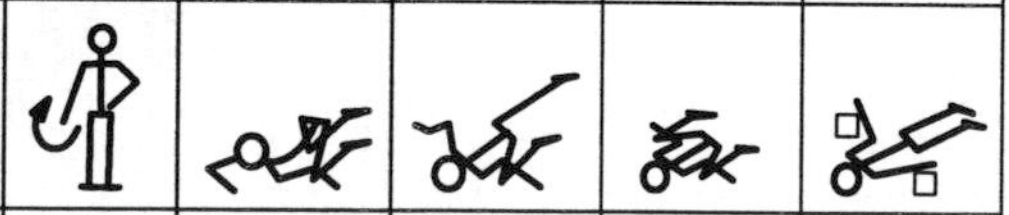				
33	Arm	Shoul-der	Inward rotation					

№	Body part	Element, joint	Movement direction	Graphic example	Asana complexity levels 1 Muscular	2 Tendon	3 Joint	4 Hollow
34	Arm	Elbow	Unbending	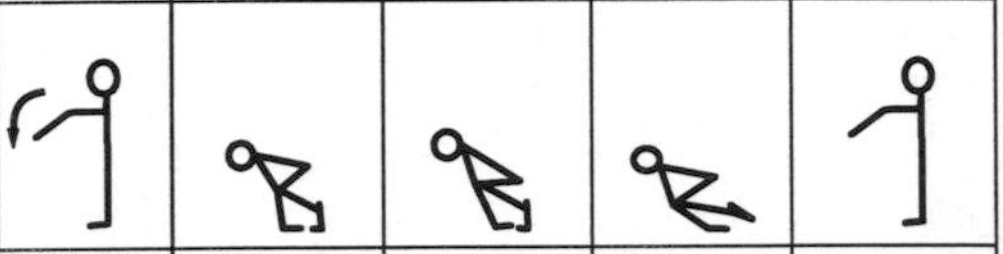				
35	Arm	Elbow	Bending outward	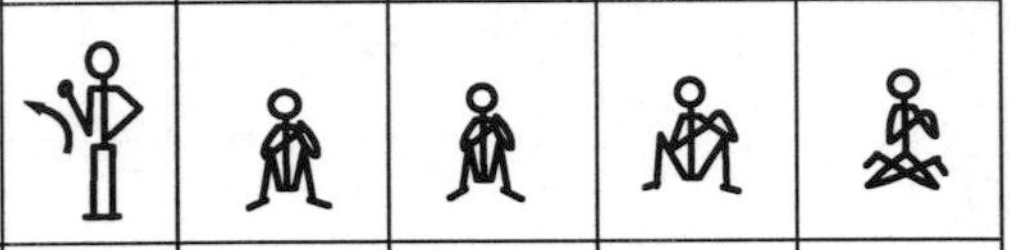				
36	Arm	Elbow	Bending inward					
37	Arm	Wrist	Longitudinal bending upward					
38	Arm	Wrist	Longitudinal bending down	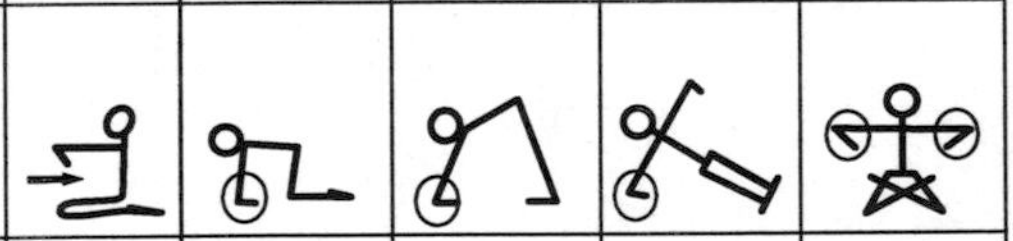				
39	Arm	Wrist	Transverse bending down	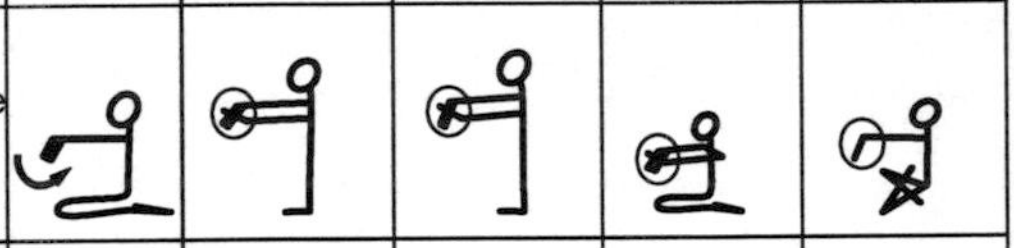				
40	Arm	Wrist	Transverse bending up					
41	Arm	Wrist	Outward rotation	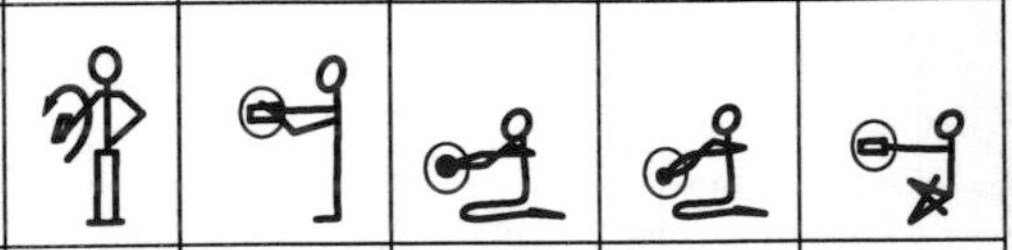				
42	Arm	Wrist	Inward rotation	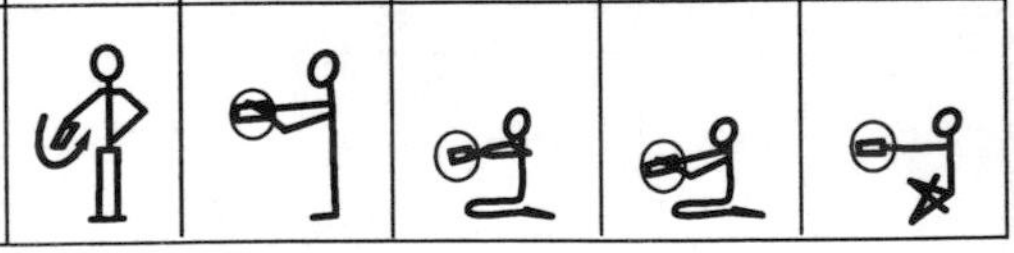				

Table. 1

Besides the degree of mobility of that or other joints is conditional upon the surrounding tissues: muscles, tendons, bursas of the joints, etc., as well as the anatomical configuration of the joints themselves. Thus four levels of restricted mobility may conditionally be taken: *muscle*, *tendon*, *joint* and *cavity* levels. These restriction levels correspond to the «four levels of all-round liberation» (Table 1). In order to simplify the understanding of the schematic body posture drawings given in Table 1 one may use the summary descriptions of these postures, which are set forth in Attachment 1.

1. *Muscle restrictions* are connected with the stiffening of the muscles. Ultimate mobility at this level allows the practitioner to perform such *Asanas* as, for example: «triangles», «passes», and the simplest back bends: *Bhujangasana*, *Dhanurasana* and forward bends: *Pacchimottanasana*, *Halasana*, and also *Ardha Padmasana* and *Virasana*.

Special cleansing measures, energy control and regular training based on the tie of the movement with the breath, combined with the use of similar preparatory exercises allows one to purify and liberate the body of toxins and stiffness, and quickly overcome muscle restrictions. In this case one's mobility may be increased by centimeters within months.

2. *Tendon restrictions* are connected with the restricted plasticity and the length of the tendons. Ultimate mobility at this level allows the practitioner to perform such *Asanas* as, for example: longitudinal and transverse splits, circular catches of legs in back bends of the type of *Padangustha Dhanurasana*, exercises with the legs behind the head, *Padmasana* and *Vamadevasana*.

Pure, balanced food, the optimum expense and accumulation of additional energy, and intensive training with prolonged times in ultimate postures, allow one to gradually change the quality of the tissues and stretch the tendons. In this case the mobility can be increased by centimeters within years.

3. *Joint restrictions* are dependent on the plasticity and size of joint bursas. Ultimate flexibility at this level allows one to perform such *Asanas* as , for example: longitudinal and transverse splits with negative angles, circle-like back bends without catching the legs with the hands of the type of *Kapotasana*, with the feet placed on the back or *Pandagustha Dhanurasana*, with the toes held by the jaw, exercises with legs under the armpits, such as *Bhuddhasana*, *Kapilasana* and *Yoga Dandasana*, as well as *Mula Bandhasana*, *Kandasana*, and *Vamadevasana*, with the feet held by the side of the waist without participation of the arms.

Special food, daily regime, increase one's psychic-energy potential and cautious training with the use of similar exercises allows to rich of vast extraordinary qualities within the tissues of the body, stretches the bursas and creates additional space in the joints. In this case mill imeters of «space» are achieved in years.

4. *Cavity restrictions* are manifested as counteracting forces. When deep hyper-mobil ity of the joints and surrounding muscles and tendons is achieved, the problem of «staggering» and uncontrolled displacement of bones in the joints can appear. The joints may start "booming" under various moves. This increases their wear. The intent of cavity-level training is the search for a reasonable balance between the expending and compression, between the greatest possible diapason of mobil ity range and the avoidance of body injury and healthy.

Strengthening the muscles surrounding the «staggered» joints, so that conscious control of joint position is possible controls extra hyper-flexibil ity at the cavity level.

Balancing the most del icate mechanisms of the consciousness, indisputably requires keeping a balance of mobil ity in all directions.

Unfortunately, not only beginners, but many experienced practitioners often have no the laws of harmony, and some of the parts of their body may contain muscle restrictions, but other parts may contain joint restrictions, etc. Usually, this is connected to initially using those elements and properties of the body that are initially in better condition, and ignoring those that are underdeveloped.

Practical use in training the system presented in this book should begin with the comparison and evaluation of your abil ity to do the example exercises presented in Table 1. This will allow you to easily determine mobil ity restrictions, and the level of individual development in any of the main mobil ity directions. Further evaluation during the course of this practice will allow you to accurately monitor your slow and fast-developing elements, and introduce corrections in the individual training program.

Balancing the «sectors» begins by working on the development of slow elements, and bringing them up to the level of fast-developing ones. After that, one can use broad-based training oriented towards the versatile development of flexibil ity in all the elements.

This, however, does not mean that the exercises involving well-developed elements should not be used. A balanced training program should act on all the elements but maximum influence must be on the underdeveloped elements. But well-developed elements must be used as much as it is possible to use the poorly developed elements. Only this approach will make the overall psychic-energy effect of the training well balanced and harmonic.

Only when the underdeveloped elements gradually improve, and will reach the ultimate ability level of the well-developed elements, the balance will be reached, and one can begin all-round ultimate practice.

Almost all Yoga practitioners face the problem of inconsistency between their possibilities and the set of exercises proposed by a particular school for training. Understanding the basic mobility directions and the level of their development (Table 1) allows the practitioner to easily adapt **any** established set of exercises to one's own abilities, both towards simplification or complication, thus controlling the power of energy flow without changing the energy configuration of the set of exercises themselves and preserve the core of training's effect on the consciousness.

Such adaptation may be realized in both independently performed sets of exercises, and in the exercises proposed at group training classes.

Of course, in-group training, fast adaptation is only possible with sufficient experience and free use of this adaptation system.

Besides the use of Table 1 allows to construct individual training programs that include all the main joint mobility directions, without omitting any of the important psychic-energy controls. In order to make these programs perfect it/is necessary to accumulate practical experience and knowledge about the effect of particular *Asanas* and their sequences on the psychic-energy structure.

Since these elements of the body are intertwined, action on any joint will result in action on an adjacent joint. Therefore, it is nearly impossible to exert selective influence on a joint or a section of the spine independent of the adjacent body elements, or with the help of particular exercises to affect only separate parts of the body corresponding to any energy centers. So, for example, bending the knee inside in «Half-Lotus» causes a simultaneous outward turning of the hip; when the first leg is drawn foreword in the longitudinal split, the second leg is drawn backwards simultaneously; or during the back bend, the dorsal section usually implies that the back is also arched in the cervical or lumbar sections of the spine. On one hand this is a drawback, but on the other hand, in real practice, this allows to use a much smaller number of basic exercises if compared to their aggregate number, as presented in Table 1. This reduces overall training time without cutting the efficiency of the impact of training in all main mobility directions.

At the same time real training exercises often contain multiple varieties of similar forms on the same complexity level, differing in minor secondary details or just in the positions of these forms in the dimensional space.

POSITION OF THE FORM IN THE DIMENSIONAL SPACE

When one of the bodily forms is set, its disposition in the dimensional space may be different depending on which of the different elements of the body serve as the supported ones, and this will lead to different energy-related results.

The Body of the One is an endless conglomeration of universal ties, which are closed including each human being. And any living being has the mechanism of ties to the Body of the One (for example, through electromagnetic, gravitational and torsion interactions).

So the ties with the most ancient and unchanging kinds of energies provide vital important processes and remain unchangeable for millions of years. And in comparison with the life of a human being, and mankind as a whole, are almost constant.

One such constant on the Earth is the tension of the gravitational field. The main basic subconscious mechanisms are oriented towards the force of gravitation. For example, our sleep cycle, blood circulation, vestibule apparatus, sexual activity, intestinal peristalsis, etc.

Are *standing* and *sitting* positions in the human life equal? Can you fall asleep while standing? Not really. And this vertical position allows for an awakened state of mind. And what happens if one lies down without any purpose? This position requires no work of the muscles to balance the body, the body gradually relaxes and the consciousness falls asleep. This is one of the reasons why eating before you go to sleep, or reading while lying down, are harmful.

Cycles of the Earth around the Sun, and of the Moon around the Earth, determine high and low tides of the oceans, and the life rhythms of all beings dwelling on the planet. But the base of planetary organization is the Field, which defines the Universal Order. And the forces of gravitation are simply a tangible manifestation of the interaction of celestial bodies.

So, the dimensional system includes six main positions for each form and a variety of intermediary positions between them, which correspond to the result of influence of these or those of the main ones.

The main group includes the following positions: head up (1) and head down (4), abdomen up (2) and abdomen down (6), on the one side (3) and on the other side (5) (Figure 3).

Positions on one side and on the other are different, because of the asymmetrical disposition of the internal organs in the human body.

The forms that involve deep hyper-mobility, where the body takes a ring shape become combined, because they create powerful reactions in

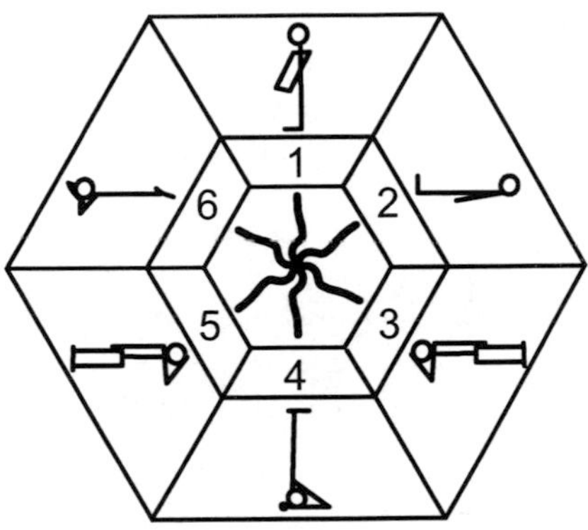

Fig. 3

the nervous system, change circulation and blood pressure, and have gravitational affects on different parts of the body in different ways.

If the position of the straight line of the spine and the head in the dimensional space are basically conditional upon the potential rest planes of the straight body: forward, backward, upper, lower and sideways, and then the deformation of the spine is completed and circular forms in the back bends or forward bends, the possible positions of the body in the dimensional space are chiefly determined by the planes of the rigid elements of the body.

For example, in the ring-shape form with back bend in *Pandagustha Dhanurasana* (Fig. 4a) or with a forward bend in the «*Lotus*» in *Yoga Mudra* (Fig. 46) the body rests on five slanting planes on which it may be supported stabley. It is also possible to use different types of resting on the hands, legs and head, which created additional positions. As was mentioned earlier, in each different position there is a different effect from the Earth's gravitational field on the psychic-energy structure. And different forms, positioned in various ways, determine relevant changes in torsion fields. Therefore, similar forms of the body with different foundations have principal differences in terms of their effect, and have different names in the Tradition of Yoga. Besides the back bend in Fig. 4a, where is rest on the abdomen in *Pandagustha Dhanurasana*, a similar bend, when is rest on the upper part of the chest, neck, and chin is *Ganda Bherundasana* (Fig. 4в); where is rest on the forearms is *Chakra Bandhasana* (Fig. 4г); also similar bend, when is rest on the feet is *Triang Mukhottanasana* (Fig. 4e), or when is rest on the knees and feet is *Kapotanasana* (Fig. 4f); and resting on the thighs, knees and toes is also another posture, which is not met in classical literature (Fig. 4g). The forward bend as presented in Figure 46, resting on the thighs, which exists in *Yoga Mudra*, a similar bend, where is rest on the forearms and the head bears the name of *Pindasana* in *Sirsasana* (Fig. 4h); resting on the shoulders is *Pindasana* in *Sarvangasana* (Fig. 4i); resting on the back is *Pindasana* in *Savasana* (Fig. 4j); resting on the buttocks is *Pindasana* (Fig. 4k); and with resting on the hands (arms) is *Urdhva Kukkutasana* (Fig. 4l).

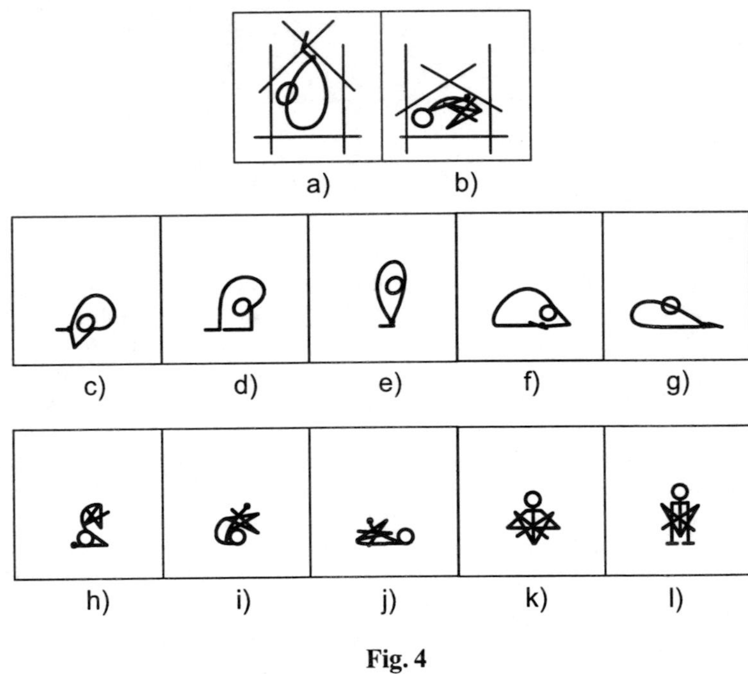

Fig. 4

Table 2 (p. 48 — 49) gives other samples of base forms which are wide-spread in the practice of Yoga, and which correspond to the four complexity levels in different dimensional positions.

Although at first glance, it appears the «main exercises» given in Table 1 will develop all types of mobility. From the point of view of the psychic-energy effect, this first impression is absolutely unjustified, since these practices result in the reduction of psychic-energy capacity, perception range and the diversity of the practice as an art.

It is also worth noting that in order to facilitate the understanding of the exercises presented in Tables 1 and 2, the pictures show not only individual parts of the body, which receive the main influence, but the entire body. This may give the impression that these exercises are devised to exert influence on some secondary elements of the body. To avoid this mis take and have the correct understanding of which of the elements is the main one on a particular drawing, please follow the additional short descriptions of the forms depicted in Tables 1 and 2, which are contained in relevant appendices to these tables (see p. 35 — 38, 46 — 47). In order to facilitate the understanding on some of the drawings, the main influence zones are circled.

The body forms presented in Tables 1 and 2 are not exhaustive and have particular «synonyms», i. e., other forms requiring the same mobility level in the «sectors» under question, but positioned in different ways in the dimensional space or having other positions of auxiliary elements (e.g., foundations). Therefore, the forms presented in Tables 1 and 2 are just the most typical, and are sufficient to understand the principle of differentiation of the main mobility directions and complexity levels of positions.

VINYASAS

Vinyasa — is the movement of the body synchronized with the breath.

The formation theory allows to classify all possible dynamic movements (*Vinyasas*) beginning from the neutral position. According to their dynamic characteristics, *Vinyasas* are divided into several groups:

1. *Direction of movement* — single-directional (for example, from the first form of the body to the second, then to the third, without returning back to the first one) and bi-directional (for example, from the first form of the body to the second one and back to the first one).

Single-directional *Vinyasas* are usually used to connect moves when making the transition from one form of the body to another, whereas bi-directional forms make ring-type movement cycles, and are used to achieve specific psychic-energy results.

2. *Number of repetitions* — single (for example, one cycle, from the first form of the body to the second, and back to the first one, and then subsequent transition to the third form), and multiple (for example, repetition of several similar cycles in succession, from the first form of the body to the second, and back to the first form).

The number of repetitions determines the accumulated psychic-energy effect. And this number depends on intermediate tasks in the general algorithm of reaching the training goal.

3. *Number of moving elements of the body* — single-element *Vinyasas* (for example, the movement of one arm, without changing the form of the other parts of the body) and group *Vinyasas* (for example, simultaneous movement of the arms, legs and the spine).

Single-element *Vinyasas* are used in the following cases: in changes of position of one of the limbs; in movements of the spine without changing

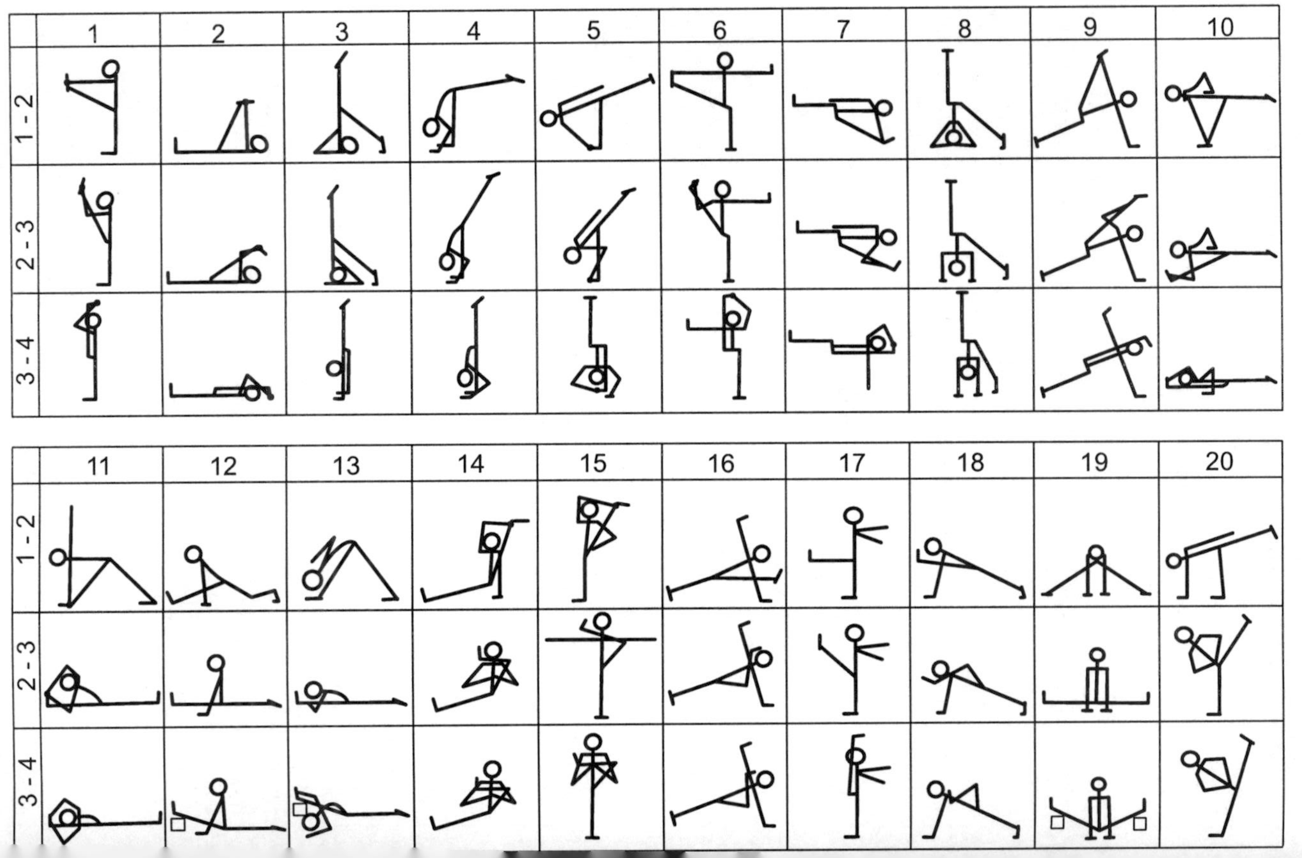
1
2
3
4
5
6
7
8
9
10
1 - 2
2 - 3
3 - 4
11
12
13
14
15
16
17
18
19
20
1 - 2
2 - 3
3 - 4

	21	22	23	24	25	26	27	28	29	30
1 - 2										
2 - 3										
3 - 4										

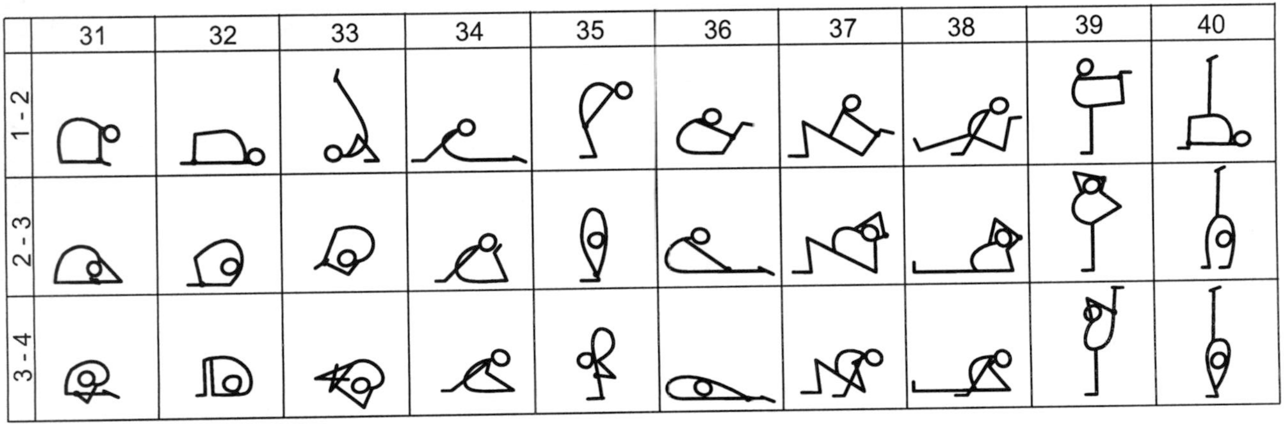

	31	32	33	34	35	36	37	38	39	40
1 - 2										
2 - 3										
3 - 4										

Table 2

UNIVERSAL FORMATION SCHEME

“Gherandasana”

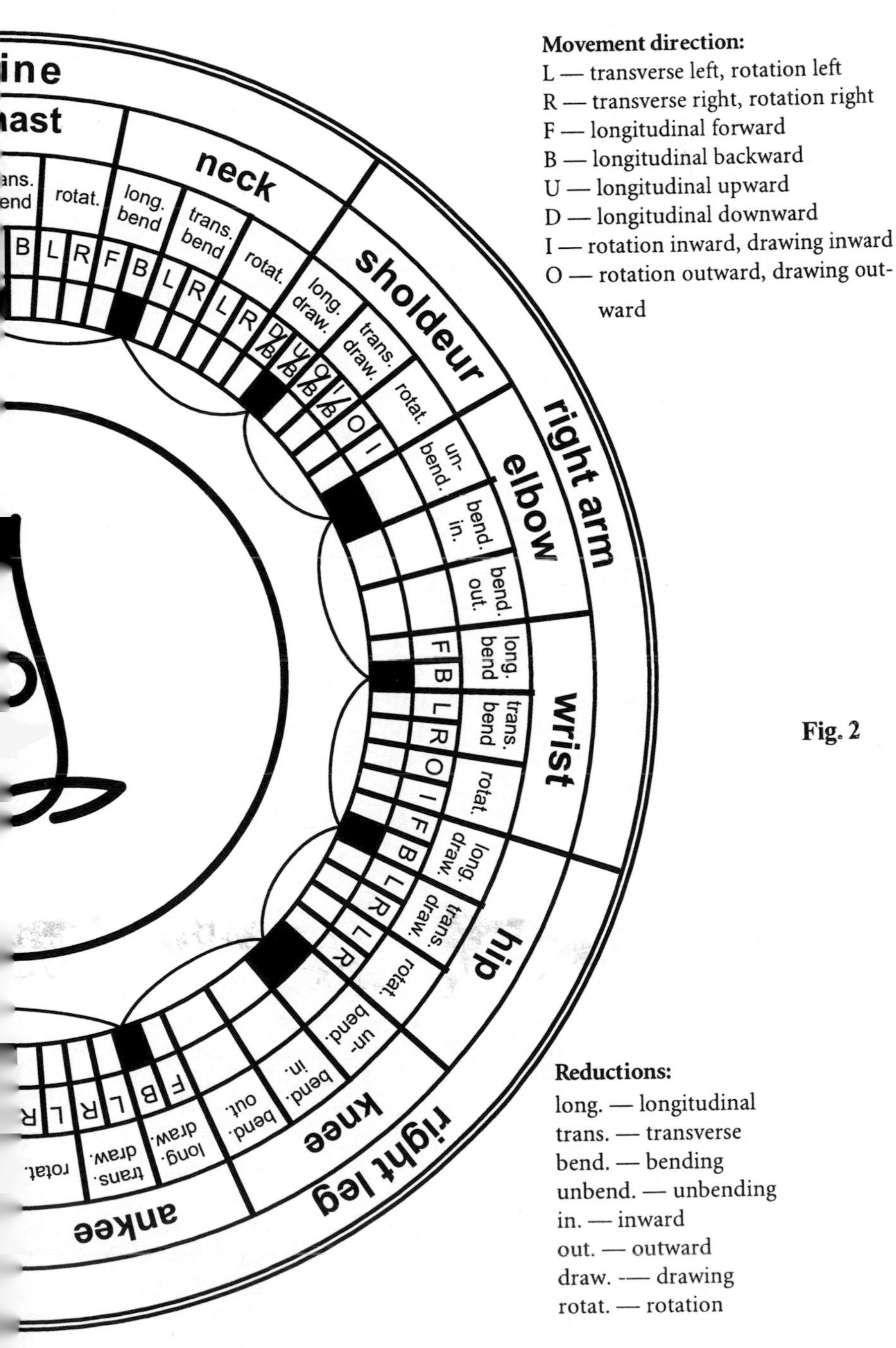

Movement direction:

L — transverse left, rotation left
R — transverse right, rotation right
F — longitudinal forward
B — longitudinal backward
U — longitudinal upward
D — longitudinal downward
I — rotation inward, drawing inward
O — rotation outward, drawing outward

Fig. 2

Reductions:

long. — longitudinal
trans. — transverse
bend. — bending
unbend. — unbending
in. — inward
out. — outward
draw. — drawing
rotat. — rotation

position of the limbs; while «push-ups» on one hand or «squats» on one leg and etc. Due to the intertwined nature of the movements of different body parts, group *Vinyasas* are used much more frequently in practice.

4. *Speed of motion* — fast (for example, movements at maximum speed without the loss of quality), slow (for example, special deliberately slow motion) and extra slow (for example, in movements, which are so slow that they cannot be differentiated if looking from the side).

Speed depends on the style of the training, and in turn determines the characteristics of the psychic-energy processes.

High speed facilitates general activation and the concentration of the Power of Spirit.

Low speed increases the density of the energy flowing to the maximum point, and is of greatest use in the development of physical strength and endurance. Low speed can also reduce injury in practice.

The extra-slow motion mode increases energy flow density to the maximum point, requiring extreme will-control, physical power and endurance. Extra slow mode almost corresponds to static fixation. Therefore, its training effect is close to the practice of static forms and develops static power and endurance.

5. *Influence on bodily form* — symmetric (for example, upon symmetrical forward bend from the standing position) and asymmetric (for example, raising one leg from symmetrical standing position).

Symmetric and asymmetric movements depend on the energy configuration of the training algorithm and the motivations generated during spontaneous training.

6. *Relation to counter-force* — superior (for example, lifting the body weight in «raising on hands» from the floor) and inferior (for example, lowering the body to the floor from the raised position).

In the superior movement phase, muscle strength dominates body weight, while the inferior movement phase allows the body weight to dominate.

It should be remembered that the inferior phase should always be smooth and slow without jerks and tension fluctuations. For example, lowering the legs to the floor from a handstand position should occur as a restrained, controlled movement rather than an uncontrolled fall.

7. *Spine direction in the dimensional space* — unchanged (for example, movement of the arms or legs with the spine remaining in vertical position) and changed (for example, in the change of the spine from the horizontal position to vertical).

An unchanged direction of the spine allows only limb movements. Therefore, such *Vinyasas* usually change positions of the limbs with respect to a relatively fixed form, or move this form along the gravitation component using various arms or legs «presses». Position of the form de termines subconscious reactions and the psychic-energy result. Therefore, *Vinyasas* with the changed spine position are used for special purposes (see below).

8. *Influence on the spine* — when curved (for example, in the back bend of the spine from upright position), and when fixed (for example, in the change of position of the spine from horizontal to vertical, keeping the spine straight).

Movement without curving the spine is only possible when the limbs move to change positions, or when doing «presses» while maintaining a fixed form of the body. Energy circulation depends on the form of the spine. And *Vinyasas* with spinal bends are often used in the practice of Yoga for special purposes (see below).

Movements in *Vinyasas* require muscular efforts, which develop dynamic strength, endurance and coordination. These efforts may be different and depend on the scope of the force necessary to move a particular body element or the whole of body. Therefore, according to complexity levels, *Vinyasas* are subdivided as follows:

1. «Turns» and «revolutions» of the body on the floor.
2. «Steps» and «jumps» while changing the relevant position of the feet in standing position.
3. «Waves» and «punches» with arms or legs.
4. «Pushups» and «jumps» on one or two arms with support on one or two legs.
5. «Somersaults» over the head, arms, or legs, and «cartwheels».
6. «Squats» and «lunges» on one or two legs while lifting the weight of the whole body.
7. «Presses» with one or two arms while lifting the weight of the whole body.
8. Various acrobatic movements of the whole body in the air like «flips» or their fragments.

Different schools and styles, depending on the main orientation, use different movements or combinations of movements from the above groups of *Vinyasas*.

All theoretical possibilities of the *Vinyasas* are, no doubt, interesting for the development of artistic training, and to obtain consciousness-developing experience. But from the point of view of time, only some of them are efficient in practice.

PSYCHIC-ENERGY MANDALA

The main peculiarity of the *Vinyasas* is a powerful psychic-energy influence, which is based on several effects:

1. Changing the position of the head and the spine acts on the «basic ties» of the sub-conscious to the Earth's gravitation field, which causes powerful reactions in the basic instincts of the subconscious and increases the tension of the psychic-energy structure field.
2. Spinal formations within opposing sectors exert strong influence on the vegetative nervous system, initiating spinal energy flows and increasing body temperature (increasing heat literally «melts» the tissues).
3. Deep breathing brings enormous energy into the system, and, like a tonometer, tunes all of the flows to a single rhythm, which produces a reverberating energy surge.
4. The connection of attention with breathing rhythm stops thinking, and in this case the mind energy becomes free and sublimates into the intellect.
5. Physical efforts actuate energy circulation in the extremities channels.

Those Vinyasas that incorporate all five of these effects provide the most powerful effect on the psychic-energy system. They provide for simultaneous positions of the head and the spine with respect to the gravitational component, spinal formation among opposing sectors, synchronization of the movement and the breath, and the training of the main groups of the body muscles. In essence, these are the *Principal Vinyasas.*

Principal Vinyasas are usually used to «start» and «untwist» the so-called Psychic-energy Mandala. This results in the rapid development of the practitioner's psychic-energy power, increase the body temperature, activation of the internal metabolism processes, comprehensive cleansing of the energy channels and the organic body of polluting substances, and efficient training of the principal groups of muscles. Usually they are performed one by one, using key forms of the body or in sequences consisting of 3, 6, 12 or more repetitions.

Principal Vinyasas are integrated into training sessions at the points requiring energy «activation» and «charging».

The value of the *Principal Vinyasas* in the practice of Yoga can not be overstated. Nothing can be compared to them in terms of the powerful impact on the psychic-energy system.

MULTILEVEL VINYASAS ALGORITHM

With regard to the six principal body positions (Fig. 3), there are only six *Principal Vinyasas*, which are critically different in terms of their effect on the psychic-energy structure (Fig. 5).

Fig. 5

The difference between the «first side up» *Vinyasas* and those with the «first side down" is important, and must be taken into consideration in the general algorithm of training. But the technique used in their performance is absolutely similar. Therefore, in further description of the *Principal Vinyasas* technique, and the algorithms of connecting them with the other *Vinyasas* and *Asanas*, only five technically different *Principle Vinyasas* will be described: «head up», «head down», «abdomen up», «abdomen down», and «on the side», as shown on the pentagram of the *Principal Vinyasas* (Fig. 6).

In this pentagram the movements are presented in only two longitudinal planes, the forward bend and the back bend, as they are usually performed, in sequences consisting of several repeated longitudinal cycles. These *Vinyasas* form the group of *Principal Longitudinal Vinyasas.*

But each of the initial positions provides the possibility to move in three planes. That means not only longitudinal, but also transversal and twisting spine-forming moves. Therefore, the pentagram of the Principal *Vinyasas* (Fig. 6) provides only a «longitudinal section» of three-dimensional *Vinyasas* algorithm. These additional transversal and twisting side movements form two more groups of *Principal Transversal Vinyasas* and *Principal Twisting Vinyasas.*

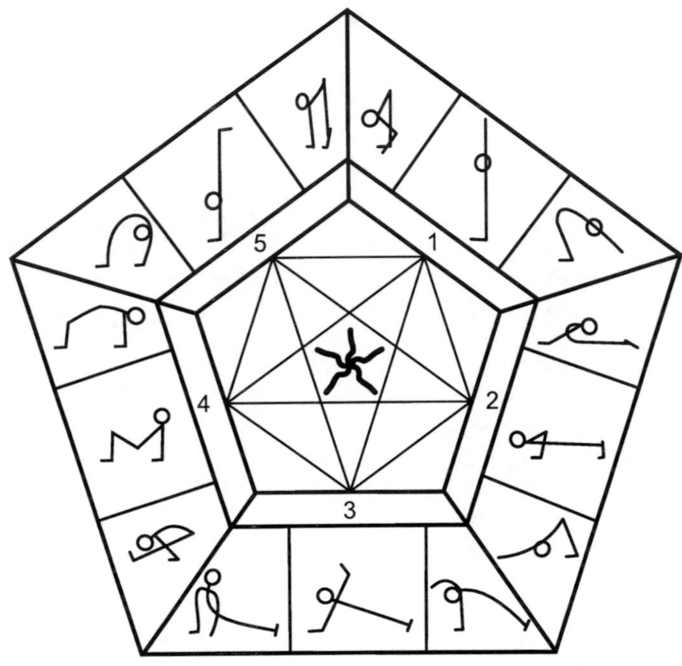

Fig. 6

For example, the «standing upright» *Vinyasa,* in addition to a longitudinal forward bend and back bend, is also performed with transversal bends strictly to the sides (Fig. 7a) and twists (Fig. 7b).

Anatomical restrictions limit a man from performing all of the theoretically possible side movements. For example, side movements from the standing position are restricted by «dead-end» bends (Fig. 7a). There are not more then ten performable movements strictly to the sides. Therefore,

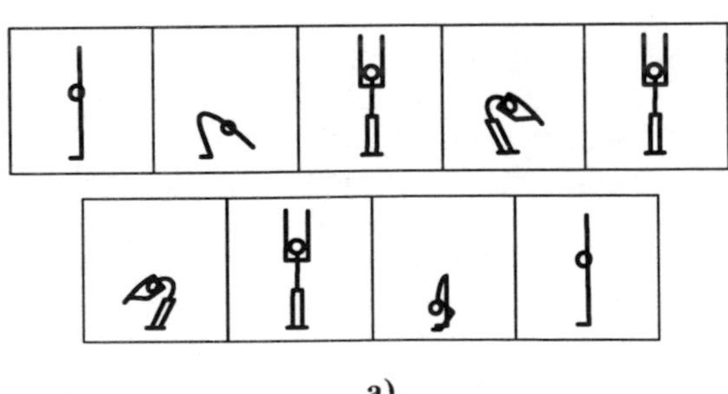

a)

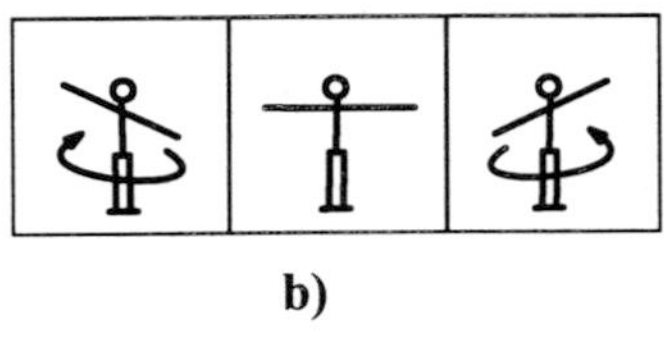

b)

Fig. 7

Yoga traditionally has used replacements to side bends, in the form of various diagonal moves: to the side and slightly forward, or to the side and slightly backward. In fact, such diagonal moves are something in-between transversal movements to the sides and twists.

So, for example, from *Sarvangasana* — «Postures for all parts of the body» — bends strictly to the sides are practically impossible. Therefore, these moves are replaced by diagonal bends with both legs in *Parsva Halasana* («Side Plough») or *Parsva Setu Bandha Sarvangasana* («Side back bend standing on the shoulders») (Fig. 8). The group of the *Principal Transversal Vinyasas*, has a few movements strictly to the sides, but mainly includes such diagonal moves.

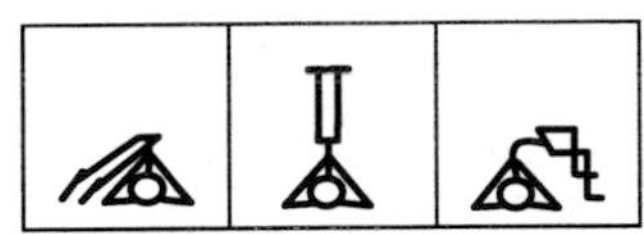

Fig. 8

The *Principal Twisting Vinyasas* have modifications corresponding to practically all of the *Principal Vinyasas* in the «head up», «head down», and «abdomen up» positions. But in «abdomen down» and «on the side» positions, twisting moves are difficult because, as a rule, the arms and the legs in these positions are used as foundation elements. Therefore, such positions limit the practitioner to only some of the *Principal Twisting Vinyasas* which are not very effective.

The *Principal Longitudinal Vinyasas* presented in Fig. 5 are the most typical *Vinyasas* and represent the different positions of the body in the dimensional space. But in fact, each of the six principle positions of the spine, with respect to the direction of the Earth's gravitational field, may be fixed with different parts of the body used for foundation: parts of arms, legs, body, neck and head. And each position, with its corresponding foundation, may serve as an initial form for relevant *Principal Longitudinal, Transversal* or *Twisting Vinyasa.*

So, for example, there is a minimum of four principally different foun dations and respective *Principal Longitudinal Vinyasas* of the «head down» type (Fig. 9):

1) «On the shoulders»;
2) «On the head and the hands»;
3) «On the forearms»;
4) «On the hands (palms)».

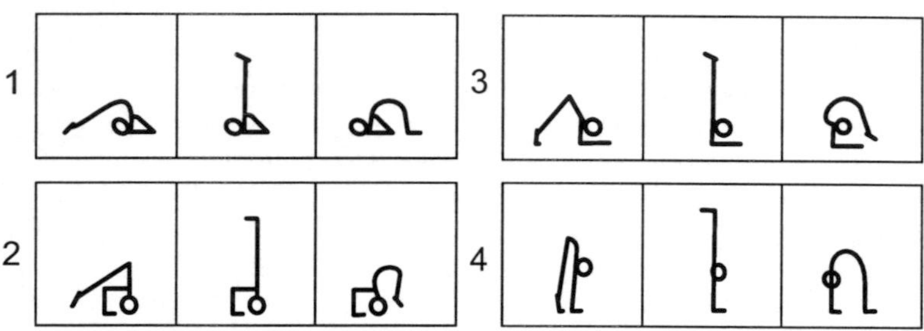

Fig. 9

And four principally different foundations and respective *Principal Longitudinal Vinyasas* of the «head up» type (Fig. 10):

1) «Standing on straight legs»;
2) «Standing in longitudinal pass»;
3) «Sitting with bent legs»;
4) «Sitting with straight legs».

Fig. 10

Some of the *Vinyasas* presented in Figures 9 and 10 may be easily performed without any training, whereas others require a couple of months of preliminary training, depending on the complexity level of the *Vinyasas* and the training form had.

Therefore, depending on the possibility of using particular *Principle*

Vinyasas in training, the practice has been divided into several complexity levels.

On first sight it may seem that besides the key exercises depicted in Figures 9 and 10, it is possible to also use others. For example, in the «head down» position — «forward bend in standing position», «stand on one arm», «stand on the elbows (only)», «stand on the head (head stand) without hand support». Or also in the «head up» position — «squat on toes», «stand in transversal pass», «stand on one leg» or «curl into ball supported on the hands». And this is actually so. But *Principal Vinyasas* are the basic elements performed repeatedly in the training complexes. And the application of the *Vinyasas* with the above foundations as «the principal ones» is not justified by practical experience, and is not as practical for use as the *Principal Vinyasas*. When performed, they are used only as specialized independent exercises.

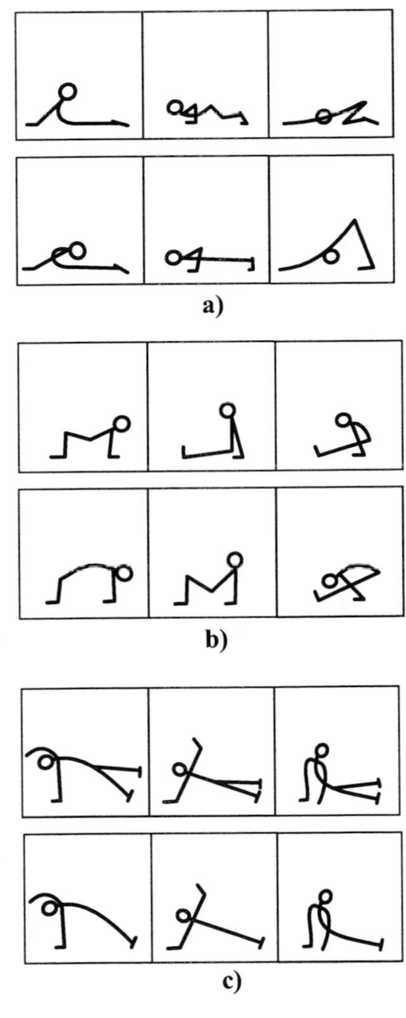

Fig. 11

It should also be noted that the contrast in the complexity level between the foundations with «head down» (Fig. 9) is much greater than between the «head up» foundations (Fig. 10). This is due to the fact that the human's habit of walking on two legs developed over multiple millennia, and shifted the energy balance of the body. This resulted in legs strong enough to «carry» the weight of the whole body, while the arms became weaker. The difference in the complexity level between *Principal Vinyasas* with «abdomen down» (Fig. 11a), «abdomen up» (Fig. 11b), and «on the side» (Fig. 11c) is so small that in practice all are first determined by the ability of the practitioner to use particular «head down» *Vinyasas* while resting on the shoulders, head or hands.

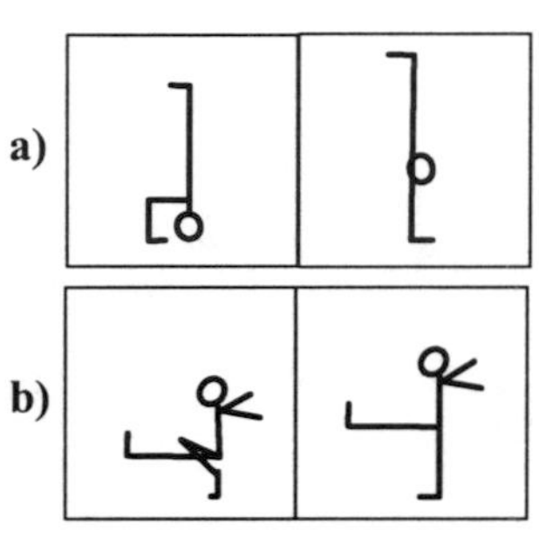

Fig. 12

Special moves forming a group of *Inter-Level Single-Directional Vinyasas* are used to connect and transfer from one «principal position» to another with foundations built from levels of complexity containing the same position of the head and the spine. For example, the transition from the «headstand while resting on the hands (palms)» to the «handstand (palms) only» may be achieved through «press with the hands» (Fig. 12a). Whereas, from the position «resting in a squat on one leg» to the position «standing on one leg» – may be achieved by means of «press with one leg» (Fig. 12b).

Besides the different principle foundations presented in Fig. 9 and 10, there are also a variety of other foundations for «head down» and «head up» positions containing different symmetric or asymmetric positions of the main foundation elements. But the practice of the *Principal Vinyasas* with the use of such foundations is not justified in terms of efficiency and time. Therefore, such foundations are more often used for performing various *Asanas*.

For example, in the «head down» position one can use a minimum of 140 variations of different foundations (Fig. 13).

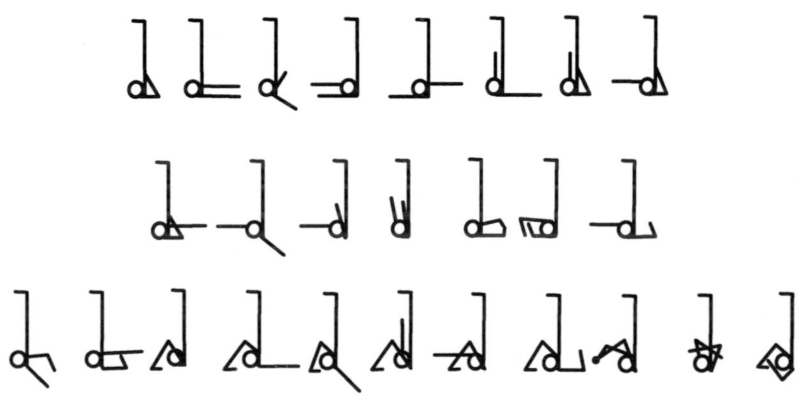

Fig. 13(1)

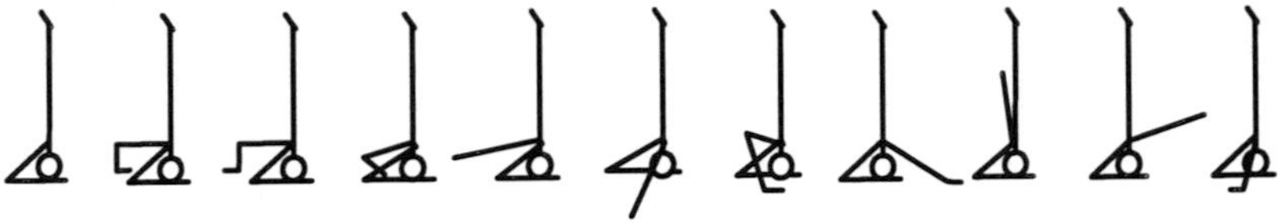

Fig. 13(2a)

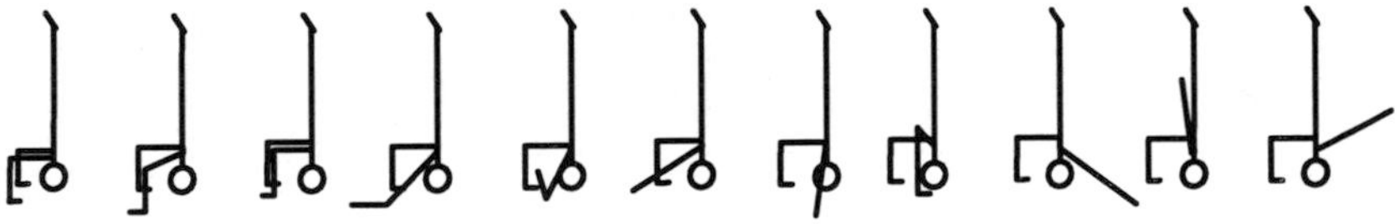

Fig. 13(2b)

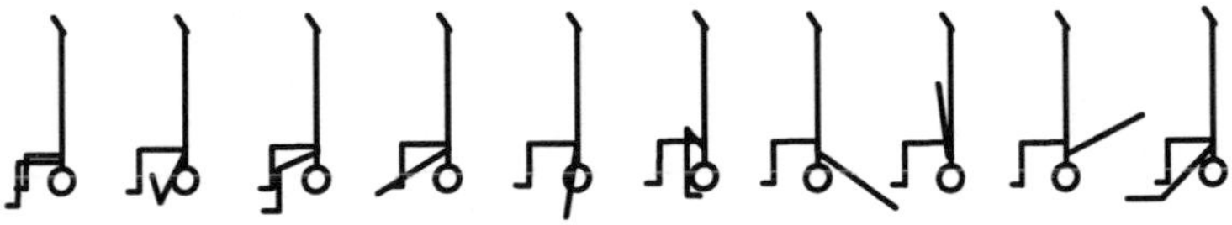

Fig. 13(2c)

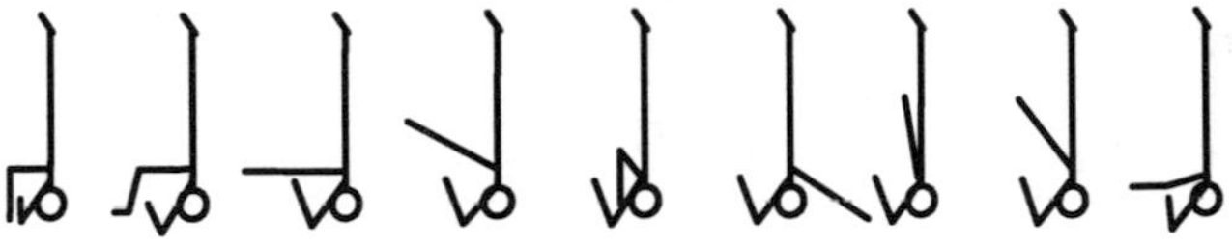

Fig. 13(2d)

Fig. 13(2e)

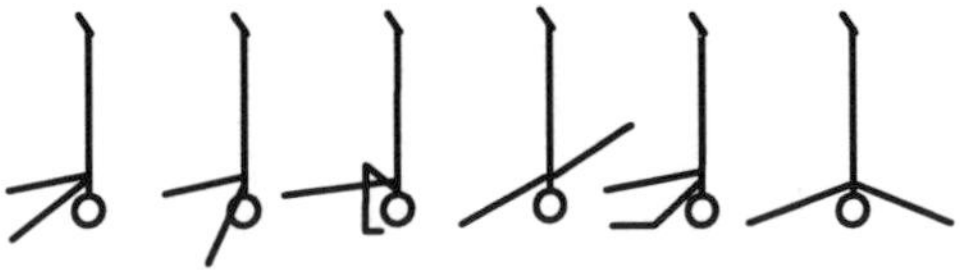

Fig. 13(2f)

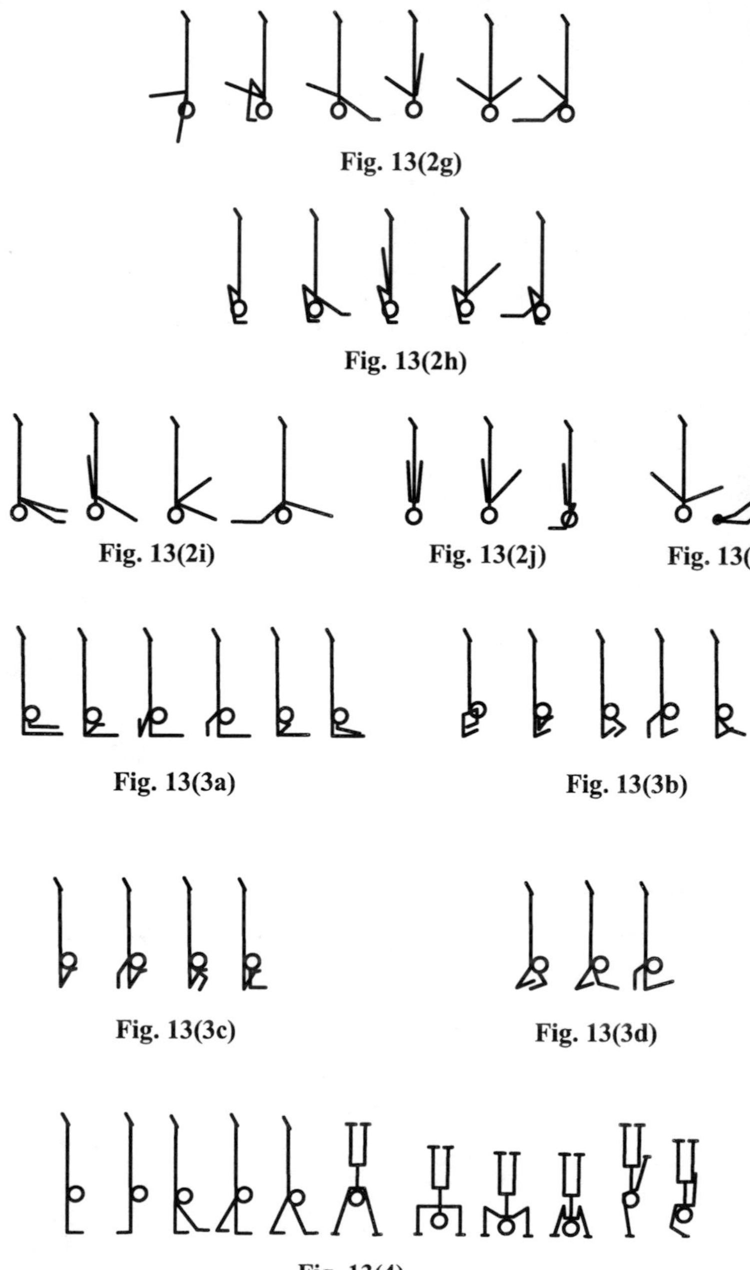

Fig. 13(2g)

Fig. 13(2h)

Fig. 13(2i) Fig. 13(2j) Fig. 13(2k)

Fig. 13(3a) Fig. 13(3b)

Fig. 13(3c) Fig. 13(3d)

Fig. 13(4)

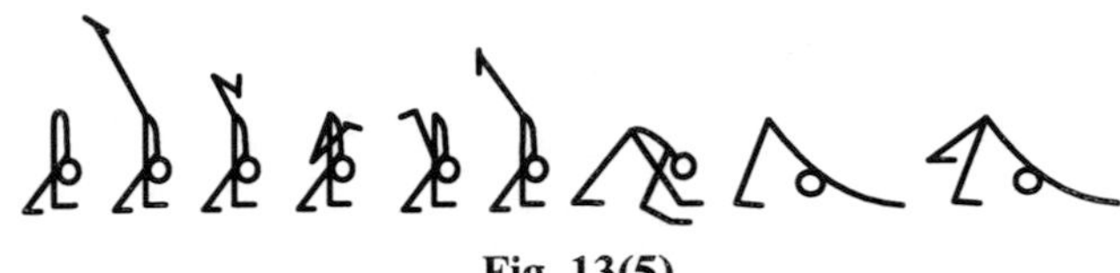

Fig. 13(5)

In the «head up» position there are a minimum of 234 variations of different foundations (Fig. 14). And in each of these postures a variety of forms (*Asanas*) with different positions of the torso and the limbs may be performed.

Fig. 14(1a)

Fig. 14(1b)

Fig. 14(1c)

Fig. 14(1d)

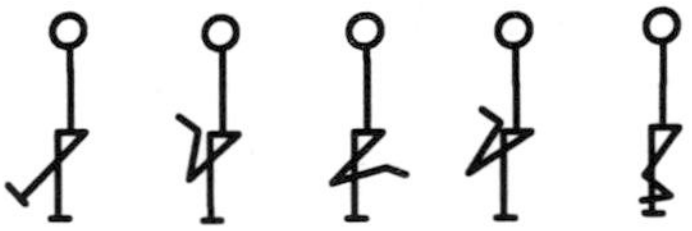

Fig. 14(1e)

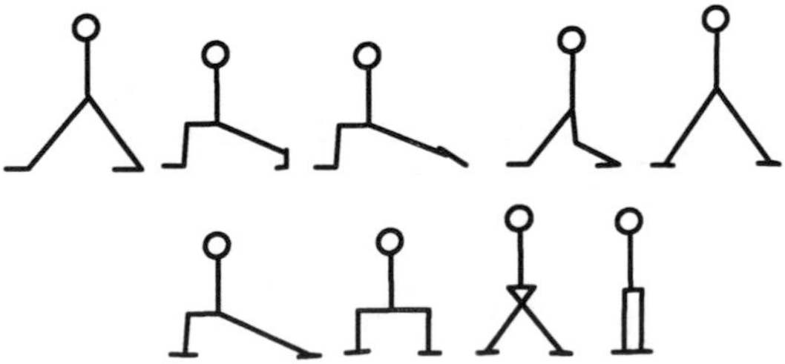

Fig. 14(1f)

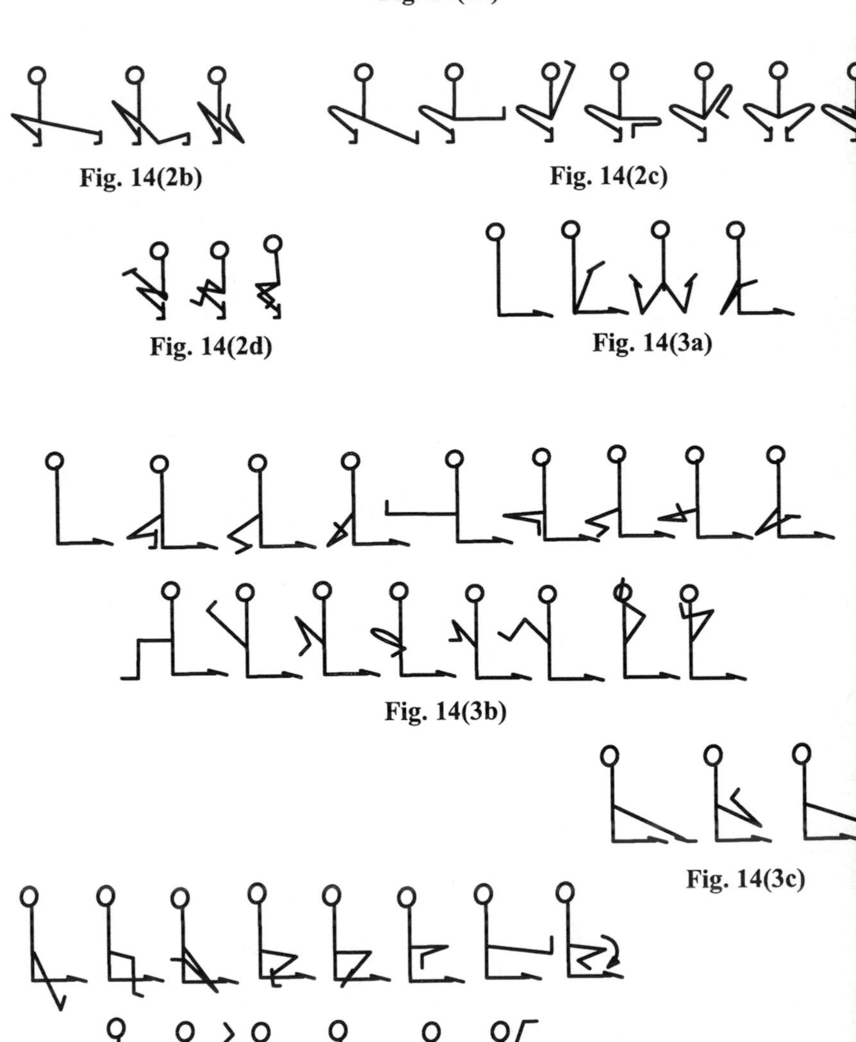

Fig. 14(2a)

Fig. 14(2b)

Fig. 14(2c)

Fig. 14(2d)

Fig. 14(3a)

Fig. 14(3b)

Fig. 14(3c)

Fig. 14(3d)

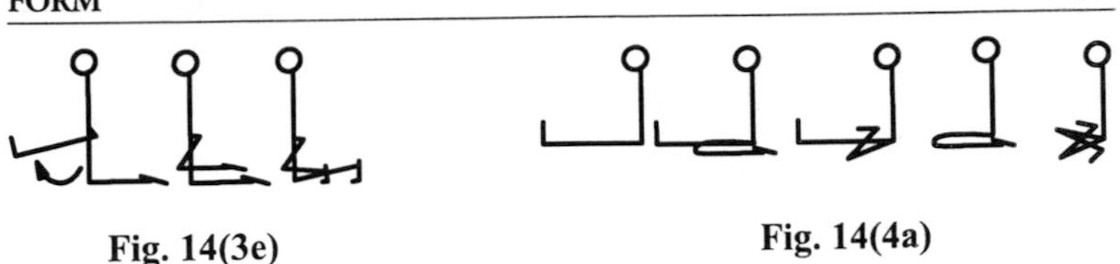

Fig. 14(3e)

Fig. 14(4a)

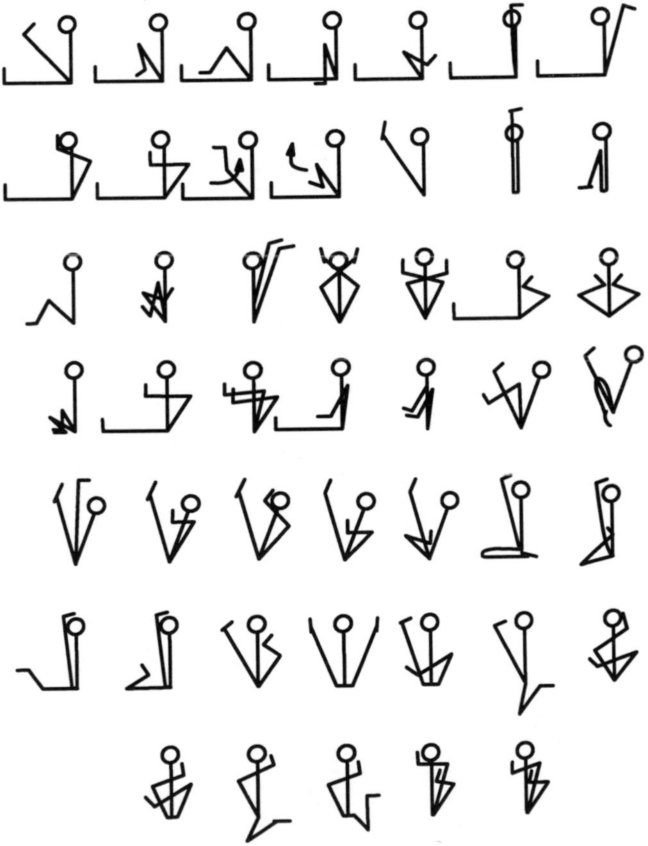

Fig. 14(4b)

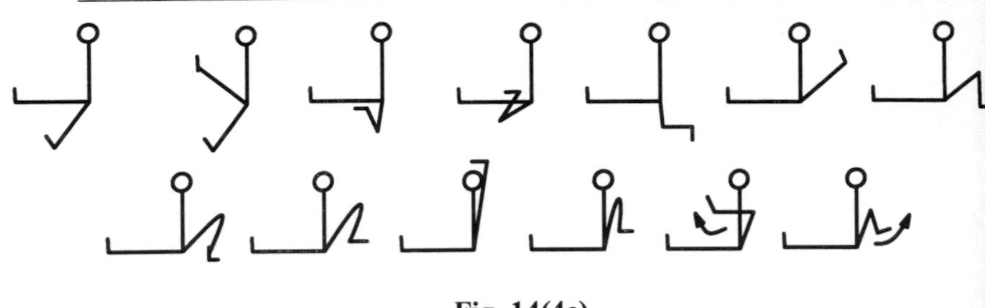

Fig. 14(4c)

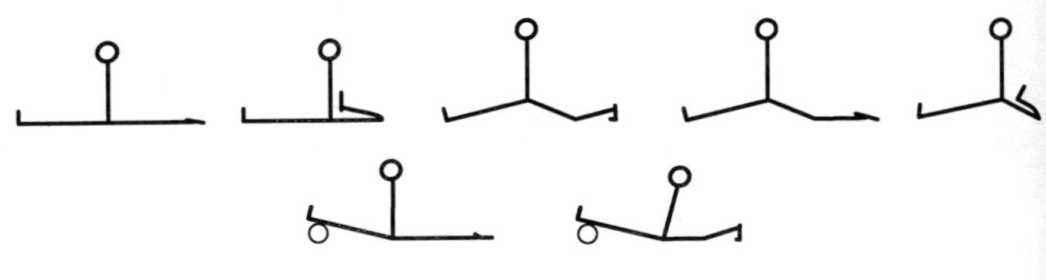

Fig. 14(d)

Fig. 14(4e)

Fig. 14(5a)

Fig. 14(5b)

Fig. 13(2i)

Fig. 13(2i)

Fig. 13(2i)

For example, each of the «head down» positions with different foundations which are given in Fig. 9 and 13 allow at least 123 variants of the forms (*Asanas*) with different positions of the legs (Fig, 15).

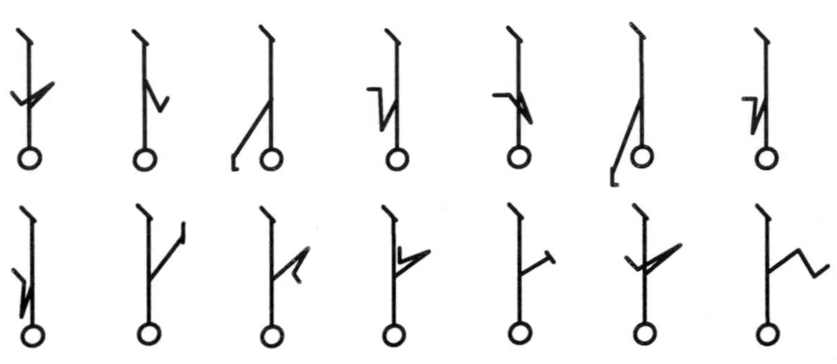

Fig. 15(1a)

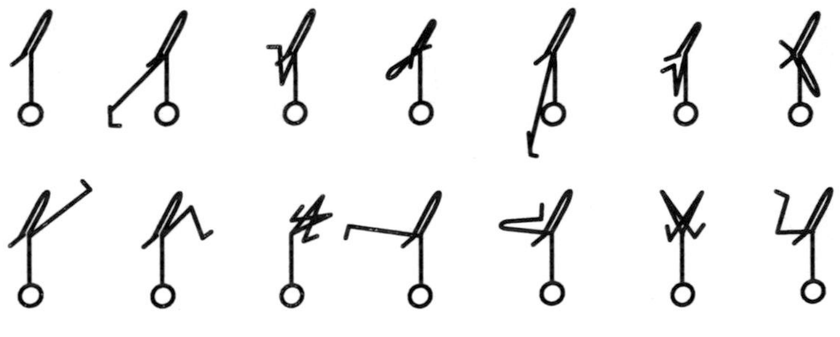

Fig. 15(1b)

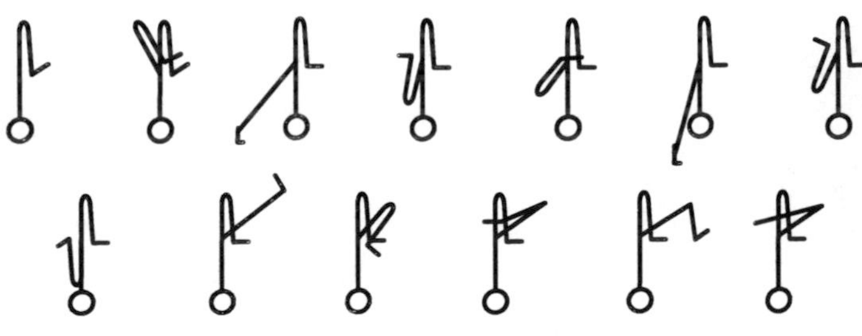

Fig. 15(1c)

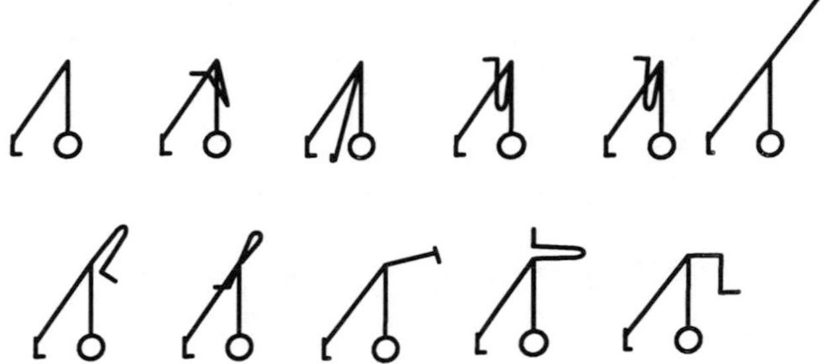

Fig. 15(2a)

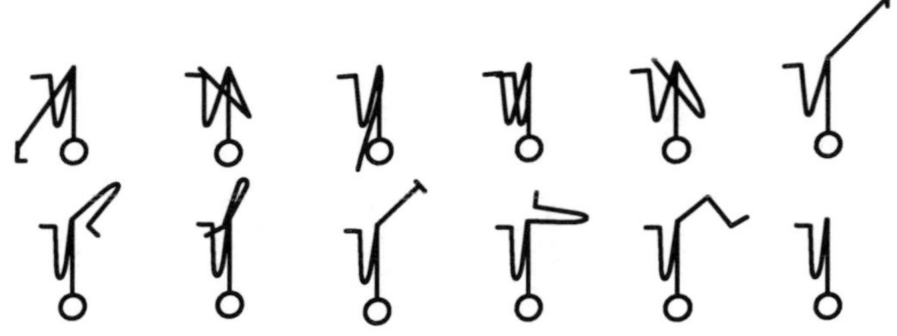

Fig. 15(2b)

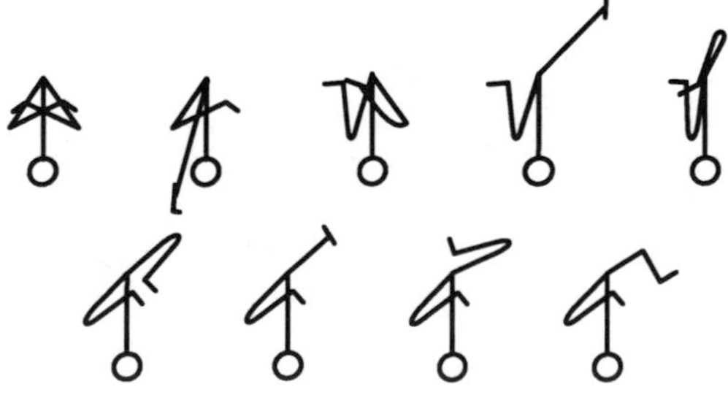

Fig. 15(2c)

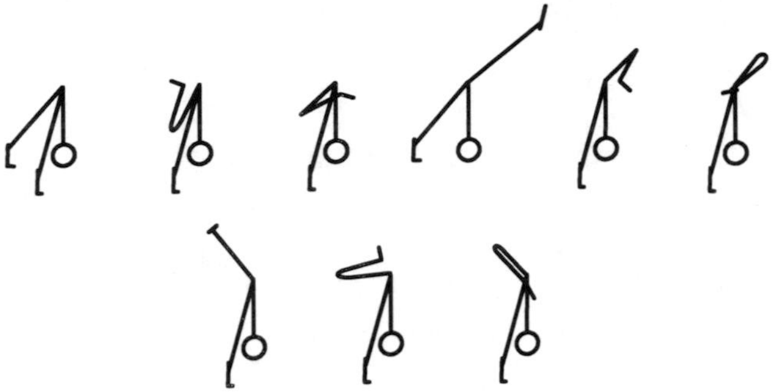

Fig. 15(3a)

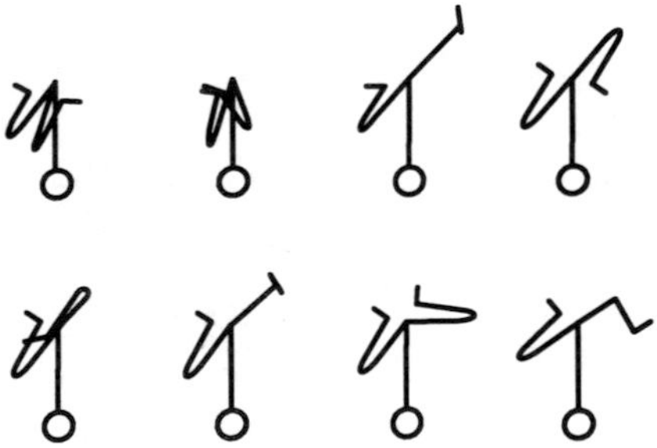

Fig. 15(3b)

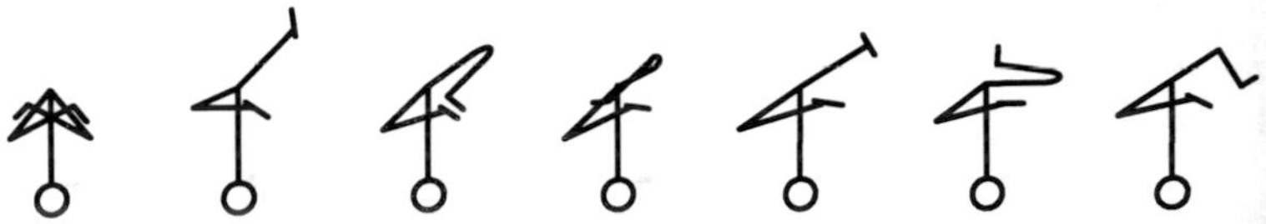

Fig. 15(3c)

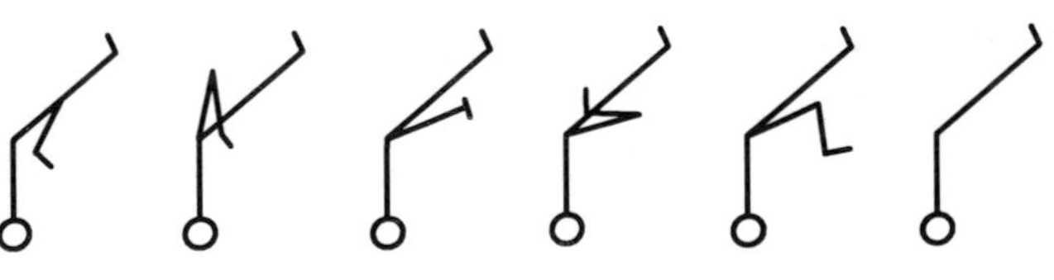

Fig. 15(4a)

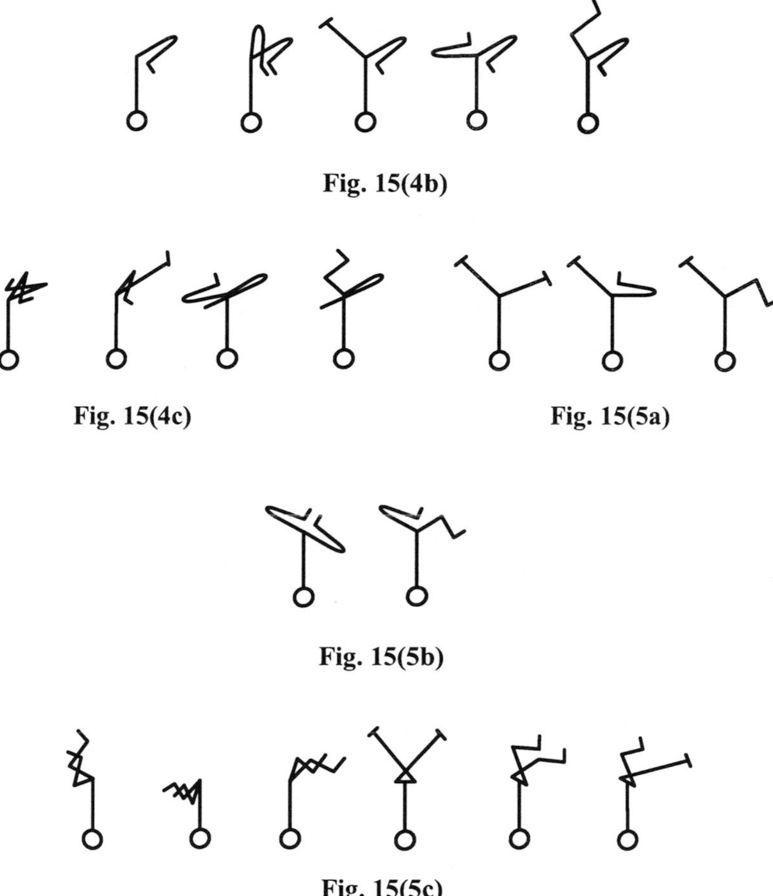

Fig. 15(4b)

Fig. 15(4c)

Fig. 15(5a)

Fig. 15(5b)

Fig. 15(5c)

This is how the network of peripheral algorithm of *Vinyasas* pertaining to various complexity levels is expanded.

Upon the change and fixation of any foundation, or during various indefinite forms of the torso, the head and the limbs (Fig. 9, 10, 13, 14, and 15), the result is additional movements which form the group of the *Specialized Non-Marginal Vinyasas.*

It should be noted, however, that during the practice of the *Principal Longitudinal and Transversal Vinyasas,* and the *Specialized Non-Marginal Vinyasas* also, maximum depth of spinal bends or of the flexibility of limb joints are not usually achieved. And when the practitioner «dives» from these *Vinyasas* to different *Asanas* with various bends, twists, and pullings

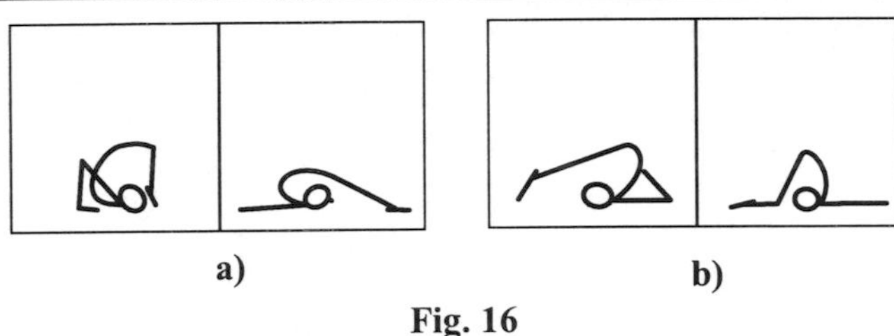

a) b)

Fig. 16

of the spine, and with asymmetrical positions of the arms and legs, the result is additional in-depth movements, which form another group of *Specialized Marginal Vinyasas*. For example, the transition from *Ganda Bherundasana* (non-marginal back bend) into *Viparita Salabhasana* (marginal back bend — «Reversed Grasshopper») results in additional fragments of the movement into the marginal back bend: lowering of the chest and the arms on the floor with marginal disposition of the feet on the floor ahead (Fig. 16a). Whereas the transition from *Halasana* (non-marginal forward bend) into *Super Halasana* (marginal forward bend) also results in additional fragments of the move: lowering of the arms and the knees on the floor far behind the head (Fig. 16b). So, all these additional movements comprise the *Specialized Marginal Vinyasas*. These form the peripheral network of dead-end branches of the complete single-level algorithm of *Vinyasas*.

Internal lines of the pentagram on Fig. 6 characterize ten possible interconnections between various positions and relevant *Principal Longitudinal Vinyasas*, which are realized through the use of special movement algorithms forming the group of *Multidirectional Vinyasas* (or *Linking Vinyasas*) (Fig. 17):

1. From the «standing upright» position (1) — to the «abdomen down» position (2) and back.
2. From the «standing upright» position (1) — to the «on the side» position (3) and back.
3. From the «standing upright» position (1) — to the «abdomen up» position (4) and back.
4. From the «standing upright» position (1) — to «head down» position (5) and back.
5. From the «abdomen down» position (2) — to the «on the side» position (3) and back.
6. From the «abdomen down» position (2) — to the «abdomen up» position (4) and back.
7. From the «abdomen down» position (2) — to the «head down» position (5) and back.

tion of the inhalation and the exhalation in such breath is approximately equal, and there are no delays between the inhalation and the exhalation.

The practice of *Pranayama* in Yoga implies conscious control of the life-power flow during the process of breathing by controlling the parameters of the breath. In this case any type of breathing, where different characteristics are controlled consciously, is called *Sahita Pranayama*. And any automatic breath is called *Kevala Pranayama* and, in addition to «normal» breathing, it can comprise any type of *Pranayama* with different automatic breathing characteristics, reduced to automatism which do not require conscious control.

SIX CHARACTERISTICS OF BREATHING

1. Harmonious breathing

Harmonious breath is breathing in which the duration (T) and the depth (V) of the inhalations and the exhalations are equal ($V_1 = V_2$ and $T_1 = T_2$) (Fig. 30).

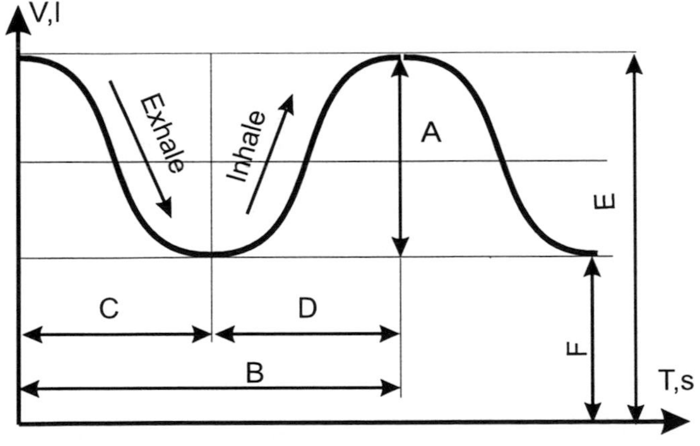

Fig. 30

Harmonious breath is called *Sama Vritti Pranayama.*

2. Shift in the Range of Breathing

A shift in the range of breathing, with respect to the preset «normal» volume of the lungs after a full inhalation (E), and after a full exhalation

(F), an increase of volumes ($V_1 + 1$ and $V_2 + 1$), or a decrease ($V_1 - 1$ and $V_2 - 1$) may occur. (Fig.31)

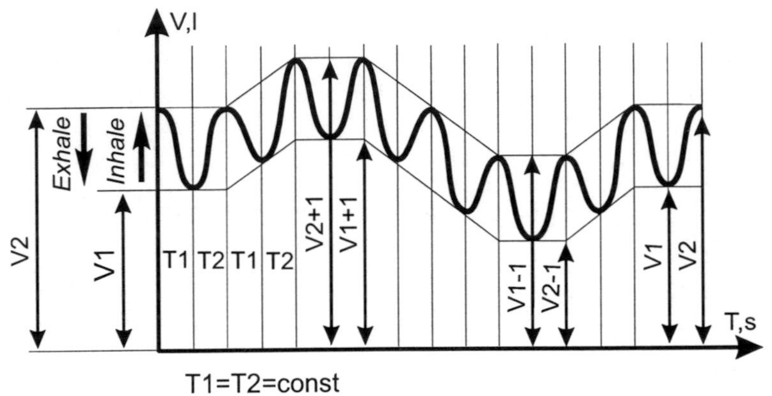

Fig. 31

A shift in the range of breath towards an increase in the volume of the lungs after full inhalation and full exhalation occurs, for example, upon the practice of psychic-energy exercises actuating the upper energy centers (*Chakras*) during the breath at the marginal point of the inhalation. Whereas the shift of breath towards a decrease of the volume of the lungs occurs, for example, during the practice of *Asanas* with deep forward bends, back bends and to the sides, and twists of the spine, compressing the thoracic and abdominal cavities.

3. Temporal Correlation

Temporal correlation between the duration of the exhalation (T_1) and the duration of the inhalation (T_2) may change both towards longer inhalation ($T_1 > T_2$) and towards relatively longer exhalation ($T_1 < T_2$) (Fig. 32).

Breathing with different temporal correlations is called *Visama Vritti Pranayama*, which has numerous variations of the correlation and is widely used in the practice of Yoga.

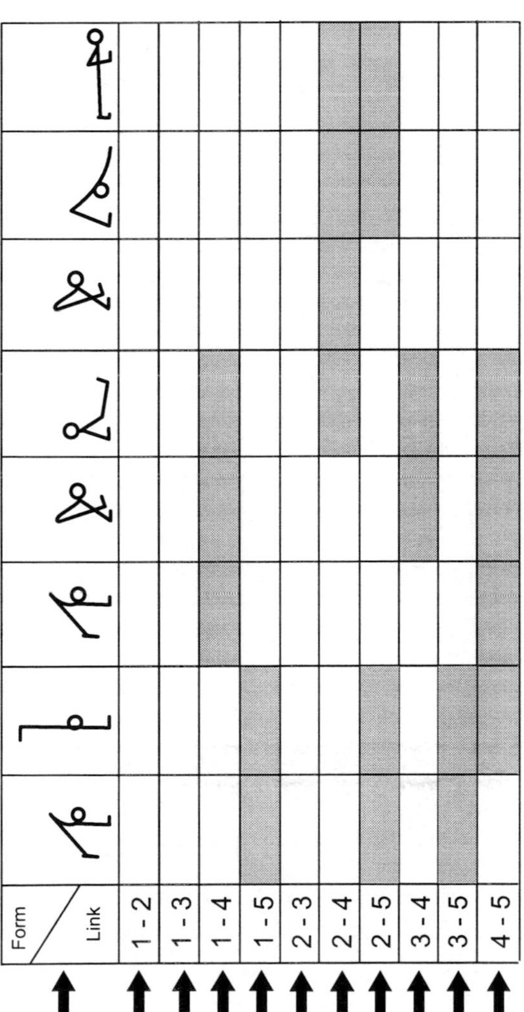

Table 3

Fig. 18

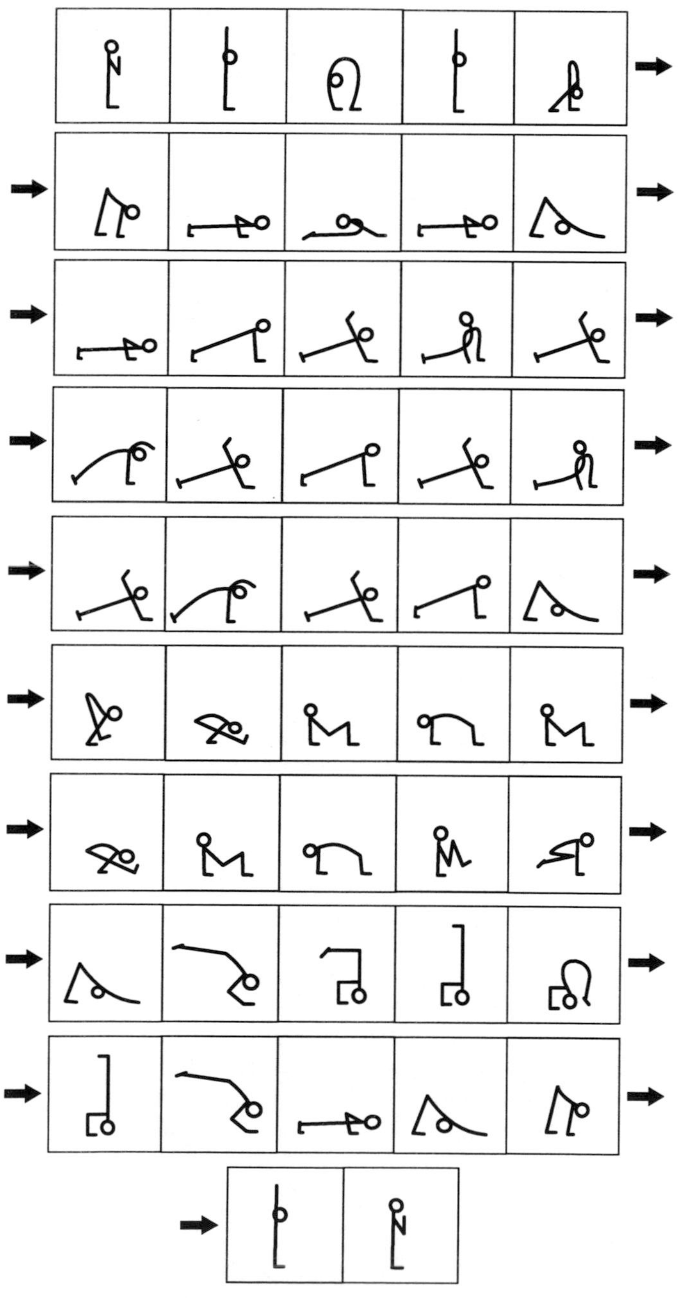

Fig. 19

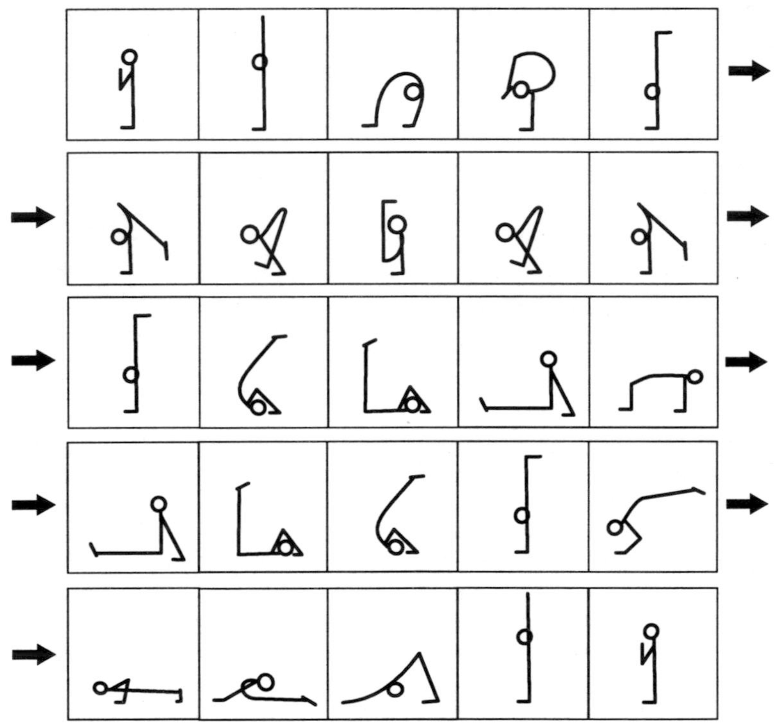

Fig. 20

The difference between the *Principal Longitudinal and Transversal Vinyasas* and the *Multi-Directional Vinyasas* (*Linking Vinyasas*) is that the *Principal Transversal and Longitudinal Vinyasas* create stress on the spinal formations with simultaneous change of the spine's angle with respect to a particular neutral position. Whereas in the *Multi-Directional Vinyasas* (*Linking Vinyasas*), the form of the spine changes insignificantly, the accent being made on the change of the position of the spine with respect to the direction of the power lines of the Earth's gravitational field.

From Fig. 17 possible to see that some fragments of *Multi-Directional Vinyasas* (*Linking Vinyasas*) are absolutely identical. Therefore, the possibility of practicing all of the *Multi-Directional Vinyasas* results in the practice of those key fragments which are not duplicated. In Table 3 they are marked with a shaded area.

Each of the Yoga practice levels uses key algorithms consisting of all such (non-doubled) movements. For example, if the initial level employs

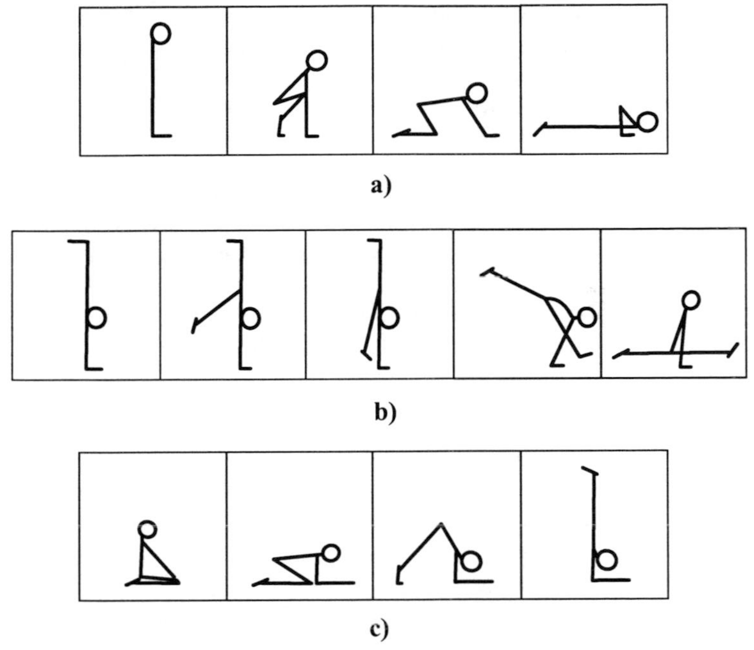

Fig. 21

sequences consisting of the simplest variants of the *Principal Vinyasas* (Fig. 18), the advanced level uses more sophisticated options of the *Principal Vinyasas* (Fig. 19), and the intensive level uses even more elaborate variants of the *Principal Vinyasas* (Fig. 20). In each subsequent level, such a sequence comprises only principally new elements and contains no familiar fragments from the previous level.

Multi-Directional Vinyasas linking the postures of one and the same complexity level form the group of *One-Level Multi-Directional Vinyasas* (or *Single-Level Links*). For example, the transition from the «standing upright on two legs» position to the «laying on the abdomen» position may, at the first level, be performed by sequential sitting-lowering on the knees, hands and to the «laying on the abdomen» position (Fig. 21a).

Multi-Directional Vinyasas linking the positions of various complexity levels form the group of *Inter-Level Multi-Directional Vinyasas.* For example, the transition from the «head down» position in the «handstand» (foundation from the third complexity level) to the «head up» position in the «longitudinal split» (foundation from the second complexity level) may be performed by lowering the legs to the floor, while simultaneously spreading them «on the move» and forming a longitudinal split (Fig. 21b).

Or the transition from the «head up» position sitting on the floor in *Virasana* (foundation from the first complexity level) into the «head down» position as in *Pinca Mayurasana* (foundation from the second complexity level) may be achieved by raising the body and the legs into vertical «stand on the forearms» (Fig. 21c).

Complete mastering of all of the *Single-Level Multi-Directional Vinyasas* (*Linking Vinyasas*) allows the practitioner to combine them into one continuous movement algorithm, which comprises all possible positions and forms a «Universal Single-Level Psychic-Energy Mandala» (or «*Universal Single-Level Linking Vinyasa*»). Whereas the mastering of all of the *Inter-Level Multi-Directional Vinyasas* (*Inter-Level links*) allows the practitioner to combine them into one continuous movement algorithm, comprising all possible positions pertaining to different complexity levels and forming the «Universal Multi-Level Psychic-Energy Mandala» (or the «*Universal Multi-Level Linking Vinyasa*).

Unfortunately, practical use of a «*Universal single-level Linking Vinyasa*» is usually not possible due to many practitioners' insufficient training and lack of experience. Even after doing all of the *Linking Vinyasas*, the first level of the program is often too difficult, until after many months of regular training. Therefore, in order to develop the lack in physical abilities and prepare the muscles of the arms, legs and torso, another group has been developed: *Preparatory Vinyasas*. They are also used in the training for warming up, general strengthening of the principal muscle groups, the cleansing of peripheral channels and the delivering of energy to the psychic-energy centers (see below in the description of the *Vinyasas* practice technique).

Also, there are number of special movements, such as «somersaults», «leaps» or «cartwheels» form the group of *Circular Vinyasas*. Usually, in these *Vinyasas*, the body rolls on the floor and there is the possibility to stop it at different points of this movement and change over to some other *Vinyasas* or *Asanas*. Such *Circular Vinyasas* allow the practitioner to connect some of the marginal positions of peripheral «dead-end» branches of the *Complete Vinyasas Algorithm* in the shortest possible ways, thus saving a considerable amount of time spent changing between these marginal positions, and through this improving training technique.

Circular Vinyasas, linking the positions pertaining to the same complexity level, form the group of *Circular Single-Level Vinyasas*. For example, the back bend with the catch of the legs in *Chakra Bandhasana* shapes the body in the form of a ring (Fig. 22). If rolled on the floor, the body will gradually change from *Chakra Bandhasana* (1) to *Kapotasana* (2), from it to *Pandagusta Dhanurasana* (3), from it to *Ganda Bherundasana* (4) from which it will again return to *Chakra Bandhasana* (1) (or, bypassing it, to *Kapotasana* (2)). In addition, in these *Asanas* there is the possibility to lay

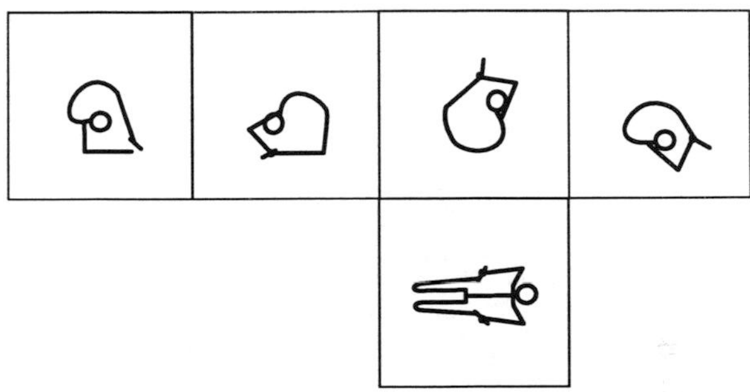

Fig.22

on the sides, which results in links with the postures performed on the sides. Fig. 22 shows such a movement to the side from *Pandagustha Dhanurasana* (3) to *Parsva Pandangustha Dhanurasana* (5). Therefore, this *Circular Vinyasa* has, besides the qualities of a «ring», those of a «sphere», which can be rolled both ahead and to the sides, allowing the practitioner to use a short algorithm that combines all peripheral branches of the complete single-level *Vinyasas* algorithm.

Circular Vinyasas, which allow the practitioner to change between the postures belonging to different complexity levels, form the group of *Circular Inter-Level Vinyasas.* For example, with the use of a *Circular Vinyasa* («somersault») one can change from the «head down» position in the «handstand (palms)» (foundations of the third level of complexity) to the «head up» position» «sitting on the floor with straight legs» (foundations of the first level of complexity) (Fig. 23).

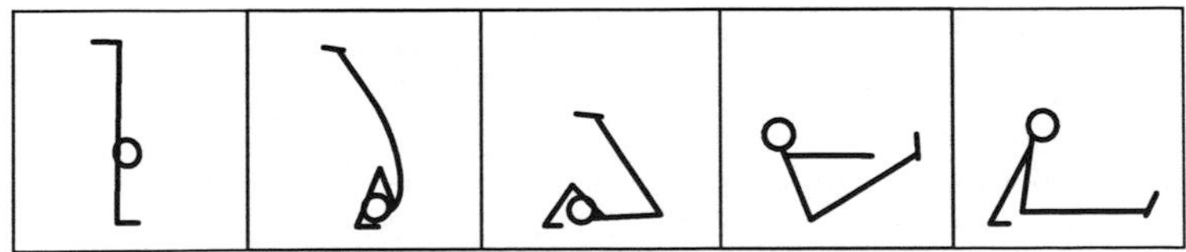

Fig. 23

Or from the «stand on the hands (palms)», (foundations of the third level of complexity), using a fragment of the move resembling a «cartwheel», one can change to the «posture on straight legs» (foundations of the first level of complexity) (Fig. 24).

MULTILEVEL VINYASA ALGORITHM

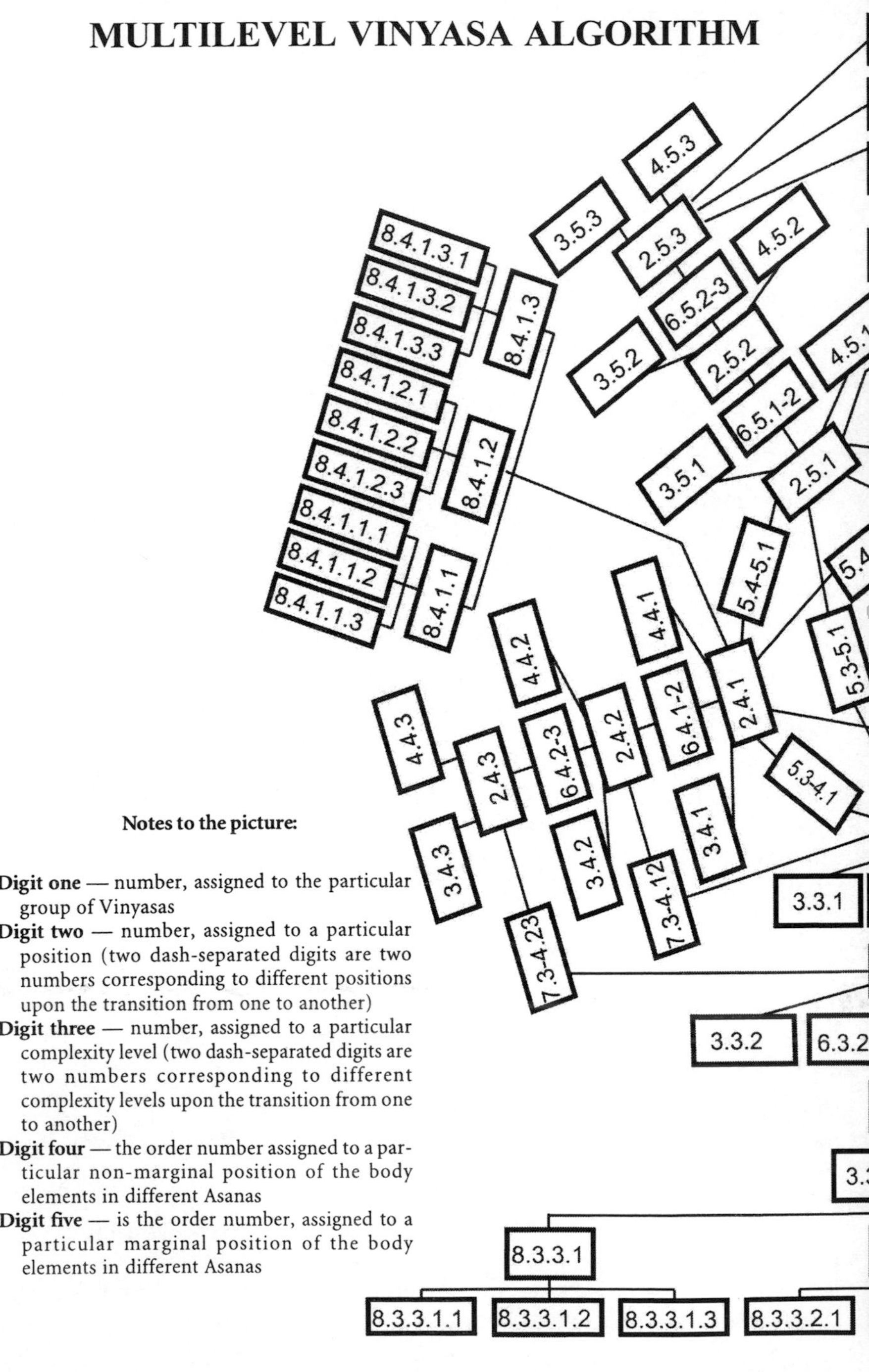

Notes to the picture:

Digit one — number, assigned to the particular group of Vinyasas

Digit two — number, assigned to a particular position (two dash-separated digits are two numbers corresponding to different positions upon the transition from one to another)

Digit three — number, assigned to a particular complexity level (two dash-separated digits are two numbers corresponding to different complexity levels upon the transition from one to another)

Digit four — the order number assigned to a particular non-marginal position of the body elements in different Asanas

Digit five — is the order number, assigned to a particular marginal position of the body elements in different Asanas

3.1.3
2.1.3
4.1.3
3.1.2
6.1.2-3
2.1.2
4.1.2
3.1.1
6.1.1-2
2.1.1
4.1.1
5.5-2.1
5.1-2.1
5.1-3.1
2.2.1
4.2.1
6.2.1-2
5.2-3.1
3.2.1
2.2.2
3.2.2
6.2.2-3
2.2.3
3.2.3
4.2.2
4.2.3
7.2-3.2-1
7.2.3.3-2
4.3.1
4.3.2
4.3.3
8.2.2.1
8.2.2.2
8.2.2.3
8.2.2.1.1
8.2.2.1.2
8.2.2.1.3
8.2.2.2.1
8.2.2.2.2
8.2.2.2.3
8.2.2.3.1
8.2.2.3.2
8.2.2.3.3
8.3.3.3
8.3.3.2.3
8.3.3.3.1
8.3.3.3.2
8.3.3.3.3
Assigned numbers:
Vinyasa groups:
1. Preparatory
2. Principal longitudinal
3. Principal transverse
4. Principal twisting
5. Single-level multi-direction
6. Inter-level single-direction
7. Inter-level multi-direction
8. Specialized non-marginal
9. Specialized marginal
10. Circular single-level
11. Circular inter-level
12. Twirling single-level single-direction
13. Twirling single-level multi-direction
14. Twirling inter-level single-direction
15. Twirling inter-level multi-direction
Position:
1. Head up
2. Abdomen down
3. On the side
4. Abdomen up
5. Head down
Conditional complexity levels:
1. First
2. Second
3. Third

Fig. 29

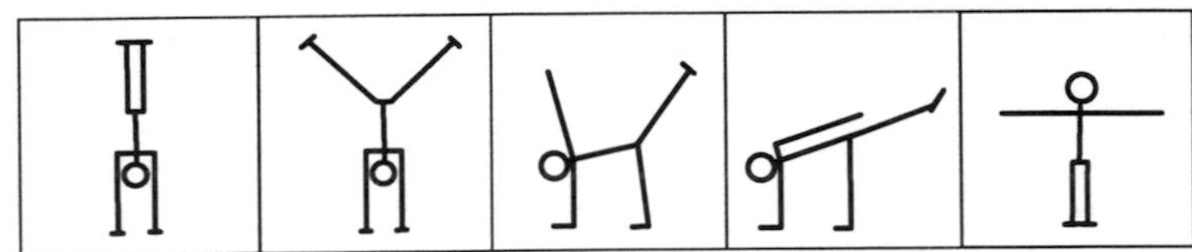

Fig. 24

Apart from the above groups of *Vinyasas* with foundations in the advanced level of practice, there is the possibility to include in training another four groups of *Twirling Vinyasas,* which represent various motions in which the body loses contact with the ground. These may be relatively simple transpositions of legs and arms and jumps or revolutions of the body in the space resembling some kinds of acrobatic «somersaults» or their fragments.

Introducing *Twirling Vinyasas* in training becomes natural, as a transformation of the quantity of accumulated psychic-energy potential and experience in performing the *Principal Vinyasas* with foundations moves into a new quality of energy-saturated «twirling motions» that are performed in the air, without a foundation.

Twirling Vinyasas, beginning and ending in the same position, are *Twirling Single-Level Single-Directional Vinyasas.* For example, when performing the «back somersault» from the position «standing on the straight legs» (Fig. 25).

Fig. 25

Twirling Vinyasas, beginning and ending in the same position, but with a change between the levels of foundations, are *Twirling Inter-Level Single-Directional Vinyasas.* For example, when doing a «back somersault» and starting by standing on the straight legs and ending it sitting on the knees (Fig. 26).

Twirling Vinyasas, resulting in a change of position without changing the level of the initial and final foundations, are *Twirling Single-Level*

Fig. 26

Multi-Directional Vinyasas. For example, upon the change from the «head up» type of position, «standing on straight legs», into an «abdomen up» position, «lying on the back», using a «frontal somersault» (Fig. 27a). Or vice versa, from the «abdomen up» type of position «lying on the back», and moving into a «head up» position, «standing on straight legs» — by vigorously pushing the legs up, and causing the momentum to raise the body in the air, and then into the standing position (Fig. 27b).

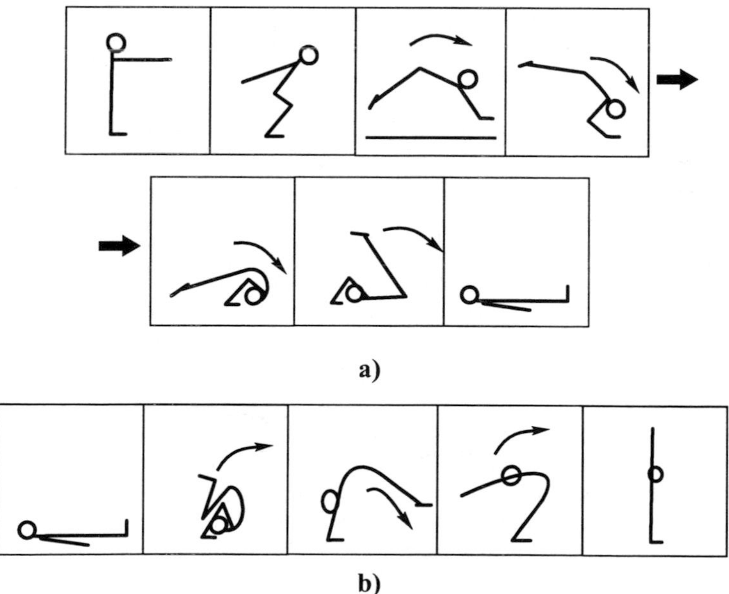

Fig. 27

Swirling Vinyasas, which change both the position and the initial and final foundation level, are called *Swirling Inter-level Multi-Directional Vinyasas.* For example, upon the changing from the «head down» position, «standing on the hands (palms)», strongly push the arms to spring, make a revolution resulting in a «head up» position «standing on the hands» (Fig. 28a). Or upon the change from a «head up» position, «standing on the legs», jump forward, and with a simultaneous revolution of the body move into a «head down» position, «standing on the hands (palms)» (Fig. 28b).

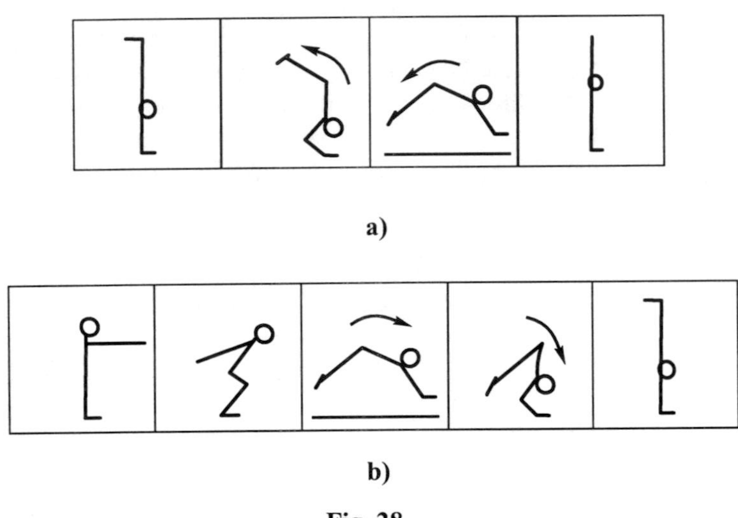

a)

b)

Fig. 28

Circular and *Twirling Vinyasas* add a torsion component to Yoga practice, and the harmony, energetic integrity and coordination expressed, advances the practitioner towards liberation.

Practical mastering of a completely branched algorithm of the *Universal Multilevel Vinyasa* (Fig. 29 at p 80 — 81) is achieved through multiple repetition of separate fragments, a gradual increase of the psychic-energy potential, and a gradual transition from easier fragments to more complicated ones, as well as through a practical investigation of various body positions and different combinations of separate elements of such positions during spontaneous training.

The transition from one complexity level to another should be natural, and should only be the result of accumulating enough psychic-energy potential to serve as a guarantee for the practitioner's safety, and the energy-based right for such a transition. Ignoring this rule, and forcing a sporting approach to practice, may result in injuries and unnecessary wear of the organism.

The multilevel *Vinyasa* algorithm presented in Fig. 29 is the accumu lation of all the sample logical chains, and is sufficient to present the whole of this algorithm. However, the complete illustration of absolutely all of its links and peripheral networks within the scope of this book is, unfortunately, impossible.

The current numbering of the *Specialized Marginal and Non-Marginal Vinyasas* are only given for the purposes of illustrating the branches of a complete multi-level *Vinyasa* algorithm and implies no particular position of the elements of the body.

Training on the basis of the multi-level *Vinyasa* algorithm facilitates the actual increase of the «psychic-energy potential and the generation of the bioprocessor», while improving and expanding the consciousness.

HIERARCHY OF VINYASAS

The hierarchy of *Vinyasas* is based on the transition from the simple to the complicated, and from less efficient to more efficient.

The use of exercises in the training program, which are a combination of elements of already mastered exercises improve the quality of the practice, diversify movements, and make them more beautiful. Besides the creative free search of previously unknown combinations of such elements, together with self-revelations, results in the establishment of new links in the psychic-energy structure, expands the abilities of consciousness, and increases the level of the bioprocessor. But at the same time, the practitioner's level of psychic and physical ability remains the same. And of this ability determines psychic-energy capacity.

For example, if a man is unable to do a «handstand», then the entire «head down» exercise series he uses in training will be variations of shoulder or head stands with the hands used as an additional foundation. Consequently, no matter how sophisticated the practitioner is in combining the forms accessible to him, he will not be able to transfer to the next level and build his practice. He will not be able to enter into a majority of *Asanas* dominated by handstands unless his training level and the capacity of psychic-energy structure increases to a particular degree. Therefore, the ability to change from one foundation to another in the *Principal Vinyasas*, as a rule, determines one's ability to transfer from one level of the practice to another.

On the first level of practice, the simplest *Preparatory* and *Specialized Vinyasas* are used: «stepping», «jumping», linking movements, and other accessible options of the *Principal Vinyasas* and *Linking Vinyasas.*

In the course of improvement, at the **second level** of practice, these simple linking movements are replaced with more complicated and efficient options from the *Preparatory* and *Specialized Vinyasas*, which are complemented with previously inaccessible, but already mastered, *Principal Vinyasas and Linking Vinyasas.*

The third level of practice implies the complete integration of the *Multilevel Universal Vinyasa.*

Circular Vinyasas are introduced into training as the practitioner develops the ability to perform them. Whereas the *Swirling Vinyasas*, although their most simple fragments are introduced at the **second** and the third levels, are only introduced in full scope at the final **fourth** level of the practice.

The similar manner the technique of practicing the *Vinyasas* given below uses a hierarchical approach.

Unfortunately the scope of this book does not allow space to consider the technique of the practice of all possible *Vinyasas.* Therefore, those included in the relevant sections are the most typical examples used to illustrate the essence of the movements pertaining to a particular group of *Vinyasas.* At the same time, in selecting them, preference was given to the most effective and useful for ones progress in training.

The *Single-Level Universal Vinyasas* and the *Multi-Level Universal Vinyasas* are not described separately, as they are defined as a group of *Linking Vinyasas.* Concerning the *Swirling Vinyasas*, presenting their technique in pictures, and teaching them by a book is a useless and even dangerous business. Therefore, there is no description of their technique given in this book.

It should be noted, and remembered once and for all, that practicing exercises of a high complexity level is not a goal in itself, but is just a test of the availability of particular psychic-energy potential and corresponds to a more developed and balanced consciousness. **The transition from simple *Vinyasas* to more complicated ones should take place naturally, as a consequence of accumulating the Power resulting from regular, gradual and careful training.**

The good physical properties of a young body are not the indication of a perfect consciousness. These are only enjoyed in youth and vanish with age. The real value for developing and expanding the consciousness happens in the process of spiritual efforts and deeds.

Therefore, in practicing Yoga, different ages require that different aspects of the practice be accented.

At a young age, for example, development should be concentrated on missing features, accumulating practical experience in performing various unfamiliar exercises and techniques, and strengthening one's health in order to be able to store Power in old age.

In middle age, the accent should be made on realization and preservation a kind of «Standard of Organizing Power», which allows one to remain young and healthy for many years, and helps one avoid karmic mistakes (sins).

In old age, one should provide support to what remains of one's life, and should make conscious conclusions in order to summarize the results of this passing life. This should serve as a basis for Wisdom and subsequent incarnations.

ENERGY FORMATION THEORY

ASSOCIATION OF BREATHING WITH THE STATE OF CONSCIOUSNESS

The breathing process is the main one among all the factors of the vital provision of a human being. A man can live without food for a couple of months, without water — for a couple of days, but without breathing a man cannot survive for even ten minutes.

The process of breathing is closely related to the state of consciousness, and its characteristics determine the quality of the psychic-energy structure of a man. It can be said that the rhythms of the breath and the consciousness are similar. Therefore, in order to achieve the principal goal of Yoga, which is the stabilization of consciousness, it is absolutely necessary to completely master the breath.

Through conscious control of breathing, one can directly affect the state of consciousness, and can cause specific effects such as stopping or accelerating the work of the heart, brain, blood, nervous, lymphatic and endocrine systems, and restoration of the organism and the accumulation of the life-power also.

When considering the process of breath, it is essential to understand the wave-like process with which all laws of the wave theory operate. The investigation of various breathing characteristics, rhythms and accompanying processes forms a complete breathing system (to the extent the wave theory is complete). This system consist of all types of breathing rhythms and exercises can. And includes, not only rhythms and exercises discovered empirically and practiced by different world schools, but also that rhythms and exercises which have been overlooked and have been unknown until now.

In the process of breathing (Fig. 30), the internal volume (V) of the lungs changes with the passing of the time (T). And different characteristics of the breath are described by such characteristics as the depth (amplitude) (A), frequency (B), correlation of the time of the inhalation (C) and of the exhalation (D), volume of the lungs after the full inhalation (E) and after the full exhalation (F).

The «normal» unconscious breath of a man is controlled automatically by a subconscious program. Its pattern is set by the brain's breathing center, and is usually close to the harmonic sine curve (Fig. 30). The dura

8.From the «on the side» position (3) — to the «abdomen up» position (4) and back.

9.From the «on the side» position (3) — to the «head down» position (5) and back.

10.From the «abdomen up» position (4) — to the «head down» position and back.

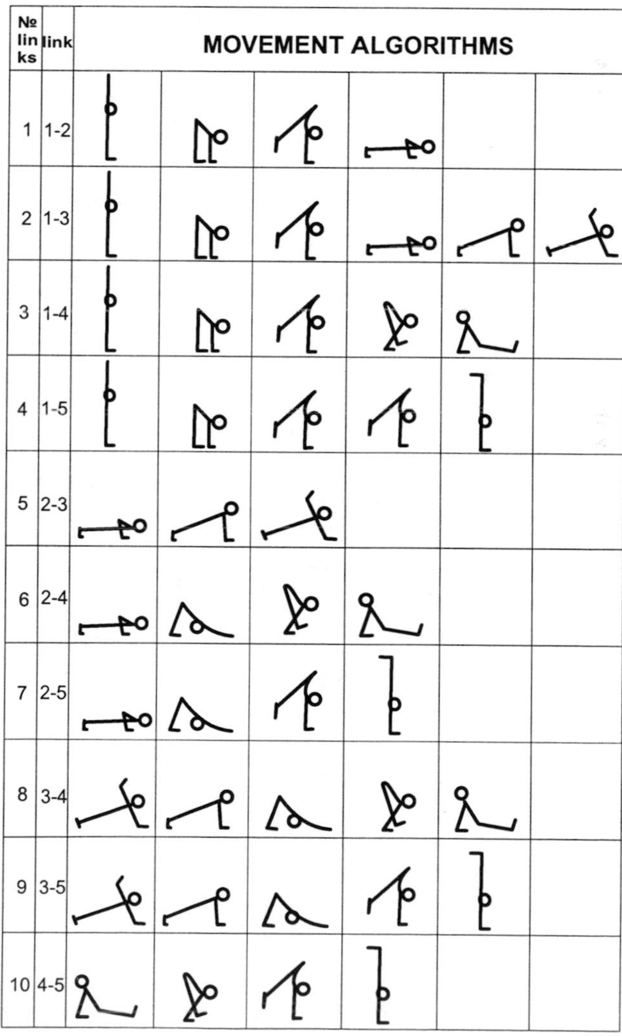

№ links	link	MOVEMENT ALGORITHMS
1	1-2	
2	1-3	
3	1-4	
4	1-5	
5	2-3	
6	2-4	
7	2-5	
8	3-4	
9	3-5	
10	4-5	

Fig. 17

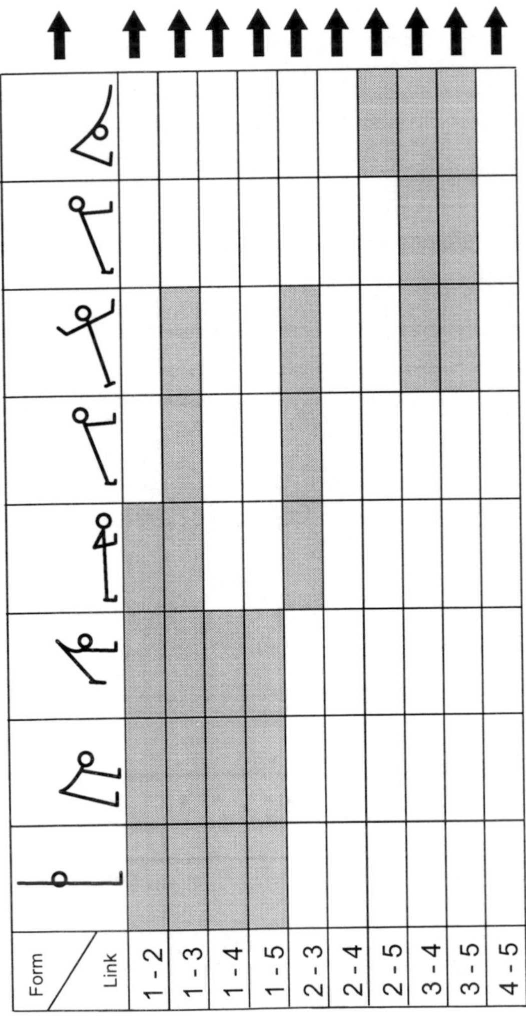
Form
Link
1 - 2
1 - 3
1 - 4
1 - 5
2 - 3
2 - 4
2 - 5
3 - 4
3 - 5
4 - 5

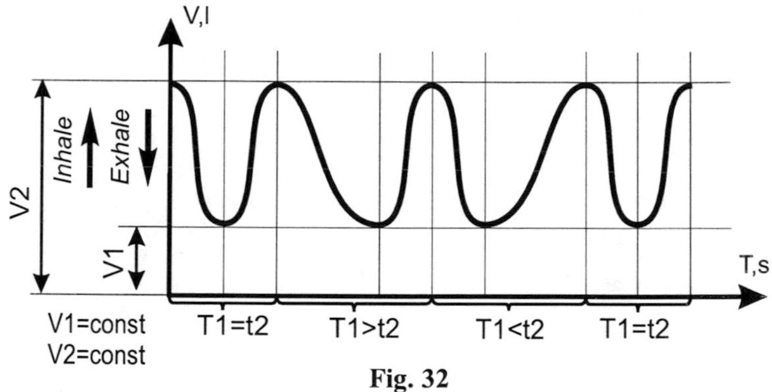

Fig. 32

4. Breath Delays

The breath may be delayed after the inhalation (T_1) and after exhalation (T_2). According to the temporal correlation, they may be equal ($T_1 = T_2$) or different. Delays after the exhalation are longer than after the inhalation ($T_1 < T_2$), or the delays after the inhalation are longer than after the exhalation ($T_1 > T_2$) (Fig. 33).

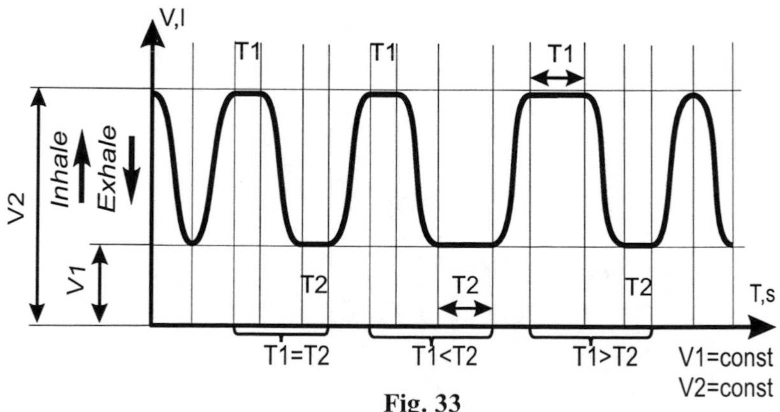

Fig. 33

Breathing with delays is called *Ujayi Pranayama*; it is also widely used in Yoga practice, and has a number of variations differing in the presence of stops and the temporal correlation of the delays after the inhalations and after the exhalations.

Breathing delays may also be performed, not only after inhalation or exhalation, but also during the inhalation (T_1) or during the exhalation (T_2) — in the form of «steps» (Fig. 34). This type of the breathing is called *Viloma Pranayama.*

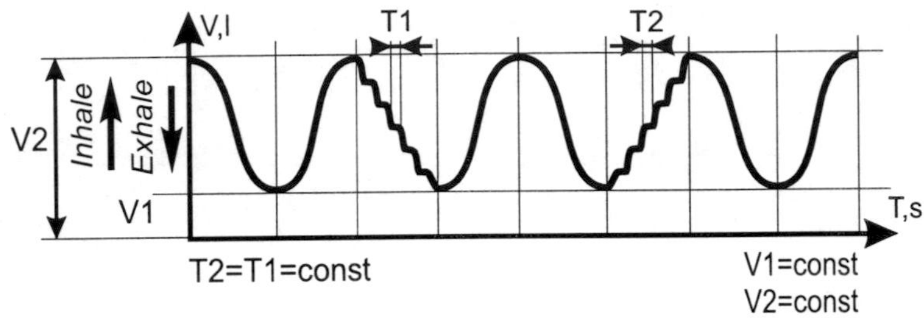

Fig. 34

5.Depth of Breath

Breathing depth (amplitude) may change independently, towards the increase of the inhalation ($V_2 \rightarrow$ max), or of the exhalation ($V_1 \rightarrow$ max); or towards the decrease of the inhalation ($V_2 \rightarrow$ min) or of the exhalation ($V_1 \rightarrow$ min). Simultaneously, it can change towards the increase of the inhalation and the exhalation (($V_1 + V_2$) $\rightarrow$ max), and towards the decrease of the inhalation and the exhalation ($V_1 + V_2$) $\rightarrow$ min) (Fig. 35). In this event, the scope of variation towards the inhalation and towards the exhalation may be equal or may vary.

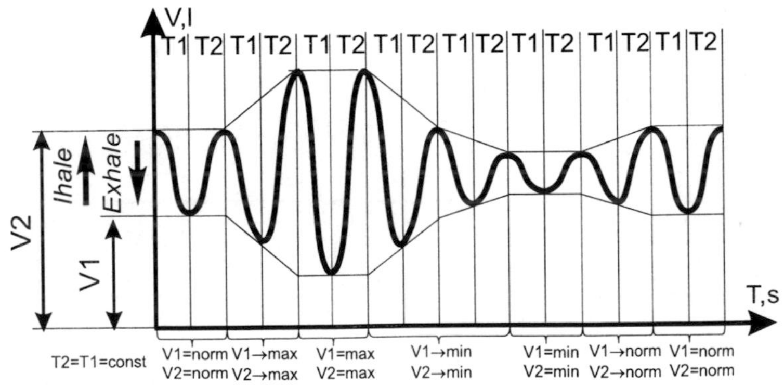

Fig. 35

Depth of breathing increases during the performance of different *Pranayamas*, requiring increased time of the inhalation and/or the exhalation, during special hyperventilating exercises facilitating fast restoration and increase of the energy potential, or during intensive physical exercises comprising the training requiring more energy resources. The depth decreases upon the transition from intensive lung ventilation modes back to «normal» breath, or during deep physical and psychic slowdown during the «dive» in relaxation.

6. Breath Frequency

The frequency of a breath may vary towards an increase or decrease in the number of breath cycles for a particular time unit. This is achieved by the acceleration or slowdown of the inhalation time ($T_1 > T_3$) or the exhalation time ($T_2 > T_4$), as well as by the acceleration or slowdown of both times simultaneously ($(T_1 + T_2) > (T_3 + T_4)$ or $(T_1 + T_2) < (T_3 + T_4)$) (Fig. 36). The rate of acceleration or slowdown of inhalation and exhalation may be equal or may vary.

Breath frequency is increased during the practice of *Bhastrika* and *Kapalabhati Pranayamas*, as well as other hyperventilating breathing exercises, and is reduced upon the change of hyperventilation to «normal» breath, or during deep relaxation when there is a slowdown of the rhythm of breath.

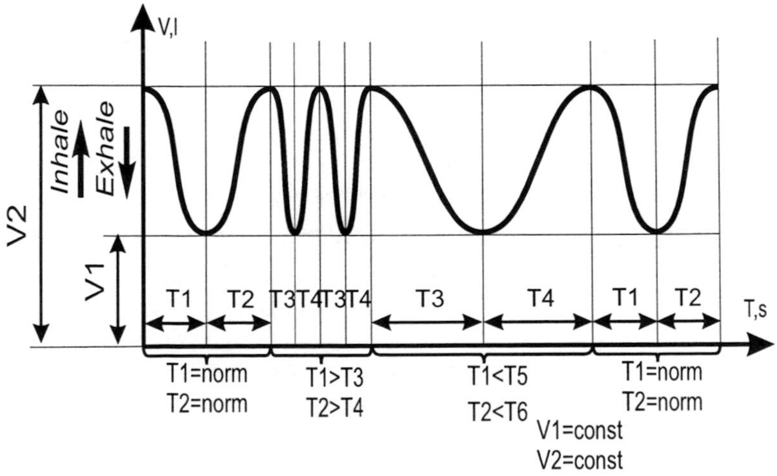

Fig. 36

SIX FACTORS ACCOMPANYING THE BREATH

The breath is related to the following accompanying factors: acoustic vibrations, temperature, internal pressure, forward signals and feedback signals, smoothness of the breath and characteristics of the respiratory pathways.

1. Acoustic Vibrations

An organism's life is accompanied by numerous sounds related to the operation of various life systems and organs. During training, the practitioner accumulates experience with these sounds, and begins to understand the meaning of the processes they represent. The sound vibrations are one of the main resources of information in the system of direct and back ties. Realization of these acoustic codes allows one to understand phenomena at various levels of your own essence, and to understand the essence of other people and animals. Also this understanding allows the affecting of behavior and reactions in yourself, as well as in others.

Loud sounds result from natural functions of the organism — heart pulse, breath, arm and leg movements, food processing (chewing, swallowing, digesting), cleansing (coughing, sneezing, burping, vomiting, defecating) and etc. Usually, these sounds are generated by contacting the walls of respiratory pathways, by movement of the air in the places of expansion in the respiratory channels, and by digested food.

There is also a large spectrum of «delicate internal sounds» connected with the blood flows in the blood group system, signals in the nervous system, tension of power fields, mental flows and various modifications of the consciousness.

With the use of special acoustic vibrations (*Mantras*), one can consciously reach different effects at a particular level. According to the «level of roughness» and «level of consciousness», *Mantras* may be divided into three main groups. Gradual transition from one level to another occurs in the process of realization the impact (essence) of a particular *Mantra*.

The first group comprises loud acoustic syllables (e.g., *Om*, *Hum*, *Lam*, and etc.) These are pronounced or sung using the same phonetic capabilities as used for words, with special position of the tongue and the lips in the mouth cavity and determine particular properties in the air flow and create the desired acoustic vibrations.

The second group includes acoustic vibrations not linked to any known alphabet counterparts. These resemble humming sounds, and are distinguished by the range and frequency of their generation. These *Mantras* are not so loud as are usually pronounced with the closed mouth. They may resemble some letter-combinations, but the resemblance is vague, not so different, and not as clear as in the articulation of syllables compris ing the first group. Using them is like using a tonometer, where one can tune all sections of psychic-energy structures to a particular frequency and achieve the «resonance splash».

A typical example of generating such sounds is *Bhamari Pranayama.*

The third group comprises externally «noiseless vibrations», which are the result of mental pronunciation or singing of a *Mantra.* They penetrate deep into the consciousness doing superfine corrections and tuning. *Nadabrama meditation* is a typical example of the generation of such sounds.

Mantras of the first two groups are in one way or the other related to exhalation, whereas the third group of *Mantras* has almost no dependence on breath, but depends on its activity by requiring a general level of silence of the nervous system and stable attention.

In natural conditions, it is possible to diagnose and judge the nature of the processes in the body by analyzing the peculiarities and the place of sound generation. When doing special breathing exercises, it is possible to obtain information about the state of respiratory channels, the uniformity and speed of airflow, etc.

Practical understanding of the essence of the first and second level sounds allows you to distinguish the truth of the words, the zone of generation, and the essence of acoustic vibrations both in yourself and in other people. This allows you to unmistakably determine the scope of truth in the words spoken by anybody.

By bringing the notional meanings of words and the vibrating essence of the psychic-energetic filling of transferring sense during one's speech into actions it becomes possible to give full information by expressing a true sense as well as the meaning of the given message.

Realization of the essence of the third level sounds allows one to see the thoughts of people, not only in the form of the words but in the form of access to the essence of their real thinking, motivations and intent. Any difference between what a person says and what he/she really thinks becomes obvious.

2. Temperature

Body temperature is one of the main indicators of the state of the psychic-energy structure. It can serve as a basis for viewing bodily processes and how with changing of temperature affect to them.

Practicing physical or breathing exercises is usually accompanied by an increase in body temperature. This is connected with the activation of the metabolic processes in the organism. This increased temperature may be used to increase plasticity of tissues in exercises requiring deep stretching, since heating any material, including tissues of the body, causes them to expand and become more elastic. Increasing body temperature in the

In normal conditions, the difference between internal lung pressure and outer pressure is not high, and it is conditioned by the necessity to provide normal breathing. Substantial muscle tensions, however, result in natural breath delays. Tension of the abdominal cavity and the diaphragm, results in an increase of pressure inside the lungs and activates energy exchange. Think about somebody lifting something heavy from the ground (a stone or a barbell). They generate sounds like «Utt». Try it yourself... What happens in this event?.. And read this paragraph once again.

The human organism consists largely of fluid. Therefore, body metabolism in it is by this or that manner linked with hydraulic effects. Blood flow, as known, occurs due to the work of the heart. Inside the blood vessels, there are one-way valves that let the blood pass in only one direction. And when the muscles work dynamically, they encourage blood flow and alleviate the efforts of the heart in moving the blood.

During static effort, this assistance is not provided, and the heart carries the whole load. Therefore, people who practice *Asanas* in the static mode, avoiding *Bandhas* or «membrane locks», will sooner or later start feeling heart pains. These pains may continue until the method of practice is changed to include dynamic *Vinyasas*, or *Bandhas*, which aid the heart to transport blood to particular zones of the body.

But beyond just blood to the muscles, there is a more important reason to control the body's internal pressure.

Increase of the pressure and the activation of blood circulation within the area of particular glands cause secretions. The flow of these secretions in the blood causes serious psychic changes and the transformation of consciousness. The energy enclosed within the secretions of these glands serve as additional power to transform the borders of perception. It is for these reasons that comprehensive training with physical exercises, synchronized with special breathing exercises, is absolutely required to receive an experience of different modifications and the real expanding of consciousness.

One should note here that the use of hyperventilation, dynamic synchronization of movement and breathing, and also others aerobic regimes, results in the secretion of endorphins. These are essentially natural internal drugs, which affect the same receptors of the brain as artificial drugs and cause changes in the state of consciousness, specific effects include slight intoxication and insensitivity to pain, which is widely used in training to anaesthetize and achieve extraordinary results. The impact of such natural internal drugs is not harmful since their presence in the organism can not be in excess of the acceptable levels. In addition, their composition is natural, because they are produced by the organism itself.

The human body has three main cavities: abdominal, chest, and cranial, which are interconnected. They are surrounded with flexible walls

In normal conditions, the difference between internal lung pressure and outer pressure is not high, and it is conditioned by the necessity to provide normal breathing. Substantial muscle tensions, however, result in natural breath delays. Tension of the abdominal cavity and the diaphragm, results in an increase of pressure inside the lungs and activates energy exchange. Think about somebody lifting something heavy from the ground (a stone or a barbell). They generate sounds like «Utt». Try it yourself... What happens in this event?.. And read this paragraph once again.

The human organism consists largely of fluid. Therefore, body metabolism in it is by this or that manner linked with hydraulic effects. Blood flow, as known, occurs due to the work of the heart. Inside the blood vessels, there are one-way valves that let the blood pass in only one direction. And when the muscles work dynamically, they encourage blood flow and alleviate the efforts of the heart in moving the blood.

During static effort, this assistance is not provided, and the heart carries the whole load. Therefore, people who practice *Asanas* in the static mode, avoiding *Bandhas* or «membrane locks», will sooner or later start feeling heart pains. These pains may continue until the method of practice is changed to include dynamic *Vinyasas*, or *Bandhas*, which aid the heart to transport blood to particular zones of the body.

But beyond just blood to the muscles, there is a more important reason to control the body's internal pressure.

Increase of the pressure and the activation of blood circulation within the area of particular glands cause secretions. The flow of these secretions in the blood causes serious psychic changes and the transformation of consciousness. The energy enclosed within the secretions of these glands serve as additional power to transform the borders of perception. It is for these reasons that comprehensive training with physical exercises, synchronized with special breathing exercises, is absolutely required to receive an experience of different modifications and the real expanding of consciousness.

One should note here that the use of hyperventilation, dynamic synchronization of movement and breathing, and also others aerobic regimes, results in the secretion of endorphins. These are essentially natural internal drugs, which affect the same receptors of the brain as artificial drugs and cause changes in the state of consciousness, specific effects include slight intoxication and insensitivity to pain, which is widely used in training to anaesthetize and achieve extraordinary results. The impact of such natural internal drugs is not harmful since their presence in the organism can not be in excess of the acceptable levels. In addition, their composition is natural, because they are produced by the organism itself.

The human body has three main cavities: abdominal, chest, and cranial, which are interconnected. They are surrounded with flexible walls and movable muscle membranes. Due to the strain of these muscle membranes (fulfilling *Bandhas*) it becomes possible to control their position, efforts created by them and degree of their elasticity (Fig. 37).

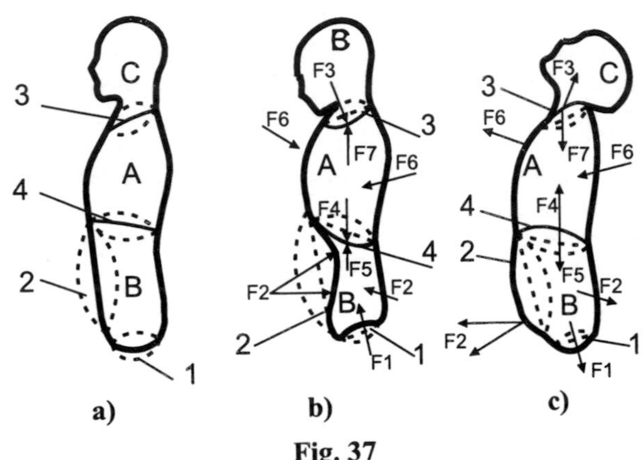

Fig. 37

A — Chest cavity, B — Abdominal cavity, C — Cranial cavity
Muscle membranes: 1 — pelvis bottom, 2 — abdomen, 3 — neck, 4 — diaphragm
- - - - - - — possible positions of the membranes

Effort: F1 — pelvis bottom muscles, F2 — loin and abdominal press muscles, F3 — front neck, gullet and tongue root muscles, F4 — diaphragm after the inhale, F5 = F1 + F2 — high pressure within the abdominal cavity, F6 — counteraction of the chest muscles, F7 = F5 + F6 — high pressure in the chest cavity.

In the natural position (Fig. 37a), the pressure within the chest (A), abdominal (B) and cranial (C) cavities is «normally» balanced.

During inhalation, the muscles of the chest and the diaphragm (4) expand the chest cavity (A), and the diaphragm (4) and the muscles of the abdomen (2) are lowered. In the majority of normal people, the muscles of the pelvic floor, abdomen and neck are not trained, always relaxed or insignificantly strained, «sagged», without actively participating in the breathing process.

During exhalation, the pelvic floor, abdomen and neck muscles remain relaxed, the ribcage sags, the diaphragm is raised and strained, and the abdomen is pulled slightly in. Topside movement of the diaphragm during inhalation increases the volume of the chest cavity, but due to retraction of the abdomen, the internal abdominal pressure remains unchanged. And the downward movement of the diaphragm during inhala tion reduces the volume of the abdominal pressure and this is now compensated by means of puffing the abdomen. Thus the internal abdominal pressure is kept unchanged.

Therefore, during normal breathing, all changes of the abdominal cavity form are a function of the breath-conditioned movements of the chest and diaphragm, and the pelvic, abdominal, and neck membranes move only passively and do not affect any of the characteristics of the breathing process.

By consciously controlling the muscle membrane tension, i. e., by the practice of *Bandhas*, possible intentionally alter the pressure in the cavities and achieve the transfer of the internal pressure and blood to particular zones of the body.

So, delaying breathing after an inhalation (Fig. 37b), and intensively drawing in the muscle membranes of the pelvic floor and abdomen, increases the pressure on the internal abdomen. This causes the transfer of the resulting force of the excessive pressure (F5) from the abdominal cavity (B) through the diaphragm to the chest cavity (A). This will lead to a pressure increase in the chest cavity and, as a result, to the expansion of the chest and transfer of the residual effort caused by the excessive pressure (F7) from the chest cavity (A) through the relaxed neck membrane to the cranial cavity (C). This pressure transfer to the cranial cavity may be blocked, if by simultaneously tensing muscle membranes of the pelvic floor and the abdominal cavity, one creates a counter-effort to the forces acting from below (F7). This blocking effect results (F3 + F6) by pulling the head down and tensing the muscles of the neck membrane (front surface muscles, gullet and the root of the tongue).

If exhaling and fully emptying the lungs, and to do this not only at the expansion of the muscles of the ribcage and diaphragm but with using the resulting force (F5), pulls in the muscle membranes of the pelvic floor and the abdominal muscles, in addition to the muscles of the chest and the diaphragm. Then, relaxing them (1 and 2) and then straining again (Fig. 37a), but this time pushing out (F1 and F2) out from the center of the abdominal cavity. The pressure inside the abdomen will be lower than in the chest cavity, which will lead to the transfer of the resulting force (F5) through the membrane of the diaphragm from the chest cavity down to the abdominal cavity. The pressure inside the chest will be reduced even more due to the counter-forces of the chest (F6) upon its maximum compression. But this will result in the transfer of the retracting force (F7) from the cranial cavity (C) inside the chest cavity (A). This will result in the reduction of the intra-cranial pressure and partial increase of intrathoracic pressure. This may not occur, if during exhalation, one keeps the neck membrane relaxed, and during the post-exhalation delay, to create contracted force (F3) by the neck membrane is made by pushing the neck up and outward from the chest, and simultaneously straining and lowering the pelvic and the abdominal membranes.

Usually, people do not realize the above processes, therefore, when performing particular muscular work, the muscular membranes of their body strain unconsciously and often inconsistently. This results in an internal pressure distribution that is in excess of the acceptable durability limit for internal tissues and damages them (common injuries include ruptures, pressure increases, headaches, etc.).

A typical example of a breathing exercise that creates a change in the internal pressure within the body's cavities is *Ujayi Pranayama.*

During conscious manipulations with *Bandhas,* should take into account the inertion character of the body's hydraulic system. After these manipulations, body returns to the «normal» breathing mode, but the difference of the blood pressure in the cavities will remain for a time. Balance and stability will return later, depending on the passive characteristics of organism's individual hydraulic processes.

Control over *Bandhas* allows the practitioner to achieve extraordinary super-power in performing strength exercises.

The internal pressure control principle serves as the basis for practical methods of many schools of Eastern martial arts, in addition to Yoga. ***Bandhas* perform the work of the heart, and use the force of some of the big muscle groups to help the heart. They are a second heart, which is stronger than the first one by several times.**

Practical experience in controlling internal pressure allows one to substantially increase the power of your psychic-energy processes during training, and to consciously control the internal pressure of daily life. Controlling the pressure inside the body's cavities becomes possible, not only during static breath delays, but also during dynamic and non-delayed breathing with controlled resistance or assistance during inhalation or the exhalation.

Sufficient practical experience allows to consciously increase or reduce blood pressure, not only within the cavities of the body and the head, but also in the blood vessels of the arms and legs.

This control allows the possibility to forget about headaches caused by hypertension or hypotension, intestinal disorders and blood circulation to the extremities.

Manipulations with *Bandhas* influence not only on the circulatory system, but also on the lymphatic and nervous systems.

4. Control over Signal System

The body's signal system is the system of direct ties and feedback ties that exchange signals between the controlling structures and the major parts of the body.

The controlling structures pertain to consciousness and subconscious and contain a set of programs of various generations, versions and complexity levels.

Direct ties serve to send commands from the controlling centers to major body parts. Whereas, the feedback ties are for signals sent by special receptors located in different organs and systems, and they carry coded information about the actual processes.

Our subconscious contains a set of our body's most ancient programs (at least 95%). These are reliable and verified by thousands of years of evolutionary trials. They support all natural functions, providing and protecting the life of the organic body, which is their material realization. Some of these programs are useless atavisms, but the majority of them are the best we can have till now. Any interference with their algorithms results in serious functional disturbances and diseases.

The consciousness, however, contains a small set of universal up-to-date programs of the last generation, which can mach more easily be changed and developed. These form the spiritual basis for a human being, which is its way of manifestation.

Every individual's sensitivity to their own signal systems differs. The development of the signal system means:

- expanded sensitivity with a simultaneous development of protective capabilities, the ability to adapt to both rough and super-powerful signals, from hypersensitivity to complete insensitivity;
- increased selective capability and degree of discretion by the controlling system;
- the change of the pathways and varying the direction of feedback signals (taking, for example, inhalation for an exhalation and vice versa);
- the special transformation of feedback signals and a connection to the program controlling modeling units, which can imitate various «feedback information signals», and lead to various reactions of the controlling program and relevant changes in the body.

By the location of the generation of feedback signals in meditation, one can monitor the condition of the body's tiniest perception receptors. By determining the location sending these signals, memorizing and concentrating your attention on them and ignoring areas which provide no information at all, one can determine more pathways for the feedback signals to the controlling centers of the brain.

For example, when speaking about the breathing process, the ability to differentiate between one of the two groups of information is of practical interest.

Group one includes the signals informing about the state of respiratory organs: their disposition, the pressure exerted on them, temperature, energy resource, characteristics of the current breath control program, etc.

The second group includes signals informing about the quality of the air inside of the respiratory organs: flow rate, temperature, energy content, presence of airborne dust, ions provoke odour and taste sensations, etc.

The signals referring to the first group are received from special receptors of the muscle groups participating in the breathing process, the tissues in contact with the air, and the respiratory center of the brain itself. The signals referring to the second group are received from special receptors located on the mucous membranes of the respiratory pathways, tongue, and teeth, along with signals from the general system informing about enough quantity of energy which is necessary for the human organism.

In this case the transformation of breathing characteristics inevitably causes changes in the feedback signals.

5. Smoothness of breathing

Smoothness of breathing depends on the rate of breathing set by the correlation between breath frequency and amplitude, and on the possible acceleration or damping of the breath during inhalation or exhalation. Acceleration or damping of the breath determines the character of the impact of the airflow on the receptors on the surface of the mucous membranes of the respiratory channels, and affects the energy exchange and other characteristics of the breath.

Increasing the frequency of breathing with the same amplitude (Fig. 38a), or increasing the amplitude with the same frequency (Fig. 38b), results in the reduction of smoothness of the breath and the «radius of the peaks» between inhalation and exhalation is reduced — «the peaks acquire a sharper shape».

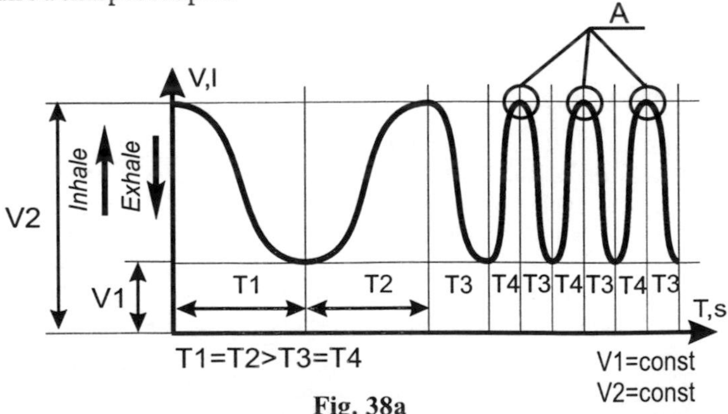

Fig. 38a

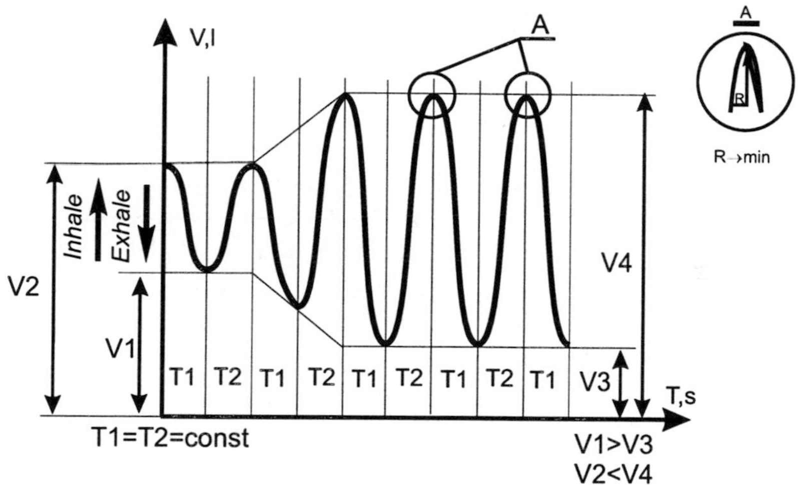

Fig. 38b

Such «sharpening» increases the intensity of dangerous «deforming» impacts on the mucous membranes of the respiratory organs. This may result in overdosing, and may also cause inflammations (colds), reduced sensitivity of the informing receptors, etc.

Reducing the frequency with the same amplitude (Fig. 39a), or reducing the amplitude with the same frequency (Fig. 39b), increases the smoothness of the breath. The «radius of the peaks» between inhalation and exhalation is increased — «the peaks acquire a round shape», eliminating the possibility of the above adverse consequences. Conscious

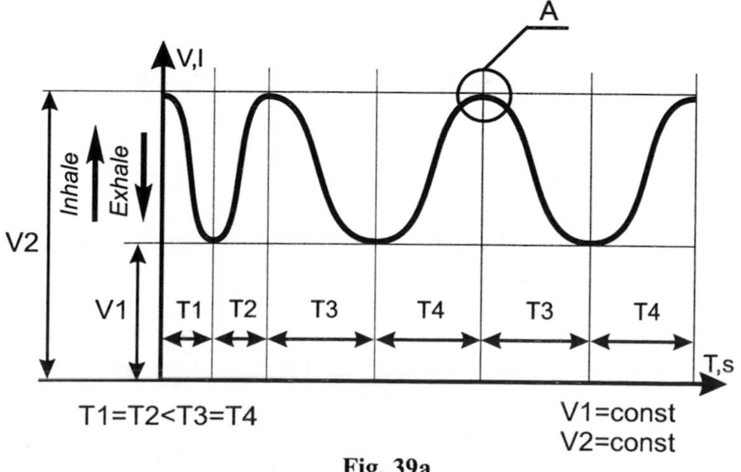

Fig. 39a

«rounding» of the «peaks» is achieved through damping the breath before changing between inhalation and exhalation, and vice versa, with subsequent acceleration after such changes.

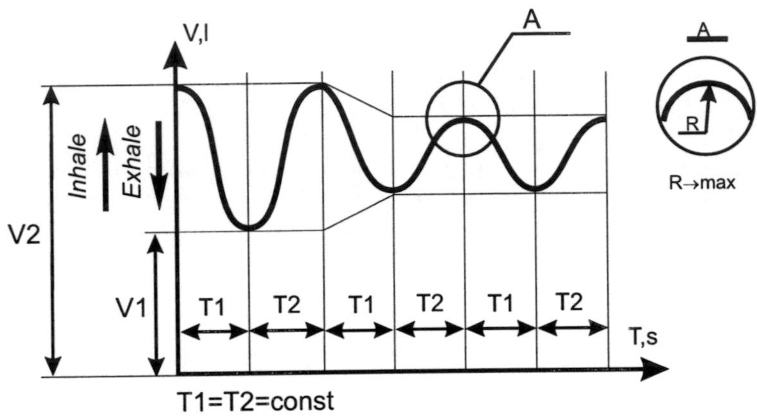

Fig. 39b

6. Respiratory pathways

Natural breath occurs through the nostrils or, in special cases, through the mouth. Our subconscious contains special programs to control respiratory pathways depending on the general energy balance of the body, disease-like defects, temperature and the quality of the inhaled air.

With the purpose of conscious influence on the characteristics of breathing through manipulations with respiratory pathways, different schools use special exercises which provide the opening or closing of the nostrils or the mouth separately, the simultaneous closing of the latter, or in a combination of two or all three openings at the same time.

Naturally, the mouth is closed by the lips, various positions of the tongue and lower jaw. Whereas, the nose is closed by contracting the sphincter muscles around the nostril openings to the gullet, and by narrowing the open flow areas of the nostrils around the nose bridge through changing blood circulation within this zone.

Artificially, the mouth and the nose are closed with palms and fingers of one or both hands by pressing on the lips and nostril wings.

The main respiratory pathways are: nasopharynx, mouth, trachea, bronchi, and intra-lungs space. But secondary respiratory pathways also exist, and they are rather important for the life of the organism. These are the gaimor cavities, syringes, ear cavities, lachrymal channels, esophagus, stomach, intestine and genital cavities.

Natural movement of the air through the secondary pathways occurs during breathing, yawning, sneezing, swallowing, blowing the nose, eating, drinking, burping, digesting food, defecation and performing physical movements.

Artificially flow of air inside the secondary pathways may be effected using special manipulations.

Ear cavities can be filled with air through syringes when the mouth is closed, and thus increase the air pressure inside the gullet. This can be achieved by exhaling with the nose held closed by the fingers. Excessive pressure in the ear cavities can be released by imitating yawning, swallowing, or with special movements of the lower jaw and the root of the tongue.

The air may flow through the lachrymal channels when imitating nose blowing.

Special exercises, which imitate swallowing, burping the air with the stomach, and filling and releasing the air from the intestines assist in achieving intensive cooling of the organism, ventilate the esophagus, and stimulate the oxidization processes in the digestive tract.

Conscious change of the open flow areas of the air channels may be achieved using a variety of natural and artificial positions within the range of ultimate mobility, from complete opening to full contraction:

In the mouth area:

1 — with the jaw

- from complete opening to full closing of the teeth
- from ultimate abduction to one side to ultimate abduction to the other side

2 — with the tongue

- by ultimately drawing up and down (in *Khechari Mudra*)
- by tightly pressing down (in *Kurma Mudra*)
- by drawing to the sides until touching the points on the internal surface of the cheeks (special energy contacts)
- by placing the tip of the tongue on the alveoli above the upper cutting teeth, above and back at the depth of the gullet (in *Nabhi Mudra*)
- by pressing in the front against upper or lower teeth (special energy contacts)
- by making it flat (in «normal» position)
- by making it a round form (in *Sitali Pranayama*)
- by rolling a tube form (in *Sitakari Pranayama*)

3 — with the lips

- by ultimate withdrawal (in *Simhasana*)
- by firmly pressing (upon the breath delays)
- by rolling a tube form (in the «*Cleansing Pranayama*»)

- by firmly pressing on the gums above the teeth (special position)
- by firmly pressing on the teeth (special position)
- by turning them inside around the teeth (special position)
- by drawing them away from the teeth (special position)
- by turning them outside (special position)

In the area of nostrils — artificially close it by pressing on the nostril wings with the fingers (in *Surya Bhedana Pranayama, Chandra Bhedana Pranayama,* and *Nadi Sodhana Pranayama*), and by natural expansion of the nostrils and raising the upper lip (in the intensive *Bhastrika Pranayama*). A combination is possible also.

In the area of nasopharynx — by natural fixation of the sphincter muscles that surround the openings of nostrils into the gullet (for example, when diving a head in water).

In the area of gullet — by natural fixation of the tongue root and muscles that surround the gullet (during breathing delays).

In the area of the glottis — by natural fixation of the glottis (during control or breathing delay).

In the area of the Eustachian tubes — by natural fixation of the marginal positions through tensing the muscles of the gullet, tongue and jaw by imitating swallowing and chewing movements (during «blowing» before a deep dive or during the release of excessive pressure in the ear cavities).

In the area of lachrymal channels — by natural fixation of marginal positions through tensing muscles when closing eyes (in special cleansing exercises).

In the abdominal area — by naturally fixing marginal positions of sphincters at the intake of the esophagus and outlet to the intestine (in special cleansing exercises).

In the genital area — by naturally fixing marginal positions of tension in the muscles of genitals in special exercises during sexual intercourse (in *Vajroli Mudra* and *Yoni Mudra*).

In the anus area — by naturally fixing marginal positions of the anus sphincter muscles (upper and lower, about 5—7 cm one above another) (in *Ashvini Mudra*).

The practice of *Pranayama* leads to conscious changing of air pathways. Typical examples of such breath exercises are *Anuloma Pranayama* and *Pratiloma Pranayama*, during the practice of which inhalation and exhalation are through one nostril only or through two nostrils in turns.

COMBINED CONTROL

Loss of control during the training period results in the periodic replacement of conscious behavior with unconscious behavior.

In some cases, subconscious programs may be most efficient or necessary from among all of the available programs, or a changeover to such programs may be the result of conscious choice.

So, for example, in order to relieve stress, one may use the transition from the conscious control over the stressful situation to the surrender of control, and allow the body to sleep deeply or to enjoy a delicious meal, relying on the Higher Will rather than conscious control.

Breathing may employ an alternating mode, for example, conscious inhalation; having controlled varied characteristics, and unconscious «normal» exhalation (Fig. 40). In this event, the change of the periods of conscious and unconscious control occurs with predefined temporal correlations.

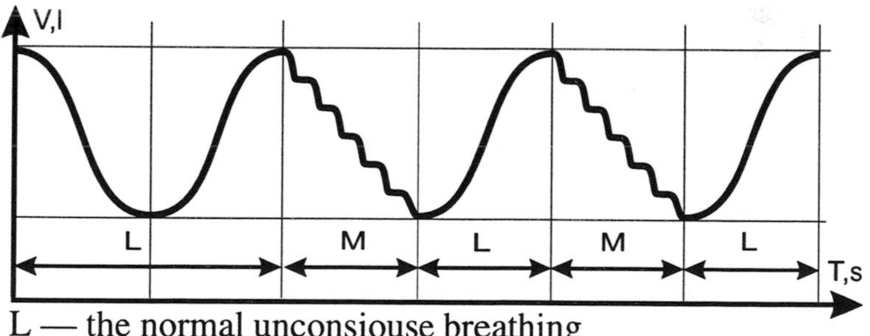

L — the normal unconsiouse breathing
M — the consiouse breathing under control

Fig. 40

For example, in *Viloma Pranayama* the inhalation may be done naturally, and be «normally» controlled by the automatic program from the subconscious, whereas the exhalation may be performed as a consciously controlled alternation of partial fragments of the exhalation and breath delays. Or vice versa, the inhalation may be a consciously controlled alternation of partial fragments of the inhalation and breath delays, whereas the exhalation may be natural and controlled by a «normal» automatic program from subconscious.

***

A similar detailed approach to these breathing characteristics has already given an invaluable assistance to many people who have strived to master *Pranayama* perfectly. It has given the possibility to investigate and use the psychic-energy effects caused by changes in breathing characteristics (which for some reasons escaped from the attention of the presently popular Yoga schools). And also, without omitting anything, it is equally important to apply the same in practice, and to investigate everything related to *Pranayama* in the Tradition of Yoga.

It appears that all *Pranayama* forms actually used in most Yoga schools are frequently the above breathing types. In this case changing any characteristic of the breath is related to the changes in biochemical processes inside the body, energy potential, psychic background and the state of the consciousness of the practitioner. These changes can be easily noticed in the course of regular practice, and subsequently, according to one's needs, learned consciously, just the same as through various *Pranayama* forms.

Traditional *Pranayama* forms, however, in most cases, consist of combinations of several of the above breathing types and, as a rule, are the most effective and powerful empirical findings of the of the Yoga Tradition's adepts.

SRI MANTRA

Sri means «saint» or «sacred». *Mantra* — is an acoustic vibration.

Acoustic vibrations differ from one another with amplitude and frequency characteristics, and they are divided into the pronounced and received. At the same time, these may be «external» or «internal». «External» *Mantras* are the sounds of the surrounding Universe, both natural and artificial. And the «internal» *Mantras* are the sounds of the breath, speech, muscle movement, tendons, joints, internal organs, food, blood, nerve signals, field interactions, mental forms, etc.

Perception and contemplation of the «external» and «internal» sounds allows the realization of the essence of their impact on particular zones of the psychic-energy structure, and on the respective changes in the consciousness, as well as their meaning in the Game of the Universe.

Articulation of sounds with particular amplitude and frequency characteristics allows special transformations in the psychic-energy structure and transforms the state of one's own or of other people's consciousness.

This mainly occurs due to resonance effects in the psychic-energy structure, respective reactions, and changes in the consciousness.

Besides *Mantras* differ by sound origination zone. They may or may not have notional meanings also. The *Mantras* which have sense are essentially prayers. They are most effective if pronounced in the native language of a man, in the language he/she thinks. It is not very effective to pronounce them in a foreign language (Mainly because, as auto-training suggestion mainly consists of affirmative sentences and the particle «no» has never being used in them. Because it is a kind of block for the direct movement of energy flow in the controlling organs. The same is with *Mantras* pronounced in a foreign language which go through a special transformer contained in the consciousness that is responsible for the translation from a foreign into native language).

Mantras in foreign or ancient languages, if applied in the training, may become efficient only after years of personal in-depth cultural reorientation that provides actual replacement of native meaning codes with foreign or ancient ones. But such reeducation is, in our days, an efficient leading of the life time and may not be justified. And it is usually a tribute to an exotic style, or the imitating of foreign or outdated training technologes without understanding and preserving the true essence of the Tradition of Yoga.

Training technologies based on energy laws, which are deeper than cultural or national differences become applicable in the modern conditions of the cosmopolitical tendencies in the whole world. In relation to the *Mantras* pronunciation technique, this means that modern universal *Mantras* should only have energy essence which does not require language translation. And which can directly, purely through vibration, lead to the same results that can be achieved using *Mantras* which have the language sense. Such universal *Mantras* may use language sounds, but these will have purely vibrational, rather than language, meaning. General names of such *Mantras*, however, only convey the meaning of the results achieved in the psychic-energy structure and the consciousness.

Among the variety of private specialized *Mantras*, there is one principal — *Sri Mantra*. This acoustic vibration smoothly changes frequency within the range from the lower to upper margin, covers the entire acoustic spectrum and realizing integrating principle at the acoustic vibrations level. Because *Sri Mantra* is considered to be a name and sound expression of the Omnipresent God.

Sri Mantra exists in three main forms: two are human and one is divine. Articulating *Sri Mantra*, a man can change the frequency of acoustic vibrations. In this case according to the first form, the frequency changes from the lower margin to upper margin. And in the second form the other way around — from the upper margin to lower margin. When sound ac companiment is used, the first form of *Sri Mantra* sounds like H-A-O-U-M-m-m, and the second form like — m-m-M-A-A-H-H. However, this is just a resemblance, not more. But in essence *Sri Mantra* is just pure vibration. It becomes more apparent, if practiced with the mouth closed and without acoustic accompaniment, as a booming sound. The vibration runs through the body along the spine from bottom to top or from top to bottom. The first variant is dominated by the ascending excitement flow from the lower energy centers (*Chakras*) to upper centers. Whereas the second variant is dominated by the descending flow from upper to lower energy centers. Traditionally, Yoga distinguishes seven principal *Chakras*, which correspond to the seven notes of the octave. In fact, the *Chakras*, as well as sounds, are much more numerous.

The first or second variants of *Sri Mantra* is used in training, depending on the stage orientation or the principal goal of the practice.

The third divine variant of *Sri Mantra* implies simultaneous sounding of all possible acoustic vibrations with different frequencies. It can be compared to organ sounds. By analogy with organ sounds, for example, if the first and second forms of *Sri Mantra* take place in consecutive order playing the keys from one side to another and back, then in the third form, all keys of the organ sound simultaneously. Perfect articulation of the third variant of *Sri Mantra* is possible only for the One. Therefore, a man may perceive it only as an absolute unified sound of the Universe.

FIELD FORMATION THEORY

LIFE SOURCE

The main source of Life is the Organizing Field Power. If the depletion of this Power is running low it results in aging and diseases. Complete exhaustion of this Power means Death inevitably followed by fast decomposition of all material systems into elementary components.

The Organizing Field Power establishes a specific organization code, provides the program for the development of all living and «inanimate» beings within the Universe, and determines their role and the sense of Being.

Universal Ties provide the cause energy exchange between all living and «inanimate» beings within the Body of the One.

This Great Unity, which a human being is part of, represents an energy conglomerate that may be provisionally divided into several "limbs", each with different vibration levels. Everything in it, from the roughest, *manifested* organic forms to the finest transparent field substances, is material that differs only in frequency and measurement, and, therefore, is subject to the Law of *Ha-Tha* Dualism.

The purpose of Yoga is transcending or overcoming this dualism and achieving (do not be surprised) the Limit of the Unlimited.

Differentiating the human being into limbs is required, but only for the purposes of primary teaching and realizing him/her its nature. This is a general approach. But different spiritual schools discriminate different numbers of such limbs. For example, the Tradition of Yoga uses seven limbs, or *Koshas*:

1. *Anna Maya Kosha* — organic body
2. *Prana Maya Kosha* — energy body
3. *Mano Maya Kosha* — psychic body
4. *Vijniana Maya Kosha* — intellectual body
5. *Ananda Maya Kosha* — body of joy
6. *Chitta Maya Kosha* — body of consciousness
7. *Atma Maya Kosha* — body of selfness

RASAS — PSYCHIC-ENERGY DOMINANTS

In fact, all *Asana, Vinyasa* and *Pranayama* practitioners sooner or later deal with strange phenomena in training. These phenomena, which at times can hardly not to be noticed, are unfortunately not consciously followed, interpreted or developed by the practitioners who meet them. These are *Rasas* — psychic-energy states which are manifested and often steadily dominate the course of the practice of Yoga.

Changes in psychic-energy states occur first of all, due to the fact that the course of comprehensive yoga training leads to changes in blood circulation and pressure in the areas of the main endocrine glands. This leads to the increased activation of their functions and additional portions of their secretions in the blood, which affect relevant receptors of the brain and facilitates in changing the practitioner's range of perception and state of consciousness.

These changes take place during the process of training in exactly the same way as a dropped item always falls to the ground, but unfortunately, very few understand the importance of conscious development, so as to transform one's psychic-energy structure in order to further ones progress in Yoga.

Depending on the specific features of the training program, the qualities of psychic-energy modifications may be different.

These qualities must be completely conscious, and used to establish direct ties between certain sequences of training exercises and the psychic-energy modifications taking place as the result of the practice of such exercises. In the beginning, these ties develop empirically during the course of persistent and regular practice, but their development is to a great extent individual, since similar modifications are based on an individual's metabolic rate. Thereafter, the accumulation of sufficient statistical data enables the practitioner to consciously define the required *Rasas* through the use of readily known combinations of training exercises. When there is enough experience and enough entries into altered states, it becomes automatic. The practitioner may develop the possibility to vary *Rasas,* not only through special sequences of *Asanas, Vinyasas* and *Pranayamas,* but also without using them, only by the effort of will. Not only in the course of special training, but also in any situation of life where social interactions may become subject to day-and-night practice of these magical abilities.

One should never tell anyone else about such practice, since people are afraid of what they do not understand, or what they are unable to do; they assume the worst — danger for themselves. They often try to dominate what is not in their power, since self-preservation is the principal instinct. The closer an effort gets to the human *Ego*, the more opposition the Ego exerts to protect itself. This is exactly why even sophisticated Yoga practitioners are often opposed to various psychic-energy effects that they witness when watching advanced students, or when new elements are introduced in the training program by the teacher, which provide previously inaccessible real psychic-energy transformation.

In order to soften this kind of resistance by those who have not yet started to realize, and use *Rasas* in their training, need to understand a simple truth: the occurrence of psychic-energy modification in the course of the practice of Yoga is absolutely consistent and inevitable. And the way to the peaks of spiritual development in Yoga goes through the complete realizing and practical control of *Rasas*.

Modification and stable fixation of various *Rasas* develops the ability to identify particular psychic-energy dominants in the consciousness, and to be free of them. Even during the initial stage this, as a minimum, allows the practitioner to get rid of the stresses and adverse effects of routine life, improve one's self-restoration capability, to become more powerful and to feel harmony in any situation.

There are a number of typical *Rasas*, for example:

- love and hatred
- charity and selfishness
- calmness and instability
- peace and aggression
- spirituality and materiality
- modesty and self-conceit
- wisdom and delusion
- activity and passivity
- industry and laziness
- audacity and fear
- assurance and cowardice
- sensitivity and stupidity
- discipline and laxity

There are many others. Each *Rasa* may also have a number of different shades, or may manifest itself as a mixture of several *Rasas*.

In the process of training, each of the practitioners shows individual psychic-energy dominants, the density of which may increase or decrease over time. These are, as a rule, the *Rasas* that facilitate successful practice. But they are absolutely different in different styles of practice. For example, *Ha*-style is characterized by firm intention and the control and tension of the «iron» will. Whereas, *Tha*-style is characterized by soft sensitivity, loss of will, and relaxation. Practice of the styles, which are based on the ascending «flow», use a number of different psychic-energy states. But the styles based on the "descending flow" are usually characterized by the «Buddhist» background of the absence of emotions and detachment.

In practice, one should never give any preference to particular *Rasas* such as those that are easily attainable, or to ignore those that are difficult to attain or are unpleasant. Without realizing the practical control over the whole *Rasa's* spectrum, it is impossible to gain power over various dominants in the consciousness. The practitioner will also not be able to fully control his psychic-energy structure and social behavior, and, consequently, will not be able to realize the spiritual ideals of the Tradition of Yoga in his life.

Given this, the practice of «negative» *Rasas* should be done impartially, as in a play or art to be anyone, or as specific «psychic makivara», which may be used to work off all the energy of the compressed springs of internal imbalance (if any), and, thereby liberate one's consciousness from them, thus achieving contentment, harmony and equilibrium.

Manifestation of particular *Rasas* depends on the domineering functions of particular psychic-energy centers — *Chakras*. Therefore, there is a principle in the Tradition of Yoga that one should first master principal *Rasas*, i. e., try to selectively fix psychic-energy properties, pertinent to a particular *Chakra*. This position is based on the following analogy: the three primary colors (red, blue and yellow) serve as the basis of all colors, the rest being the combination of these basic colors in various proportions. So, various *Rasas* are manifestations of the mixture of psychic-energy dominants of the seven principal *Chakras*:

1. *Muladhara Chakra* — simplicity, durability, materiality (Pic. 1 a, b).

2. *Swadhisthana Chakra* — sensitivity, jocosity, sexuality (Pic. 2 a, b).

3. *Manipura Chakra* — purpose, willfulness, industry (Pic. 3 a, b).

4. *Anahata Chakra* — compassion, mercy, charity (Pic. 4 a, b).

5. *Visuddha Chakra* — insight, creative inspiration, persuasion (Pic. 5 a, b).

6. *Ajnya Chakra* — clarity, assurance, rationality (Pic. 5 a, b).

7. *Sahasrara Chakra* — spirituality, content, wisdom (Pic. 7 a, b).

Complete mastering of these principal *Rasas* allows you to achieve the eighth *Rasa* (Stumbha), which is, on the one hand, a potential ability to manifest the whole spectrum of the above *Rasa* properties. On the other hand, it allows one to be ambiguous, unpredictable, and spiritually free (Pic. 8). If the seven *Chakras* listed above are characterized by the general properties of availability, manifestation and presence, the eighth *Rasa* is characterized by the opposite qualities of absence and non-manifestation.

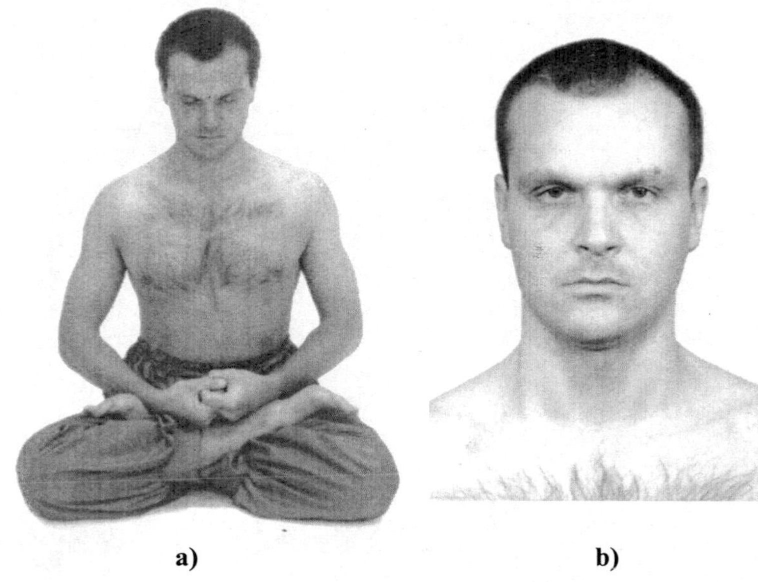

a) b)

Pic. 1

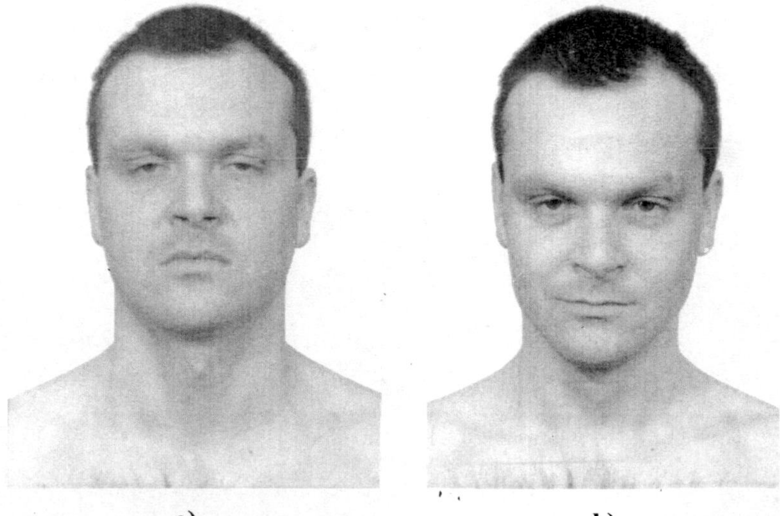

a) b)

Pic. 2

In practice, one should never give any preference to particular *Rasas* such as those that are easily attainable, or to ignore those that are difficult to attain or are unpleasant. Without realizing the practical control over the whole *Rasa's* spectrum, it is impossible to gain power over various dominants in the consciousness. The practitioner will also not be able to fully control his psychic-energy structure and social behavior, and, consequently, will not be able to realize the spiritual ideals of the Tradition of Yoga in his life.

Given this, the practice of «negative» *Rasas* should be done impartially, as in a play or art to be anyone, or as specific «psychic makivara», which may be used to work off all the energy of the compressed springs of internal imbalance (if any), and, thereby liberate one's consciousness from them, thus achieving contentment, harmony and equilibrium.

Manifestation of particular *Rasas* depends on the domineering functions of particular psychic-energy centers — *Chakras*. Therefore, there is a principle in the Tradition of Yoga that one should first master principal *Rasas*, i. e., try to selectively fix psychic-energy properties, pertinent to a particular *Chakra*. This position is based on the following analogy: the three primary colors (red, blue and yellow) serve as the basis of all colors, the rest being the combination of these basic colors in various proportions. So, various *Rasas* are manifestations of the mixture of psychic-energy dominants of the seven principal *Chakras*:

1. Muladhara Chakra — simplicity, durability, materiality (Pic. 1 a, b).

2. Swadhisthana Chakra — sensitivity, jocosity, sexuality (Pic. 2 a, b).

3. Manipura Chakra — purpose, willfulness, industry (Pic. 3 a, b).

4. Anahata Chakra — compassion, mercy, charity (Pic. 4 a, b).

5. Visuddha Chakra — insight, creative inspiration, persuasion (Pic. 5 a, b).

6. Ajnya Chakra — clarity, assurance, rationality (Pic. 5 a, b).

7. Sahasrara Chakra — spirituality, content, wisdom (Pic. 7 a, b).

Complete mastering of these principal *Rasas* allows you to achieve the eighth *Rasa* (Stumbha), which is, on the one hand, a potential ability to manifest the whole spectrum of the above *Rasa* properties. On the other hand, it allows one to be ambiguous, unpredictable, and spiritually free (Pic. 8). If the seven *Chakras* listed above are characterized by the general properties of availability, manifestation and presence, the eighth *Rasa* is characterized by the opposite qualities of absence and non-manifestation.

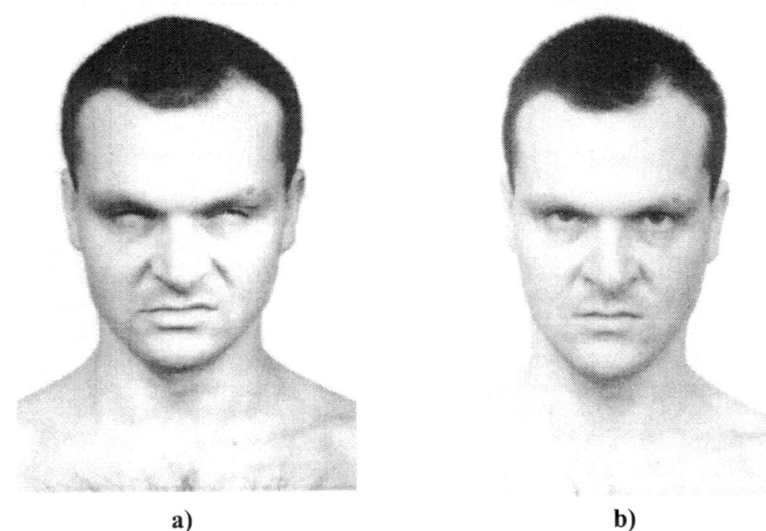

a) b)

Pic. 3

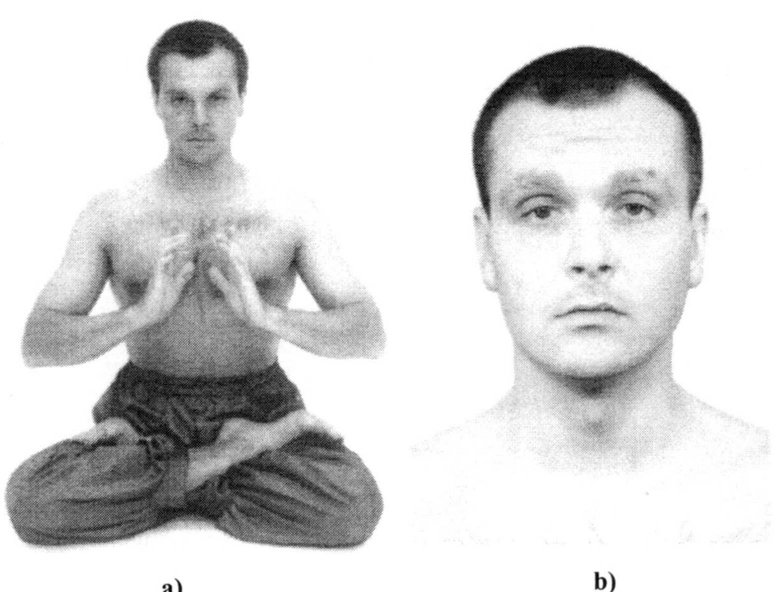

a) b)

Pic. 4

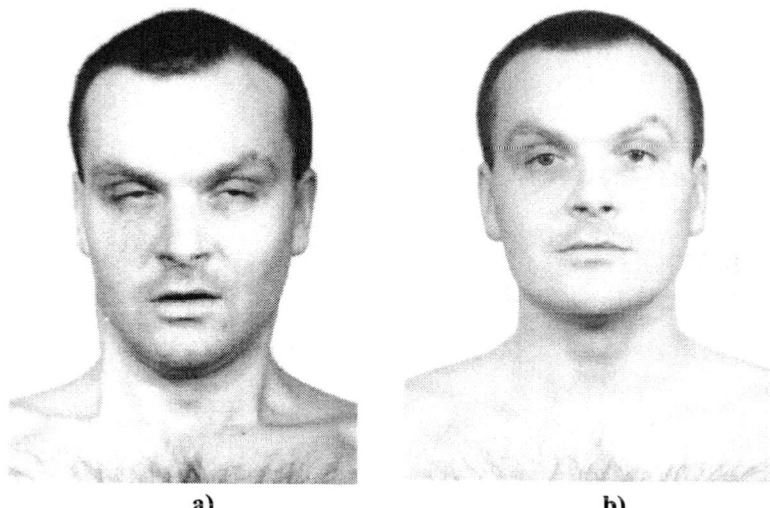

a) b)

Pic. 5

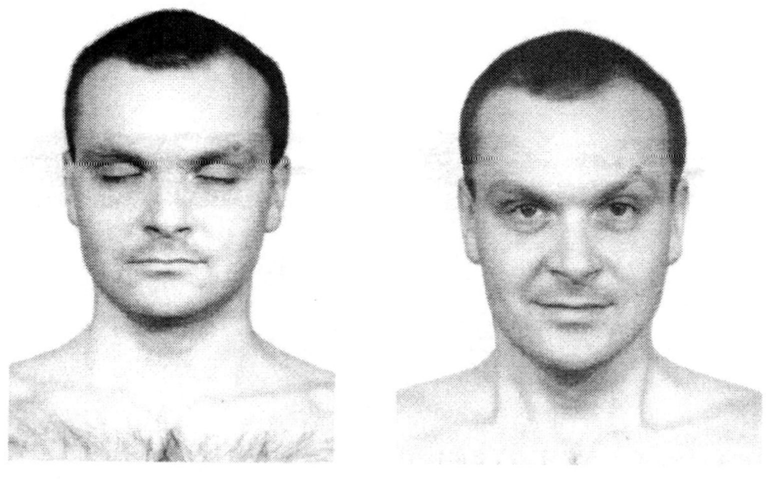

a) b)

Pic. 6

a) b)

Pic. 7

Pic. 8

Beside the seven principal *Chakras*, the psychic-energy structure of a man contains a variety of other *Chakras*. The scope of this book, however, will not allow the illustration of the complete diversity of the potential psychic-energy states. Therefore, all of the above properties pertaining to particular *Rasas* are simply examples, sufficient to understand the main orientation in practicing conscious control over *Rasas*.

Complete transfer of the qualities of **Rasas** by means of photography in the distracting conditions of a photo studio is quite a complicated task, since the requirement of giving commands to the photographer about the readiness of taking pictures of a particular **Rasa** distracts and modifies the required states at that moment. Therefore, the pictures presented should not be treated with criticism. Nevertheless, these serve as an example, sufficient enough to allow the readers to catch some peculiarities of particular **Rasas**, and to later learn to distinguish between them in oneself and other people. This develops the ability to make the **Rasas** more and more conscious and proficient on the level of one's own psychic-energy modifications and interactions with surrounding living beings.

One should also note that each *Chakra* might be manifested in two ways, i.e. in positive and in negative quality. If, for example, the fourth center is manifested in the positive quality, this leads to concerned behavior, and the ability to be sympathetic, compassionate, and merciful to all living beings requiring help. If this center is manifested in the negative quality, this can lead to cruelty, indifference and the inability to be compassionate and merciful.

In addition, the properties of each *Chakra* may be manifested through the remaining centers. If, for example, the second center is active, its sexuality will condition the respective themes for the creative efforts of the fifth center, or direct all thoughts to a single purpose, coloring one's thinking with sexual tendencies. There are numerous examples of poets and artists who manifested creative abilities of their fifth center exclusively through the use of the energy of the second center in love poems and paintings depicting something sexual.

Therefore, each *Chakra*, being linked to the remaining psychic-energy centers, may be manifested in different ways under the influence of the properties of the other centers.

Differentiating and controlling *Rasas* opens a whole world of interactions, existing in parallel to organic metabolism. The perception of life manifestations becomes of absolute interest to anyone who begins developing their abilities and reaching more sophisticated levels of Yoga practice.

Due to the fact that psychic-energy practice is extremely individual, it would be ill advised to suggest a generalized *Rasas* practice method, since it is most likely that it would not suit the majority of followers. These skills are unmistakably conveyed, and much more effectively adopted, only through direct contact with a teacher.

SRI YANTRA — UNIVERSAL YOGA TECHNOLOGY DIAGRAM

Sri means «saint, sacred». *Yantra* — an object for contemplation, realizing the qualities of which allows one to penetrate into the essence of the object.

Sri Yantra means the main sacred object for contemplation, for which our case uses the «Universal Yoga technology diagram» (see Fig. 41 on page 144 — 145).

Sri Yantra includes the graphic representation of *Asanas* consisting of forty two main sectors and four levels of mobility of the organic body; *Vinyasas* — five principal «psychic-energy Mandalas»; *Pranayamas* — twelve principal characteristics and factors accompanying the breath; *Rasas* — eight main psychic-energy types; and the double-sided *Swastika* — a symbol of equilibrium of the natural and reversed flows within the Unity of the Universe.

Contemplation on *Sri Yantra* allows one to realize various aspects of the practice and to penetrate into the essence of the ancient and modern Tradition of Yoga.

MRITA MUDRA

In the second, third and fourth Raja-Yoga (Astanga-Yoga) sutras of Patanjali says:

Yoga is a restrain (control, termination) of *vritti* (fluctuations of consciousness), pertaining to the mind.

When *vrittis* are restrained, the meditator stays in his own nature.

Otherwise he has the shape of *vritti* (fluctuations of consciousness).

Therefore, training in Yoga is a means for controlling feelings and stopping of the mind, resulting in complete perception and the gaining of complete control of all of the material nature of one's own being, as well as in understanding particular aspects of one's own being.

The principal, in perceiving ones own nature in the practice of Yoga, is the «personal turn off mode», which is usually actuated by practicing *Mrita Mudra* in any «perfect sitting posture» («meditating») or in *Savasana.*

Mrita means «dead», *mudra* is a «state». *Sarva* means «corpse», whereas *Asana*, as you know, means «posture».

All exercises comprising Yoga complexes, i. e., *Asanas, Vinyasas* and *Pranayamas*, are varieties of actions: preparatory, auxiliary, or compen sating, with respect to *Mrita Mudra*, which in any event implies concentration. But the *Mrita Mudra* itself is the absolute absence of actions and the termination of concentration. In order to enter correctly into it, one only needs to fully stop all activity and concentration.

Usually, people start to learn *Mrita Mudra* with various auto-training relaxation exercises, which, if perfected, are substituted with a quick deep relaxation of the whole body. Detecting the flows of imbalance in the "signal body" follows this. These will also balance and quiet down by themselves, like waves on the water. After that, only the «breath-mind» remains, and deep detachment from such «breath-mind» and the loss of interest in its «toys» leads one to stop thinking and to the voluntary attenuation of breath.

This state also has some background qualities, but they finally dissolve too. Contemplation itself loses any quality and the Contemplator dies away in *Shanti* (Peace), *Movna* (Silence) and *Nirvikalpa Samadhi* (no-quality balance of consciousness)...

Absent of energy consumers, i. e. the body, feelings and mind, require no energy for their activity. This state does not require even the slightest breath, and so breath is delayed naturally. The only thing that remains is *Sat Chit Ananda* — direct contemplation and pure perception in absolute non-action and bliss.

The process of such step-by-step detachment results in the perception of the «internal» human nature, appearance of the ability to disable particular organs and systems of the organism, so the practitioner becomes independent and free from any «external» impacts. This is how *Moksa*, Spiritual Liberation, is achieved.

Diving into *Mrita Mudra* results in becoming experienced in terminating suffering, which removes the fear of Death.

All acts of humans are, virtually, done without will, and their life energy and the Power of Spirit are irrevocably wasted. This volition is manifested through non-action with the absence of desires and striving for the objects of feelings, rather than through persistent actions. Only this process actually involves the Will and increases the Power of Spirit.

In conditions of modern life, diving into *Mrita Mudra* is, as a rule, time-restrained and not deep. However, even if this is the case, the dive still results in transformations of the consciousness, which make a man partially inadequate from the social point of view. In this state, a man may make some mistake or perform an inattentive deed, which may cost him his life or somebody else's. Therefore, an obligatory element of the practice of Yoga in society is the «adaptation to social norms». A conscious «protective filter» is put into place, preserving «extra-marginal zones» of perception, or restricting perception to the generally accepted «norm».

This is achieved by special actions, which are contrary to the «personal turn off mode» which must be practiced after *Mrita Mudra.*

KUNDALINI — ORGANIZING POWER

Kundalini rests with any living or «inanimate» object as a Power, supporting its life and organization. There are methods to make it change. This leads to the total reorganization of the material structure, its transformation or transmutation.

Kundalini is an organizing Power, free energy of transformation. Its manifestations should be treated with honor. Some esoteric schools erroneously believe that the manifestations of Kundalini may be fatal. But this opinion only belongs to those who do not have a complete understanding of Universe, no practical experience of interacting with it, or are pathologically afraid of changes.

The process of «raising» the *Kundalini* is simple, but... where are those, strong in Spirit, who have intent to realize it?

The arousing of *Kundalini* only requires three regular components:

- complex cleansing of the organism (in particular, of the psychic-energy channels);
- at least six months' accumulation of a strong life power potential through maximum control of various wastes of energy (minimum actions, food, sex, words, thoughts, and social contacts);
- activation, putting in good order and sublimation of energy in the course of intensive training (*Asanas, Uijajai* and *Bhastrika Pranayamas*).

In the event the «burning» has taken place, it is absolutely required to be alert and remain detached. The ascending energy is sublime, transiting from one energy center to another, and causing confusing temptations in each of them. The process of raising the energy resembles a ball being taken up by a fountain spout. And if the «water of the fountain» is pulsing, i.e., there is no internal detachment and balance, the ball will, at some moment, slip and fall down.

When *Kundalini* enters any of the energy centers, the psychological events that are determined by these centers begin to manifest themselves in an extremely powerful manner, simultaneously, on «both poles». For example, upon reaching the second center there is simultaneous feeling of sexual temptation and sexual disgust. Upon reaching the fourth center, the practitioner is overfilled with love, charity, friendliness and, at the same time, hatred, antipathy, and hostility. Reaching the sixth center results in manifestation of super-capabilities, allowing simultaneously curing and creating or destroying and burning to ash.

Desire for any of the factors diverts the rising energy towards this desire. It is experienced in a very powerful manner. For example, going through the second center, one can experience autonomous sexual satisfaction of such power that after such experience the opposite sex will never cause serious interest, since the person who experienced it will subsequently understand that no sexual partner will ever be able to satisfy him so entirely.

Having reached the fourth center, the practitioner may exhaust himself with the tears of joy, universal love or total grief, or may stream hatred to all beings.

The diverting power of feeling the object of desire satisfies and fills the adept to such extent that the desire itself is «burned out». This is the «Fire Gehenna»; and it is a deep spiritual cleansing. But this also burns all of the free energy accumulated in the course of a long-term ascetic life. And further psychic-energy practice will again require long months of diligent accumulation of such energy, drop-by-drop. There is also a slight risk of «going out your mind», «burning out» desires in such a manner. And the majority of practitioners usually do not know what their future life will be, or whether they will be able to accumulate a sufficient amount of energy once again. It would be better to orient towards faultless movement only upwards, using intuition, without being distracted by the objects of desires...

> *The centers which were passed are «turned inside out» and become cold... Sitting in lotus, drop your hands down and find no floor below (levitation). The hair on the crown seems to be pulled upward by somebody. The stormy sound of «all keys of an organ pressed all at the same time», increases like a snowball... Ultraviolet transiting into a blinding white light... Hop-p... And the usual Picture of the World no longer exists... Only the Unique, silver-streaming, Substance, vibrating with myriad shades... vibrating... lines, lines, lines... There is no Onlooker and objects... There where was a chair, a carpet, you ... One... there is only a different rate of vibrations... Half a step "up" and... Death. You go?.. A numb feeling of the presence of Death... «The last switch of auto-turning off»... The Blackness of the Absence...*

The High Power alone is capable of switching back. In this event, everything returns back: thoughts, images, perception reappear spontaneously again. But alredy will never be the same again. Everything that was of any value is destroyed within minutes.

Now it is not the literature, but personal experience that tells that All is One! You Saw It, Felt It, You Were In It. No Doubt. Begone heresy of splitting and dualism. Simplicity and Wisdom leave no place for the hunger for power.

Kundalini is a spiritual teacher. When «raising» It, It shows everything which is required and important to know about oneself. And when acquire such a Master, reading books and being a student of other teachers looses its meaning. *Kundalini* opens the entrance to Tantra, where the Energy shows and teaches everything.

One should not be afraid of raising *Kundalini*... If this is your destiny from the incarnation, you will survive it. So what? Of course, there is some danger. Life is generally dangerous. But if one uses intuition and determined intent, there is a chance of success. And there are those who manage to survive it alone, without any teacher-assistants. This is possible even here, far from India... and, in fact, this was always possible and happened everywhere, in all times, even for the ones who did not know the word «*Kundalini*».

But this way is not for old, exhausted and wornout people. They have wasted themselves, and their *Karma* will no longer allow them to «take wing» in this life. Young people, however, have many more chances. They are pure, and their energy stores are active...

Besides, this practice is not meant for «dummies». They have no chances as they always rely on someone's prompt...

Believe in yourself!

It happens that the «raising» is effected in several stages. During the first day, when a person manages to wake up *Kundalini*, it only becomes possible to deliver it into *Susumna*. On the next day, one may manage to «lead» it higher and achieve the second or the third center. But if the amount of the free energy is insufficient, it «descends» again. The process of «raising» *Kundalini* may last for months. And even the complete «raising» may be followed by the return back.

But sometimes it happens so that the «raising» is not followed by a «descent».

> *For the first time the feeling is strange... A dead body alive... Cold and senseless... There is a mute question hanging in the air: Why is the body still alive?.. Through Vision and Abnormal Abilities... Unclaimed Might and Power... But everybody around is warm... They want and want and want something... Strive for something... Why are all these?.. Cool peace... Later — you get used to it and take no notice of the transmutation...*

What happens during the years of transformation related to the «awakening» and «movement» of *Kundalini* may have a «feedback reaction» of at least the same duration. When the inverted descending flow is effective for the same period of time, the activation of the lower centers and the relevant lunar biological dominants return.

And happened just one. When everything comes to an end and is balanced, «the mountains become Mountains, and rivers turn into Rivers»!

One should not mix up wide warm flows inside the body, which occur during the practice of oriental martial arts or Taoist Yoga with the movement of *Kundalini*. These flows are connected with the movement of blood and some reactions of the nerve system. But they are too far from the subtle electric ray of cold ultraviolet *Kundalini*.

During the raising of *Kundalini*, inside *Sushumna*, there is a «biological chain reaction».

Each nerve cell has several sprouts linked to other nerve cells. When the potential of the sexual «burning» (*Kanda*) gives the first impulse to the nerve sprouts at the bottom of the spine, the adept makes spiritual efforts promoting the spreading of the excitement upwards, towards the brain, rather than towards sexual organs. If this comes off, the excitement starts to spread upwards.

Each nerve cell conveys the excitement to several rather than one cell, each of which, consequently, conveys the excitement to another several cells, etc. The organization of the spine becomes more sophisticated and expands from bottom to top.

> When the excitement reaches the brain it flashes, radiating bright psychic light... Like a 220 V electric lamp connected to 550 V... Burns... And how it is burning bright... But not a long time... At the same time with the rousing of Kundalini there is a swelling loud sound and the blinding bright light increases... The eyes radiate psychic power of such capacity that you can «shoot» with them, «firing» other people. The people surrounding you «flash» and start «radiating» too, without understanding anything, and, smiling, bow with gratitude. And you go on «firing» the next people, without being distracted to the latter...

This is all the result of the biological chain reaction.

Part III

TRAINING

TRAINING AT VARIOUS YOGA PRACTICE LEVELS

The beginning level of yoga practice includes exercises that can only be practiced in special «hothouse» conditions — in a temple, gym or at home. Therefore, beginners who do not have sufficient knowledge about the Purpose of the Tradition of Yoga and the essence of practical rituals, associated with physical, breathing or contemplation exercises, with an atmosphere of «prayered» Place, with mystery and participation to something special and mysterious. But, after completing the training and leaving this special Place, beginners return to the swirl of their routine life and usually forget about the practice of Yoga. They become normal and ordinary. Then they become licentious and make a great many karmic mistakes (sins).

In the course of accumulating practical experience at advanced Yoga practice levels, all of life's actions turn into particular varieties of training. They become conscious, oriented towards the realization of one's intent in life and the achievement of the harmony of being.

Then, the «esoteric mist» surrounding all things related to the dogma and mystery of special ritual practices dissipates and changes into ordinary but conscious actions based on the Knowledge of the Essence of ritual actions.

Various exercises, which can comprise the training program, are varieties of *Dharaha*, the exercises in concentration of attention, which promote the strengthening of one's personal Power of Spirit and serve as the foundation for *Dhyana* — contemplation. When the spiritual concentration level reaches some critical point, the result is a spiritual «explosion» that turns one's whole life into *Dhyana* — contemplation. Then personal motivations in life are replaced by divine predestination. When this happens, one's self-assurance and one's feeling of «self-exclusiveness» are replaced with Wisdom and Simplicity.

The growing up of the Spirit is the natural process where leaps by wish and by mind are impossible. That is why there is no sense to try to become perfect in one's mind. Fictional properties, which are not confirmed by sufficient practical experience, will remain only fantasies. Perfection can only be reached within the Spirit. And no one will say when the explosion of «ego» will take place, or when enlightenment occurs and divinity comes. Will this occur in the present life, or is this destined only to happen far in one's remote future? Everything depends on when the concentration will reach the required limit, and sufficient personal Power of Spirit has been accumulated. Therefore, the best thing to be done is to strive, truly and tirelessly, for the Purpose of the Tradition of Yoga, which implies irreproachable actions and uninterrupted concentration in life.

PROTECTION AND SAFETY

The forms requiring deep hyper-mobility are not by themselves a pur pose. But at advanced levels, their practice in the course of training is absolutely required as a means for coming into contact with the Limiting Margin. And the principal meaning of working out the physical plan lies with the expansion of the psychic-energy range.

But, despite the understanding of this general orientation, there is still a risk of particular physical traumas during the training due to a lack of experience. Reducing the possibility of traumatizing the organic body is secured through the use of the «body elements disposition rules», which are subject to the **Balance and Phases Laws.**

The Phases Law secures protection of the practitioner from traumas and the wear of the body due to excessively forcing the practice modes. Usually, such forcing results from overestimating personal readiness and the desire for excellence, which is delusion and leads to the loss of true sence in practice.

The Phases Law implies the transition, when ready, from simple to complicated, and from a sufficient quantity of practical experience to a required new quality. One's measure of readiness is the margin of one's capability to adjust to the training mode of the highest complexity level.

Protection is the first and main principle of any action. Because any action loses its meaning if it causes damage of the action participant. Descending the practitioner from the «ethereal heights» of fantasies caused by the romance of fiction books on «esoteric» topics. It is also caused by the injection into the practitioner's consciousness of a substance containing the True Knowledge virus, which will prepare the perception of the technological content of the practice, and facilitate real Protection of the practitioner.

Protecting of the organic body in the course of practice is secured by the understanding of the **Law of Balance**, mechanics of movements and the «disposition» of the vectors of forces in the forms being practiced. Protection is also achieved by applying the «body elements disposition rule» to all the technical elements of the training program.

Presently, all modern Yoga schools throughout the world use the «body elements disposition rules».

Knowing these rules, and their application in the course of practice, is a special characteristic of the elementary literacy of both the practitioner and the professional Yoga teacher.

It is also required to understand the practice formation principle on the basis of energy forms. This is done with the «closing» or «opening» of channels in the appropriate manner. For example, Chinese QiGong practices are a perfect means to develop energy capabilities, but almost always within the limits of an existing body-conductor channel. If, from the point of view of opening or closing the energy channels, the Body Elements Disposition Rules, with the legs, arms or fingers spread apart or kept together (that does not include the development of hyper-mobility in joints) are expedient, then in the system orientated towards expanding the already attainable amplitude of mobility arsenal of readily achievable forms and perception range, the critical factor securing protection of the organic body from injuries and traumas is the «mechanical disposition principle». It is the sole means that can secure reliable balance of the body in the space and such kind of application of efforts by all of the auxiliary body elements, so that the resulting force can precisely reach the zone or point where going beyond the Limiting Margin is supposed.

The form of skeleton and its dimentional position serve the basis of the «Body Elements Disposition Rule». In this case the psychic-energy configuration is conditional upon the form and direction of the spine.

Looking at the skeleton one can see that the spine is a flexible system with two lines of joints, which allow one to do forward bends and back arches without causing defects in the joint connections of the vertebrae (spinal bones). And, on the contrary, rotations of the spine lead to changes in the mutual disposition of the vertebrae in the double-axis joint system.

According to the results of practical experience accumulated in various Yoga schools throughout the world, it is possible to say that the most vulnerable places of the human body are the lumbar and cervical section of the spine, as well as the knees, elbows and fingers.

Safety from trauma of these elements is secured through consciously controlling the mutual disposition of the bones in the joint connection and by strengthening the muscles and tendons, which fix and control th joints.

Extremely harmful impact on the spine is exerted when turning combined with forward bends or back arches. Such movements loose the lumbar section of the spine in such a way that even healthy people ma develop vertebral osteochondrosis. In «normally-atrophic invalids», it ma be enough to rest one knee on the floor and make the bend combined wi turning to cause mutual misplacement of the vertebrae and disks of t spine, resulting in unbearable pain and a visit to a doctor.

Concerning the knees and the elbows, which are the joints that move in a single plane, a serious problem for their construction is turning and overstraightening. This example is widely found within groups of enthusiastic *Padmasana* (*«Lotus-pose»*), *Mula Bandhasana* and *Kandasana* practitioners, too many of who may «boast» knee meniscus traumas.

Yoga is not a sport, and comparing one practitioner's achievements with those of another is not important in its Tradition. Moreover, if a comparison of external forms is made, everybody who reaches his personal Limit, even if practicing exercises pertaining to absolutely different levels of practice, are, in terms of absolute categories, at one and the same level of practice. The complexity level only determines the power and rate of the practice, but it is only the Power of the Limit, which transforms consciousness and strengthens the Spirit.

Therefore, the transition to more complicated practices and forms should occur naturally, only in line with the accumulation of experience and Power as the result of regular, gradual and cautious practice.

HIERARCHY OF COMPLEXES

When, in the course of development, one changes from simple training complexes to more complicated ones, one should allow for the specific features of impacts on vulnerable body zones to insure their safety.

When using the feet as a foundation, the pelvis is the «reference point» with respect to where the position of the spine should be. And the position of the pelvis in the majority of exercises is determined by the mutual disposition of the thighs, which support it.

When using the arms as a foundation, the position of the shoulders are the «reference point», with respect to where one can consider the position of the spine to be. In this event, the position of the shoulder line is determined by the mutual disposition of the arms.

Therefore, **at the initial level of the practice**, special attention should be paid to developing the flexibility of the thighs in all directions, as well as to the strengthening of the shoulder muscles. One should also remember that the construction of the thigh and shoulder joints allows them to move in practically all directions. Whereas, the knee and elbow joints, which move in a single plane are vulnerable under heavy side shifts. Therefore, for example, *Padmasana* (*«Lotus-pose»*) should be performed generally with the rotation of the thighs and with limited (minimum) formation stress on the knees. *Vamadevasana*, however, should be performed with the ankle-joint lowering to the floor as close to the thigh as possible, with limited (minimum) spreading to the side.

In order to avoid «loosening» in the loin or neck, the initial level complexes should contain a sufficient number of exercises that strengthen the muscles surrounding and fixing the lumbar and cervical section of the spine from all sides. For example, with respect to the lumbar section of the spine, one has to develop «iron» protection of the loin by training. One must additionally develop protection for the straight muscles of the back (back protection), all muscles of the abdomen (front protection), and last but not least, all the small muscles of the paravertebral corset, which surround and fix the position of the spine. It is also necessary to develop the thighs in order to allow easy practice of splits, and to control the position of the pelvis in such a manner as to fix the pelvis perpendicularly to the central longitudinal plane of the body in all asymmetrical forms with back arches (e. g., *Kapotasana, Natarajasana, Gherandasana*, etc.) and forward bends (e. g., *Utthita Hasta Pandangusthasana, Ardha Padma Paschimottanasana, Bhajravasana*, etc.), and to secure that the back arches and forward bends can be performed in one and the same plane of the body. Then, despite the asymmetric disposition of the thighs, forward bends and back arches will be practiced in the same manner as in symmetric back arches (e. g., *Bhujangasana* or *Vrshchikasana*) or symmetric forward bends (e. g., *Paschimottanasana* or *Kurmasana*).

In general, according to readily available practice-based statistics, it can be said that in order to secure traumatic safety, asymmetric back arches and forward bends must be introduced in the program only when the thighs are developed so greatly, that this allows easy practice of passive longitudinal splits with a negative angle and an absolutely perpendicular pelvis (with respect to the direction of the thighs).

Possibly, this is exactly why in sequences of Ashtanga-Vinyasa-Yoga of Krishnamacharya - Pattabhi Joices's, the initial state pays special attention to the thighs and forward bends, which create the foundation, stretch the tendons and prepare the legs for the pure practice of longitudinal splits. In the first and second sequences of Ashtanga-Vinyasa-Yoga of Krishnamacharya — Pattabhi Joices's, asymmetrical back arches are not presented at all. They are only introduced at the end of the third sequences, after deep split stretches in *Viparita Salabhasana* («*Inverted Grasshopper*») — a variety of the «*Scorpion-pose*» (one of the deepest symmetrical back arches). At the same time the third sequences of Ashtanga-Vinyasa-Yoga of Krishnamacharya — Pattabhi Joices's already requires the ability to practice passive «splits in the air» with the pelvis hanging below horizontal line.

This is completely justified, since after completing the first two levels of this school, at the third level there already exists a well developed ability to safely use asymmetric back arches in one's practice. Here, for example, two hands hold the leg in the asymmetrical «*Pigeon-pose*» with the body being in a symmetrical back arch (as in the «*Cobra-pose*»).

Besides the above, it is also important to pay attention just to the «actuation» (contractation) of the muscles. If there is hyper-mobility in the joints against the background of weak muscles, which can often be observed in women, than assemetrical contractation of the body muscles may cause traumatic displacement of the mutual disposition of the vertebraes and the disks. For example, if, starting with the «*Cat-pose*» (standing on all fours) one raises a leg and an arm of the same side, preserving balance will require an asymmetrical compensating contractation of the body muscles, which may lead to traumatic displacement in the lumbar section of the spine. In the event that similar exercises are combined with the back arch, the risk of sustaining a trauma is increased substantially.

Similar adverse effects may be obtained by performing asymmetrically:

- longitudinal *Vinyasas*;
- «head down» *Vinyasas* with a push up with one leg;
- entering (exiting) the «*Scorpion-pose*» by waving one leg;
- entering (exiting) the «head down stand» (on the hands, head, shoulders, etc.) by waving one leg; and etc.

At the advance levels of practice, which uses multiple overturned forms with «stands on the hands» in order to reverse the Flow, the accent is shifted to developing the strength of the shoulders and torso muscles, securing balance of the spine in dynamic transitions and static forms.

In this case any bends or arches of the spine must be practiced with obligatory conscious control of the fixating muscle corset.

Summarizing the above, it is possible to define the focal points of physical development at different levels of practice.

Level one:

- Cleansing the organism and reducing the fat content in the body to a minimum through accumulating and burning harmful substances.
- Strengthening all the body muscles with the accent being made on the muscles of the paravertebral corset of the spine, abdominal muscles, the straight muscles of the back and the shoulder muscles.
- Stretching the muscles and tendons of the back leg planes.
- Developing the thigh joints in different directions.

- Accumulating Power and Endurance through composing the training form in the course of regular and educated practice.
- Mastering splits, until one has the ability to practice them in the ideal passive manner in various positions, including negative angle splits.
- Stretching the spine and torso muscles in deep symmetrical back arches.
- Controlled and cautious development of the single-plane joints (knees and elbows) in side directions, the same refers to ankle joint and wrists.

Level three:

- More intensively accumulating Power per weight unit and developing «unkilled» endurance by precisely balancing energy consumption and collection, adaptation and regeneration.
- Developing the body in synthetic forms, employing different positions of arms, legs and the spine.
- Mastering asymmetrical back arches and forward bends, including during handstands, on one leg, one hand and one leg.
- Mastering the technique of interaction with the Inverted Flow, during the various forms of handstands.

Level four:

- Retaining and using Abnormal Powers.
- Using paradoxical exercises and unexpected technical combinations on the verge of the Real (all possible stands: on one hand, on the elbows (only), on the hands (palms) with fingers directed back, on the fingers, on the head without using the hands, etc.).
- Freely combining the elements of all possible forms from previous levels.
- Controlling the Primary Flow.

RELATION OF THE LIMITS IN THE BODY AND THE SPIRIT

The state of the physical body of a man is a materialized memory of his style of life within the last couple of months. The qualities of the physical body are the indicators of what motivations are driving this man, what the essence of his life is, and what he/she actually is. At the same time, the in-born, and the acquired qualities of the body, determine the moral and *abilities* of the human consciousness.

So, it is not hard to trace the connection between the qualities of the body and the abilities of the man.

If the body is solid, tendinous and muscular the man is, as a rule, active, categorical, sometimes psychically firm, ascetic, easy-going, concentrates easily, and manages to do a lot of things in his life. On the contrary, if the body is tender and weak, the man is, as a rule, lazy, has a lot of desires, is weak in character, absent-minded, slow, always late and hardly completes duties which require concentration. Of course, these relations are not absolute, but, nevertheless, can be traced quite clearly.

Any regular training grafts particular qualities of both the body and the Spirit. Long-term development of the *Tha*-qualities in the body (such as flexibility, calisthenics, and gentleness) will sooner or later be reflected by the state of Spirit. Initially, a concentrated man will gradually become calm and balanced, but slow and, possibly, phlegmatic. It will be harder and harder for him to concentrate and pull things together. On the contrary, that one, who initially was slow, and could hardly concentrate, will, after starting with strength exercises in the *Ha*-style, in time become pulled together, will learn to concentrate, fight in life and completely perform his duties.

In order to develop the unusual and broader characteristics of the Spirit, it is necessary to totally develop the body's qualities in the course of training, qualities such as: flexibility, static and dynamic strength, static and dynamic endurance, coordination and speed (reaction).

Practicing the marginal Asanas develops **flexibility, static strength and endurance**. These assist in obtaining «internal» peace and balance in the consciousness, and call for the ability to strongly concentrate on any life task and to remain in this state for a long period of time without getting tired.

Dynamic strength and endurance are developed by the regular practice of various *Vinyasas* and by dynamic strength exercises. This burns harmful substances and extra fat stored in the body, improves health, brings contentment, and increases life tonus. A man becomes active, «easy-going» and cheerful.

Coordination and speed (reaction) are developed, by practicing balance *Asanas* and the dynamic movements of the *Dance of Shiva* (see below). This calls for an ability to instantly and to effectively react to changes in a given situation, to easily control and coordinate different events, and to keep a balanced social life.

Through complex training, the Spirit acquires a worthy instrument and perfect carrier — the Body, possessing all the abilities and qualities required for the complete realization of spiritual ideals in life. Ignoring this simple rule usually leads to the situation where the Spirit is ready to «fly», but the feeble body is incapable even to crawl.

It is only the first impression that leads one to believe that the essence of complex training implies only the development of physical qualities. In fact, the main work is at the level of controlling structures and their functional abilities. And the results, which are the fastest and closest to reality, occur within the Spirit through physical training, rather than through any other purely meditative or speculative mind techniques. Although this may seem strange, but practice, which employs the physical plane, is the closest to the Spirit. This is possibly why throughout history, and in all the spiritual traditions of the world, the most spiritually advanced people developed themselves and strengthened their Power of Spirit through various physical and ascetic deeds (up to «self-excruciation»), thus allowing the placing of Personal Spirit over bodily matter.

VARIETIES OF PHYSICAL LIMITS

In the course of the training-based development, there are seven types of physical limits to be overcome: flexibility, static and dynamic strength, static and dynamic endurance, coordination and reaction.

1. **Flexibility** is developed by overcoming the «mobility margin» of the joints.
2. **Static strength** is developed by increasing muscle loading in the static mode of applying efforts.
3. **Dynamic strength** is developed by increasing muscle loading in the dynamic mode of applying efforts.
4. **Static endurance** is developed by increasing the static training time.
5. **Dynamic endurance** is developed by increasing the dynamic training time.
6. **Coordination** is developed by gradually complicating special exercises, requiring control of various body elements.
7. **Reaction** is developed by performing special speed-based exercises, requiring the fastest and the most precise actions possible.

Referring to the above list makes it clear where the maximum effort should be applied in particular types of exercises. For example, there is a principal difference between performing static forms (*Asanas*), fixed inside the «Marginal Mobility Circle Limit», without the intent to exceed it, and in performing *Asanas* oriented towards overcoming this «Limit». The first chiefly, have the time limited, and first develop in most cases, static strength and endurance. The second, besides time limitation, also has limitations of flexibility, related to pain signals and other reactions of the stretched elements of the body. And besides the static strength and endurance, the second group also develops mobility in particular joints.

The exercises that develop static strength and endurance or dynamic are different in principle, since their practice employs different muscle fibers (respectively white-static or red-dynamic). And long-term static training with the application of *Asanas* alone does not develop dynamic strength and endurance. In the same manner, dynamic training with many *Vinyasas* does not develop static strength and endurance.

The exercises that develop coordination and reaction do not require substantial physical efforts or deep flexibility, as they first develop the controlling centers of the brain, the nervous system and muscle reaction mechanisms, rather than strength and flexibility. And these qualities can be better achieved by mastering the movements of *Shiva Nata (the Dance of Shiva)* (see below) rather than by practicing *Asanas* and *Vinyasas*.

TRAINING VARIETIES

A **individual training** contains in its basis a «closed to itself loop» model. It allows one to achieve a one hundred percent ideal relationship between the training program and the needs of the practitioner, both in respect to structure and timing interrelations. It gives the best possibility to «work for oneself», achieve any individual narrowly specialized training purposes, develop one's «poorly developed elements and weak qualities», harmonize one's feelings, balance one's consciousness, and realize the «know yourself» principle.

A group training contains in its basis an «looped to the Universe» open model. It allows one to understand various energy-based interconnections between different individualities. It enables the practitioner to work out different forms of interactions, reactions and social behaviors of people, while «working for everybody, including oneself» to achieve group purposes and mutual assistance, and realize the following principle: «know the world and your place in it».

An independent training by the definition means that the «leader» and the «follower» (student and master) are one and the same person. It implies that the practitioner must possess his own knowledge and experience sufficiently, in order to independently define the purpose of the training and make the correct choices among relevant methods and means in order to achieve the goals.

A guided training implies that the «leader»-master, using his knowledge and experience, determines the goal, the methods and the means of the practice for the «led pupil», who has no requisite practical experience and knowledge.

A training under a predefined program means that a goal is defined before it is started, and there is a definite algorithm for achieving this goal through specific methods and means. In this case such a program may be defined by both the master and the student himself.

Spontaneous training has no predefined program and is determined solely by the free choice of the practitioner at the present moment of time on the basis of spontaneous motivations.

There is a principal difference between these types of training. There is a number of arguments which ground pros and cons with respect to each, but, coming from the essence of Yoga, one can make a conclusion that these varieties of training are in addition to, rather than in lieu of each other, and each being necessary in its own fashion.

The drawbacks, as a rule, result from the incorrect application of a particular type of training to achieve a specific goal, rather than from the types of training by themselves. The goal and the methods for achieving it in the training must correspond to each other.

Consider a number of examples of such non-compliance.

1. The first example. There is a wide spread critical opinion that group training does not provide the possibility to achieve results which would conform 100% to the needs of each practitioner comprising the group, that in the group one cannot achieve deep peace or achieve the «dive» in contemplating practices, etc. And this is completely true, but the point is that the individual training exists to achieve the goals listed above. But the attempt to achieve them in a group is an example of the non-compatibility of the goal and the method for its achievement.

The main goal and principle of group training is the group psychic resonance, which allows the practitioner to achieve a great capacity of psychic-energy processes, which is considerably inferior in the individual training. The main intent of the group training is «energy feeding» and «energy pumping».

Such «energy feeding» and «energy pumping» do not mean that some people in the group «rob» somebody. Psychic exchange is fundamentally different from physical exchange. According to the laws of Newton physics, if something is added to something, then something is decreased by something. Under psychic laws, however, this situation is only true in the events of unconscious energy exchange. If it is conscious, then something may be added to something, without reducing anything else.

This means that every member of the group receives energy feeding without anybody being «robbed». This is due to the fact that first, the psychic-energy potential is increased due to resonance, and second, because everybody is feeding off each other. But the difference is that everyone is generous about giving off energy because they know the boundless «ocean of energy» can restore it. Also keep in mind that the «one who loves» will be bestowed with all the love that has been given off by the «ocean of energy».

And if somebody comes to class tired after a work day, the person who is feeling perfect that day undertakes the initiative in the course of group training, thus generating a powerful determined intent to achieve the goal in the united group field. In this situation the first person will be charged and use the drive of the second person, and as a result, will achieve more than if he/she trained independently, based on his/her tired state. The next day, they may switch roles. This is the model of unification, mutual assistance and practical love, which serves as the basis of all tantric techniques.

In psychic exchange, everything is conditional upon one's attitude. The one who gives off energy without desiring to will definitely feel «robbed».

If he/she understands that in this world everything is based on the natural energy balance, he/she will not burden themself with egoistic thoughts, will not be afraid to give off energy, thus becoming a perfect conductor and, as a result, receiving much more.

For example, if parents do not wish to put out energy without keeping some for themselves, they feel that their kids have «robbed» them. But the reason for such parental discomfort is the lack of love they have for their children, and without understanding that, in fact, they and their children are one and the same. Some may deem it «hard to believe», but, in fact, all the people and all the things in this world are One.

Besides if a group has been «getting along» and every member of the group behaves in a sincere and open fashion, the group may produce such «miracles» which are simply inconceivable in independent training. In this event, all the drawbacks that are usually assigned to group training are completely absent. That means that the results of training, the level of peace, depth of contemplation practices, etc. considerably exceeds an individual's maximum margin (which, with respect to the majority of people, is high only in their dreams and fantasies).

2. The second example involves the critical confidence of students with respect to teachers, and their attempts to self-affirm in the presence

of the teacher. Such mistakes are based on the «feeling of personal greatness» and the inability to take off the «ego-crown». Here, coordination of the purpose and the method consists of determining the purpose in this actual situation. If a student is absolutely sure that he/she knows everything, and can't even assume that in this world he/she may meet somebody knowing and capable of doing more than he/she, so he/she should train himself/herself and not encroach upon the teacher's time!

If, one assumes that there is something that they do not know, this "something» may come through anybody and anything. And if somebody intends to learn it, do not «show off», learn to take off the «ego-crown», while taking guidance with gratitude.

Guided training implies conveying knowledge and experience from the master to the student. For this occurs naturally and easily, there should be no personal opinion of the student, unless, of course, if it is asked by the teacher. The student must only receive everything that the teacher conveys to him and follow the teacher sincerely.

Another mistake also exists when training independently. The practitioner seems to be waiting for somebody to do his practice for him. Such training will be of no use. If somebody has undertaken to train themselves and to pull themselves together without relying on anybody, then they should «guide» themselves and show themself what kind of teacher they are.

3. As the last example of the inconsistency between the goal and method is «distraction to spontaneity» when one practices under a predetermined training program. This is not a grave mistake. Often such a distraction is justified, and manifestations of spontaneity are specially provoked. But not to make mistakes it is necessary to understand the following: if there is a particular goal and there is a special training program developed beforehand to achieve it, it is best not to digress from this program whatever «esoteric» things may happen. For example, the growth of Power through gaining a training form requires multiple repetition of the same exercises within a limited period of time. And becoming distracted by new sensations, internal «pictures» or movements of Power though has cognitive interest, but breaks the process of achievement of the contemplated.

On the contrary, in spontaneous training there is no room for a plan or definite goal other than removing barriers to the manifestation of spontaneity itself. And that one who sets the «*goal*» before training spontaneously, but does it in a *planned* fashion is, in no doubt, applying the wrong method to achieve the goal.

Spontaneity may not follow a program. All that is required at the beginning of spontaneous training is to remove mental control and stop impeding the energy and active forces to control yourself. Having feelings and reactions without the participation of the mind is crucial to spontaneous training. In this event, the controlling and protective function is performed by the intuition instantly reacting to passing signals and determining what can and cannot be done, but, exclusively, as a «live reactive feeling» rather than with the mind. But the mental logical explanation for all that happened is possible only after the completing of the spontanity. The attempt to switch to it immediately cuts off spontaneous training.

Depending on the main orientation, training may be comprehensive or specialized.

Comprehensive training implies the development of all of the body elements equally, varying the training effect on all principal muscle groups. It comprehensively influences the nerve, lymphatic, blood and endocrine systems and creates necessary conditions for psychic-energy plasticity, which may be used to achieve different abstract (comprehensive) or particular (specialized) modified states of consciousness.

Specialized training implies selective development of particular body elements by exerting specific training influence only on particular joints and muscle groups. This has a local effect on the systems of the body, and creates conditions for special psychic-energy shifts required to achieve typical modified states of consciousness.

Comprehensive or specialized approaches may happen in both the process of training under a predefined program and in the process of spontaneous training. In this event he difference is only that the algorithm of training under a predefined program is defined by a predetermined comprehensive or specialized goal of the training. But the algorithm of spontaneous training is not known beforehand and is only defined by the spontaneous development of the processes that may be of both a comprehensive and a specialized nature.

Comprehensive training in the Tradition of Yoga is ideal because it is harmonious. But there are no limits to comprehensiveness. And willingness to it leads to the necessity to include an excessively large number of possible components in the training program. And such training is conditional on the endurance of the practitioner and his time resource.

This does not mean that comprehensive training is, in principle, impossible. There are a number of options of comprehensively developed and well-balanced training complexes, but these are deemed comprehensive only with respect to narrowly specialized programs. Real (time-limited) training, however, is, as a rule, specialized and aimed to achieve particular physical, psychic-energy or spiritual results.

Based on the above, all yoga therapy exercise sequences are also specialized.

But specialized training should not be seen as defective. One should understand that it is either supplementing, or compensating for, particu lar motivations in the process of human development, or compensating for particular influences (stresses) on a person in his social activity. When this happens, the aggregate program of various day-to-day and special training effects within the day, form a comprehensive training scheme.

So, for example, if a person's major type of activity is physical work with substantially little scope for mental concentration, a special training aimed at harmonizing his feelings should be carried out with an ascent to both the muscles stretching and relaxation. And also this program should include training the muscle groups which are not used during his work activity. This will facilitate the redistribution and distraction of energy from the zones of physical stress to free zones. Such training should also include special exercises developing the concentration of attention and coordination, which are not present in his/her day-to-day work in a sufficient scope.

And on the other hand, if the main type of work activity is psychic concentration, which does not imply any physical actions, then special training should be oriented to increasing the training form and tonus of the organism. Such training should include comprehensive strength-based training and improvement of the mobility of all body elements. And it should also include special psychic-energy exercises to relax the mind and release attention from the «stress situations».

From the point of view of harmonious development, each practitioner has underdeveloped or unequally developed body elements which require more attention. Each practitioner has habits fixed in his consciousness, which create obstacles to practicing psychic-energy exercises. Removing these habits requires individual contemplation devices to realize the pollutions of consciousness, and experience liberation from them. And each practitioner fills the lack of energy for expanding his consciousness, since there are no limits to the perfection and growth of the Power of Spirit and the Infinity of the Universe.

Therefore, standard programs, developed according to common principles for all followers, are used in the practice of yoga at the initial preparatory stage. Because this is only «the way to the base of the mountain». The more conscious the practice becomes, and the stronger its orientation towards overcoming personal defects, the more individual and the more increasingly specialized training becomes. And the striving for harmony in one's comprehensive practice grows larger and larger in this Battle.

ONE OF A THOUSAND ALGORITHMS OF SPECIAL TRAINING

A full algorithm of special training usually supposes several consecu tive stages:

1. Prel iminary determination of initial imbalance of the consciousness, and the formation or antici pation of the goal of the training.

2. Starting creation of mood — focusing the rays of attention from the peri phery to the center.

3. Activation and increase of the capacity of the psychic-energy processes with the aid of *Pranayamas, Surya Namaskar, Chandra Namaskar* sequences, or the *Shiva Nata* (Dance of Shiva) movements (see below).

4. Comprehensive or selective influence of body's elements with the help of warm-up non-marginal *Asanas* and *Vinyasas.*

5. Assault of one's l imits and the l iberation of bio-nuclear energy of the l inks (see below, page ###) in the practice of over-the-l imit *Asanas.*

6. Physical compensation, relaxation and psychic-energy stabil ization by using compensation *Asanas* and psyche-controll ing willpower exercises.

7. Using the generated free energy for isolated psychic-energy practice of *Rasas*, expanding the range of perception, contemplation and real isation of the unity of the «internal and external subspaces».

8. Adapting to one's «social environment» by placing a flexible psychic-energy filter to protect oneself or narrowing the range of perception down to the boundaries of common social «norm».

«FIRST SIDE»

In practicing asymmetric exercises, one may face the question: «What is the first side?» or «What side should I start with?»

Different schools suggest their own rules for this answer. One school claims that men should start with one side and women from another side, due to the different direction of the flows of energy in men and women. There is also an opinion that in view of energy circulation and different

SRI JANTRA: UNIVERSAL TECHNOLOGICAL DIAGRAM OF YOGA

Fig. 41

functions of the left and right cerebral hemispheres, one of the sides should be selected as the first one, etc.

The first position over stresses the physical differences between the male and female body, ignoring the generality of human consciousness. And the second position is, for some reason, based on the opinion that one and the same of cerebral hemispheres is dominant in different people, (which is totally wrong).

But one should remember that the purpose of Yoga is balancing and harmonizing consciousness. And the exercises comprising training are nothing but a means to achieve this purpose, but the balance indicator pointer of the scale is the state of the body at a given concrete moment of time.

It is easy to find out that all beginners have asymmetric capabilities and the development of different sides of their bodies.

Therefore, the answer is as follows: «The first side should not be the right or the left, but it should be "underdeveloped" side».

Most often it is the left side of right-handers and the right side of left-handers.

Often, however, it happens that one side has better flexibility, while the other side is superior in terms of strength. In this event, stretching exercises should be started from the side with inferior stretching characteristics, whereas the strength exercises should be started with the underdeveloped side.

Why? This is because the state of the body itself demonstrates the complex impact of multidirectional flows of powers on the balance of the cerebral hemispheres and anything else in the body. The state of the body unmistakably reflects the true situation as the total result of one's state of being.

One should start with the inferior side and apply maximum effort to develop it. And when changing to the superior side, one should exercise to the same extent as was achieved by the first side, but not more, even if one has such ability and there is its reserve.

With such an approach first of all the underdeveloped side will be improved, whereas the better side will be «waiting» for it to catch up. This is how balance of the sides and harmony of consciousness is achieved.

When beginning with the better side and applying possible maximum effort, it is natural that this side will perform better and achieve better results. But changing to the inferior side, even using great effort to achieve the maximum, one will not manage to exercise with the same range as was possible with the superior side. And the effect of this practice will not be symmetrical or harmonious.

Better side plus maximum is not equal to the inferior side plus maximum, since the sides were not equal from the very beginning.

Having initially understood what side should be first, it is important to not forget that, by continuing the training over time, the inferior side «catches up» with the better side and the problem of choosing the «first» side still remains and can not be avoided. And if to follow the habit of always starting with the side which was weaker, statistics prove that it begins to outpace the ex-superior side. Sides as if exchange their development levels. If this happens the ex-better side, which has now become the weaker side, should be used as the first side for the purposes of training harmonization. But it would be more correct, if upon achieving balance in the development of the sides, one begins to practice regular interchange and at each training beginning with one side and then the other. This is how the balance of the sides will be preserved, and the assault of the Margin will be double-sided.

SELF-RESISTANCE MODE

Self-resistance mode may allow one to practice any press-derivative ex ercises, where in addition to the weight of the body, muscles must also overcome the resistance of their respective opposing muscles. In this event the muscles alternate and exchange the dominant role by one side, then by the other. So, for example, it is possible to fold the arm in the elbow joint by straining the biceps and triceps at the same time. In this struggle between the two muscle groups, they both win alternately.

A group of exercises exists in which the self-resistance mode is presented in the dynamic movements of joints. This, for example, happens in self-resistance-based turning in any of the arm, leg, loin or neck joints.

In the contest of self-resistance between muscles, it is possible to always reach a vibrational effect. The energy intensively flows to the joint centers around which the movement is affected. This feeds tissues, and facilitates their warming and regeneration after exercises that use deep hyper-mobility.

CORRECT MOOD

Development is your personal business. And training should be prac ticed only for yourself, not for other people, not for those who may pay attention to your own success, not for your own prestige, not for your own carrier and not for your teacher. Try to do everything in a correct and qual ity fashion not because somebody thinks that you need it, but for yourself. This is the only approach that may lead to quick results and move «the main» in the consciousness.

Training consists of elements (exercises) that require, first, concentration and the focusing of attention, and secondly, relaxation and contemplation.

Complying with the first requirement means *expressing will*, whereas the second is the *depriving of will.*

The method of practice should correspond to the type of action. And the set should correspond to the elementary exercises being practiced. Neglecting these rules is a grave mistake that reduces the effectiveness of training to practically zero.

It is necessary to master different training techniques and apply them as required in accordance with the exercise being practiced.

One should learn to mani pulate training methods with the same speed as the elements-exercises. And should learn to do this perfectly and without mistakes.

For example, strength-based training, lazily oriented towards minimum efforts and «recollections about sandwiches» and home coziness, or the development of flexibil ity and relaxation with preserving internal hardness and «bell icosity».

A special case is preparatory or intermediary elements-exercises. So, for example, relaxation during intervals between *Asanas* should only comprise peri pheral coverings and should only extend as far as physical, emotional and mental bodies. But it should not try to effect the intention of training and the Power of Spirit. In this event concentration and hardness of the Crystal of Spirit should be always preserved. Otherwise, the resulting process will break the advancement of the true training goal.

HA, THA AND HA-THA STYLES

In the tradition of Yoga, *Ha* and *Tha* are two counter-qualities originating from the same source. They represent the dualistic principle contained in the matter of the World. And as far as everything in the World, beginning with «primitive» organic forms to the most «exquisite» organizing fields, is interconnected material, so *Ha* and *Tha* qualities cover every thing existing in this World.

Traditionally *Ha* quality corresponds to light, sun, activity, absence of inertia, maleness, etc, whereas *Tha* quality corresponds to dark, moon, passivity, inertia, femaleness, etc. It is absolutely obvious that a detailed analysis of all the material and energy manifestations in the World would make a list extending to infinity.

From the very beginning, it is necessary to understand that *Ha* and *Tha* are not matter and energy as such, but their qualitative states.

For example, in a question such as: «Is electric or nuclear energy good or bad?» The question is not clear, isn't it? It requires qualitative clarification. Because verything depends on how the energy is generated and used, and what results will be obtained from this.

Answer: «Energy or matter may not be bad or good, but it can possess *Ha* and *Tha* qualities, which may have beneficial or adverse effects on a particular phenomenon».

Energy may not be «dirty», and it is stupid to become free from it and lose it. It can just be in the unfavourable quality, which may be transformed into something beneficial, which is a matter of practical experience in tantric energy control.

Energy control implies the presence of a controlling will. All things under control are, with respect to the controlling will, controlling instruments, means and objects.

Any active will source expresses *Ha* quality. And any passive object or processes transformed by this active will manifests itself in *Tha* quality. According to definition, instruments are subject to their master and are controlled by his will program.

Human physical organs, senses and mind are controlled instruments and, with respect to the Power of Will, they posses *Tha* qualities. The will may be conscious or unconscious, and respectively pertain to consciousness or the sub-conscious.

Any exercises designed to overcome personal weaknesses require effort, expression of will and the *Ha* quality of the Power of the Spirit, whereas any exercises related to the relaxation of the body, senses, and the mind imply loss of will and *Tha* quality of the Power of the Spirit.

Therefore, it is necessary to realise what is happening with the controlled instruments during training and what the state of the Spirit is. With this understanding one should strive to reconcile the state of the Spirit with the qualities required to perform particular exercises.

Asanas, Pranayamas, Pratyahara or *Dharana* — regardless of whether while practicing them one strains or stretches the muscles, whether the breath is deep or relaxed, or whether the rays of attention are distracted from the object or are fixed on it — all require will-based control, concentration and *Ha* of Spirit.

Dhyana requires contemplation on natural processes «left to themselves», moving into a deep relaxation, and «dismissing» the instruments of the body, senses and the mind. It also means spontaneously restoring or releasing all forms of will concentration and control. Then up to *Samadhi*, when there is said to be a complete balance in all systems, achieving unity and identifying it with the essence of the object of contemplation. This corresponds to *Tha* of Spirit.

Ha-style training means ultimate capacity in all exercises and concentration of the Spirit. This is a fight for new qualities in all subordinate bodies under the control of the will. Compression and concentration of the Fire in the ultimate limiting point reaches a critical level, which is followed by an essence-transforming explosion. In this style the active male energies of self-assurance and worship of the Personal Power dominate.

The technique of exercises in this style requires high functional training, practical experience with a number of different strength elements, «unkilled» endurance, lightning-like reaction and impeccable will control.

The majority of tough styles in Oriental martial arts, Southern-Indian dance styles (Bharata Natyam) and Tensgheriti are featured by *Ha*-style.

Ha-style training is the same as climbing to the top of a high mountain. The mountain represents a concentration of Personal Power of the Spirit. This climb occurs during the whole process of training. In this event, of course, a discharge of concentration may occur at the times when it becomes unbearable, but not all the concentration, only its part - the unbearable excess of energy concentration.

In general, all elements of *Ha*-style training are a challenge worth accepting. Personal heroic feats provoke strengthening concentration and Power of the Spirit in order to «jump from the top of the mountain to the bottomless abyss» of relaxation, liberation and fusion with the High Power at the end of the training session.

Tha-style training means ultimate sensitivity and plasticity. The release of the Personal Spirit concentration implies the transfer of personal instruments to the High Power. This is pure spontaneity and contempla tion of the flow of exercises in the course of training. This is the development of the ability to perceive and conduct through oneself the qualities of the High into the World. At the breaking point of dissipation and release of Personal Spirit, the loss of form occurs, and the quality of the Emptiness that contains everything becomes clear. This style is featured by passive female energies, renunciation and self-sacrifice in the triumph of the High Power of the One.

The technique of exercises in this style requires high sensitivity, a broad range of perception, the ability to be submissive and give oneself to the spontaneity of the energy flows, knowledge of personal limitations and Wisdom.

The majority of soft styles Oriental martial arts, Eastern-Indian temple dances (for example, Odissy), and Buddhist, Hindu, Sufi and Christian tantric practices are featured by *Tha*-style.

Training in *Tha*-style resembles the collapse of a mountain and its dispersal on the boundless flat plain. This is a gradual deep dive into the Ecstasy of Unification with the High and surrender into Its hands. It is related to liberation from mind-imposed limitations until they are completely stopped. At this time, the senses and an accurate reflection of all energy-related motivations by one's the relevant actions occupy the foreground. Concentration is reduced, increasing softness, plasticity and disengagement. At the end of the training, one achieves a perfect translation of the High Will and identification with the essence of the One.

Ha-Tha-style requires alternating *Ha*- and *Tha*- styles in the process of training, developing abilities required in the practice of both styles, and making a conscious choice of the most beneficial method for achieving a goal at a particular stage. This is a fusion of personal heroic feats with worshipping the High. It is the development of various qualities and the expansion one's functional ability to be different. This style is featured by the harmony of active (male) and passive (female) energies as the realization of the Unity of the individual and the Universal.

A few of the schools existing in the world aim from narrow specialization to integrating all of the previously accumulated experience and harmony of the Overall. As an example, we can suggest Aikido, Indian Hatha Yoga, some ancient and almost lost traditions in the Danube and Dnieper basins, Egypt, and Scandinavia, a few true followers of the Israeli and Middle Eastern schools, as well as the «Polyglot-Masters», followers of any kinds of world schools.

It is hard to convey the differences of training in *Ha-Tha*-stile with respect to *Ha*- and *Tha*- styles. It is possible, however to, note that it is the optimum combination of the best qualities of both *Ha* and *Tha* opposite extremes and the balance between them results in the manifestation of third quality of the Middle Way, which differs from the first and the second ones and posesses absolute advantage.

Naturally, *Ha*- and *Tha*- styles are only milestones that illustrate opposing poles of orientation and development during the course of training. However, a great variety of transitional *Ha* and *Tha* modes of the Middle Way are shared between them. These are oriented towards one pole in the beginning, in the middle or at the end of training, or whichever preserves a stable and balanced correlation of *Ha* and *Tha* during the whole duration of training.

FEMALE AND MALE TRAINING STYLES

Female and male styles of training differ in the dominance of particular qualities pertaining to the majority of women or men at birth. In fact, these match *Tha* or *Ha* orientation of styles and only have different names, with the accent on natural strength or flexibility abilities.

Female or male styles are usually formed by the people who first exploit the qualities given to a child at birth, and who do not strive to balance the opposing gender.

Female style is based on deep hyper-mobility of the joints, smooth movements and plasticity. At the same time for dynamic links this style usually uses simple (in terms of strength) stepping, jumping or somersault-based techniques.

And the male style is based on strength functional training form, power and fast actions. For dynamic links, this style uses different classical gymnastic and exotic handstands, headstands, acrobatic «somersaults», «sklepki», and «flips», requiring advance coordination and strength endurance.

Since the moving principle of Yoga practice is harmony and overcoming duality, the female and male approaches become mutually complementary components of a united practice. In this event assault the Margin of the Boundless begins with underdeveloped elements and lacking qualities, i. e., men's primary goal is to gain lacking female qualities (plasticity, sensitivity, logical ambiguity, etc.), whereas women strive for male qualities (strength, endurance, purpose, etc.)

This approach develops an understanding of the opposite origin and shows Tolerance to be the main moral principle. It terminates rigid convictions, removes different gender conflicts, and supports Peace in the World.

Spiritual transformation occurs solely through the heroic action of overcoming personal defects and gaining previously unattainable qualities. There are numerous examples of women being initially flexible (but weak) entering a Yoga group which practiced female *Tha*-style and featured stretching exercises. From the very beginning, they were capable of doing the most complicated stretching exercises, but since they achieved such results without any spiritual effort, they usually undervalued it, and quickly lost interest in Yoga practice and stopped training.

In the same manner, having initially superior strength, men start to «parade» with handstands, etc., without noticing their own stiffness and ignoring physical and psychic plasticity. This only leads to strengthening their feeling of personal physical superiority, and blocks spiritual development.

Many say that they want to develop, without realisation that they are lazy and reluctant to change what is rooted deep in their sub-conscious. This laziness and reluctant in sub-conscious covered by the masks of beautiful gestures and words, exploiting the qualities given to one at birth. But this is only an illusion of development when compared to people who were deprived of such natural superior abilities at the birth.

Most often professionals make this mistake. In the race for superiority during competition, they exploit readily available qualities that enable them to take a «head start» and feel superior to their competitors. Such «teachers» should remember the main moral principles of Yoga — honesty and truth, since ignoring them is subject to karmic punishment and inevitably leads to defeat, and terminates the spiritual way.

Spiritual advancement and development is an absolutely personal business, and it should be sought only for oneself, rather than for self-assurance in the superiority over anyone else.

Rarely it is possible to meet a correctly oriented Spiritual Warriors who had developed by themself the qualities that were not given to them by birth. Truthfully, practical realization of deep Human Origin is worthy of admiration.

STATIC AND DYNAMIC MODES

Everything in the World exept Universal is varying, since all common processes are in the dynamic flow of changes.

Therefore, *Asanas* look static only on the outside. But by they are dynamic by their essence.

Fixing the body in any form requires muscle work to keep this form. And, therefore, all *Asanas* involve muscle work or stretching and are, in fact, not static, because any tension is related to the dynamic process of fatigue and relevant changes in all bodies. Exceptions to this rule are *Shavasana*, the posture of «conscious self-shutdown», and the «perfect meditating posture», done with the body fully balanced and relaxed in the sitting position.

The remaining postures, although they look static externally, but «on the inside» they require the technique of «diving into depth» and overcoming the limits of the Marginal Mobility Circle. This is usually achieved by increasing the tension of necessarily switched muscle sectors shaping the body, and by lengthening necessarily stretched muscle sectors.

The summary vector of efforts in such «static postures» is always directed perpendicular, with respect to the line of the limit of the Marginal Mobility Circle. And in accordance with the main goal, which is overcoming this limit, such postures are «extra-marginal».

If a «static posture» (for example, strength or balance-based posture) does not employ «diving into the depth» and is fixed «inside» the Marginal Mobility Circle without overcoming mobility limitations, the dynamics of change are created by increasing muscle fatigue.

As to dynamic exercises of any complexity level can be referred to as «links» (dynamic transfers from one extra-marginal posture to another «inside» the Marginal Circle), or to the group of energy distribution movements, and they are dynamic by the definition. At the same time their practice is also related to overcoming the Limit, but of another nature, i. e., the limit of dynamic endurance or energy tendencies.

Training always requires actions related to transition processes. In the course of training, directions of vectors transforming «extra-marginal» efforts, methods and techniques may vary from stretching-based (extending the limits of the Mobility Circle) to those aimed at developing endurance and adaptation to the density of energy flows. But the essence of the dynamic characteristic of the flow in this case always remains unchanged.

A truly static stage may only be achieved in the non-doing of the contemplation practices, however, not at the early stage of learning these techniques and not during starting creation of one's mood when transitory processes are still presented, but at the final stage of a perfect *Samadhi*.

RELATION OF BREATH WITH FORM AND MOVEMENT

There are varying opinions regarding proper breathing during the yoga practice of static forms of dynamic movements.

Some schools insist on constant sinusoidal breathing at all times during training, based on the law that «action = counteraction». And for example, breath delays increase *Ego*.

Other schools suggest special types of breath for different exercises, for example, use breath delays with *Bandhas* when it is necessary to realize «superpower».

Who is right?

Both. Everything depends on one's goal and the methods one chooses for achieving it.

The following may be stated categorically:

- all movements related to complex formations and decreasing the chest volume are naturally accompanied with the exhalation, and vice versa;
- change of volume in the abdominal cavity changes breath characteristics;
- contracting the chest muscles connected to the ribcage imposes limitations on the breath;
- static forms, requiring complex formations of the chest, limit the depth of breath and shift its range towards reducing the inhalation;
- synchronizing movements with hands, which assist the expansion or compression of the chest, makes the breath easier and deeper, increasing its range;
- breath delay, with subsequent complex formations of the chest or contraction of the muscles attached to the ribcage, changes the internal pressure inside the chest, abdominal and cranial cavities;
- the breathing process is directly linked to consciousness and its characteristics determine the state of consciousness;
- exhalation facilitates relaxation and makes stretching of the muscles easier;
- inhalation assists the activation and makes contraction easier;
- breathing delays after the inhalation facilitates concentration of the mind and the breathing delays after the exhalation facilitates stop of thinking.

Upon detailed analysis, this list may be extended, but it sufficiently illustrates that the uniform approach (breathing rules) may in rare cases lead to the required results. Therefore, at the initial level of development, it is absolutely necessary to realize the impact of forms and movements on breathing characteristics. And at the advanced level, to know these peculiarities in order to consciously determine particular breathing characteristics during training, thus helping the body and consciousness to transform in the required direction.

TRAINING TIME

At the advanced level, practical training comprises all phenomena of life. Therefore, we can only discuss training time in the context of the initial stage. That is the training time intended for the special exercises of the beginner.

When choosing the time for such training, it is necessary to understand and consider the specific features of planetary and biological rhythms at a particular time of day. Morning features an increase of activity, which reaches its maximum from 11:00 till 13:00.

Then there is a decrease, the down point of which falls between 15:00 and 16:00. And, activity increases again, with the peak from 17:00 through 19:00. It is followed by another decrease, followed by a sleeping time during the night. In this event the evening activity increase is not as strong as the daytime peak.

In the early morning, the greatest results may be achieved after practicing psychic-energy complexes such as *Surya Namaskar* («*Sun Salutation*») or the *Shiva Nata* (*Dance of Shiva*) movements (see below), breath and contemplation practices. Good results at this time may also be achieved after such generally restorative techniques as morning jogging, swimming, and tempering.

At mid-day, one may develop all physical qualities, such as: strength, flexibility, coordination, reaction or endurance.

Evening time is ideal for development flexibility and deep relaxation exercises. Good results may be expected from psychic-energy complexes of the type of *Chandra Namaskar* («*Moon Salutation*») breathing and contemplation exercises.

Unfortunately, the majority of practitioners must use whatever time is available, after work or family, rather than the time most suitable for training. At first sight, it appears that nothing can be done about this, but among people who have already obtained the Spirit of the Tradition of Yoga, there is the popular opinion that the Pathway is the main thing in their lives. Work and other obligations become the means to provide greater capabilities and increase the effectiveness of this Pathway. A practical use of yogi capabilities in real life develops outside the special «hothouse» conditions of the training hall.

Many experienced Yoga technique practitioners change their whole life and organize their working day in such a manner as to adjust it to training.

But, of course, the ideal option is a rare combination of personal creative interest and professional obligations. These are the only conditions, which allow the best capabilities of a person to develop, and for the practitioner to realize the purpose of his life.

Whatever conditions you are in, it would be useful to remember to allow for some peculiarities with respect to the time of the day you train and the results obtained.

All Yoga schools deem the transition time between the day and night the best for practice. In the morning, it is sunrise and one hour thereafter. In the evening, it is one hour before sunset and one hour thereafter. This is the time when a deep psychic-energy transformation takes place in the consciousness, which is so powerful that even the most insensitive individuals can not ignore the related processes. This is the time when the organizing Power is most active.

During this time the consciousness becomes bipolar, not as active and awake as in the daytime, and not as passive and sleepy as during nighttime. One's conscious and unconscious functions combine into a non-dualistic balance, which does not have a dualistic nature. During this time, one can easily and consciously penetrate into the sub-conscious, trace the actions of subconscious programs and reprogram them as required. This ability is directly connected with rapid consciousness growth and the ability to adapt to any conditions. It gives a chance to survive at least to separate representatives of the mankind.

Subconscious programs, comprising at least 95% of the whole life activity of any «normal man» control all material shells and rhythms of a human being.

It is possible there is not any reasonable sense in this, but even if the acceleration of the human civilization progress is accepted as necessary and useful then overcoming of lack of human biological foundation from demands required to him is possible only through counsious bioprogramming and substitution of old fashioned programs with new more perfect and progressive ones. Human nature has adjusted through thousands of years of evolutionary selection. Because it is impossible to make the correct improvements into such an ancient and evolving mechanism. The responsibility and opportunity to personally evolve depends on the abilities and caution of the person who chooses to «train the Beast»…

People who only have time to train in the evening should construct the training algorithm in such a manner as to avoid over-stimulating the nervous system before going to bed. Violations of this rule may result in late nights (and, as it is known, going to bed after ten o'clock in the evening is harmful for health). Therefore as a rule after training, one feels like eating, which is also extremely harmful before sleeping, and leads to diseases of the internal organs. Because, one should pay special attention to avoid becoming over-excited during evening training. It is advisable to use special relaxation exercises at its final stage, this will facilitate a slow-down of the whole system. Also avoid eating before going to sleep (in extreme cases, restrict yourself to liquid and easily digested food such as honey dissolved in warm water, which appeases hunger and quenches thirst). Eating before going to sleep is harmful and contributes to obesity, body pollution, and change of weight and proportions of the body, restricting the training process.

Evening training will be of higher quality if you manage to take a nap before, which helps the interaction of consciousness and the sub-conscious in the same way as during the post night-sleep period.

It's clear that early in the morning, all these training difficulties vanish by themselves.

First of all, morning-time training is practiced right after a night's sleep, so there is no need to spend additional time for rest, which is advisable before evening training. Also, the organism is fresh and restored, and interactions between consciousness and the sub-conscious are most favorable.

Secondly, the activation of internal rhythms after training does not interfere with the requirements of the coming day, on the contrary, in most cases it helps stimulate effective and fruitful actions.

Thirdly, the hunger one feels after training is easily appeased by a harmless morning breakfast. In this way, there is the possibility to easily control the time of the evening meal and eat earlier, which facilitates the reduction of weight and polluters in the organism, cleansing energy channels and making the body proportions more delicate, which substantially accelerates the training progress.

And fourthly, the day becomes longer because people who sleep in the time period from 9 p.m. to 2 a.m. get enough sleep in a shorter period of time than people who go to bed after midnight. Remember: morning begins in the evening. And when one goes to bed early, the foundation is laid for feeling energetic and having a complete training in the morning.

The above mainly refers to non-professionals, for which even one training a day is a gift of Fortune. What concerns the people who have devoted all their lives to the Tradition of Yoga, is that their daily schedule includes several specialized training cycles at different times of the day.

With the development of Mastership, this gradually transforms into a Special day-and-night training program with alternating special conditions and Real («Martial») Actions, in accordance with the requirements of life. In this event, dreaming is completely or partially replaced with specialized relaxation and meditative practices.

Non-professionals cannot afford more than one (even short-term) training cycle a day. And it is quite enough for them to have one complete training cycle per day. Moreover, their training level would not allow the organism to regenerate between two complete training cycles within one day even if they tried to do so. This would sooner or later lead to over-training and frustration with practice. If you use short-time training, the algorithm will not include the required amount of exercises. Therefore, a sufficient load will not be created to develop enough endurance, the transition to the a second wind will not happen, one's Personal Power will not be increased, and other similar effects verified by centuries of training experience at many schools around the world will not happen. Moreover, short-term training complexes may not include all mandatory exercises, required for complete development of only basic elements of the body and the psychic-energy structure. Such training would become restricted and incomplete.

It is desirable to train at the same time of the day for the biological rhythms of the organism to get used to a particular schedule. Then, it will adjust and activate during a particular training. This will result in an increase of the training form, and, consequently, an increase in the Power, opening new horizons for the evolution of consciousness.

In the long run, the duration of one complete training cycle is absolutely individual and depends on many factors such as initial state of the practitioner, his general training form, experience, speed of practice, purpose of training and the conditions available.

For the people who aim at a «protective» approach and the «conquest of colds» two-three training cycles a week will suffice.

Training once a week or less is not worth doing. In this event, each session will only mean stress, related to regular muscle pains and other unpleasant things.

Training methods and conditions should not be diluted by adapting them to personal «deficiency», on the contrary, one should develop oneself and organize life by coordinating it with the ideals of the Tradition of Yoga.

TRAINING PLACE

At the advanced stages, life itself is a Place for training. And this Place is not to be chosen.

You can only choose the place for special training, which should correspond to the main tasks and the goal of your practice as much as possible.

It is desirable to have a fixed place for training, and, if possible, avoid changing it. The longer you stick to the same place, the farther you can advance in your development and the more efficient your training will be.

The matter is that in the new conditions attention, in one way or another, is distracted by the peculiarities of the new place, and an effort is necessary to get used to the new conditions. Of course, it is interesting to develop one's ability by consciously adjusting to anything and «survive», but distracting attention wastes Power that could be used in practice and this reduces the intensity and quality of your training.

If one is familiar with the Place «prayered» (i. e., a place charged by habitual prayers), it becomes similar to a tuned instrument: «a wave of the fiddlestick and the music is flowing». In this «place» specialized training takes minimum time, and there is the possibility to regularly measure training effects, which is absolutely necessary for progressing in practice, mastering training form and increasing the Power.

At different stages of evolution in training, one has to resolve different tasks. Resolving them, accordingly, requires different training conditions.

The best place for training is untouched nature. Unfortunately, the number of such places on the Earth decreases every year. But it is still possible to make the conditions as close to ideal (at least partially) by choosing a forest, beach, park, etc.

But in the real conditions of modern life, there is often no time to get to a natural place even if it is not very far away. There should also be no people in this place who might interfere with your practice. But the main restrictions on training out in nature are weather and season.

Of course, for some types of psychic training, the weather and climate conditions are not important, and adverse weather conditions can be used as special stimulating factors. First of all, such exercises develop the ability to adjust to any conditions and ignore whatever weather restrictions exist. As a result of this training, you improve your immunity and get rid of diseases. At advanced levels, this allows you to develop superior endurance, strength and abilities.

It is the weather conditions that make a Himalayan yogis migrate to the valleys in the winter. During this time, snow covers all the high mountains and the temperature is often fifty degrees below Celsius.

Outdoor practice is often distracted by the unevenness of the ground, stones, grass, and other objects on the surface. Problems also arise from the temperature of the ground, humidity, mosquitoes and other distracting factors. This is why the most valuable and popular places for training have always been those which do not have adverse conditions. Quite logically, this leads to establishing special places for practice in monasteries and training halls.

The possibility to avoid being distracted by outside effects, and get the additional energy given by special training places, leads to the rapid development of training techniques and progress in practice. This makes clear the importance of a special place and equipment (if necessary) in order to achieve the best results and to save time.

Among numerous training techniques, we can differentiate several types requiring similar conditions and places. These are complex psychic-energy and breathing exercises on the floor, standing position exercises for controlling attention and contemplation, and such generally restorative techniques as jogging, swimming, etc.

The best place for jogging is nature. And it is healthier to jog barefoot. Jogging is also more effective if you practice on hilly rather than flat terrain.

The best place for swimming is a swimming pool if, of course, the goal is training rather than a pleasant rest at the beach.

Nature is also an ideal place for breathing exercises, *Shiva Nata* (*the Dance of Shiva*, see below), development of the ability to concentrate attention and to contemplate (if there are no restrictions in terms of weather conditions and mosquitoes). Although, a place specially equipped for these purpose (Temples) is in no way inferior to the outdoors.

Referring to complex psychic-energy training, a specially equipped hall is the best place to take advantage of modern training techniques. Of course, specialization and equipment are conditional on the method of the school «but all questions regarding training must be answered here». And there will never be a uniform standard for such a place, as it always progresses with the development of the methods of the school.

Traditionally from ancient times, Himalayan yogis used warm tiger skins for meditation; cotton or woolen material for training; and vines, ropes or slings on which they could hang for some special compensation and antiorthostatic exercises.

The proliferation of Yoga in western countries in the twentieth century, led to the development (in Krishnamacharya's and B. K. S. Iyengar's schools) of special modern props. These were devised to assist beginners, and to compensate for various problems related to the lack of flexibility and physical atrophy. These props are now wide spread among *Iyengar-Yoga* practitioners.

Besides Western countries have also developed special *yogi-mats* (modern substitutes for training mats), timers to count static form and keep time during breathing control exercises, electronic glasses with programs that model meditative objects for contemplation, special training clothing, special phonograms and music for practices, and many other things.

Attitudes to all these products vary and depend on the level of the practitioner's consciousness. The direct physical contact of the practitioner with any surface, atmosphere, sound, form, radiation, etc., of these external effects must be taken into account. Individually, it is necessary make a conscious choice, from the many possible options, and choose those that provide the most efficient training.

A yogi-mat may be taken as an example. Can it be called perfect if the practical experience of many practitioners has connected it with a number of inconveniences, such as: insufficient length to practice? (Many people who practice Krishnamacharya's - Pattabhi Joice's Ashtanga-Yoga order a special longer yogi-mat.) There is insufficient width to train in Tri-Yoga style (Kali Ray uses two yogi-mats, laying them crosswise), and there is insufficient stability during dynamic practices when it wraps, distracts and requires to be constantly put right. On the other hand, it proves insufficiently soft. The mat provides no compensation for the rigidity of the floor, and it distracts beginners by causing pain signals when they stand on knee or elbow joints, spine lumps, ribs, chin or head.

Of course, at advanced levels of practice, all these difficulties are minimized since practitioners have already acquired enough experience to ignore the problems listed above. But even the most efficient practitioners will never be absolutely free from the requirement to choose the qualities of the place for special training.

Unfortunately, the above drawbacks of the training place limit one's freedom and ability to creatively develop training techniques.

Traditionally, small-sized spaces for practicing Yoga were mainly conditioned by the culture and life conditions of overpopulated and poor countries in the East (where people lived tightly), or by the inability for a travelling yogi to have a sufficiently large or thick mat.

But presently, when numerous places for training are available not only in the East, but also in the West, it is simply not necessary to restrict the creative development of training techniques by looking back at the oriental atavisms or at the lack of free space in small-sized apartments.

For example, by the way why should a yogi-mat look as it has been designed in the West if in the East, it never existed in such a form and has a lot of imperfection? Aren't people simply used to it? Don't they get ac customed to the limitations which it gives and forget that Yoga's purpose is Liberation (*Moksha*)?

Special gymnastic equipment, which is more advanced than a yogi-mat, and allows one to avoid the above listed problems, has been designed and widely used throughout the world. For example, the «tatami»-mat covering used for judo optimally combines all the qualities required for free training in any Yoga style. The weight and thickness of this cover prevents wrinkling, and remedies the unevenness of the floor. The hardness of such mats allows you to stand firmly on one foot or on your hands. Their softness compensates for the pressure on body tissues in any exercise, and alleviates pain, which allows you to avoid being distracted during practice, and guarantees safety in intentional or accidental falls on the floor. If required, the smooth surface of the cover allows the mat to slide during the training, whereas a special wavy surface stops slipping.

A large area of such special mat relieves the practitioner from sense of the constraint and nesessity to be depended on a minimum area, limited by the square of the small mat. This allows him to use a wider arsenal of various forms, movements and combinations during the training.

Preserving balance, while standing on one foot or on the hands on the «soft» surface of these mats, may be hard just in the beginning. But when one learns to allow for the «softness» of the mat, this inconvenience ceases to be of substantial importance. Besides, if all these balance exercises are mastered on the «soft» surface, it will be much simpler to practice them on a firm surface.

In summary, it is possible to say that there are no minor details in choosing the right place for training, and that the place should have a number of important qualities consciously selected by the practitioner.

ANCIENT HEALTH STANDARD

Presently, the whole world is experiencing the active development of «ecological human support systems» (complex recreation systems) that do not wear out the body of the man or woman practicing them. On the contrary, these systems restore and improve the body with the lapse of each year, irrespective of the age. It is quite obvious that these systems should consist of the elements that are closest to the *natural* motor functions of the human body.

Humans have existed as a biological type for many thousands of years, but during the last several decades we have faced a very serious problem:

our way of life has changed in an increasingly fast and radical manner, and this way of life is ruining our bodies. People spend more time sitting and laying, and less time in physical motion.

This sedentary life causes progressive physical degradation for the majority of people living in civilized countries, and physical degradation, as was established in the section entitled «Yoga and Morality», is directly connected with spiritual degradation.

If this persists, mankind will inevitably face a crisis. Is there a way out of this terrible situation? Yes, there is one. It is contained in the restoration of the «ancient health standard».

It requires us to abandon our comfortable and lazy way of life, and actively pursue the types of physical activities that contain the Challenge. Constantly overcoming the Challenge should become the means for encouraging the triumph of the Power of the Spirit.

Modern science says that aerobic exercise is the most natural for a human body, and this is quite correct. But the aerobic exercises that are widespread and popular at the present time are usually practiced in «the standing on the legs position».

Their creators didn't have enough courage to place a man on *four* limbs, thereby returning him to the ancient position of his ancestors is not practiced... Why?

It has been known for a long time that the lumbar section of the spine is man's «Achilles heel». Almost 80% of the adult population of the World have problems in the area of the fourth and the fifth vertebrae of the lumbar section. In animals that walk on four feet, these chronic diseases are almost absent.

It is possible to say that the construction of the human body is *naturally designed* for activities using a bar or rope, or swimming and jogging in the rhythm of breath... on four limbs in an «abdomen down» *Vinyasa* manner. Imitation of this position occurs in the process of practicing dynamic yoga styles, the arsenal of which includes *Vinyasas*. Particular positions of the body (*Asanas*) constituting *Vinyasas* that are drawn from among all living creatures on the Earth. For example, «dog face down», «dog face up», «cat arched back» are practiced naturally every day by many animals. In the same way, spiral and radial movements of the legs, arms and spine in the hyperventilation movements of the Dance of Shiva are functionally close to swimming movements, etc.

A considerable part of this book is devoted to the natural ways of training. It is written for people, who proudly see themselves as «modern» and «civilized», yet can understand the true value of this fabulous natural program for restoring animal health (in the best sense of this word).

Even limited experience with Yoga practice allows one to feel how strong the changes in energy circulation and the state of consciousness are in the «head down positions».

Vinyasas constantly alternate the «head up» and «head down» positions. In addition, these positions employ the spine, which twists in different directions, powerfully stimulating the nerve system.

This changes the balance of blood pressure and affects the glands in high-pressure areas. Additional secretion of the glands strongly shifts your psychic background and changes your range of perception. This results in a change of perceiving «picture of the world».

When our ancestors started to walk upright, their psychic-energy structure changed drastically. There were both advantages and disadvantages to walking upright in our biological and psychic energy structures. And these disadvantages definitely need to be compensated for. This happens to some extent in the horizontal position duiring sleeping. In this time our organism is ruled by pure biological instincts, but sleeping alone is not enough for restoring the ancient energy structures of the body and consciousness. Regular natural training is of great importance. When the energies of a straight-walking man flow from the head to the abdomen, they must be returned upward to stimulate the brain. This flow radically changes the energy balance between the upper and lower centers of the body.

Natural types of training give fantastic results — «beastly strength and health» (in the best meaning of this word), unhuman endurance, plasticity, coordination, peace and balance of consciousness.

This should not be understood as the appeal «to return back to the caves». We do not speak about consciously returning to the lower beings beastly instincts. By no means! It is only important to understand the organization and mission of the human organism's biological system, and also the essence of phenomena it undergoes during the progress of human civilization. It is necessary to assist this system to completely meet the requirements imposed on it and secure strong health as the foundation, which is absolutely required for effective manifestation of the Spirit.

It is necessary to preserve all valuable ancient biological programs that have empirically evolved to guarantee life on Earth for millions of years. And on their base it is necessary to build the practice spiritualizing and introducing through oneselves on the Earth those that are possible for a human only.

Part IV

LESS KNOWN PRACTICES

LESS KNOWN YOGA PRACTICES

Some literature on Yoga repeatedly mentions different and, on first sight, untraditional types of Yoga training. They told about mysterious Himalayan *respa*-yogis who cover great distances on mountain pathways at night, stand under ice-cold mountain waterfalls for hours, or compete in the number of wet sheets that can be dried on their backs in a minus thirty degrees Celsius frost. Stories about traveling pilgrims who cover many kilometers in the Himalayas in groups consisting of several hundred persons marching to a drumbeat, and about fish-yogis who do not drown or spend hours in cold water, etc. But still there have been no publications that could give at least partly reasonable explanations about how and why these methods were practiced by these yogis.

These practices have been used in Yoga not first millennia and have a deep sacral meaning. In this book we will remove the mysterious veil and present some aspects of these special practices in the context of the material under study. Even more so, as the supposed readers of this book are the residents of a region with cold winters, and the experience of the Himalayan yogis living at high altitudes, where the climate is also cold, may not only be of cognitive interest to them, but may also be of practical use.

Among man's numerous actions, the most natural ones have been polished by hundreds of thousands of years of evolution, and have been critical to life for this entire time. Such actions, first of all, include walking, running and swimming, as well as the ability to adjust to any climate changes (instead of creating for yourself a «hothouse» climate in modern apartments).

Walking, running and swimming have one common characteristic. These activities are performed as multiple rhythmic movements, synchronized with the breath and assist concentration of attention. The same is applicable to the all *Vinyasas*. So, it is possible to say that walking, running and swimming are also varieties of natural *Vinyasas*.

In modern times, these actions are still important in terms of the evolution of the consciousness, preserving health and life, as well as the vitality of humans as a biological variety. With the continued development of these natural activities, a man does not break the line of one of mankind's most ancient evolutionary achievements, and may achieve many new qualities that were not attainable by him before.

The Yoga Tradition developed special walking, running, swimming and tempering methods that continue to live in the rituals of particular Hindu and Buddhist religion sects.

These rituals assist the practitioner in entering into changed states of consciousness. They are practiced as heroic spiritual deeds that develop the body and strengthen the Power of Spirit.

PRANAYAMA IN WATER

All known swimming styles are varieties of natural *Vinyasas*, and hy drodynamic laws determine their techniques. These movements have been thoroughly studied and practically adjusted in sports swimming that it is hard to add something to them. And it is possible to see that the last word in the most effective movements of swimming techniques belongs to professional sportsmen. Therefore, the best thing that can be done to achieve purely yogi goals is to borrow technical methods of sports swimming and combine them with *Pranayamas* and other psychic-energy Yoga exercises.

From the very beginning, it is necessary to remember that sports swimming and *Pranayama* in the water are oriented towards different goals. The main goal in sports swimming is speed, but when practicing *Pranayama* in water, a yogi does not aim at swimming fast. The speed factor is not critical, but psychic balance and the timing of the inhalations, exhalations and breath delays are the most important factors.

To master the initial water *Pranayama* level, first it is necessary to master the breaststroke and a hyperventilation technique. (This is a synthesis of *Bhastrika Pranayama* with a «complete yogi breath through the mouth») and *Ujaya Pranayama* with breath delays after inhalations and exhalations, combining it with *Mula*, *Uddiyana* and *Jalandhara Bandhas.*

The initial-level training may begin by purely a warm-up, swimming in any style.

Thereafter, it is possible to attempt «breath mountains» which are usually practiced on the basis of breaststroke swimming on the water surface with delays of breath for different time periods after the inhalation. At the beginning, the duration of such delays gradually increases, thereafter, it decreases in the same gradual fashion. This is how the «breath mountain» is formed. The duration of a breath delay is measured by the number of arm strokes taken without raising practitioner's head above the water level. Therefore, during breath delays practice become a kind of diving on the water surface.

After the «breath mountains» (breathing warm-up), it is possible to begin a series of dives under water surface with maximum delays of the breath. These develop the life capacity of the lungs. And the training may be ended with swimming distances in any style.

The technique of using the breaststroke during the practice of «breath mountains» with a breath delay, for example, for three strokes, looks as follows:

1. Normal inhalation above the water surface, breath delay.

2. Three strokes with the breath delayed, head down in the water. The front part of the neck is fixed in *Jalandhara Bandha* («throat lock»).

3. Exhale into the water at the fourth stroke.

4. Normal inhalation above the water, breath delay, etc.

The technique of «progressing dives» (maximum) looks as follows:

1. Hyperventilation — fast and deep breathing with the mouth for 20 — 30 seconds standing by the side of the swimming pool.

2. Right after hyperventilation: deep inhalation, breath delay and shallow dive into the water.

3. After the stroke, it is not necessary to hurry and to make another one but should stretch in the water while the body moves on inertia. This saves energy and allows practitioner to delay breathing for a longer time and swim underwater for a longer distance.

If the distance of the dive is longer that the length of the pool, turn underwater without emerging on the surface and try to press the chest and abdominal cavities as little as possible, so as not to break the breath delay or cause psychic anxiety.

During the dive, it is important to pay special attention to psychic balance, avoid anxiety and stay calm. It is necessary to psychically join with the element of Water and «dissolve in the peace of it».

4. If the breath delay and the dive are completed somewhere in the middle of the pool, it should emerge without stopping and reach the end of the pool, swimming in any style. Then take a rest before to go on to the next dive.

The Pranayama training in water at the initial stage may look, for example, as follows:

#	Exercise	Distance	Style	Note
1.	Warm-up	200 - 400 m	any	
2.	"Breath mountain"	8 x 50 m	"brace	
		50 m		No breath delays
		50 m		Post-inhale breath delay for 1 stroke
		50 m		Post-inhale breath delay for 2 strokes
		50 m		Post-inhale breath delay for 3 strokes
		50 m		Post-inhale breath delay for 3 strokes
		50 m		Post-inhale breath delay for 2 strokes
		50 m		Post-inhale breath delay for 1 stroke
		50 m		No breath delays
3.	"Distance diving"	4 - 8 x 50 m maximum	"brace"	Dive after 20 - 30 second hyperventilation
4.	"Swimming'	200 - 800 m	Any	

In the course of developing your training form, you can increase the duration of breath delays up to 12 or more strokes and practice several «breath mountains» during the same training cycle rather than just one.

It is important to remember that excessively forcing the water *Pranayama* program during the training does not show effects immediately, but could eventually result in particular breath organ disorders or diseases: colds of the nasopharynx, bronchi, ears, etc. Therefore, water *Pranayama* should not be treated as sports training, and when practicing it should practice with regularity, gradation and caution.

In the course of developing advanced levels of *Pranayama* in water, the practice should include various *Bandhas* and *Mudras,* and more attention should be paid to the psychic-energy aspects of the training.

AWARENESS IN RUNNING

There is a special regime of contemplation. That is the contemplation in running. It is one of the best means of actually stopping mental activity and developing the practical ability to react instantly and accurately while being close to the risk of physical injury. This is a correct formula, but those who are concerned about the consequences of injury will only worry.

Awareness in running should be practiced in a proper place. Mountains or hilly terrain are the best for this practice. At the very outside, it is possible to practice on flat terrain, but it should be in the forest or in the park. The main thing in choosing the place is that the terrain should be complicated and varied.

The technique of such running is very simple. It is necessary to run non-stop as fast as possible over the rugged terrain, slightly slowing down when moving uphill and speeding up when moving down, but in such fashion that have no time to think about where to place the feet. There is a special mode of operation of the controlling structures, which is manifested in such a run. In this mode, possible to have a «beastly» feeling born inside when the feet firmly hold on the ground and know exactly where to be placed themselves: on the protruding angle of a stone, a hole between the stones, a root sticking out, vertical side-walls of the hill or a tree trunk. In this mode, a fabulous feeling of foresight of an unknown situation comes and the ability of quickly finding the way out of it. If the sudden step on a «live» stone or sandy ground happens, the speed regime of life saving will give protection from the situation of the fatal hazard. In that time errorless instant «out of mind» actions which drive out of dangerous situations. These dangers, by themselves, are not the goal of such running, but they happen from time to time, and the one who is not thinking overcomes them.

At the initial stage, such running is better to use on familiar terrain but at high speed, so that the wind always «whistles in the ears». Also, it is necessary to try to run in a non-standard fashion, for example, crossing the pathway from one side to another and back, running on the sides of a hill around the pathway, jumping on the trees and pushing off them, etc. And, of course, it can be manage all that only if the practitioners are not lazy and run actively, close to the boundary of his/her abilities.

The training goal may be achieved if the feet are unerringly placed on stable places, or they instantly jump from unstable places to stable ones. If the speed becomes extraordinary and endurance becomes «unkillable», even twenty kilometers does not take much time and gives pleasure. The only thing that is remaining in consciousness at this time is the noise of the wind and the exaltation of flight at reckless speed.

Running in the nighttime further complicates the task of foreseeing obstacles and provides extra-sensations. Night running awakens the mechanisms of the consciousness that are used by animals hunting at night. And these mechanisms sleep in every man because people do not use them. But they are very ancient and strong, and are still available and alive. These have evolved over hundreds of thousands of years, and the age of modern civilization is insignificantly small in comparison to their evolutionary importance.

But the main reason for the respa-yogis to run in the nighttime is that in tropical climates the heat drops only at night. Running in the daytime, under the baking rays of the sun, with temperatures over 40 degrees Celsius simply disables consciousness.

As to a risk, it exists everywhere. To live is generally risky. Risk is a part of any situation faced in life. But those people who are careful and not silly don't make mistakes... and continue to live.

RELAXATION IN RUNNING

The Tradition of Yoga has another special type of running which provides maximum body relaxation through self-suggestion, as done in *Shavasana.* If to use this running technique in freezing temperatures, it changes the status of the psychic-energy structure so much that it is possible do not feel the cold at all. This allows to run for many kilometers without feeling any fatigue or cold, although the running speed is relatively low.

Relaxation in running is practiced on the basis of «jogging». All parts of the body are relaxed in turns, as is usually done in *Shavasana.* The relaxation technique may vary depending on the individual experience. And how the relaxation effect is achieved is not as important as finally achieving it .

Learning to relax in *Shavasana*, beginners usually use the self-suggestion method: «My leg is relaxed, it is heavy and I can hardly lift it», etc. Later, when he knows the result and is familiar with the sense of relaxation, such relaxation is achieved much faster and without any self-suggestions, by direct will-driven transition from the feeling of being «geared» to the feeling of complete relaxation. The same refers to relaxation on the run: first it is necessary to use special self-suggestions, whereas later the same result is achieved by direct will-driven control of the status of the senses.

Given below is an example of one of the possible relaxation schemes with self-suggestion in relaxation in running, which may be creatively changed in accordance with the individual experience, orienting it to efficiently achieve the result.

It is possible to start from the top and move to the bottom. Using the self-suggestion formula used in the familiar *Shavasana* technique, it is necessary to first relax the muscles of the torso and the neck. Thereafter, go to the arms. The arms should be dropped down along the body, and one should run so that they «dangle» as two leashes. Then, subsequently relax each of the arm's elements, from the shoulders to the fingertips, using the standard formula, for example: «My arm is relaxed, the forearm muscles are relaxed, the hand freely moves on the fly, the wrist joints are relaxed, I can't lift my arm, my arm is very heavy, my wrist is hot, the wrist is filled with heat, my wrist breathes like a fire...», etc.

After the relaxation of all the parts of the arms is completed, similarly relax all the muscles of the legs, from the thighs to the toes. While doing this one should not raise the relaxed hands, they should remain dropped down and dangling during the whole time of the run.

An extended relaxation scheme may also include relaxation of the internal organs. Or one may not relax them if sticking to a short variant of the relaxation run.

The cold should never be met with resistance and internal strain, on the contrary, but to relax and tune to harmonious interaction with the temperature of the surroundings and try to enjoy the «goosebumps» caused by the cold, rather than resisting them.

Having achieved complete relaxation and warmed the whole body with «internal fire», it is possible to get down to various psychic concentration models, for example, on «breathing through the *Chakras*», perceiving the surroundings (trees, mountains, skies, sea, sun, moon, etc.) and interacting with them.

In such a way, one can run for many kilometers in freezing weather and achieve the benefits of running, while accumulating yogi experience by adjusting to the conditions of the surroundings. Relaxation in running may be used in a warm season by creatively changing the scheme and ori entation of the self-suggestions in accordance with the specific features of the surroundings.

The body status during relaxation in running is often on the margin between being asleep and being awake. So one should be careful in order to avoid getting into unexpected dangerous situations.

PRANAYAMA IN WALKING

Walking movements may be synchronized with the breath rhythm. When doing this, each part of the breath: inhalation, exhalation or delays may correspond to a different number of steps. For example, you can inhale for four steps, delay the breath after the inhalation for eight steps, exhale for four steps, and delay the breath after the exhalation for two steps.

The possible correlation between the breath parts can be taken from the breath models that have already been developed and are widely used in Yoga literature covering the systems of *Pranayama*.

It is necessary to note that the synchronization of movements and breathing leads to the increased capacity and general endurance of the organism. So, walking in the rhythm of the breath becomes quite easy. In such a way, it is possible to walk for tens of kilometers without feeling any fatigue. It also relieves the mind from different thoughts, and the conscious is only occupied with the sound of the breath *Mantra* in the rhythm of walking.

Today there are still rituals of religious sects in India, which include multi-kilometer processions along Himalayan mountain roads as part of their religious practice. These are made by groups of hundreds of people who march in columns, in step, like soldiers. Their breathing rhythm is substantially increased by regular group outcries of sacred syllables (*Mantras*) and a drumbeat.

Such groups experience powerful mutual psychic-energy feeding. The most experienced and enduring marchers set the rhythm, whereas the weakest, who are in a trance, follow them, thereby exceeding their «super maximum» individual achievement and entering into deeply transformed states of consciousness.

The only thing to remember when practicing *Pranayama* in walking is that walking creates physical stress and, therefore, the modes of *Pranayama*, which have already been mastered in a quiet state, may create an overload while walking and lead to different functional disorders. Therefore, while walking one may only apply the breath modes that are not marginal in a quiet state. It is required to obey the rules of regularity, gradation and caution. Or, if there is enough experience, it is possible to compensate a lack of physical training form with psychic-energy transformations in order to enter into transformed states of consciousness.

FUNDAMENTALS OF YOGI ADAPTATION

It is no secret for anybody that the larger the contrast between the tem perature of the surroundings and the body temperature, the more active the metabolic and thermal regulation processes are in the organism, which determine the ability to live in any climatic conditions without becoming sick.

Diseases are caused by disorders in human homeostasis, where adaptation mechanisms are unable to cope.

Through regular training it is possible to influence homeostasis, and gradually develop the ability to adjust to increasing deviations from its norm without causing any diseases. This training principle serves as the basis of almost all adaptation techniques, for example: cold, hot, sun radiation, tempering, etc. But another principle exists that allows one to adapt to the surrounding «external» conditions by consciously harmonizing the external surrounding conditions with the internal processes in the organism by will-driven control alone, rather than by training.

If "polar bears» can bathe in ice-cold water regularly, they are supporting their trained capability to withstand cold. But yogis may not bathe in cold water for several months, and if it is necessary, they can tune themselves to harmonious interaction with the surroundings, bathe in cold water and avoid diseases by using their ability to influence change by using their Power of Will. They tune to the rhythms of nature in any given season or to the natural surroundings at any given moment of time and psychically shift the «internal» energy processes of their organisms, so as to make them correspond to the «external» conditions. For such psychic adjustment, yogis often use special types of breathing, which accelerate the changes in «internal' rhythms. For example, before going into ice-cold water, yogis inhale and simultaneously lift their arms above their heads, and delay their breath. Then, with a post-inhalation breath delay, they lower their arms down in front of their chest, and move the air from the chest cavity to the abdominal cavity, thereby filling the lower center with energy. After that, when they exhale, they subjectively do not feel any loss of the energy they received. This is followed by another inhalation, with arms raised above the head, etc. After several breathing cycles the yogis firmly walk into the ice-cold water and dive into it completely (including the head).

The yogis' ability to stay in ice-cold water for a long time, or to dry several wet sheets on their backs at one time, shows the evidence of the power of metabolism and energy processes inside the body. And their eccentric competitions, which at first sight may seem strange, have deep meaning.

Using similar yogi techniques independently, it is necessary to remember that thermal output is very fast in water. In order to avoid possible diseases, one should never overestimate his/her real psychic-energy capabilities, and should follow his/her intuition and sense of reason

YOGA IN SEX

By definition, Yoga in sex means the fusion of two into one during sexual intercourse.

Before beginning to consider the peculiarities of such unification, it is necessary to determine the options of possible personal programs with respect to sex.

There are three main approaches towards sex.

First: the unconscious biological approach, which is based on the passion of sexual attraction and the spontaneous biological development of relationships, which does not imply mastering the culture of sexual relationships.

Second: the conscious ascetic (religious monks') approach, which implies the «destruction of flesh» and refrains from sexual contacts, both self-suggested sexual stimulation and even thoughts about them. In other words, obeying a complete taboo with respect to sex, and liberating consciousness from dualism and the dependence on the human partner for strengthening the Power of Spirit and realizing the Unity with the High Partner.

Third: the conscious tantric approach, which allows sexual relations but with mandatory understanding of all components and mastering the culture of sexual relations. It implies the understanding that the High manifests itself in all the diversity of the world, and sexual relations with a human partner comprise the model of Unifying with the High, allowing the consciousness to evolve without disclaiming anything.

The unconscious approach is based on the operation of the endocrine system and the biological program of reproducing living beings. It is powerful and reliable as an instinct, but its manifestation is not purely what is called human.

However, in some cases of functional disorders, biological stimulation of this instinct may be useful and relieve these situations.

The unconscious approach to sex in modern social conditions usually facilitates the development of an individual's sexual desire and «disturbs society», so that this way can often lead to maniacal behavior. Many current criminal sexual activities have appeared due to people's unconscious attitude toward sex.

The conscious ascetic approach to sex is one of man's most audacious challenges to the High and Unknown. The biological instinct of reproduction is one of the most ancient and strong programs in human beings, because it is related to the importance of prolonging human existence. There is only one instinct which is stronger that this one, i. e., the survival instinct.

The conscious ascetic approach is the «art of pacifying the Beast».

History shows numerous examples of the «fallen», and how people became crazy on the ascetic way. And at the same time, there are numerous examples of spiritual leaders who have added to their Power of Spirit and their magical abilities by overcoming the sexual instinct.

The most important rule in overcoming any habit or instinct is to distract attention from the object and direct this attention to something else. If basic instincts are suppressed by taboos, these instincts will continue to live and operate because they remain in the field of attention. And attention feeds and enhances everything that comes in contact with it. Therefore, the strength of a habit or instinct will increase in proportion to the efforts taken to suppress it, and sooner or later this results in a breakdown.

If attention is peacefully distracted from anything related to a habit's manifestation as soon as anything reminding one of it attracts attention, it will not be fed and its impact will be reduced until it gradually ceases to be of any substantial importance.

In this way, everyday negative habits and desires can be gotten rid of: eating meat, smoking, drinking alcohol, taking drugs, filling the sexual excess, etc.

Each instinct, desire or habit consumes life energy for its existence. And liberation from them is related to the liberation of the energy involved in their manifestation. And the stronger the instinct, desire or habit is, the more energy is liberated that may then be used consciously for spiritual purposes.

Isolating the reproduction instinct from other basic instincts does not cause any defects in the body's sexual functions. In fact, this instinct may be demonstrated to its best advantage, with power exceeding regular instinct.

Sexual self-restraint touches deep layers of the sub-conscious and makes the psychic background of the ascetic seem unusual to normal people. People think he/she is strange, and suspect that he/she is impotent, cold or frigid (every person seeks explanations in accordance with his mentality and culture). But these assumptions are totally different from reality. It is that the sexuality of an ascetic is directed towards the Supreme.

The conscious tantric approach to sex is an even a greater challenge to the Supreme Unknown than a conscious ascetic approach, since it implies control of the reproduction instinct in conditions of its active manifestation, rather than in the «hothouse» conditions of its isolation. The conscious tantric approach is the «art of pacifying the Violence of the Beast».

And the «fallen» on this way outnumber the followers of the conscious ascetic approach. Many literature sources have been published about the tantric way, and many fans have appeared who overestimate themselves and start to «play with the Beast» without sufficient knowledge of its power, guile and strength. And the majority of them devolve to unconscious biological sex. This happens due to numerous mistakes.

The conscious tantric approach requires the Power of Spirit which should not only be superior to a «normal» man's, but it should also be superior to the Power of Spirit of an ascetic who has managed to overcome the reproduction instinct. And from the beginning, the Power of Spirit should defeat and overcome sexual instinct, and one should not fall going through comprehensive ascetic training, and thereafter, cautiously try the conscious tantric approach. And although if few people managed to skip the ascetic stage, their percentage is so small that it is better to adopt the requirement of preliminary concentration and the accumulation of the Power of Spirit through the ascetic stage before practicing contemplation in the tantric approach.

And go slow. The reproduction instinct should be restrained completely. Early transition to sex with insufficient Power of Spirit causes the «Power of the Beast» (which is instinct) to start dominating. It takes control from the hands of the adept, and the his accumulated Power of Spirit is taken away and «gobbled by the Beast». This is followed by degradation of the consciousness with all resulting immoral consequences. But the point is that the reproduction instinct is a very ancient and powerful program, and a hasty «adept» has not accumulated sufficient Power of Spirit to control this powerful instinct and falls into trivial sexual satisfaction.

If you do not have problems with this control, a whole world of ener gy interactions opens with the partner. And the art of mastering this has no boundaries.

The reproduction instinct is based on the ecstatic resonance caused by the amplification of repeated signals going from the nervous system as the result of rhythmical movements and excitations of the primarily tactile receptors of genitals. This resonance is substantially assisted by prior or simultaneous excitation of individual erogenous zones situated on the whole surface of whole a human body.

The biological sexual behavior of men and women is different. But their common behavior is the continuous or stepped increase of excitement to some peak, which corresponds to ecstasy, followed by the decrease of this excitement. The only difference is that the rate of both excitement and recession is relatively long for females, and male recessions occur much faster. As well as the period of excitement and recession is quite longer when compared to a male's period.

When analyzing sexual relations, it is necessary to understand that, first of all, this is a game of senses and exchange of signals between the nerve systems of the partners. The behavior of one of two partners is not correct if their attention is directed only to their individual feelings. Roughly speaking, if one of them behaves «like a log». Such behavior is more pertaining to some women, but, as a rule, this happens due to the lack of experience and with the lapse of time many women become more active. But similar things can happen with men and, in this case, there is a real pathology.

Harmonious sexual relations imply the fusion of the partners' energy structures into one, and each of them can feel that one as themselves. So that, if something happens with one of the partners, it is noticed by the other one and they both act in unison helping each other to achieve happiness during the resonance of unification.

Where there is love and unification there is no place for egotistical behavior.

Prior ascetic experience, in at least one of the partners, allows him/her to control the senses. This is more essential for men, considering the relative transience of their excitement.

In the «Kama-Sutra» Tradition, it is customary to use the abstract of the «fire» and «water» model with respect to the senses. It means that, on the one hand, it is required to make and maintain «fire» of excitation, and, on the other hand, to extinguish it with «water» if the excitement is going out of control. Of course, this is a provisional model but it explains the principle of how one should treat the excitation signals.

If biological excitation can be characterized as a narrow «mountain» with a high peak, with fast ecstasy on top, tantric excitation can be characterized by a very broad and sloping mountain, with a plateau on top, where the ecstasy lasts very long. In this event the degree of excitation and the intensity of ecstasy are almost the same as in the event, of a «mountain with a sharp top». The difference is purely subjective, only because the contrast between bottom and top is not very big in tantric variant.

The ecstasy on a «sharp top» is essentially a momentary flash of a real ecstasy of unification.

Never it is necessary to hurry. And help each other feel when to delay or avoid overexciting the partner, and, on the contrary, when it is necessary to be more active and help the partner to «make fire». Also, it is necessary to feel yourself better, and if one gets overexcited, stop and take a pause, signal ing the partner to «work for himself/herself» and burn his/her own fire, assisting him/her in it.

It is also important to understand the partner correctly if she/he gives the same sign, and, without being distracted, continue «burning the fire», of course with the assistance of the partner. And one should not lose control by too rapid of an increase of excitement, which is followed by frustration.

Smooth building of the excitement with control allows a «rise» in the degrees of passion that is much higher and experienced much longer. It builds a powerful ecstasy of unification that transforms consciousness and completely removes the feel ing of separation and dual ism.

It is known that any signal, if it is too strong, turns to pain. And if it is too weak, dissatisfaction is felt. But if it is neither strong nor weak (optimum) and pleasant, it carries enjoyment and satisfaction.

Practical experience of yogi training develops sensitivity and control of the senses, strengthens the heart and expands the arsenal of possible forms. The functional tone of the body and its endurance are the best assistance to the harmonization of sexual relations. It expands the abil ities of personal and mutual adjustment and sensory control. A higher capacity energy flow appears and carries the partners for a long time without any negative consequences, while the potency is increased very substantially.

Combinations of various yogi postures during sex open broad opportunities for mutual creativity, as well as many new energy loops and circulation contours that considerably expand the spectrum of feel ings experienced and refine the style of l ife.

The development of Yoga practice allows for the removal of many problems that often disrupt family l ife.

First of all, you should get acquainted with the «Kama-Sutra» technique, l iberate yourself from any sexual complexes and apply the whole arsenal of available forms and means of mutual satisfaction.

There should be no l imitations as to mutual stimulation instruments and means between partners.

One should not forbid their partner to do anything, if only it is not related to pain.

The more natural the behavior, the closer to the goal.

The reasons for various problems usually stem from ill iteracy or psychological complexes.

Sometimes a problem may be caused by incompatible dimensions or by the form of genitals. This is easily overcome by selecting particular postures that compensate for such incompatibil ities.

For example if the event the penis is too small, the woman may, by contracting the perineum muscles, constrict the vaginal orifice, or change postures to provide the easiest access for deep penetration.

In the event the penis is too big for the woman, the man may take time to arouse the woman with his li ps, tongue, and hands in different postures (preferably «on all fours») until her vagina increases to the required dimensions.

There are no sexual problems that can not be resolved by yogi training. And no one will want to change partners with those who have sufficient experience in applying Yoga achievements to sexual relations.

The main problem for men is quick excitement, ejaculation, and further inabil ity to «speak to the woman». The reason for this is weak Spirit and a lack of sexual control. It is also egoism and a reluctance to put energy into self-control, not only for the sake of a woman, but also for his own sake, which means the absence of love for both the woman and himself.

According to Tantric canons men should «creep» to ejaculation «without loosing the Power» enjoying long and powerful ecstasy for hours, l ike a women. Or, against the canons, «unload» when they want, if they do not wish to share the Power. And if a woman continues to assist him without ceasing her caresses for a single moment, then, even with the «loss», male ecstasy may last rather long, l ike a female's.

However, men should remember that the body does a lot of work to process food products to produce sexual hormones. And the presence of hormones in the organism is very important for a man's health. Nature's intention of this hormone was not to satisfy ordinary lust, and its loss inevitably causes the worsening of health and changes the man's constitution. In order to receive required substances to produce a new portion of hormones, a man starts to overeat, his body becomes polluted, fat, weak, and starts hurting and aging (look at any «common family man»).

In fact, a partner, who is experienced in yoga-based control of the signal system, is not a simple man. His potency has no l imits. The Kama-Sutra says that the Master is capable of satisfying three women at a time without losing anything...

During «normal» (biological) sexual intercourse, male energy, driven by excitement, flows from *Kanda* (the source of *Kundal ini* energy) to the genitals. If a man has experience «raising the *Kundalini*», he can change the energy flow when the excitement increases. To do this, he uses his will to block the energy flow, running from *Kanda* to the genitals and redirects it, as in the practice of «raising the *Kundalini*», in *Sushumna*, by driving the excitement signal through the *Nadi* (energy channels) of the spine to the brain's excitement centers. This flow will bring an incomparable ecstasy. It will make one completely forget all the «toys» of biological sex. Thus tantric-followers «use» the natural initial passion caused by the partner's sexual influence, as a «burner» for the complete «raising of *Kundalini*» and Spiritual realization.

The technique of controlling the «raising of *Kundalini*» may also be used to decrease excitement when it is necessary to continue «working for a woman» without being overexcited. So, distracting the excitement signal from the genitals and redirecting it to the brain or through other channels decreases the degree of «narrow» excitement and initiates energy flows of another type, which expand the passion spectrum and the sphere of delight.

If a man has no such experience, he can't do something and cannot control his sexual passion, and over-excitement begins to get the best of him, he may to leave alone his penis and, without frustration, continue interactions with the woman using lips, tongue or hands, and, when his excitement is restored, he can revive his penis without interrupting intercourse. And it is possible to continue so all the time. In this case each partner follow its own rhythms and with understanding helps each other.

From the energy point of view, women, unlike men, are lucky by birth. Their body is constructed so that they do not need to ascetically accumulate sexual energy for «raising the *Kundalini*». For them a man is a universal «burner». Possibly, this is why the majority of women subconsciously long for a man like a God. Because it is through the connection with him, and the «raising of *Kundalini*», that divine realization occurs.

Often, a problem for women is achieving a complete orgasm and ecstasy. The reason for that is usually lack of experience and insufficient sensitivity, or the lack of an experienced and uninhibited partner.

A woman should understand what arouses her sexual excitement, and let the man understand this. She must literally teach the man if he is «stupid» and has not yet understood himself what he should do to stimulate her and how he should do it. And she should part with him if he always makes haste and cares only about himself.

The lack of sensitivity is, in fact, not a problem, as it can be developed in the course of Yoga practice. And the main thing during sexual intercourse, however, is to «surrender» and to stop thinking. Each woman's nature is inclined to this. And this is a problem for a masculine woman only.

A woman must always be a conscious Magician and remember the necessity to be mysterious and inaccessible. She should never allow a man to surfeit completely or become sure «that this woman is always in his pocket». Assurance decays unconscious people. Few pass this test. But the way out is simple: a woman only needs to provoke a man's interest in her and, thereafter, manipulate this living energy, constantly using special magical tricks, not only during sexual relations, but throughout life, ALWAYS. This should become the life style for every woman.

And do not be deluded into thinking that these behaviors are insincere toward the beloved creature, of course, if we speak of real love. It is important to understand the psychology of men, and know that, in fact, they like the process of longing and contesting the beloved woman rather than the resulting process. Even if it is connected with a kind of "suffering". And one should strive to assist men to extend this process infinitely. But in such a fashion that he should never even guess about this «assistance».

A woman should never tell her tricks to a man. This should be kept in secret. She should always account for the male unconscious psychology. Men betray even beloved women in the event they become sure of them.

Even if love is strong and there is nothing else to be desired, nobody should relax and seduce themselves, because the feelings are filled with life power that has a dynamic nature. Feelings are always variable: they flow, transform and, sometimes, run dry.

Each woman is a Magician by the nature. And the art of magic, as any other training, requires spiritual effort. Understanding this, one can not be lazy. It is only necessary to understand how and what a man reacts on and it is possible to control a man's energy completely for the sake of the harmony and happiness for both partners. Men should be controlled for the sake of preserving eternal love.

A woman who possesses the magic of Kama-Sutra has no problems in the life. No one can be equal with her. And, once contacting such a woman no man will be able to think about any other woman.

(However, the above female magic technique also pertains to men. In the majority of one-sided love cases, men should also resort to it.)

And, of course, the most important thing to make a woman's life successful is the presence of a loving tender man and her assurance in him.

In some cases it may be justified, both for men and women, to let the control go and allow the reproduction instinct to violently manifest. This is justified in making children and in particular moments of sexual relations as a combined mode of consciously alternating special controlled actions with spontaneous instinct-based ones.

A very interesting aspect is «field» sexual relations, i. e., sexual rela tions without physical contact: through emotional and mental communication, looks, gestures etc.

Many call out-of-marriage sexual relations a betrayal. At the same time the same people flirt at work or in social situations, just without physical contact, and for some reason this is not considered as a betrayal. But «gentle» contact-free sex is no less complete than contact-sex. This division is strange, as well as the lack of understanding that it is the same thing, even if it is completed silently in dreams and feelings. In this event, there occurs a «gentle» energy-level unification of emotional or mental shells of the partners and complete sexual energy exchange.

There are no boundaries for sex, as there are no boundaries for unification. Possibly this is why tantric followers see the whole world as divine sexual intercourse.

The ascetic approach towards sex allows the realization of the nature of the human body and feelings. But complete knowledge about human nature implies the realizing of two origins: male and female, as well as their meaning to one another. And this is only possible through the complete realizing of the psychic-energy processes of not only your own, but of a human being of another sex. And tantric experience allows one to completely realize peculiarities in the nature of male and female origins, transcend the existing differences and achieve universal, non-dual, human Vision and Being.

Having experienced biological, ascetic and tantric sexual approaches, it is possible to apply any of them in accordance with changes in the life situation, be satisfied with life and avoid suffering in any twists of fate.

TWELVE DIET RULES

In the conditions of modern style of life, civilization-imposed habits, and the influence of mass attack of advertisements offering «foodstuffs» unfit for consumption and harmful for health, it is impossible to speak of a natural diet. In exactly the same way, it is not possible to speak of a natural state of human consciousness. Therefore, it is absolutely necessary to follow special diet rules that can restore and protect the body's natural functions and strengthen health.

1. Eat to live rather than live to eat.

Diet is a means for achieving a goal rather than a goal in itself. Through realizing the High Sense of life and personal life mission, one should con sume only useful products that assist in the acquisition of the physical and psychic qualities required for effective actions on the Pathway for achieving the High Goal.

2. Hunger is truth, and appetite is lies.

Appetite is a desire to eat something tasty, whereas hunger is on one side the readiness to eat any food (as, for example, after a long walk in nature or after active physical work). And on another side hunger is also an indicator of exactly what particular food is required by the organism at a particular time (high-calorie or rich in vitamins, sweet or salty, liquid or solid, usual or unusual, for example chalk or salt, etc.).

Appetite is the result of old rakish desires and the absence of the will-humbleness. Food preoccupation or appetite may also be connected with the unconscious striving «to tune out» from stress influences and become distracted by the sensations of eating. A similar situation may cause other desires that are not conditioned to the real needs of the body, such as a desire to have sex, etc. This is usually connected with the psychic overloads of a modern stile of life.

Animals eat only when they are hungry, whereas humans, corrupted by abundance, have long ago become an exception to this rule of nature.

Restraint and self-control in any life situation liberate one from obtrusive desires and allow the body to live with preservation of natural motivations, achieving complete hunger.

The state of hunger produces an exact intuition-based knowledge of the quality of food needed by the body. Eating food based on the feeling of hunger quickly eliminates «extra weight», facilitates the cleansing of the body and returns ancient natural health. In this event, food is only taken when it is really needed.

It is necessary to stop eating before one feels the stomach is full. After half-filling the stomach, a quarter of its volume should be left for water and another quarter for free movement of digested food and expanding gases.

The digestion process often consumes large portions of the readily available energy in the body. If one overeats or eats food that is hard to digest, there is often a situation when the quantity of energy received from the food is compared with the quantity of energy spent for its consumption. When this happens, one usually becomes sleepy, lazy and feels the falling of the power still for a long time after having the meal.

Besides overeating is also a «striking» load for the digestive organs and leads to their diseases.

Reduction in the amount of food consumed by people partly resolves the ecological problem of preserving natural resources through conserving their use and allowing them to regenerate.

3. You live as you drink.

Water comprises a substantial part of the human organism. And metabolic processes are largely conditioned by the quality and quantity of water the body takes in. By controlling drinking, it is possible to substantially impact the internal rhythms and the overall condition of the body.

Many people think that drinking large amounts of water leads to putting on weight, and for this reason they try to drink as little water as possible. In fact, people put weight on because along with water they take in excessive amounts of salt, and it is the salt that causes the body to retain water.

But water is the juice of life. And, without sufficient amounts of water, plants, for example, dry up, or, on the contrary, blossom when they have a sufficient amount of water. Of course, humans are not plants, but their metabolism is equally dependent on the required amount of water in the organism.

Besides people also acquire excessive weight by ignoring the balance between consumption and used energy, i. e., balance of the amount of food consumed and the amount of calories burned for active physical and psychic activity.

In countries with a moderate climate, the human organism requires 1.5 — 2 liters of water daily in winter and 2 — 3 liters in summer.

By controlling drink regime one can affect one's feelings of hunger. And depending on the style of life and life conditions, it is possible to provoke hunger or on the contrary to delay it. So if it becomes clear that the possibility to eat appears at a particular time and later one will not have such chance, but the hunger feeling will scarcely come one can stimulate their hunger by drinking half a glass of water every 15 — 20 minutes. Then, the hunger will come faster. Or, on the contrary, if one is already hungry but there is no possibility to have a meal, it is necessary not to drink any water at all. Or it is possible to drink some herb tea. This will appease the hunger until it is possible to have a meal.

In any event, it is better to drink half a glass of water or herb tea a half an hour before a meal. And after the meal, drinking water or herb tea for washing the mouth and gullet should be restricted to prevent the dissolution of the gastric juices, and the impairment of digestion.

4. Drink solid food and chew liquid food.

In the digestive process the contact of food with salvia is of great importance. Salvia is an active biochemical substance that is absolutely necessary for complete digestion. To insure saliva secretion during digestion, solid food should be chewed until in turns into a liquid mixture without any remaining pieces of food. At the same time, liquid food (milk, soups, compotes, juices, herb tea, etc.) should not be swallowed instantly. Before swallowing them, make «taster» movements with the tongue and the jaw mixing the food with salvia. Only after this procedure is it possible to swallow liquid food.

Washing the food down does not substitute for the salvia's digestive function. Fluids dilute digestive fluids and are of no assistance in completing digestion.

5. Enjoy an empty stomach.

One should live in peace. And should not hurry the meals, or strive to eat as much as possible, even if eating a delicacy. Food should remain in the mouth until it is possible to taste its flavor thoroughly. This technique allows the receiving of the maximum taste sensations from a minimum amount of food. Using this technique it is possible to enjoy the taste sensations for a long time and become full after consuming only a third of what would normally be eaten. As repletion of brain centers depends on the number of signals received from the mouth cavity, teeth, and other receptors, rather than from the stomach actually being full. Following this eating technique allows one to avoid overeating, polluting the body and growing fat.

6. Do not try to kill two rabbits with one shot.

What is done without distraction of attention is accomplished with a substantially higher quality than something that is accompanied with «parallel» activity.

One should not integrate a meal with something that distracts attention from it, such as reading, talking, watching TV, etc. When the attention is distracted, the brain centers do not receive sufficient amounts of information signals about the quality and quantity of the food consumed. This leads to voracity, poor-quality chewing, incorrect food combinations and overeating with all the resulting effects.

While eating one should think about the food, about its perfect qualities, its usefulness and the delight it gives. Enjoy it and receive all the positive emotions that eating good food gives. Receiving a meal is an indivisible ritual, a prayer to the Supreme Ideal.

7. Morning begins in the evening.

One should not take any food less than four hours before going to bed, or even better 7 hours before going to bed. This may seem strange for many people, but there are a number of advantages to following this proposition.

Firstly, food is normally digested and moves through the stomach and the intestine only when a man is awake and active or, what is most important, when his body is vertical, as the direction of the gravitation component assists the movement of food in the intestinal tract. If some body eats before going to bed, then during sleep, when all the life processes are slowed down, the gravitational component, directed perpendicular to the body of a lying man, is of no assistance to the movement of food in the intestine. This leads to stagnation, fermentation, toxication of the body, formation of feces stones on intestinal walls, an increase of the volume of the stomach and the abdomen, worsening the intestinal tract, the development of diseases of the digestion organs, bad sleep and insufficient restoration during the night. And in the morning it is difficult to awaken, it is possible to feel swollen, an unpleasant smell comes from the mouth, as well as other complications.

And secondly, the suggested pre-sleep mealtime is connected with the real digestion rate of particular foods. Carbon-rich foods (vegetables, fruits, grains, etc.) are fully digested and pass through the intestine in about 4 hours. Whereas protein food (meat, beans, nuts, etc.) takes about 7 hours.

In general, the best meal schedule for stimulating powerful metabolism, increasing endurance and physical strength, improving health, and increasing the duration of life is to take food once a day, at a midday time.

Healthy people, who not sick or «maimed» by civilized habits, will not want to eat in the morning after sleep at once. Slight desire to eat should not appear earlier than an hour after waking up, but it is far from the sense of hunger. True hunger really comes into force about 4 hours or more after waking up. The next feeling of hunger rarely appears before it is time to sleep. But the phenomenon that makes people become «food-obsessed» is, as a rule, a reaction to life's stresses in the modern conditions of life rather than hunger.

8. Do not force yourself.

Violence is as harmful over yourself as it is to other people.

One should never make «abrupt movements» in life. And it is much more useful to alleviate contrasts.

If it is necessary to change the normal diet and exclude particular foods, this should be done gradually to enable the metabolic system to readjust and decrease the «pressure» of the habits.

One should never eliminate the habits instantly with strict will-taboos and suppression (violence). This approach is oriented towards the struggle with the result rather than the cause.

Will-driven taboo does not remove the roots of habits (desires), and, on the contrary, feeds and consolidates them. When the will acts against the habit, then (action is equal to counteraction) memory cells store «attributes» of the habit, are fed with the energy of attention and are amplified. This leads to an increase of desire to eat the forbidden product (this is like a river, blocked by a dam, but the source of which still exists). Such a misguided approach will sooner of later lead to an «explosion», and in the overeating of the forbidden product in amounts substantially exceeding the amount which would have been consumed by the person if he had continued to eat it as usual.

Habits are stored in memory. First of all, one should act at the level of controlling the attention.

If the attention returns to the memory cells that store sensitive information about the taste of products for which the habit (or desire) was formed, it should be softly and unobtrusively distracted from these cells and switched to something else, until no memories remain. Without being fed by the energy of attention, the information contained in the memory declines and gradually disappears (the river source drys up). In such a way, it is necessary to gradually replace the existing habits with new ones, containing information that this food is not for you, and that it is not consumable at all, like straw or soil. Such changes in consciousness require some time and active self-training, but this is the true way to success.

9. Cleanliness is a sign of the divine.

Preserving health requires that one support both external and internal purity which substantially depends on the quality of food and water that is consumed, and the natural and special organism cleansing processes.

Any car owner is well aware that the car's operation depends on the purity of gasoline, oil, and air inside the engine. And, of course, he knows that the engine's power is directly dependent on the content of foreign particles in the engine's crankcase, as well as the quality of gasoline. But it is somehow hard to understand for many people that the human organism needs clean fuel, lubrication and regular preventive cleansing in exactly the same way. They smoke, drink alcohol, take drugs, waste vital power through sex, eat products which, judging by their natural criteria, cannot be considered as food at all, etc. They are pressed for time or lazy. They simply lack the time to care for themselves, although they find the time to strive for something which is prestigious (but stupid). But the living organism requires much less than a car, because it is much more efficient, and struggles to correct itself with self-cleansing and self-regeneration mechanisms. And if one ceases interfering with it, no parts will need to be replaced for many years. And if one makes some effort to assist it, however, it will serve one well until old age.

The Tradition of Yoga has accumulated a wealth of experience concerning the cleansing measures used to regenerate, recreate and strengthen the human organism. Many of these are still used by the majority of people engaged in «re-creation» activities throughout the World. From individual enthusiasts to large medical corporations, they all cultivate body cleansing and rehabilitation methods. Presently, there is a large variety of special and popular literature where it is possible to find the answers to many questions about special organism cleansing methods.

With respect to natural self-cleansing of the body, it is necessary to introduce a regular rule to fast 24 to 48 hours weekly. During this period, all digestive organs rest, self-clean and regenerate themselves. It is better to fast on the weekend, when it is possible to avoid stress, and it is possible to control the status of the psyche, i. e., be calm.

For better cleansing and normalizing metabolic processes, fasting may be accompanied with drinking water or herb teas.

In special cases the fasting may be «dry», i. e., without drinking anything.

If the organism is polluted and weak, or if there are already internal organ diseases and metabolic disturbance, this may be corrected by long-term fasting, which may last 3 to 50 days. But this can only be done after prior, detailed theoretical preparation, and under the guidance of specialists.

Speaking of the clarity of food and the clarity of consciousness, one should not ignore not only the purity of foodstuffs, but and the «purity» of the means of getting the food and ways of life support. This determines the clarity of the «subtle» — karmic «cause and effectv» plans of a human being.

10. You are what you eat.

The organism is formed from the elements it receives. And it acquires the qualities of these elements.

Eat only fresh, clean, tasty, live, vitamin-rich, and energy-filled food. It is necessary to forget about what is called «junk food» by experienced western people, forget about all these chips, hamburgers, canned sausages, mayonnaise, etc.

And it is stupid to use expensive and rarely available, or «prestigious» products also. Using these, one is feeding their self-assurance by being exclusive, rather than «feeding» their body. For the organism there is no use in such food, there is most likely only harm.

Many people in the world have started to understand that it is really prestigious to be healthy and strong, look smart and always feel well.

By controlling the diet, it is possible to consciously affect the formation of the body, the state of the senses, consciousness and the karmic cause-effect ties (Destiny). Numerous naturalists have verified this fact by centuries of practical experience.

11. Do not combine the incompatible.

The digesting of different foods is performed by different biochemi cal reactions: acid or alkaline. Combining such foods in one meal causes acid-alkaline neutralization and the formation of useless minerals that substantially hamper the digestive process.

To avoid these phenomena it is necessary to consider the combining ability of different foods in one meal. There are numerous special food combination theories developed for these purposes. The food combining compatibility table, composed by A. Sidersky on the basis of works of

	1	2	3	4	5	6	7	8	9	10	11	Notes
1			✓					✓				
2			✓					✓				
3	✓	✓						✓				
4			✓					✓				
5												I
6												II
7			✓									III
8	✓	✓	✓	✓								
9												IV
10												
11	✓											V

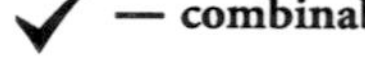 — **combinable**

Notes:

I — used separately (interval 40 minutes)

II — combinable only are fresh milk with rice.

III — 7 with 3, weight proportion 1 : 3

IV — If there is a sharp necessity to receive a big amount of energy without loading the digestive tract.

V — and with nuts

Table. 4

Ventseslav Yevtimov, a Bulgarian author of books on Yoga, and other literary sources (see Table 4).

1. Starchy vegetables: potatoes, old carrots, old beets, turnips, etc.
2. Grains: corn, wheat grain, flour and products containing it, sprouted grains.
3. Non-starchy vegetables: grasses, young root crops, white roots, cabbage, lettuce, radish, tomatoes, cucumbers, etc.
4. Protein products: beans, nuts, eggs, caviar, etc.
5. Fresh berries and fruit.
6. Dairy products, other than melted butter.
7. Meat and fish (preferably to be gradually excluded from the diet).
8. Vegetable oils and melted butter.
9. Melons and bananas.
10. Chocolate and cocoa (in restricted quantities in conditions just of large energy consumption).
11. Dried fruit.

12. Dogma first says: « dogmas are absent».

When determining the diet and schedule, one should consider all of the above prescriptions and rules, but it is important to never forget to stick to the rule of feeling well and be guided by the intuition-driven sense of common sense.

YOGA DIET

Yoga distinguishes three qualities (Gunas) — *Tamasic*, *Rajasic* and *Sattvic* which are incidental to the material World. And all food products subdivide into three relevant groups:

Tamasic: dead, tasteless, non-vitamin, dry, floury, cooled and warmed many times, technically processed, refined, not fresh, fermented, decomposing and foul smelling, synthetic, etc.

Rajasic: arousing desires, salted, sour, bitter, spicy, sickningly sweet, roasted, fat, smoked, canned, etc.

Sattvic: live, rich, full of vitamins, sprouted, fresh, pure, tasty, etc.

Sattvic products exert a «gentle» effect, and cause natural and «soft» taste sensations. Whereas *Rajasic* food causes a «rough» effect, and its consumption is accompanied by «firm» taste sensations. As to their impact on the sensory system, *Sattvic* food is accompanied by weak signals, whereas *Rajasic* food has strong signals. But the human body usually adjusts to regular sensations, and this is accompanied by the sensory system becoming accustomed to the level of signals relevant to one's regular sensations.

The stronger the sensations, the stronger the dependence on having them is, and the easier it is to develop desires for this sensation. This sensory cycle makes Freedom of Spirit harder to obtain.

When the signal system is transformed and the *Sattvic* food has been gotten used to, the enjoyment one will have from eating it will not be inferior to the enjoyment of tasting *Rajasic* products (although yogis do not use the categories of enjoyment). But this transformation results in purifying the energy system, developing sensitivity and reducing the load on the signal system and psyche, which leads the person to become calm, balanced, healthy and happy.

It is better to determine the *Guna* of the product by *sensing* and *sniffing* it like animals do before eating, rather than by analyzing it with the mind and knowing «what is what». In this way often it is possible to find that the food which seemed delicious a minute ago is now inedible, «synthetic» or «plastic». Or the food, which according to all canons, corresponds to healthy and nutritious food, was, in fact, polluted from the karmic point of view when it was obtained or processed.

All living beings on the Earth are fed from the energy of the Sun and the obligatory availability of water.

Sunlight feeds the plants. Herbivores eat plants, and carnivores eat herbivores. Carnivores eat other carnivores. There are animals that eat carrion. These processes are all fed by the sun's energy, but with each transition from one living creature to another substantial qualitative changes are undergone.

The elements of a burning tree disintegrate into elementary components. When this happens, the sun's energy, which was previously accumulated in the tree, is released in the fire, and the tree turns into ashes, which will no longer burn, since ash no longer contains the relations of sun energy, which have already been released.

In chasing new taste sensations, people have developed numerous recipes, many of which imply multiple thermal processing. But they did not take into account that each thermal impact on food products like their slow combustion (oxidization) with qualitative change and the sun's energy loss.

With each subsequent warming of cold food, it continues to decompose and «live» products turn into «dead» ones, in terms of the quality of their energy-related activity.

When one living being eats another one, this results in oxidization processes similar to combustion. But, the main point is that the quality of the consumed food and the activity of life energy are changed, that causes a deep change in the state of consciousness of that living creature. Observing the psychic types of a herbivorous elephant and a carnivorous hyena, it is easy to «catch» the difference. Compare their «intellectual», «warm-heart» and «generosity» levels. Of course, such comparison is not absolute, but one can easily «catch» the difference.

Digesting food is like a fire. It is possible to try to make the fire of digestion with heavy billets (eating meat and fish). This takes a lot of time and effort, and the ashes after such a fire will be rough and solid. Whereas, you can easily make a fire of brushwood (eating easily consumed products: grains, fruits, vegetables, and etc.) throwing it into the fire regularly. This will not take much time and effort, the fire is made easily, and burns brightly and warmly. There are almost no ashes after such a fire, and, if something remains, it is easily taken with the wind of digestion.

The outdated diet theory of calorie capacity and the energy value of different products, was misunderstood in western countries for several decades. Whereas, the East never used such a theory in selecting the diet, their primary was on the qualities of the food and to its impact on consciousness, a fruit diet being preferred.

Fruits contains concentrated forms of all the valuable life elements produced by nature. Nature's intent being to extend life on the Earth in two ways: reproduction from a fruit seed to a living organism, and extending the life of an existing organism through feeding on what was produced.

This is exactly why nature provided for the production of an abundant variety of fruits, i. e., much more than would be required for extending the life of a particular variety. This abundance is produced to provide for the creatures that eat these fruits.

The Tradition of Yoga prefers *Sattva Guna* in selecting food products and recommends a vegetarian fruit diet: fruits, vegetables, grains, nuts, milk, non-refined vegetable oil and honey. Of all animal products, some Yoga schools allow eggs and caviar to be eaten. Others exclude even milk from the diet, ignoring all animal products.

Moreover they eat food raw, «live» or, in exclusive cases, at minimum thermal processing with minimum quantities of salt and sugar.

A *Sattvic* fruit diet is based on natural nutrition and implies no violence. It facilitates rooting out numerous body and consciousness diseases of the present times, endows a man with strong health, vigor, sensitivity, contentment, balance, deep internal peace and joy.

Speaking impartially, if a man is capable of controlling his senses and eats consciously, he controls the characteristics of his body and consciousness, rather than his sensational satisfaction controlling him. His convic tions, moral foundations and life goals require strength, and the qualities of a predatory wolf or a carrion-vulture, then he can eat carrion, making everything on the contrary and he will quickly succeed in attaining these goals.

In the conditions of the present abundance of food, in order to make the diet correspond to this ancient standard, to have robust digestion, to have the organism clean and healthy, and to make the body qualities assist in the development of Yoga practice, one should consciously each oneself always live with hunger.

SHIVA NATA — DANCE OF SHIVA

Transitions from one *Asana* or *Vinyasa* to another one are accompanied with the movements of the arms or legs. In general terms, these movements are variations of *Vinyasas*, as they are synchronized with the breath. But these do not form any particular group of *Vinyasas*, which is a functional element of the «Universal Multilevel *Vinyasa* Algorithm», but they comprise parts of these *Vinyasa* groups used when transiting from one *Asana* or *Vinyasa* to another one.

Such arm and leg movements may be done with a number of similar options. For example, if standing upright, start to bend forward with the arms raised above the head and lower the hands onto the floor. During this move, there are a minimum of three optional ways of how the arms will move: forward and down, to the sides and down, and back and down.

In addition, there are a number of special breath exercises that are accompanied by similar movements of arms or legs. The arms are associated with the chest by means of muscles, and the legs are associated with the abdominal cavity, and both participate in the breathing process. This means that breathing characteristics largely depend on the trajectory and movement characteristics of the arms and legs in breathing exercises.

Unfortunately, in many Yoga schools with many progressive technical elements and methods, these movements are performed with extreme simplicity, primitively and without exaggeration. But at the same time these movements largely determine characteristics of energy flows in peripheral channels, it is still necessary to study the main dynamic principles of the limbs and their impact on breathing characteristics. That is why it is important to introduce the nature of such movements into the practice of Yoga, and to make conscious all the movements with arms and legs made during training. This increases the effectiveness of breathing exercises by using specifically selected movements with the arms and legs.

* * *

Analyzing a theoretical model of the moving arm or leg, attached to a tentatively immovable body, we can see that these movements may be performed in one, two or three planes.

Single-measured movements are performed by «directly» extending an arm or a leg. Double-measured movements are performed by their "plane" ones. And triple-measured movements occur when performing «three-dimensional» spiral movements.

In this connection, there are three groups of limb movement: linear, plane and dimensional.

Theoretically, when performing purely linear or single plane movements, the elements of the skeleton are required to be driven by a single muscle or by several parallel muscles set in the same plane as the direction of the movement. But, since the human body is constructed so as to provide movements in different directions, the limb controlling muscles are attached to the elements of the skeleton at different angles. And observing the natural dynamics of the body, one can see that almost all of its movements are effected by the operation of muscle groups rather than by individual muscles. When a particular movement takes place, the load is completely or partially transferred from one muscle to another. This is accompanied by changes in the angle of the application of the driving effort. Therefore, natural movements can rarely be purely linear or single-plane (only within a short track). Most often these occur upon the abrupt relaxation of the muscles when a particular part of the body falls freely.

To make the technique of liner or single-plane movements more sophisticated and natural, they should be complemented with specific motions that make the movement three-dimensional. So for example, linear bending (unbending) of an arm (leg) may be effected in a «whip-like» way or be rotated around its axis. And in a single-plane radial movement of an arm (leg), it can be simultaneously rotated around its axis.

Compared to linear and single-plane movements, three-dimensional spiral movements have a number of benefits and positive qualities. Firstly, these are the most natural and balanced movements. Secondly, they are performed in three planes and their trajectory consists of both linear and radial motion moments, and subsequently, this implies the ability to perform and control these movements also. Thirdly, three-dimensional spiral movements cover almost all-possible positions «within the Marginal Mobility Circle» of the arms and the legs. This allows one to control this space and link any points inside this space between themselves. Fourthly, performing such spiral movements employs all muscle groups of the arms, legs, shoulder and hip girdle, which results in powerful and comprehensive strengthening effects during training.

Since movements with the limbs include overcoming gravitation, there is a relationship between the force lines of the Earth's gravitational field and the «inner energy flows». According to the «action equals counteraction» rule, the upward movement of the limbs against the gravitational force relates to actively overcoming energy flows. Or it is possible to say that the active component of the gravitational force is transferred to the channels of the arms and legs. And on the contrary with moving the limbs down, on the gravitational force movement, the activity of energy flows decreases. For all that the activity of gravitational force carries out the work of falling down the limbs and a passive anti-flow is filled in the energetic channels of the arms and legs.

Continuous spiral movements consist of two complete counter-directional sine curves. Therefore, performing such movements sets a series of alternating active and passive fragments of the energy flow. These energy impulses purify energy channels and balance the circulation of energy inside them.

Synchronizing spiral movements of the limbs with the breath creates a constant and intensive energy consumption from the surrounding space, translation of it through psychic-energy structure channels, and accumulation and radiation into the surrounding space.

Such spiral motions were widely used in early Buddhist practices. Initially these were the elements of the Dance of Shiva, a Yogic art which develops conscious control, coordination and the potential abilities of the body, without specialized application in life.

Later, Boddhidharma exported them to Shaolin, and on the basis of these movements applied martial art techniques were developed with the use of one's own body and various weapons: a sword, a pole, a spear, etc. These techniques became the perfect means for developing the functional abilities of the body, increasing the organism's energy potential, the controling and coordinating several «sectors» of various body parts at the same time.

It should be noted that having a weapon in the hands promotes an increase of density energy flowing through arm channels, and more intensively develops the strength and endurance of the fighter. But there is another side of using weapons in training: it reduces the requirements to the twisting capability of the joints.

Therefore, the Far East schools of martial arts allowed practitioners to exercise with weapons only after many years of practicing base exercises without any weapons.

Some of these exercises have become widely known today, for example «rotation of cups filled with water» which should not be spilled during radial spiral movements. In the Ancient Dance of Shiva, however, such cups contained oil and wicks, which were burning throughout the dance. And in rotating the cups no oil should be spilled, and the fire should remain burning.

This dance, performed against the background of starry skies, made an inexplicable impression...

The Dance of Shiva uses sixteen principally different basic movements and sixteen positions for two arms. And this number may be neither larger nor smaller.

The helix always has a central axis around which the rotation is effected. When rotating a cup, its upper surface and the palm should always be in the horizontal position, whereas the spiral movements should be around the vertical axis. In this event, the rotation of the cups is done simultaneously, as if in two parallel horizontal planes, and are connected by diagonal fragments of the transition movements from one such plane to another. Therefore, such spiral movements are called «horizontal».

At the same time, such horizontal rotation of the cups consists of two continuous radial movements along spiral trajectories: ascending and descending. Performing such exercises results in the integration of the upper and lower horizontal subspaces.

There are several levels for the practical learning of these movements. But, at the very beginning, it should be noted that the difference between these levels is not in physical complexity. It is in the level of control and coordination, as well as in the ability to follow a preset program for a long period of time, without being distracted. Then, faultlessly changing from one movement to another, performing them with technical perfection. But on the physical level, the complexity of these movements has little difference.

Transition from one level to another requires knowing a greater number of various combinations of these simple movements and supplementing linking movements, which correspond to improved coordination of the arms and legs. And the ability to avoid being distracted for a long time, and faultlessly follow a preset program corresponds to the increased level of controlling various positions of the arms and legs within the «Boundaries of the Marginal Circle» of their mobility.

Mastering the first level is sufficient for introducing the nature of such movements in *Asana*, *Vinyasa* sequences and breath exercises. But the first level will not be sufficient for the purposes of special development of control and coordination. Therefore, two development levels in this direction are considered below.

When analyzing the Dance of Shiva, it is required to understand from the very beginning that the word *dance* is applied provisionally, based solely on the external features of this phenomenon. It is necessary to imagine what happens with the energy body in the surrounding space during the spiral movements with the hands and cups. First of all, a spiral is a three-dimensional sine curve. And, as it is known from physics the movement of the energy media, e. g., electrons, along a spiral conductor creates an electromagnetic field. In this event, the electromagnetic force acts along the central axis around which the spiral movement is effected. Similar phenomena occur in the space around the human body if a man performs spiral movements with his arms or legs. In terms of physic science, such movements are accompanied with a definite movement of the life energy through the channels of the arms and legs. There are respective forces operating along the central axis, around which such spiral movements are performed, which interact with the surrounding space. The pulsating change of the ascending and descending directions of such spiral move ments, with the cups being continuously rotated, causes such forces to pulsate and reverse.

Gaining experience in controlling energy flows opens many abnormal abilities. But, despite the temptation of mastering them, it is important to always remember the main purpose of this practice.

Despite the powerful energy-related effects occurring during the Dance of Shiva, these movements cannot be directly compared with Qi Gong, Tai Chi, Zong Shin, Kung Fu and other martial arts of Chinese, Vietnamese or Japanese heritage. It is important to remember that in these techniques, the main accent is made on the development of the energetic results connected with the feeling of movement and the accumulation of Power, and on the development of the strategic and technical qualities of a fighter. But in the Dance of Shiva, the main accent is made on the development of the multi-sector control of the body's controlling structures, the increases of the speed of the controlling processes, and the forms of the new algorithms of transcendental links in the consciousness. These new links increase the power and generation of the bio-processor.

Of course, these controlling processes may be developed for special purposes through various exercises without the participation of the physical body. For example, the development of mathematical thinking, playing chess games and modern computer games leads to such narrow and lopsided development, and for some people, this narrow and one side development will possibly suffice. But the Dance of Shiva, however, allows the preservation of harmony in the developing of the body and Spirit. Since the body's physical abilities are more easily developed than the spiritual abilities, the tasks of conscious control in the Dance of Shiva are rather simple compared to the tasks which may be required in purely «conceptual» practices. But, at the same time, these tasks correspond to the real level of the instrument (the body). Here one will never face the situation when the Spirit is ready to fly but the weak body is not even able to crawl, because there is balance between the Sky and the Earth, between the evolution of the ideal and material.

Level one

The first level of practice implies the mastering of sixteen basic movements with the arms, two basic movements with one leg and eight basic leg steps. These help facilitate an increase in the volume of the lungs, cleanse the peripheral channels, develop coordination, develop mobility in the joints, and strengthen the muscles of the arms and legs.

Movements of arms

To facilitate practical training, spiral movements of the arms are divided into four quarters. As was mentioned earlier, during the practice of horizontal movements, the palms should always be horizontal and face upward. In the first and third quarters, the fingers are turned outward (Photo 1 and 3), and inward in the second and fourth quarters (Photo 2 and 4).

To further simplify the description of the technique of these movements, each of the quarters is assigned a relevant number: for the first quarter - 1, for the second quarter — 2, for the third quarter — 3 and for the fourth quarter — 4.

The movements should first be learned separately with each hand, turning it in the same direction (the one which is easier for you) for several times without stopping. Then, it is possible to try to make the reverse rotation. In order to memorize the correct trajectory of the movements from the very beginning, it is better if one begins to learn these movements standing before the mirror, paying attention to the smoothness and continuity of the movements and the twisting capability of the wrist. To make the feeling of horizontal surfaces easier, it is possible to take cups or something flat and heavy in the hands.

When the separate spiral movements with each arm are learned well and it is possible to easily practice them in both directions, one can move on to the next stage of practice of the first level, i. e., moving both arms simultaneously.

The positions of the two arms are also assigned a two-digit code, in which the left digit means the position of the left arm and the right digit that of the right arm. For example, if both arms are in the position of the first quarter, such position shall correspond to — 11. Or if the left arm were in the position of the third quarter and the right arm in the position of the second quarter, this position would correspond to — 32.

Photo. 1 Photo. 2

Photo. 3 Photo. 4

The simplest movements of both arms simultaneously are synchronous single-direction movements in which both arms simultaneously pass through the same quarters.

Photos. 5 - 8

For example, in sequences 11, 22, 33, 44, 11 and etc. or in the reversed order (Photos 5 — 8). Although, viewed from the top, the arms move in different directions. The sequence of practicing these and all subsequent movements is the same: initially it is necessary to practice synchronous movements with powerful breath, in which the arms turn in the same direction (the one that is easiest) and then in the reversed direction. During the movement all inhalations should be through the nose and the exhalations through the mouth. And each inhalation (exhalation) corre

Photos. 9 - 12

sponds to two quarters (one half of a complete trajectory) of spiral movements.

This stage is followed by the learning of single-direction movements of two arms, in which each arm passes through different quarters, but in the same sequence. There are only three variants of such movements. The first one starts with the shift of one arm one quarter ahead of the other and is done in the following sequence: 12, 23, 34, 41, 12 or in the reversed sequence (Photos 9 — 12).

Photos. 13 - 16

The second movement starts with the shift of one arm two quarters ahead of the other and is done in the following sequence: 13, 24, 31, 42, 13 or in the reversed sequence (Photos 13 — 16).

Photos. 17 - 20

And the third movement begins with the shift of one arm three quarters ahead of the other and follows the following sequence: 14, 21, 32, 43, 14 or in the reversed sequence (Photos 17 — 20).

Photos. 21 - 24

When single-direction movements are learned and can be easily practiced in both directions, it is possible to advance to the next stage of practice of the first level: counter-directional movements, where arms simultaneously pass through different quarters in reversed sequence. In total, there are four variants of such movements. The first movement starts from the no-shift position, but the arms are moving in reversed directions in the following sequence: 11, 24, 33, 42, 11 etc. or in the reversed sequence (Photos 21 — 24).

Photos. 25 - 28

The second movement starts with the shift of one arm, one quarter ahead of the other, and the arms move in different directions in the following sequence: 12, 21, 34, 43, 12, etc. or in the reversed sequence (Photo 25 – 28).

Photos. 29 -3 2

The third movement starts with the shift of one hand, two quarters ahead, the hands moving in different directions in the following sequence: 13, 22, 31, 44, 13, etc. or in the reversed sequence (Photos 29 — 32).

Photos. 33 - 36

And the fourth movement starts with the shift of one arm three quarters ahead of the other, the arms moving in different directions in the following sequence: 14, 23, 32, 41, 14, etc. or in the reversed sequence (Photos 33 — 36).

Besides the above eight options of horizontal movements with two arms, there is another group of spiral movements, which is distinguished by the direction of the central axis around which these spiral movements are effected. So, if in horizontal movements, the central axis is vertical, then, theoretically, there exist two more main directions: horizontal longitudinal and horizontal transversal. More over spiral movements around these axes will, respectively, be called vertical transversal and vertical longitudinal. But, in practice, spiral movements around the longitudinal horizontal axis are substantially limited by the lack of mobility in shoulder joints when the arms are brought back. Therefore, they are only used in practical martial arts exercises with the use of weapons: nunchacku, swords, sticks, etc., which extend the arms and compensate for the poor twisting of the shoulders. Therefore, the arsenal of movements without any weapons uses spiral movements only around the horizontal transversal axis. Also, in terms of technique, such movements around the horizontal longitudinal and horizontal transversal axis are absolutely the same. And if the movements around the transversal horizontal axis have been learned, then, if necessary, these can be easily performed around the longitudinal horizontal axis with the use of weapons.

Vertical spiral movements around the horizontal transversal axis are also learned at the first level of the practice. Similar to horizontal movements around vertical axis, these are divided into four quarters, which are assigned relevant digital codes with a view to simplifying further description of the technique. First quarter — 5, second quarter — 6, third quarter — 7 and fourth quarter — 8.

The palms in these movements are always turned to the outside and are kept vertical. In the first and the third quarters the fingers are directed always ahead (Photos 37 and 39), and in the second and fourth quarters – backward (Photos 38 and 40).

Performing these exercises causes the integration of the internal and external vertical subspaces.

When one can easily perform spiral movements with each arm separately in both directions, it is possible to continue to the next stage of the first level, which implies spiral movements of both arms simultaneously. These are also assigned a two-digit code in which the left digit stands for the position of the left arm, and the right digit stands for the position of the right arm. For example, if both arms are in the first quarter, such position corresponds to 55. Or, if the left arm is in the third quarter position, and the right arm in the second quarter position, such position corresponds to 76.

Photo. 37

Photo. 38

Photo. 39

Photo. 40

Photo. 41 - 44

Similar to horizontal movements, there is the aggregate of sixteen different quarter-based combinations of movements with both arms. The simplest vertical simultaneous movements with two arms are synchronous single-side movements, in which both arms simultaneously pass through the same quarters. For example, in the following sequence: 55, 66, 77, 88, 55, etc., or in the reversed order (Photo 41 — 44).

Photo. 45 - 48

This stage is followed by mastering one-sided movements with arms, in which both arms simultaneously pass through different quarters, but in the same sequence. In total, there are three options of such movements. The first movement starts with one arm shifted one quarter ahead of the other and is performed in the following sequence: 56, 67, 78, 85, 56, etc., or in the reversed order (Photos 45 — 48).

Photo. 49 - 52

The second movement begins with one arm two quarters ahead of the other and is performed in the following sequence: 57, 68, 75, 86, 57, etc., or in the reversed order (Photos 49 — 52).

Photo. 53 - 56

And the third movement begins with one arm three quarters ahead of the other and is performed in the following sequence: 58, 65, 76, 87, 58, etc., or in the reversed order (Photos 53 — 56).

Photos. 57 - 60

When single-side movements are mastered and are easily practiced in both directions, it is possible to advance to the next practice stage of level one, i. e., different-side vertical movements in which arms simultaneously pass through different quarters in the opposite sequence. In total, there are four variants of such movements. The first movements start with no shift, but the arms move in different directions in the following sequence: 55, 68, 77, 86, 55, etc., or in the reversed order (Photos 57 — 60).

Photos. 61-64

The second movement starts with one arm one quarter ahead of the other, and the arms move in different directions in the following sequence: 56, 65, 78, 87, 56, etc., or in the reversed order (Photos 61 — 64).

Photos. 65 - 68

The third movement starts with one arm two quarters ahead of the other and the arms move in different directions in the following sequence: 57, 66, 75, 88, 57, etc., or in the reversed order (Photos 65 — 68).

Photos. 69 - 72

And the fourth movement starts with one arm three quarters ahead of the other and the arms move in different directions in the following sequence: 58, 67, 76, 85, 58, etc., or in the reversed order (Photos 69 — 72).

Movements of legs

From an anatomical point of view, the legs and the arms have a similar construction and can perform the same movements. Dividing leg movements into quarters it is possible to use the same system of shifts as are applied for the movements of the arms, by simply substituting the arm symbols in the above diagrams with the symbols of legs. But, in reality, moving both legs simultaneously in the standing position is impossible, or in the sitting and lying position there are restrictions in the range of movement, such as the floor, which substantially decreases the number of theoretically possible movements. Operation of the legs upwards is not possible in full scope, since it is restricted by the time period spent in a reversed position (on the shoulders, for example) and is connected with the overloading of the cardiovascular system. Therefore, the movement model devised for the arms is not natural or «practical» for the legs.

So, the technique of movements with legs is based on their natural inclinations. In the standing position, it is necessary to only move one leg at a time and to move one or two legs in a jump or on the floor. Parts of the movements in the standing position are differentiated and combined using a system of step sequences, which follow the fragment trajectories of these movements. (There is one school in Kyiv that uses variants of movements with two legs simultaneously while on the floor).

The sequence of practicing all of the above movements is similar. In the beginning, one learns the movements on the easier side, and then on the more difficult one. And all movements follow the rhythm of powerful breath: inhaling through the nose and exhaling through the mouth.

At the first level of practice it is possible to perform horizontal, longitudinal and transversal movements with one leg, the second leg serving as a support. Compared to the simultaneous movements of both arms, practicing movements with one leg looks much simpler, but movements with legs require much greater physical effort. But, in practice, performing leg movements that are technically «pure» requires similar effort. And, in terms of effect on the psychic-energy structure, these leg movements are not less effective.

Theoretically, one leg may perform two main spiral pendulum-like movements: longitudinal and transversal, forming four loops with crossing trajectories (Fig. 1). Forward and backward movements with a leg are only restricted by the «Limit of the Marginal Circle» of mobility. Transversal movements outwards are also not restricted, but when moving inwards, the free leg clashes with the supporting leg. Therefore, the impossible transversal loop towards the support leg is reversed towards the possible loop. As the result, the transversal spiral is performed in the following fashion: initially the leg moves to the side and close to floor level, and makes a small loop. Thereafter, it moves to the same side, but high above

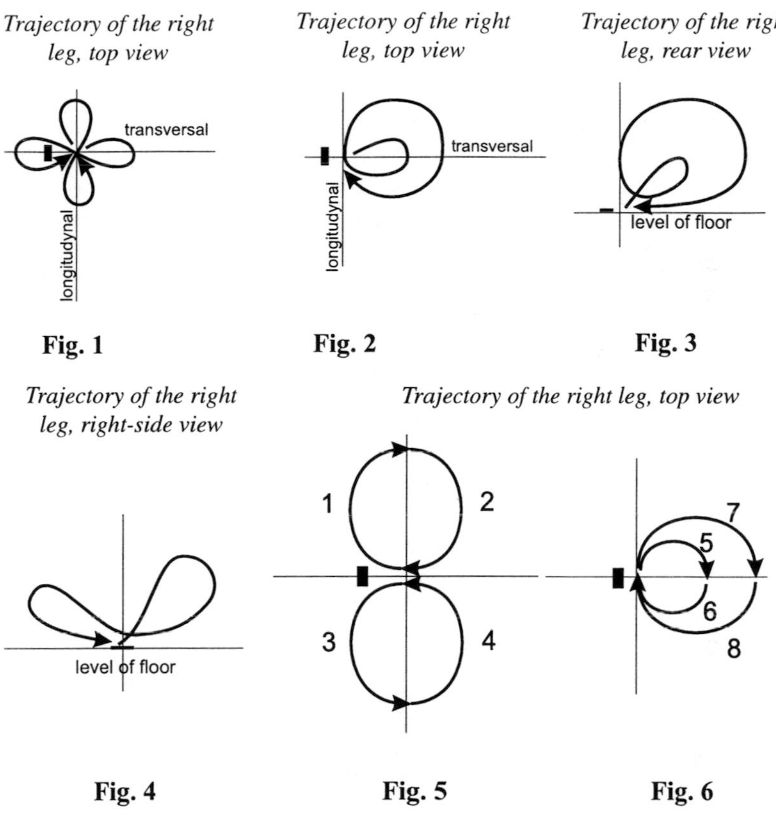

the floor level and makes a big (reversed) loop or to the reversed direction (Fig. 2).

Therefore, transversal spiral movements go to the side and upward in the vertical plane (Fig. 3). Whereas longitudinal spiral movements go forward-upward and backward-upward in the vertical plane (Fig. 4).

Trajectories of longitudinal and transversal movements may be divided into two sections, and each assigned a relevant digital code. Looking at the longitudinal spiral on top (Fig. 5) its trajectory is divided into four quarters: internal front arch — 1, external front arch — 2, internal back arch – 3, and external back arch — 4. Similarly, looking at the transversal spiral (Fig. 6) it is possible to see: small front arch — 5, small back arch — 6, big front arch — 7, and big back arch — 8.

When practicing all subsequent movements with the legs, the back of the hands should be fixed on the waist. The practice of leg movements

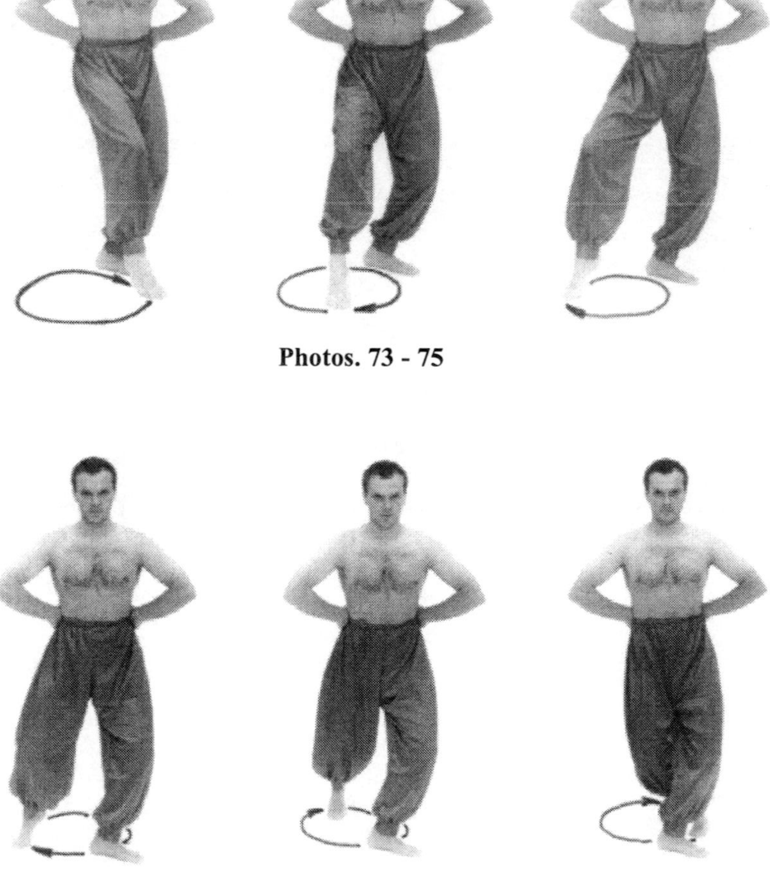

Photos. 73 - 75

Photos. 76 - 78

begins with mastering the circular movements in the front (Photos 73 — 75 and Fig. 7), back (Photos 76 — 78 and Fig. 8), on the side in a small loop (Photos 79 — 81 and Fig. 9), and on the side in a big loop (Photo 82 and Fig. 10).

Photos. 79 - 81

Trajectory of the right leg, top view

Fig. 7 **Fig. 8** **Fig. 9**

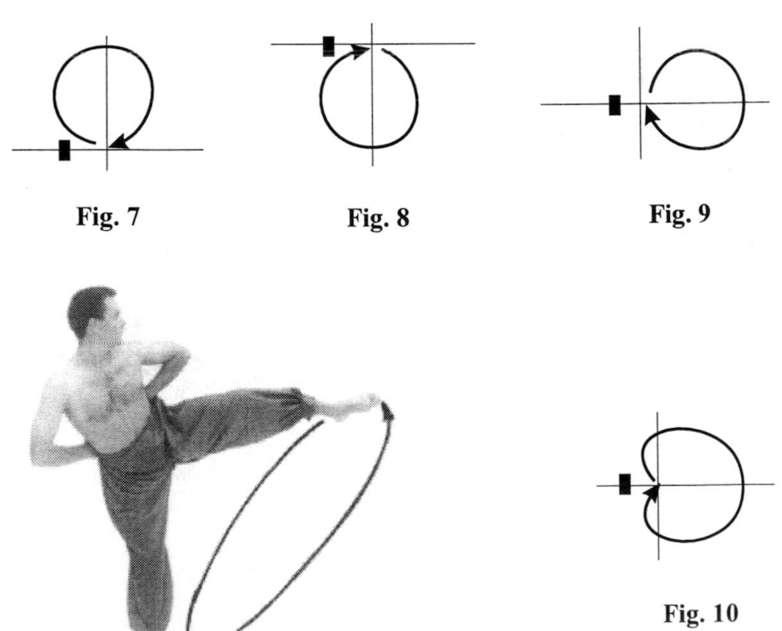

Fig. 10

Photo. 82

These movements, accordingly, are comprised of front, side and back subspace movements. They are performed several times in succession without stopping, one side after another. These movements should not be excessively broad, but one should try to do them smoothly and radially. The toes should move low above the floor level with the foot rotating as if continuing a whip-like movement of the leg. The support leg is always slightly bent. It is necessary to have the feeling that the foot is gripping the floor and to instantly react to any deviations in the gravity center and compensate for them.

When such circular movements are performed easily and correctly in both directions, it is possible to progress to the next stage of the first level. At this level, the integration of front and back subspaces takes place, performing longitudinal spiral movements with one leg (Fig. 11), and side subspaces during transversal spiral movements with one leg (Fig. 12). These are performed in the rhythm of the breath, several times without stopping, one side after the other. The movements should be smooth and radial.

After that, it is necessary to start differentiating longitudinal and transversal movements into quarters by using relevant steps forward, backward and to the sides (Fig. 13 a-c). These steps are made in pairs by the same leg, starting from the initial position of standing, feet together and leg slightly bent, and returning to this position at the end. In the beginning, it is necessary to practice clockwise steps, and then counter-clockwise. For example, the clockwise step forward goes forward following the internal arch and backward following the external arch (Fig. 13a), or the clockwise step sideways goes to the side following the front arch and back in following the back arch (Fig. 13c), etc. In total, there are four clockwise steps and four counter clockwise steps.

Trajectory of the right leg, top view

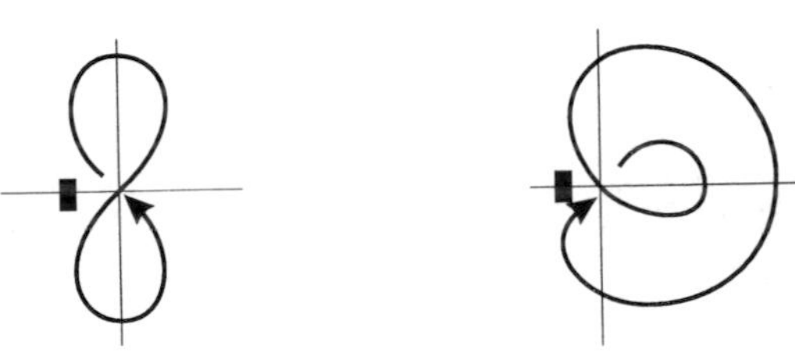

Fig. 11 **Fig. 12**

Trajectory of the right leg, top view

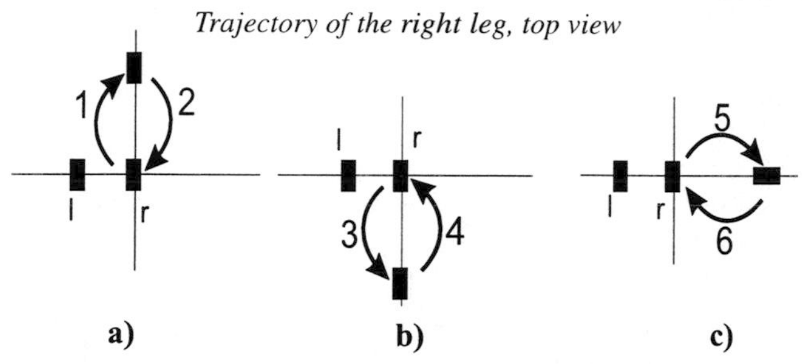

Fig. 13

The difference between the side step following the small arch and on using the big arch is not the width of the step alone, but the height at which the leg is raised. Thus, if using a small-arch step, the leg remains bent and the foot moves high above the floor following the front arch (5) and back arch (6) (Fig. 14). In the big-arch step the leg is completely straight and raises high above the floor moving outside (7) (Fig. 15a) and on the reverse trajectory it moves inside (8) (Fig. 15b). (A similar step to the side (outward) is often used in Sumo wrestling to take the main position).

When these steps have been learned, it is possible to begin to practice longitudinal or transversal steps with two legs one by one. In longitudinal movements, there are four options of such steps and four more in transversal. Such movements should begin from the initial standing position, feet together and legs slightly bent.

Trajectory of the right leg, top view

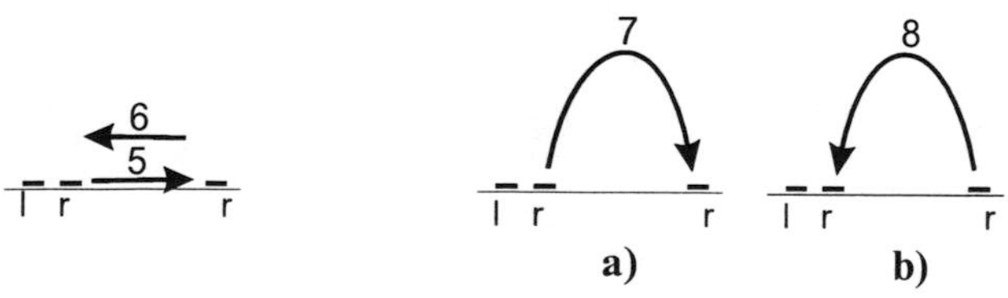

Fig. 14 **Fig. 15**

Longitudinal movements

Option one

Step forward with the right leg following the internal arch (1) then bring the left leg forward following the external arch (4), (Fig. 16a). This is followed by backward steps following the same trajectories, but in reverse sequence.

Option two

Step forward with the right leg following the external arch (2) then bring the left leg forward following the internal arch (3), (Fig. 16b). This is followed by backward steps following the same trajectories, but in reverse sequence.

Option three

Step forward with the right leg following the internal arch (1) then bring the left leg forward following the internal arch (3), (Fig. 16c). This is followed by backward steps following the same trajectories, but in the reversed sequence.

Option four

Step forward with the right leg following the external arch (2), then bring the left leg forward following external arch (4), (Fig. 16d). This is followed by backward steps following the same trajectories, but in reverse sequence.

Trajectory of legs, top view

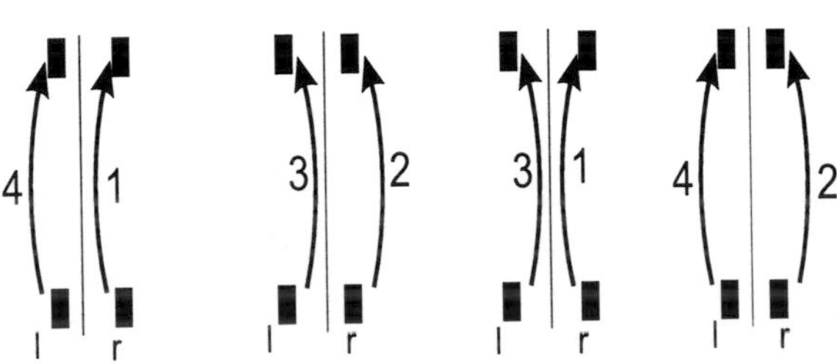

Fig. 16

Transversal movements

Option one

Step to the side with the right leg following the front arch of the small loop (5) then step to the same side with the left leg following the back of the small loop arch (6), (Fig. 17a). This is followed by steps to the opposite side, following the same trajectories, but in reverse sequence.

Option two

Step to the side with the right leg following the front low arch of the small loop (5) then step to the same side with the left leg following the high arch of the big loop, moving inside (8), (Fig. 17b). This is followed by steps to the opposite side, following the same trajectories, but in the reverse sequence. The high outward step becomes nothing but a second arch of the big high loop (7) (see above).

Option three

Step to the side with the right leg following the back arch of the small loop (6) then step to the same side with the left leg following the front arch of the small loop (5), etc. (Fig. 17c). This is followed by steps to the opposite side following the same trajectories, but in the reverse sequence.

Option four

Step to the side with the right leg following the back low arch of the small loop (6) then step to the same side with the left leg following the high arch of the big loop, moving inside (8), (Fig. 17d). This should be followed by steps to the opposite side following the same trajectories, but

Trajectory of legs, top view

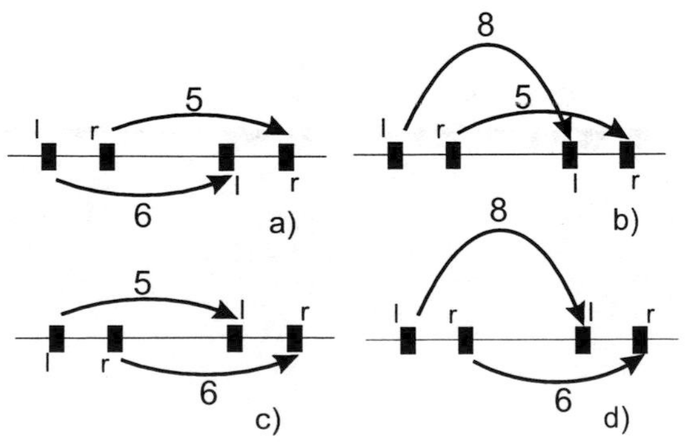

Fig. 17

in reverse sequence. The high outward step of the left leg becomes nothing but a second arch of the big high loop (7) (see above).

When practicing the steps that follow the low loop, the foot must move low just above the floor almost touching it. In the initial position (feet together) inhale and make two steps during each exhalation. Thereafter, in the initial position, make another inhalation and take another two steps, etc. When changing between the steps, slightly slow down the exhalation. All inhalations should be through the nose and all exhalations should be through the mouth.

Such steps are practiced in series by two, four, six or eight steps in succession, depending on the length of the training.

(At the advanced levels of practice these steps are performed in a more natural fashion. The trajectories of the leg movements are slightly shifted. The second leg slightly oversteps before the first leg. As a result, the first leg always starts to move from behind the second leg.)

Level Two

Arm Movements

Horizontal and vertical spiral movements comprise, respectively, horizontal and vertical subspaces, which are within the «Marginal Circle» of the arm mobility. When these movements are learned in practice and easily performed in both directions, it is possible to advance to the second level of the practice. This level is the integration of horizontal and vertical subspaces. The arms move in different subspaces controlled by independent programs. This mode of practice further develops coordination and requires a considerable increase in the degree of the concentration of attention.

In the beginning, it is necessary to learn 8 options of single-side horizontal-vertical spiral movements. These represent four pairs of sequences, each pair consisting of «mirror reflected» movements.

Movement one begins from the position when both arms are in the first quarter but in different planes: horizontal and vertical. And from this position the arms move to the same side in the following sequence: 15, 26, 37, 48, 15, etc. and in the reversed order (Photo 83 — 86).

Photos. 83 - 86

Photos. 87 - 90

Movement two is performed «mirror reflected» in the following sequence: 51, 62, 73, 84, 51, etc. or in the reversed order (Photo 87 — 90).

Photos. 91 - 94

Movement three begins from the position with the horizontal arm shifted one quarter ahead in the following sequence: 25, 36, 47, 18, 25, etc., or in the reversed order (Photo 91 — 94).

Photos. 95 - 98

Movement four is performed «mirror reflected» in the following sequence: 52, 63, 74, 81, 52, etc. or in the reversed order (Photo 95 —98).

Photos. 99 - 102

Movement five begins from the position with the horizontal arm shifted two quarters ahead in the following sequence: 35, 46, 17, 28, 35, etc., or in the reversed order (Photo 99 — 102).

Photos. 103 - 106

Movement six is performed «mirror reflected» in the following sequence: 53, 64, 71, 82, 53, etc. or in the reversed order (Photo 103 — 106).

Photos. 107 - 110

Movement seven begins from the position with the horizontal arm shifted three-quarters ahead in the following sequence: 45, 16, 27, 38, 45, etc., or in the reversed order (Photo 107 — 110).

Photos. 111 - 114

Movement eight is performed «mirror reflected» in the following sequence: 54, 61, 72, 83, 54, etc. or in the reversed order (Photo 111 — 114).

When single-side horizontal-vertical movements are learned in practice and can be easily performed in both directions, it is possible to move on to the next stage of level two, which requires multisided horizontal-vertical movements. These also consist of four pairs of sequences, and each pair consisting of «mirror reflected» movements.

Photos. 115 - 118

Movement one begins from the position with both arms in the first quarter but in different planes: horizontal and vertical. From this position the arms move in different directions in the following sequence: 15, 28, 37, 46, 15, etc. or in the reversed order (Photo 115 — 118).

Photos. 119 - 122

Movement two is performed «mirror reflected» in the following sequence: 51, 82, 73, 64, 51, etc. or in the reversed order (Photo 119 — 122).

Photos. 123 - 126

Movement three begins from the position with the horizontal arm shifted one quarter ahead in the following sequence: 25, 38, 47, 16, 25, etc., or in the reversed order (Photo 123 — 126).

Photos. 127 - 130

Movement four is performed «mirror reflected» in the following sequence: 52, 83, 74, 61, 52, etc. or in the reversed order (Photo 127 — 130).

Photos. 131 - 134

Movement five begins from the position with the horizontal arm shifted two quarters ahead in the following sequence: 35, 48, 17, 26, 35, etc., or in the reversed order (Photo 131 — 134).

Photos. 107 - 110

Movement seven begins from the position with the horizontal arm shifted three-quarters ahead in the following sequence: 45, 16, 27, 38, 45, etc., or in the reversed order (Photo 107 — 110).

Photos. 139 - 142

Movement seven begins from the position with the horizontal arm shifted three-quarters ahead in the following sequence: 45, 18, 27, 36, 45, etc., or in the reversed order (Photo 139 — 142).

Photos. 143 - 146

Movement eight is performed «mirror reflected» in the following sequence: 54, 81, 72, 63, 54, etc. or in the reversed order (Photo 143 — 146).

Leg Movements

Level two implies the integration of the front, back, and side subspaces by combining different fragments of longitudinal and transversal spiral movements in performing sequences of continual movements with one leg and a series of longitudinal and transversal steps.

When practicing continual movements with one leg, the beginning side subspaces are connected to the front and back subspaces by diagonal spiral movements. In total, there are four such sequences, performed in direct and reversed order of numbering (Fig. 18 a-d).

Trajectory of the right leg, top view

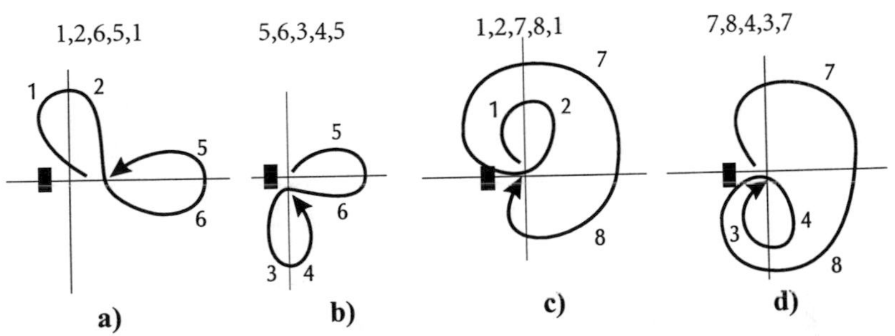

Fig. 18

After that the front and back subspaces are interconnected by one continual movement trajectory consisting of three loops, performed in direct and reversed order of numbering. In total, there are four such sequences (Fig. 19 a-d).

Trajectory of the right leg, top view

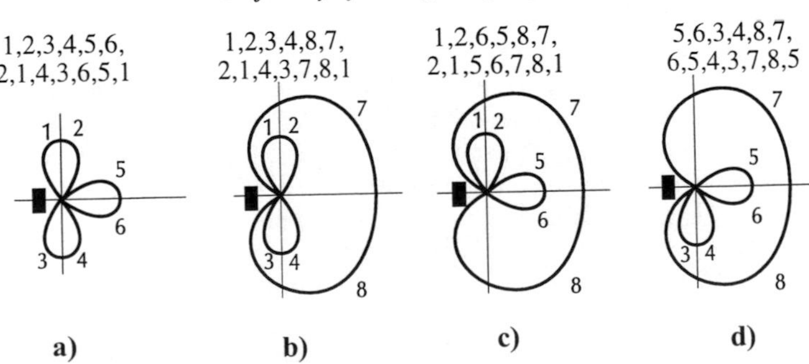

Fig. 19

As it is possible to see from these sequences, the direction of the movement of a leg is always reversed in a natural fashion. These movements are practiced in the rhythm of breath without stopping. First in one direction and then the other.

Thereafter, after mastering longitudinal and transversal spiral movements, which are connected in one continual movement trajectory, consisting, now, of four loops. In total, there are six such sequences (Fig. 20).

Trajectory of the right leg, top view

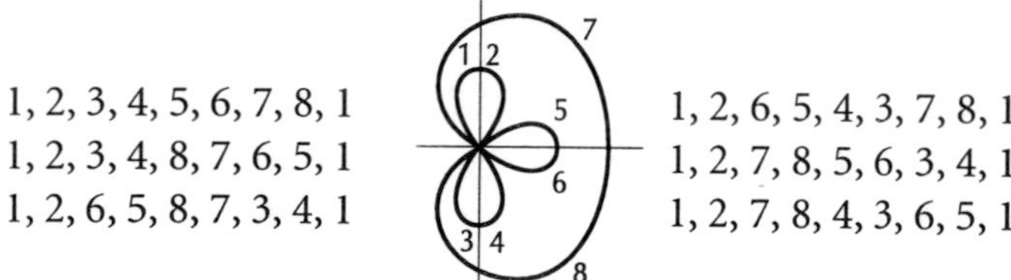

Fig. 20

All these movements should not be too broad, they should be radial, and accurately preserve balance on the supporting leg. They are practiced several times in succession, without stopping, in direct and reverse order, in the rhythm of normal breath, inhal ing through the nose and exhal ing through the mouth.

Combining different fragments of longitudinal and transversal spiral movements is also achieved by performing a series of alternating longitudinal and transversal steps. It is better to start learning them from the standing position symmetrically, with legs positioned broad and sl ightly bent in the knees. It is possible to begin with either leg. For example, put the left leg beside the right leg by making a step following the front arch of the small loop (5), and, without stopping, continuing the movement of the left leg, make a second step back in a longitudinal pass following the internal arch (3) (Fig. 21a). Thereafter, from this position, step back with the right leg, drawing it to the left leg following the internal arch (1), and, without stopping, continuing the movement of the right leg, make second step aside, to the right, in a transversal pass following the back arch (6) (Fig. 21b). After that, repeat these steps for a couple of times, alternating already known steps inward and back with the left leg, and, thereafter, step back and to the side with the right leg, etc. (Fig. 22).

Such steps should be practiced on both sides: diagonal to the right and back, and in the reversed direction, i. e., to the left and forward. From the initial standing position (legs positioned wide), draw the right leg to

Trajectory of legs, top view

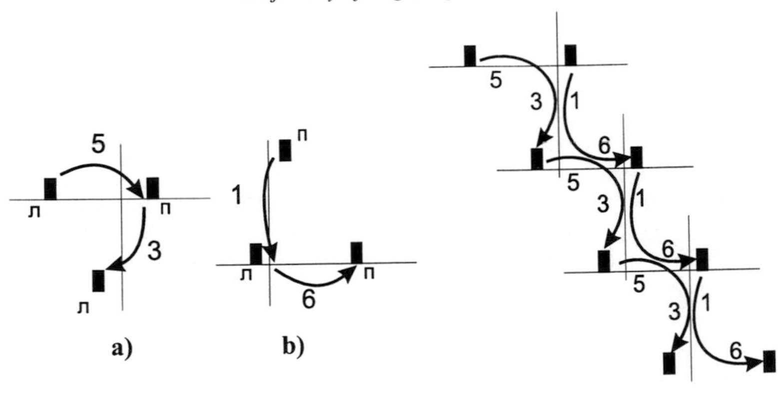

Fig. 21 **Fig. 22**

the left - step inward following the back arch (6). Then, without stopping, continuing the movement with the right leg, make the second step forward in a longitudinal pass following the internal arch (1) (Fig. 23a). Thereafter, from this position, step forward with the left leg, drawing it to the right leg following the internal arch (3), and, without stopping, continuing the movement of the left leg, make second step aside, to the left, in a transversal pass following the forward arch (5) (Fig. 23b). After that, repeat these steps for several times, alternating already known steps inward and forward with the right leg followed by the step forward and to the side with the left leg, etc. (Fig. 24).

Trajectory of legs, top view

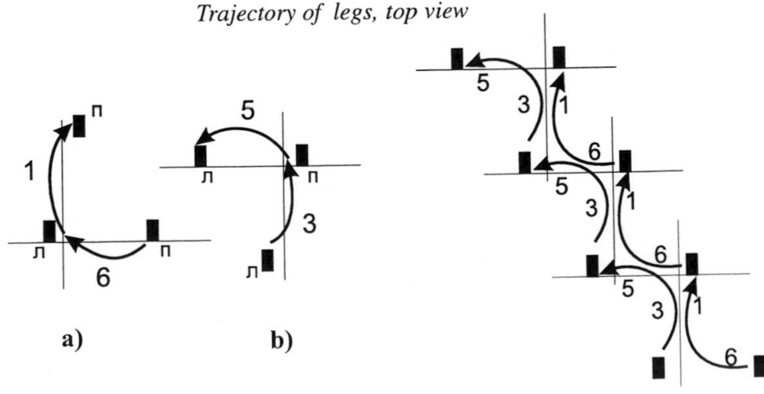

Fig. 23 **Fig. 24**

To begin the motion backward with the right leg, the general direction of the movement will be done diagonally to the left, and all steps will be done «mirror reflected». For example, bring together the right leg to the left, step inward following the front arch (5), and, without stopping, continue the motion with the right leg, make a second step back in the longitudinal pass following the internal arch (3) (Fig. 25a). Thereafter, step with the left leg back drawing it close to the right leg following the internal arch (1), and, without stopping, continue the motion with the left leg. Make a second step to the side, to the left in the transversal pass following the back arch (6) (Fig. 25b). After that, these steps are alternately repeated for several times using the already known steps inward and back with the right leg followed by a step back and to side with the left leg, etc. (Fig. 26).

These steps should be practiced in both directions. After several steps moving with a left and back bias, it is necessary to reverse the motion to bias right and forward. In that case from the initial position, standing legs spread wide, draw the left leg to the right by making an inward step following the back arch (6), and, without stopping, continue the motion with the left leg making the second step forward in the longitudinal pass following the internal arch (1) (Fig. 27a). Thereafter step forward with the right leg, draw it to the left leg following the internal arch (3), and, without stopping, continue moving the right leg, make a second step to the side, to the right in the transversal pass following the front arch (5) (Fig. 27b). Thereafter, alternately repeat these steps for several times using already known steps inward and forward with the left leg followed by the steps forward and to the side with the right leg, etc. (Fig. 28).

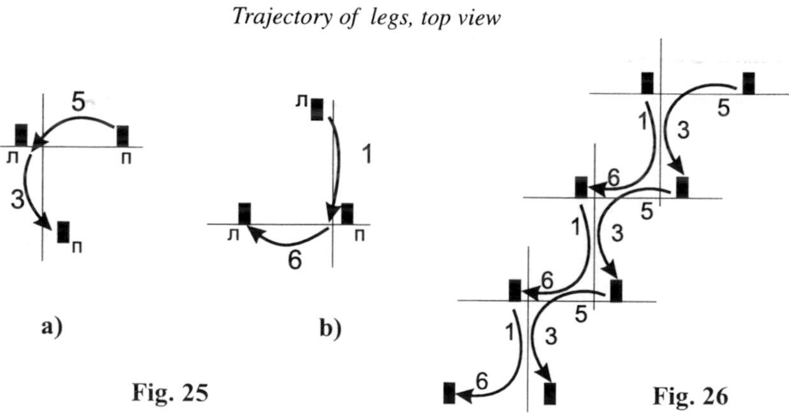

Fig. 25

Fig. 26

Trajectory of legs, top view

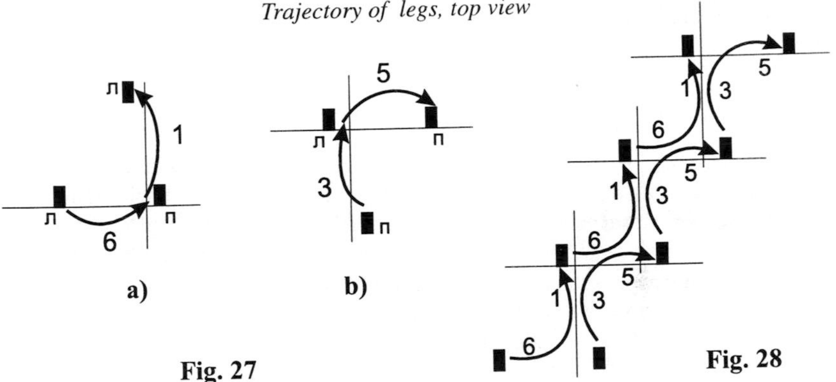

Fig. 27

Fig. 28

When these steps are learned in practice, these should be practiced in a complete form, i. e., it is necessary to make an equal number of steps back and forward to both sides. In that case the general movement will make a diagonal cross (Fig. 29).

Trajectory of legs, top view

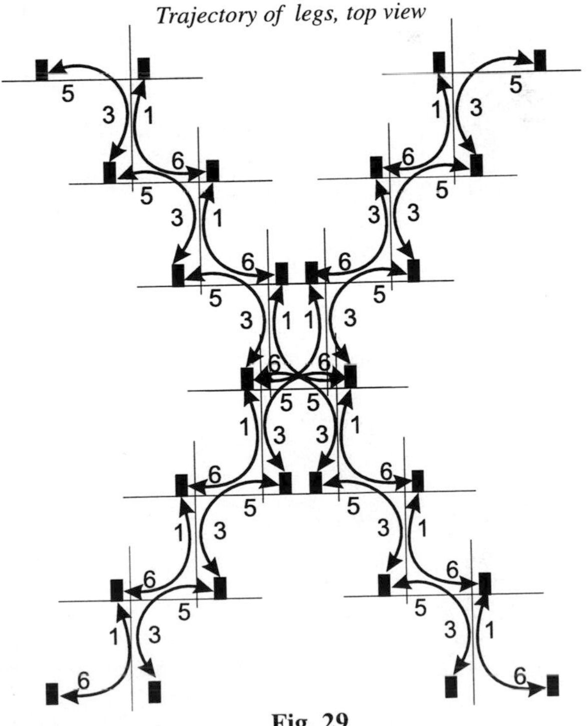

Fig. 29

SUBSEQUENT LEVELS OF THE PRACTICE

The scope of this book does not allow the depiction of all levels of practicing the Dance of Shiva, but the first two are sufficient to develop for several months, or possibly, years. By the time of completion of this training program, there will be new publications containing the next levels of training algorithms. To introduce their content to interested readers, it is possible to mention that by transition from level to level together with the increase of the training form, the spiral motion with legs becomes higher and higher, and the steps become wider and more low-set, although the general principle of spiral trajectories always remains unchanged.

Photo. 147

Photo. 148

Photo. 149

Photo. 150

Subsequent levels use the inertia of the arms and legs to transfer motion momentum to the body and secure its free twirling motion in the dimensional space. These levels complete the integration of all sixty four, horizontal, vertical, and horizontal-vertical arm movements, complete integration of all longitudinal, transverse, and longitudinal-transverse leg movements, and complete integration of all arm and leg movements between themselves. And only in the final stages, when there is sufficient skill and the culture of movements have gone far from the primitive and have become very sophisticated, is the mode of the Free Flow used. Moreover if at initial stages of practice, the hands are always kept stiff and flat, at the advanced levels of the practice the spiral motion of the arms is also extended to the hands. In this case the fingers always move

Photo. 151

Photo. 152

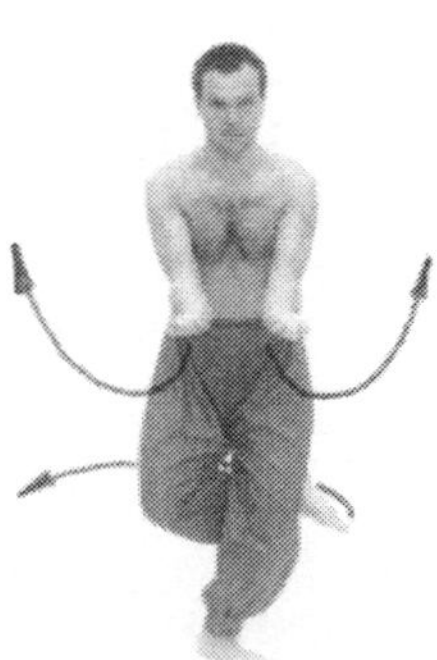

Photo. 153

Photo. 154

simultaneously with the arms and hands, folding in a pinch and opening like a fan.

As the simplest example of such integration and simultaneous control of the movements of arms and legs, it is possible to be given an exercise that is practiced even at the first level. It is practiced in the position standing on one leg, the second leg and both arms move simultaneously. In this case the leg moves along a longitudinal spiral trajectory and the arms move symmetrically (or shifted two quarters) along horizontal (Photos 147 — 150) or vertical (Photos 151 — 154) spiral trajectories. The fragments of such movements of arms and legs in the Dance of Shiva, with simultaneous control of three sectors, are engraved in the canonized statue of Shiva dancing in the fire aureole. This famous statue is well known to the whole world. Unfortunately, due to the lack of communication between the true Keepers of the Tradition and the producers of these statues, the latter are completely ignorant about the technique of the Dance of Shiva. And, copying these statues from other copies over the centuries, they have made these statues with annoying inaccuracies.

ASSOCIATING MOVEMENTS OF THE SPINE WITH THE BREATH

Practicing movements of the arms and legs in the Dance of Shiva, the corresponding momentums of forces change the form of the spine. And there are two general approaches to take when performing these movements. The first and simplest one is to constantly strive to keep the spine fixed and straight. This demands sufficient control of the muscles manipulating the position of the spine to achieve this fixed state. The second approach demands knowledge of various movements of the spine, which naturally occur when moving the arms and the legs. Having such knowledge, movements of arms and legs are consciously accompanied with relevant special movements of the spine. These movements facilitate a more natural motion of the arms and legs. They also substantially increase the psychic-energy effect of such exercises, since as spinal formation has a powerful impact on the vegetative nervous system. In this case the impact will be roughly the same as when performing basic *Vinyasas* with or without spinal manipulation. Symmetrically horizontal or vertical movements with both arms result in the deepest amplitude of spinal motions. In this case, whip-like movements of the spine are conveyed throughout the whole body to the neck and head, from coccyx to the crown of head. Such motions

Photo. 155

Photo. 156

Photo. 157

Photo. 158

Photo. 159

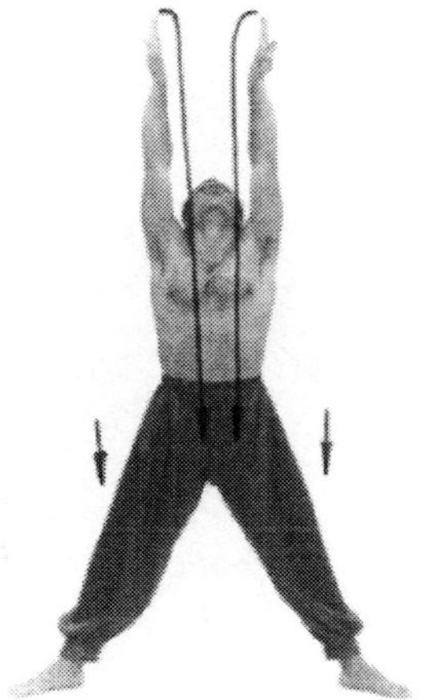

Photo. 160

Photo. 161

Photo. 162

Photo. 163

Photo. 164

are the best assistance for expanding and compressing the chest. Additionally, they are accompanied by powerful and complete breath. All inhalations are done through the nose, and all exhalations, like in cleansing breath, are done through the mouth. Moreover such movements of the arms and the spine are accompanied by rhythmic squats on broadly-position feet. In this case, simultaneously with intensive exhalation, the head is bent forward, the ribcage stooped and compressed, the arms move down and making a slight squat on two legs. And during the next deep inhalation the head is tipped back, the ribcage is opened by a «not deep back bend», the arms move up and the legs are completely straightened (Photo 155 — 159 and 160 — 164). In essence, the breath, as practiced in such exercises, is a synthesis of the *complete yogi breath, cleansing Ha-breath, and Kapalabhati Pranayama*, each of which possess a number of powerful and useful effects.

What concerns spinal motion during the practice of asymmetric horizontal, vertical or horizontal-vertical movements of arms with shifts are that they usually lack harmony. And they are not so deep in amplitude as sine-curve movements. Repeating such first and second level movements for many times results in an asymmetric formation of the chest. This causes different volumes of air in the left and right lungs. Each of these movements sets a special rhythm of oscillatory effects on the spine. By remembering this rhythm as a melody, it can be oriented by the vibration of the spine and maintain this melody, paying almost no attention to the mutual placement of the arms. In this case the correlation of quarters will be preserved automatically.

Each of the asymmetric motions with shifted quarters has its own spinal rhythm and «vibration melody». These are hard to describe, but easy to feel in the process of practice.

ELEMENTS OF THE DANCE OF SHIVA IN YOGA TRAINING COMPLEXES

Since the movements of the Dance of Shiva help to increase the concentration of attention, it is reasonable to practice them at the beginning of the training complex. In this case the energy of attention which is usually spread on the periphery will be quickly distracted and returned from all kinds of contacts, which had preceded the training, into the ancient state. And all of these will give the starting flow of Power.

More over practicing the elements of the Dance of Shiva activates the energy flows in peripheral channels and blows the Fire inside them. It is also a perfect physical warming-up for more complicated exercises, especially in the cold time of the year.

Symmetrical spiral arm movements, synchronized with spinal motion and intensive breathing, are one of the most efficient means to restore and increase the potential of the psychic-energy structure in training complexes. Therefore, these are built in Yoga training algorithms in places requiring rest, restoration or «acceleration of Power». Such hyperventilating movements and breath are often practiced standing on two feet in a transverse pass and also in a longitudinal pass, on the knees, sitting on the floor and in other positions.

More over the culture of arm, leg and spinal movements of the Dance of Shiva also serve as the basis for all the transitional movement techniques connecting *Asanas*. And in addition, fragments of the circular and spiral movements are used in performing different grips with hands in *Asanas* when one changes the initial positions of legs, in different *Vinyasas* or *Asanas*. Therefore, absolutely all movements of arms, legs and spine in training complexes, both basic and auxiliary, have special techniques that must be practiced in a conscious manner.

In general, the Dance of Shiva may be practiced as a separate type of training, as it has an independent goal and complete arsenal of technical devices to achieve this goal, which makes its technique independent and self-sufficient.

Using the elements of the Dance of Shiva has advantages for the practitioner of oriental martial arts. The motor centers of the brain that are acquainted with the movement algorithms of the Dance of Shiva, have stable schemes of various combinations of moves formed inside. Many of these moves will obviously be unexpected for the contestant's opponent who knows a lesser number of all possible kinds of combinations. This «arsenal» will, no doubt, be useful not only to fighters, but also to magicians, considering life in society as a vast field for practicing the «art of stalking».

THE JOY OF DOLPHIN MYSTERY

«Dolphin», the basic style of underwater speed swimming, is one of the most efficient types of cyclic *Vinyasa.* Looking at the body position and the dynamics of movements of this style in terms of Yoga technique, it is possible to see a combination of the most efficient technical devices from the arsenal of Yoga. In this swimming style, the body performs rhythmical wave-like movements with the spine, from shoulders to pelvis and with the legs, from thighs to toes. These whip-like movements resemble a classical yogi *Vinyasa* «abdomen down». The necessity to overcome the water pressure by using a mono-flipper (one large flipper designed for both feet) with a surface of not more than half a square meter, requires a great effort from the largest muscle groups: abdominal press, straight back muscles, buttocks, leg quadriceps, and calf muscles. But these are the same muscles that accompany the most efficient yogi *Pranayamas,* facilitating the achievement of psychic-energy effects, which are directly related to the spiritual goals of Yoga.

In the «dolphin» style, the arms are raised and stretched above the head, and the head is tipped up and back by the muscles in the back of the neck. This position corresponds to the yogi *Setu Bandha.* The eyes are raised up and look up from under the forehead foreword, which corresponds to the position of *Sambhavi Mudra* in Yoga. These positions of arms and eyes promote the flow of energy along the spine from the lower to upper centers.

More over technically correct swimming in the dolphin style is accompanied with long breath delays after inhalation. To make a mono-flipper stroke efficient and made in a layer of water rather than in the air (swimming on the surface may cause the mono-flipper to show above the surface), the swimmer quickly inhales «on the move», delays the breath and slightly dives. He swims at a shallow depth with his breath delayed until he requires a new portion of oxygen. Then, without stopping, he slightly emerges, makes a sharp full exhalation, then quick full inhalation, delays breath and slightly dives «on the move», etc., similar to a swimming dolphin. Along with these dives and breath delays after inhalation, the swimmer makes several strokes with the mono-flipper by making a wave motion with his body (spine) and legs. These kicks require the powerful operation of muscle groups. But these are the operations that are used in the main classical Yoga *Vinyasas.* And these are the operations that are made with the breath delayed during the practice of *Ujayi Pranayama,* but march more powerful.

Therefore, strange as it may seem, the «dolphin» style of underwater speed swimming contains all most efficient technical devices of Yoga, required to «raise the *Kundalini*» and make spiritual progress in Yoga.

It is known that the «raising of *Kundalini*» is accompanied with a number of profound physical, psychic-energy, and spiritual transformations. And although these are not the subjects of detailed discussion in this chapter, it should be noted that such effects, as increasing the sexual energy potential, cleansing energy channels, perceiving human nature, and a general state of contentment and joy, changing of the outlook with respect to everything that happens in the life are parts of this raising. And it is interesting to note that, according to the personal acknowledgments of many well-known under water sportsmen: the USSR sport masters, the World Class sport masters, members of the former USSR national teams in spite of the fact that they did not have any esoteric knowledge, they often noticed some «strange» phenomena. These sportsmen could not help paying attention to them. These are: hyper-sexual potential, complete breath delays during sleep, spontaneous vibrating flows in the body, rampant joy pouring out, change in perception of the world and many other phenomena. They hesitated to talk about these things, thinking themselves a bit «abnormal». The ones who later started to practice Yoga on the basis of the experience of the breathing-motion they already had, the concentration of attention and Power of Spirit, achieved the raising of the «*Kundalini* energy» in half a year. They used already acquired achievements of the motion-breath, concentration of attention and the Power of Spirit. At the same time, many Yoga veterans with many years of experience were not able to achieve such motion of the organizing Power at all. They remained theorists for their whole life, and in the depth of their soul doubt the existence of *Kundalini* and the reasons to strive to «raise» it… But the mystery of the joy of dolphins is in the nature of their natural movements…

Part V

POWER

BIO-NUCLEAR ENERGY

The body's bio-nuclear process has not been studied completely. But practical observations show that after practicing exercises that deeply stretch the muscles there is a feeling of the «in-flow» of free energy. This energy is used in Yoga to expand consciousness.

It is known that the straining of muscles is controlled by the impulses of the nervous system. When muscles tense, the chromosomes of the cells forming the muscle tissue slide into one another. This process results in the consumption of life energy.

Interestingly, there is not usually complete relaxation of the muscle tissue cells in a so called «normal» state. They are likely to possess a residual potential of the strain, i. e. stiffening, which constantly consumes life energy.

Stretching the muscles, the chromosomes slide out of each other. This process results in a feeling of free energy in the system, which now is not consumed by the residual «normal» tone of such stiffness.

Now it is not searched to which the extreme stretching of the cells will lead, when a gap (uncovered free space) between the chromosomes is opened, has not been studied yet. Possibly, this causes an additional potential for actively generating energy.

It would be useful to note that long-term *Tha*-orientation in training that is dominated by stretching and relaxation exercises, gives a lot of free energy, and, of course, develops plasticity and flexibility of the body. But with the lapse of time, this tendency «drains» into the Spirit and starts to manifest itself as the «*Tha* of the Spirit».

A man who finds it harder and harder to concentrate or manage to do things on time, etc. expresses this. Laziness easily roots in the tendency towards relaxation. But this is the completion of any forms of development and the evolution in this man's consciousness.

The decrease of residual strain in the tissues (purification from *Ha* quality) causes reduction of the discharging energy to practically zero.

What is the sense of further practice? And where is the way out?.. The answer is: in strength training, to obtain the external energy of *Ha* quality.

The point is to use regular physical loads to overcome the Force of Gravitation. The muscles were created with the purpose of overcoming the gravitational force of one's own body or external objects during particular movements. All muscle activity is related to overcoming the force of gravitation. The basis of lifting the elements of your own body, or overcoming the weight of a dumb-bell is absolutely the same. Stretching rubber or springs is overcoming of the force of gravitation between the atoms of the materials being moved (rubber or metal). Whereas pushing off the Earth when running, or pushing water during swimming is the overcoming of the force of gravity that exists between the body and the earth.

Look at this phenomenon from the following point of view. Muscles are «mouths» which «eat» the energy of gravitation. And to preserve and strengthen your health, your body requires regular gravitational feeding. This results in a special type of energy, which is accumulated as a training form, and gives the brain centers the ability to adjust to the load and act in a powerful fashion when necessary.

If you feel perfect, then instead of wasting your power and health for worthless «lusts» or on something futile, it is better to do intensive training, turning the available active energy into the training form.

This is similar to storing something. For example, if you have some money and do not want to lose it gambling, but put it in a bank account and collect interest until the time you need to buy something really important. And if in the modern world, some people may be rich, but can anybody really boast of a real abundance of health? Only the young and inexperienced may think that their health will be eternal, but, as a rule, this illusion is cleared away very soon.

Power training allows one to accumulate gravitational energy in the training form.

What follows is **the algorithm of end-to-end consumption and the sublimation of gravitational energy**, which one should understand and learn to use in practice:

Ha-exercises (strength) allows the accumulation of gravitational energy at the physical level, whereas *Tha*-exercises (stretching) convert it to a more refined psychic-energy structure, where it appears as free energy. Subsequent breathing exercises direct it to the brain, charged with additional energy expands the «band» of your perception range, resulting in the ability to «See Outside the Limits». The spiritual experience acquired as the result of such vision allows one to «live a life of several «normal» people, who live all of their lives without going beyond the limits of «normal» perception range.

Wisdom comes with Spiritual experience, and then life acquires True Sense.

It would be useful to note that the perception range of some «esoterically advanced» individuals, flying in the clouds, remains narrow because they ignore powerful training. The attraction of Heavenly forces dominates the forces of the Earth's attraction, and these people have no understanding of current events and the actual status of things. It is absolutely necessary for them to balance their energy with ordinary strength-based training in pure yogi's complexes or training in a weight-lifting gym with out any esoteric speculations and reminiscences. This can «ground» anybody in a fast and efficient manner.

So, if you have formed the intent to go till the end, complete your intention without complexes and prejudices, understanding the essence of phenomena occurring during the training. It is possible to use of any developments in sports science and use the best training tools of professional athletes.

And if Yoga's training complexes will prove to be unpracticable because of an extreme body mass which is difficult to raise then it is necessary to use special weight machines for the development of weak behind groups of muscles and reducing body mass.

Bionuclear effects have place and at different social contacts. So, for example when people break undesirable relations a free energy also liberates. This energy may be sublimated or used for formation of new ties with other people.

Unreadiness to part with people in case of their death or one-sided decision to part comes to the loss of energy by those who are not ready or do not want to part. And this loss of energy will continue until the necessity to part is accepted without residual regret as regards this.

TEMPLE OF POWER

One who understands the essence of Yoga sees Universal Links in eve rything that surrounds him. He is free from complexes and is not burdened with prejudices.

Where Yoga ends, Tantra begins. The Tantric sight is Energetic Vision and Thinking in every situation, when you seem to be far from Yoga…

A weight-lifting gym is the Temple of Power, a magic space of multidirectional effusion of the Gravitational Force…

Weight is always active, attacking Power. And the strategy of conscious interaction between them determines the future results…

Treat training machines as agents redirecting the Gravitational Force Vector under different angles with respect to your body. Absorb this force, since action equals counteraction. And at the very moment that pulls the handle of a training machine its Power is transmitted into the body and becomes one's own.

Do not follow the goal of bodybuilding, which is the chase for muscle mass. Do not use excessive weights. Do not lose the central idea of interacting with the Power. Otherwise, you will accumulate micro-injuries in joints, tendons and muscles, which will gradually change the structure of your muscles, the nature of the movements and the state of the psyche. In some cases, this may result in an injury that imposes long-term restrictions in the development of yoga training. Or, if one has a weak Spirit, you it is possible fall under the control of the false spirit of external forms (which is wide spread abroad) and lose the essence of spirituality, which was received from the ancestors...

When using training equipment, it is necessary to coordinate movements and breathing in exactly the same fashion as in yogi training. Remember three main breathing rules:

1. When straining muscles and overcoming any weight, make a powerful and noisy exhalation through the mouth, and inhalation through the nose, relaxing the muscles in the retreat phase of the exercise.
2. (The second rule dominates the first rule) If the exercise is connected with changing the form of the chest and abdomen, their compression with the forward bend of the body should be accompanied by an exhalation, whereas opening them by bending back should be accompanied with an inhalation.
3. There are a number of paradoxical exceptions.

Try to feel them and find them in the course of the training...

The initial stage of training should be at a medium or low speed, using moderate light weights. This is much better than using heavy weights at a high speed. By doing this, the risk of injury is reduced and the joints are not worn out, but the result of training is just as efficient.

Investigating new exercises requires determination and repetitions, which cuts the psychic flow of the training state, but develops a creative approach and the ability to find new ways to solve old problems...

Receive joy from realizing to use the instrument correctly. The Master is delighted to have the Power and Grace of perfect control the instrument...

To prevent consciousness from degradation in the course of Power training, it is neccesary to concentrate the attention to the Universal Links...

Portioned application of your Personal Power, which interacts, with the Power «emitted» by a training machine, develops controlling structures...

Use *Bandhas* to achieve super-power.

Fuse mental activity with the sense of motion... Accumulating Power is only possible when the practice becomes Doing Nothing.

Realize biochemical transformations during the course of training...

Do not be distracted from the continual flow of feelings in intervals between attempts, or when changing machines...

Use muscle *Pranayama...*

Music always has a Master in Spirit. Music in a training gym may cause conditions that «whip up» and force training. This forced energy kindles emotions and results in becoming tired quickly, or the Personal Spirit may also fall under its influence... The flow should be forced only if there is sufficient amounts of free energy from an excessively developed training form... And in this event the Personal Spirit remains free...

Be alert and remember that dropping a weight or moving the weights of the machine may cause injuries...

Avoid surrendering to the goals and thoughts of an athlete. They know how to do exercises correctly, and it is possible to learn this skill from them, but they do not always realise what they are doing at the psychic-energy level. They accumulate gravitational energy in their muscles, but do not stretch the muscles afterwards to transform it into «refined bodies». Nor do they develop their psychic-energy structure and consciousness.

And remember that you are a temporary visitor in a weight-lifting gym. This is a hospital for modern people, where they walk on crutches and use artificial limbs. And your task is to get well as soon as possible and leave its walls, and beginning complete natural yoga training with all its strength-based manipulations using only the weight of own body.

MODERN SHAMANISM

Instructors of various types of group training, be it Yoga, martial arts, shaping, dances or aerobics, which follow the «follow me» principle sooner or later deal with SOMETHING mysterious and strange, i. e., group transformation of consciousness.

The group Spirit in various types of training may, of course, be completely different. But this phenomenon is always present. The longer the group has been together, the more powerful the group Spirit.

Overcoming physical loads during the course of any training is in one way or another connected with super-efforts, requiring abnormal psychic durability.

Each «leader-instructor», striving to provide psychic support to his «followers», tries to lead the trainees into transformed states of consciousness. He helps them overcome difficulties and lose their sense of pain, uncertainty or fear of the impossible during training.

Depending on his talent and experience, he manages to transform them for better or worse, and eventually he understands that some magic takes place between him and his followers.

He is in the center of attention. He is an active psychic-energy center. He creates and controls «magic space», whereas the «followers» do their best to play up to him and become more and more submerged in this space, gradually experiencing the ecstasy of group resonance.

Newcomers usually do not understand this, but are subjected to IT. And IT pulls them inside. And this process is so fast that they do not understand how they manage to do something that seemed impossible fantastic for them yesterday.

When training comes to an end, everybody leaves happy and «psychically cleaned». They feel like winners, who have engaged in a heroic effort and have successfully surmounted an unbelievable challenge...

A miracle happened...

In essence, these group psychic-energy actions are nothing but a modern form of shamanism.

HATHA-YOGA — METHOD OF RAJA-YOGA

Presently, there is a wide spread mistaken opinion that Hatha-Yoga is a system, which only includes the initial limbs of Raja-Yoga, which is also called Ashtanga-Yoga (eight-limbs Yoga) Pantanjali. Some think that it comprises the first four limbs: *Yama, Niyama, Asana,* and *Pranayama.* Some ignore the first two branches and think that Hatha-Yoga only refers to *Asana* and *Pranayama.* And others speak of Hatha-Yoga exclusively as just the practice of *Asanas.*

The basis for these opinions has been the first sutra from «*Hatha-Yoga-Pradipika*» by Swatmarama. In this sutra he says, «I worship Shiva, who taught the science of Hatha-Yoga, which is a stage that leads to achieving the peaks of Raja-Yoga». Taking this idea further, analysts concluded that Hatha-Yoga simply meant the initial levels of Raja-Yoga.

As a matter of fact, this sutra tells of Hatha-Yoga as a dialectic method of Raja-Yoga. Dialectics in this case means understanding the truth through the unity and struggle of contradictions. In Yoga, these mutually complementary opposites are *Ha* and *Tha* qualities.

Of course, these are easily noticed at the third and fourth limbs of Ashtanga-Yoga, i. e., during the practice of *Asanas* and *Pranayamas.* Here, *Ha* and *Tha* are usually connected with the straining and relaxing of par ticular muscle groups and with the two phases of breath: inhalation and exhalation. But what then do the initial two limbs of Hatha-Yoga, i. e., moral and ethical principles, self-discipline and hygiene have to do with this?

It is not nesessary to think that Hatha-Yoga comprise only the first four limbs of Ashtanga-Yoga, because it also deals with the «fine» controlling structures of the human organism and to a lesser extent with the «coarse» instruments.

Pratiahara and *Dharana* require active control of the direction of the attention rays and energetic flows. This is *Ha* at the level of personal Power of Will (Spirit). *Dhyana* and *Samadhi* are passive contemplation and *Tha* at the level of Personal Power of Will (Spirit). But the organizing Power, although a «fine» matter, is still material. And these practices, as all matter in the Universe, are covered by the principle of dualism (*Ha-Tha*).

According to the «*Yoga-sutras*» of Patanjali, there are seven types of *Samadhi.* And only achieving Nirvikalpa-Samadhi is liberation, a step beyond matter and dualism, or *Nirvana* as it is called in Buddhist Tradition.

The first two limbs, *Yama* and *Niyama*, really become possible only after achieving *Samadhi.* Their being placed first in the list shows the strategic genius cource of Patanjali. He suggests «starting from the completion» and laying a foundation that facilitates fast development and evolution of your consciousness, without wasting time for delusions and making karmic mistakes.

The dialectic *Ha-Tha* method of *Raja-Yoga* *is* the best assistance to realizing various phenomena and processes during your course of practice at *any* stage of yogi development. Ultimately it allows you to balance the opposing forces and achieve Complete Satisfaction and Serene Peace in the harmony of dualism and the Unity of Universe.

THE WAY OF THE LEADER

Raja means, «king».

Raja-Yoga practice facilitates the understanding of your own nature and your mission in life. It liberates you from harmful evolutionary habits and delusions conditioned by cultural norms. The exploits of day-to-day training develops self-control, assist in accumulating life energy and strengthens the Power of Spirit. «Opening» Chakras as a result of «raising the Kundalini» gives you a deep Vision of human nature and Universal Links; abnormal Will Power; absolute control of the senses, speech, and thoughts; the gift of persuasion and many other effects. In the course of development along the Yoga Pathway, the nature of a human automatically manifests the qualities of a Leader.

«Normal» people usually do not realise why they follow a particular man's ideas and actions. It is just that when they feel a store of knowledge, experience, self-control, assurance, and the Power of Spirit in his actions, their sub-conscious automatically reacts, and they are attracted to this man. Often the essence of his ideas and actions have no meaning, but the self-control, assurance and the Power of Spirit are absolutely required for a real Leader.

There are numerous examples can be given when all those that hear doubtful ideas, expressed with «Spirit», unconditionally accept them. After a time, people wonder how they «swallowed» such crap. This happens because of the assurance and «power disposition», i. e., relation of the Personal Power of the speaker and the audience, which decides everything.

It should be remembered that the emergence of leadership qualities is not a goal in itself, and is a *consequence* of the increased Power of Spirit. And leadership is not an award, but a *trial* for moral qualification to further spiritual development. With the development of Personal Power, a man's actions become more and more powerful and the level of karmic responsibility for any deeds increase *pro rata* to the Power available to him. And among those who achieve the highest stages there are always more who have torn down than raised higher.

Those who read this and have an excessive feeling of self-importance without a Vision of the actual status of things and one's true Place in the Game of the Universe, may delude themselves and «decide(!?)» that they are now leaders and will not follow anybody or be «influenced» by anyone. But... If there is not an energy basis for this, they will only be satisfying themselves with egoistic illusions and will also be «influenced» under some concept such as the leadership concept mentioned above.

People that specifically strive to become Leaders do not achieve this because the very desire lacks high spiritual orientation, a «super-task». There is one very wise rule: «Be realist and achieve the unrealizable». Life seldom awards you an unattainable goal, but easily rewards the intermediary stages as one moves toward achieving the goal.

It is interesting to watch two or more real Leaders when their activity spheres meet. Their interaction, whether explicitly or implicitly, reminds one of a «conversation» between samurais. Few of tham are capable of remembering that they are not the «ultimate authority», that for any Power there is a Greater Power. And that any Leader, whether a saint or a prophet, is always just an ordinary performer of the plans of the Higher Hierarchy.

And one should not be afraid to follow the Leader. But should not fully dissolve in his will also, as no one can be a Leader in everything. Different experience gives Power of different quality. You can even follow a child if he is more experienced in something than you. It is the age of the Spirit, rather than the age of the body that is a key factor for leadership.

And, of course, it is not nesessary to struggle for spiritual leadership. A moderate and modest person has many more chances to preserve the Power of Spirit and be useful to people. But let the Power decide who will be a real Leader.

If your profession corresponds to your calling, strive for leadership in your professional sphere. Even if not, sincere striving for development will sooner or later result in the accumulation of experience and acceptance of leadership. Where you are not a professional, where you do not have personal talent and experience, you should not be afraid to be a common soldier, and learn to follow another Leader. That is how all the Leaders integrate within the society.

Also, you should not be afraid of the increase in the number of Leaders. Experience shows that worldwide, societies based on subordination and oppression of the leadership initiative develop slowly, or fail to develop at all. At the same time, societies that value leadership qualities flourish and become the most powerful and capable. These societies allow for the best development of individual personalities, which facilitates human evolution. And the larger the number of Leaders in the society, the more potent is the Spirit of Society.

Honest competition between Leaders should be similar to a sports contest. A good athlete is not distracted by the desires to block or disable an opponent; he is simply doing his best to achieve the best result. His advantage is Power, but not cruelty. Unfortunately, few in this world have this understanding of competition.

Those who ignore this rule by hiding behind the realities of modern life, and insisting on the necessity of «military action» aimed at disabling the contestants are only trying to convince themselves that evil action is necessary. They want to justify their personal karmic defects, as well as their inability to compete fairly. Possibly, for people who have gotten into «karmic trouble» and sinned quite enough, the yogi approach becomes impossible, and the Spirit of Unification becomes alien. The effect of cowardice inside such individuals causes a reaction that sends shivers through them when magic and Power are mentioned. They are offered a chance to become worthy and strong, but their very depths are based on nullity and weakness. Only those defected and weak-spirited are attracted by Power, but lack the Power of Spirit.

A True Leader is not guided by the desire for Power, but by how to use it correctly.

ORGANIC IMMORTALITY

Immortality becomes possible upon achieving a balance between the wear and the restoration of your biological system.

This requires the use of various means and methods to activate the restoration processes and to mitigate wear that degrades your health, destabilizes your energy structure, exhausts your body and wastes your life power. All religions in the world are aware of the Spirit of Destruction. Its energy is manifested in sinners who perform activities that are grimly followed by the degradation of health and ultimately in Death. It is the Spirit of Destruction that takes your health and your spiritual balance and Power of drug-addicts, alcoholics, heavy eaters, the sexually possessed and other immoral sinners.

Every action requires life energy. Therefore, all actions should be conscious and have meaning. It is necessary to remember that for any deed a man is paying with his life, and it is necessary to learn to avoid doing what wears your life down.

Economy of energy means its accumulation which is necessary for achieving the Goal having the sense.

It was known from the ancient time in the East and recently stated by the science in the West, that the duration of a human life and the lives of all living creatures in the Universe were determined by the number of biocycles.

Each living creature's organism has invisible «counters» measuring how long it will live. They count the duration of life by the number of breath cycles, heart beats, meals, ejaculations, stresses, diseases and other rhythms, as well as by the number of cigarettes smoked, amount of alcohol taken, drugs injected and a number of other factors that people see as their ordinary needs. This idea raises no doubts by old people who, before dying, «pay the bills» for what they have committed in their youth.

The problem lies in habits, desires, and dependencies that a man aquires then has no power to free himself of. Most often he does not try to be free because he thinks these habits and desires satisfy his sense of purpose.

It is necessary to love yourself for the sake of the Higher Sense of Life, and gradually replace harmful habits by conscious control of the physical effort, sexual energy, emotions, words, thoughts, money or any other life energy.

The body is a perfect self-restoration instrument when it is not hampered, or even better when it is assisted by cleansing its systems, psychic-energy structure, and its surroundings from any pollution. Restore body's life energy through natural training, reducing the number of free radicals, supporting biochemical balance with a pure and correct diet that contains sufficient amounts of vitamins and microelements. Train your body to adapt to different climatic conditions by water tempering, steaming in a sauna or banya, by spending maximum time in the open air or by any other means, which are already known or which will be found in future.

Long life is not a purpose in itself. It is not important how long a man lives, but most important *how* he lives. And if he lives not only in a dignified fashion and for a long time, this is just that very ideal case which allows him to rise to the top of the Perfection of the Spirit.

Leadership qualities depend on Personal Power, and Wisdom depends on the age of the Spirit, rather than on the age of the body. But there are things, which can only be realised with age of the body.

It is possible to understand that young «sages» with a cigarette in their mouth and a syringe in their pocket who understand the pitiful price of the life of a «civilized man». But it is hard to accept the weakness of the Spirit, the desire to shirk in the life, referring to hopelessness of the history course and the numerous examples of those who have fallen on the way to perfection.

FREEDOM

To make practice individualized and perfect, it should be con stantly upgraded. This may be done by a good teacher, who is always beside you, or by yourself, tete-a-tete with the Source of Infinite Knowledge.

The times of lazy people willing to follow preset models are in the past. They leave the True Pathway automatically because of their negative reaction to all independent phenomena. Their dependency possesses, a feeling of inferiority, which becomes ingrained by «living in a flock».

It is so simple to rely on the authority of the master and «sleep» for your whole life hoping to get to the Heavens without any effort... Question: «For what merits?» If everything is decided by Personal Power and the age of the Spirit, which only come through practical experience and independent realization.

One can quickly develop by following correct instructions and being inspired by the «splendor» of the master and the «grandeur» of his theories... and «RIDE» on his Power of Spirit for the whole of life. But what will happen if he disappears, but the Source of Personal Power has been forgotten?

Of course, we can understand the people who hopelessly disbelieve in themselves and do not think themselves entitled to follow an independent pathway, supposing that they will make «a mistake from which they cannot recover». Because a newcomer needs to start at some point to understand the main important, and it is necessary to reach out to assist him by providing training programs and «base complexes» of various levels and orientations. But, following the Sense of the Tradition it is important to understand that the True Path begins with the independent Challenge into the Great Unknown. And everybody always has access to the Source of Universal Knowledge even if he does not believe in it.

Real things start with the assault of the Limits of the Boundless. And the right to independence and Freedom can never be taken away from us by anybody, since all limitations are not imposed by external circumstances, but by our attitude towards those circumstances. And if one has sufficient Power of Spirit for a heroic effort, and capable of overcoming their own habits, there are no forces that can enslave or restrict Freedom. Because you are not afraid of losing something.

All fears are the causes of our habits to desire things, to own things and also the cause of our extreme fear of death as an Unknown. But diffidence in the rightness of practice means the delusion based on the weakness of Spirit.

There is not and there cannot be any improper experience, since everybody knows the common rule that a negative result is always positive.

Whole the history of the development of the Yoga Tradition illustrates how each generation of practitioners made its contribution to the creative rethinking and improvement of Yoga methods. In this century, principal steps were taken to upgrade practice, while preserving the Essence of the Tradition. Integrating all the known experience accumulated by various schools, these changes effectively achieve ancient goals by modern methods. All this was not done by Gods, but by people just like you. Because you have the same right for creative search, heroic efforts and victory in the Spirit.

WESTERN STUDENT

In the East the human master is EVERYTHING for the student. Few westerners can follow this, and it is even hard for them to understand what a master means. Western people are bred in the spirit of freedom and the very fact of being obedient to a master turns their stomachs. But eastern students are delighted with the guidance of their Master.

Western students always discuss and criticize their masters. Their feeling of self-importance is exorbitant and they often feel themselves «Great» simple because that they are spoken about, or they feel themselves «even more Greater», if they represent by themselves at least something. But, of course, they do not realize any of these ego-actions. Where can we find room for resignation, love and pure perception?

For the majority of western students this is a problem for their whole life. They wander from one school to another, doubting whether a particular school deserves to accept them. Life passes and they achieve nothing. They lack the Belief and Vision of the One in every thing. And it is the One who you should learn from.

Criticizing a teacher gives western students self-assurance and raises an ungrounded self-conceit.

Some of them, after running from one school to another, finally begin to understand something in some next school and mistakenly attribute this to the merits of the master of this last school. They negate and condemn previous masters, stating that previous masters had insufficient knowledge and taught poorly. But in this situation they do not understand that without the foundation laid by previous teachers, their «flight» in the new school would have been impossible. Just the new situation and uncertainty in oneself in the new school helped the student to concentrate better and apply all the experience they acquired before. This causes a miracle, i. e., the «flight» of new realization and skills, but they have applied the skills acquired in previous schools...

The process of teaching is endless and there is no purely «esoteric» and «exoteric» knowledge. It is just that some knowledge can be applied and some cannot. But is it possible to say with certainty that the teachers who taught to speak and read in childhood were not real spiritual teachers and have no relation to the development of adepts in the esoteric tradition? Would it be possible to go on learning and understand «real» masters without understanding language or without being able to read? It certainly depends on the method of passing on the torch of Knowledge in a particular school, but every school has semantic codes and they are not less important as conceptual components in the overall teaching process.

In fact, there should be no antagonism between former students and Masters, since the Knowledge is One. It is just some the stage of their interaction has been completed, and they have become more like a companions rather than strangers to each other. And if to look at the people whose lives are guided by completly different principles, who are at the same closer? These people? Or former teachers, the ones who conveyed all the best that they had? Masters are elder brothers, and the learning process in everybody's life is one an uninterrupted line.

It should be noted that disension between the followers of different popular schools results from self-centeredness and an exaggeration of personal merits for mercenary reasons. The names of Yoga schools, and additional specialized, patented or copyrighted, names contain the weakening traditions of separation. But there is ONLY ONE Tradition. And Yoga means Unification... which will, no doubt, save the World.

The societies which realize this and are guided by the principles of national, spiritual, professional, human and other unification develop and flourish in the World.

To follow the master and completely use his practical experience through methods and exercises developed by him. And it is absolutely necessary not just to trust in him, but to believe him without any doubts. This is a common problem for western students. They need to see the demonstration of the master's superiority with their own eyes, and this causes teachers to use various «traps» for students. These traps are not devised to harm them, but, on the contrary, for the purposes of compensating for their lack of belief, overcoming self doubts and achieving True Knowledge.

Bat there is also the reverse problem. Among the most dignified human Masters, very few are ideal ones. The same as all of us, they are only parts of the Whole and servants of the One. And it is the maximum what they can do is to reflect the uncomparable Power and Magnificence of the One. We will not speak of the fact that some of them use their position for mercenary purposes. Therefore, it is necessary to love them and learn from them, but one should never leave the watch and idealize them.

Remember that when you bow to a priest, you bow to him not as to a man, but to his cassock and divine mission. And the mystery of spiritual initiation does not lie in someone being suppressed, but in one's ability to be submissive, kneel and perceive.

HEALTH AND CONTENTMENT

Disease and health are two notions which should be distinguished in order to correctly understand and interpret the transformation of one's personality in the course of Yoga practice.

The foundation of these notions is the same source of concentrated and balanced form that supports all manifestations of human existence. If all the energies that form a human being are in a relevantly balance state, that person feels well. Moral status and mental-sensory notions of «happiness» are affected by the balance between what a man desires and what he actually has.

When a man wants more than he can have, he is dissatisfied and unhappy. When he wants less than he can have (which is an extremely rare case), he is absolutely satisfied with life, and is generous and happy.

If the external circumstances and possibilities are often connected with the personal interests and actions of other people, create the likelihood that personal transformation and adjustment toward this balance will be restricted. But there is always the possibility to expand your abilities by mastering your own potential, and you should be continuously working on yourself and your abilities. Besides the best way to find balance is to control desires and strivings since they can always be under conscious control if one has not lost control by becoming dependent on some habitual desires.

Modern social tendencies create an unlimited increase of desires and destroy what remains of Spiritual independence. These appetites whip up uncontrolled desires so that it becomes impossible for even the richest people on the planet to feel satisfaction and happiness, and they fail to find a true sense of life in their sophisticated amusements.

Balance of the desired and the attainable is mainly achieved through restraining and controlling the feelings and everything desired together with them. And this does not lead to the loss of joy and delight in life, but life simply acquires a true sense.

If somebody really reduces his needs, wishes and ambitions to the level of his possibilities, he becomes satisfied. If his needs are below his abilities, he becomes generous and capable of loving, giving off the excess.

True love is not a wish to be loved, and it is not a wish to receive the energy of the one that loves you in different kinds. It is rather an ability to give up one's excessive energy with love to other people, but give only that which exceeds what is essential for one's needs because, in absolute categories, one would then become worse off than others. And if one deprived of your minimum needs, this is the same sin of violence, only toward one self rather than others. One should not love oneself less than the others, and vice versa. This is purely energy-conditioned phenomena, and there is no moment of stopping and achieving final balance point in it for ever. And only feelings of joy and total contentment with life are the indicators of harmony and balance in each moment of life.

DOCTOR AND «SCHIZO»
(or «BEYOND THE "NORMAL"»)

Each man has own psychic-physical «frequency band», but the individual bands of different people overlap just partially. And that, what is within this overlap band is accepted as a «norm», but while going beyond its limit is classified by the doctors as a «disease».

For example, the level of hyper-mobility in the joints that is absolutely customary for yogis, practitioners of martial arts and circus performers, doctors unanimously classify as a pathology of the locomotor apparatus. People, having a psychic range which is substantially different from the norm, are referred to as schizophrenics. And it could be possible to consider correct, but with one a very important reservation, if the humans get in such transformed states of consiousness without any control and are unable to navigate in them.

However, what a man consciously achieves, while maintaining control, may not be classified as a «disease», since the ability to independently return to the initial «normal» status and behaviour can be controlled.

So, if somebody allows the atrophy of his muscles due to his lazy way of life, there is a dangerous hyper-mobility in the joints that is mistakenly taken for flexibility. And in some life situations, such people may have shifts in the joints, which can lead to serious injuries to the locomotor apparatus.

With respect to yogis, martial artists and circus performers, their hyper-mobility is developed in a controlled way, and is reinforced by continuous practical experience. They can consciously change energy characteristics in their system, the plasticity of their tissues and consciously enter into «pathologic» (for a normal-underdeveloped «modern man») states, showing wonders (for the same «normal man») and in the same conscious fashion return back without any damage to their body or any harm to themselves.

The same can be said with respect to «esoteric energy practitioners». «Normal» people who enter into transformed states of consciousness un der circumstances beyond their control, without any understanding of how they entered them, what the dangers are, or how to return, are dangerous to themselves and to the people around them. These people can be called «diseased». For the Masters of Kundalini-Yoga, controlling energy of transformation, expanding, narrowing and shifting of the boundaries of their perception of the World, is an absolutely normal practice. These Masters deal with the phenomena that the official medical world classifies as schizophrenia or epilepsy, i. e., diseases. For them, however, this is no disease, but a result of conscious energy control at «fine» levels of the practice. They maintain social normalcy, and because their altered behavior is under their conscious control it is not dangerous for society, but it is interesting in terms of the acquisition of new progressive experience. It also provides a means to access abnormal phenomena and realize life in all its manifestations.

Because realization and stable control are the guardians of safety and health. And it is not a coincidence that «control» is one of the meanings of the word of Yoga.

Progress in Yoga is accompanied with the cleansing of energy channels and the improvement of their conductive capability, as well as by the increase of the energy capacity of the psychic-energy structure of a human being. Being clean, a man becomes similar to an amplifier. A sensitive and powerful man reacts to various distracting factors more actively than a «normal» man, if of course, he does not control himself.

The loss of «normal» control is often connected with the enormous contrast between the level of «fine» signals that the purified man has adjusted to in his practice, and the «coarse» signals that surround him which are absolutely «normal» to other people. A sensitive man has «the shift of the perception band» with respect to the «middle», common for all people, «normal band».

With his expanded perceptions he can make psychic blows of extraordinary capacity, that substantially exceed the initial impacts of anybody «coarse». This especially manifests with the people closest to one (in the family), where social links and dependencies are stronger. People close to you often think that they have the right to dictate to you (especially perents concerning their children), and are often unaware that they infringe on the Freedom so valued by every person.

Many people who begin to advance in Yoga are surprised to notice that they become easily angered. But this is an absolute contradiction to the yogi image which implies peace and balance! The reason for all this is the ignorance of a key rule: during the course of progressing in Yoga one should, pro rata to the development of sensitivity, increase control of all thoughts, feelings and actions, since the loss or absence of control in a situation is anti-yoga (separation rather than unification).

Living in society makes it absolutely necessary to understand current social phenomena and undertake necessary measures to preserve the ability to act within the range of the «social norm». The coverage of the band of the perception fully depends on the availability of the controlling energy. And expanding the perception range without losing at least a part of the «normal band» is possible only if one applies additional energy in the controlling system.

This additional free energy may be generated during the course of practice by the bio-nuclear effects of freeing previously used energy of links, and also by total «not doing» to reduce the loss of energy.

If the striving for perception over-the-margin bands with respect to the «normal band» is not supported by additional free controlling energy, the expansion of the perception range beyond the «normal band» is not possible, but a shift of the whole range is possible. On one hand, this introduces a completely new range in the active perception field, but on the other hand, it also is accompanied by the loss of the previously attainable perception range. A substantial shift results in the development of social inadequacy, and an inability to concentrate or perform family and work duties. In general, one can no longer understand and tolerate another people.

In some cases, bio-nuclear effects become a «avalanche», where one's range of perception is expanded so much that it leads to the manifestation of various abnormal abilities (*siddhi*), which become impossible to conceal. In this event such an «enlightened man» may face social problems. Usually, in such cases, people around of him/her start to condemn him/her without understanding the essence of the phenomena he/she can control, they are afraid of him/her without being aware of their fear.

When this happens, the best way to return to the "normal" range is to reroute the additional free energy to the «training form bank» by strength training.

The greatest number of human motivations come from the sub-conscious, and it is absolutely necessary to pay close attention and to learn about yourself. Self awareness and understanding give the possibility to truly comprehend and realize the World.

Regular reviews of all the internal systems during practice of yoga allow one to make timely corrections and stabilize the system as a whole, as a result the contentment with life and the spiritual progress become constant.

And those able to go beyond the «normal perception range» should not show it to anybody, especially to parade. Not because there is something criminal about it, but because all creatures on the Earth, including modern people, are afraid of anything they do not understand or anything they cannot control. Noticing abnormal abilities, without understanding what is going on, people start to be afraid and prefer to isolate or liquidate those whom they are unable to understand or control, assuming the worst, i. e., danger for themselves. They will never be able to believe that this may be safe for them because the source of their fear comes from the depth of their sub-conscious. Even if people recognize this fear, they are afraid to admit it. Actually this fear lays in the base of abstruse philosophies which justifies violence for the sake of protecting society from the spiritually developed individuals.

All abnormal achievements should be kept secret and should not be used to tease the unconscious, i. e., the biological, beastly origin of a human being. This ancient origin, when it is afraid, is a Beast... but with all the attributes and armaments of a modern man. Fighting with this Beast is not a matter of interest for the seekers of the True Knowledge. This mistake may only be made by religious fanatics, claiming that they know the «Absolute and Last Truth».

Fanaticism is the worst of sins. Being stuck to one mental idea, you are unable to accept the World in all its manifestations. You are also unable to real love and forgive people who are under a delusion. And inability to understand that in the body of the Infinite always will find a stronger counter-power to any super-power.

The Tradition of Yoga has always insisted on detachment and development of only those abilities that have natural tendencies. And in all times warnings against the practical use of abnormal abilities (*Siddhis*) sounded. Because the true seeker must be only interested in the awareness of Power that enriches the Spirit, rather than competing in Power. That who strives to develop in the Spirit understands that the kinetics of the action causes reactions in the body of the One, and the conseqences imposed by the Universal Links on the state of the Spirit of those who use abnormal powers and also understands the degree of responsibility for the actions before the High Power.

Part VI

VINYASA TECHNIQUE

AUXILLARY VINYASAS

1. «Press with one leg in longitudinal pass»

Standing in a longitudinal pass on straight legs (Photo 1) and position the feet on parallel lines, on the floor at the hips width. Direct the toes of the back leg forward and push with the heel up. Stretch straight arms out to the sides at the level of the shoulders and push them as far back as possible. With a noisy exhalation through the mouth, bend the front leg and move the pelvis down as close to the floor as possible (Photo 2). Inhaling through the nose, straighten the bent leg and return to the initial longitudinal pass on straight legs (Photo 1), etc. When doing this Vinyasa, the pelvis should always be kept perpendicular to the direction of the pass.

The distance between the legs should make the line of the front leg from the knee to the ankle perpendicular to the floor when you lower the pelvis as low as you can. If this line is forward of the vertical line, the legs should be positioned broader, and if the line does not reach the vertical line, place the legs close to each other.

The warm-up variant of this *Vinyasa* is practiced in series of 3, 6, 12 or more repetitions with progressively deeper passes. In each subsequent pass, the pelvis is lowered with incremental depth and the thighs are increasingly opened. In the block of strength training, it is practiced within the fixed non-marginal range of thigh mobility.

Photo. 1

Photo. 2

2. «Press with one leg in transverse pass»

Standing in a transverse pass on straight legs (Photo 3), and position the feet under the angle formed by the thighs when you sit deep in such position. Stretch straight arms out to the sides at the level of the shoulders and push them as far back as possible. With a noisy exhalation through the mouth, bend the first leg and, drawing the thigh to the side, move the pelvis down as close to the floor as possible (Photo 4). Inhaling through the nose, straighten the same leg and return to the initial pass on straight legs (Photo 3), etc.

The distance between the legs in this *Vinyasa* is determined in the course of practice and should allow the pelvis, chest and face to always be in the same plane with the pass. The abdominal press muscles should be drawn up to avoid the body bending forward or to the sides when you make the maximum possible pass.

The warm-up variant of this *Vinyasa* is practiced in series of 3, 6, 12 or more repetitions with progressive depth of the passes. In each subsequent pass, the pelvis is lowered with incremental depth and the thighs increasingly opened. In the block of strength training, it is practiced within the fixed non-marginal range of thigh mobility.

Photo. 3 **Photo. 4**

3. «Press with two legs in transverse pass»

Standing in a transverse pass on straight legs (Photo 5) and position the feet under the angle formed by the thighs when sitting deep in such position. The heels are placed under the knees, and the knees are opened to their maximum width to the sides. Stretch straight arms out to the sides level with the shoulders and push them as far back as possible. With a noisy exhalation through the mouth, bend both legs and move the pelvis down as close to the floor as possible (Photo 6). Inhaling through the nose, straighten the legs and return to the initial pass on straight legs (Photo 5), etc.

The pelvis, chest and face in this *Vinyasa* must always be in the same plane with the pass, the abdominal press muscles should be drawn up and it is important to avoid the body bending forward or to the sides. The warm-up variant of this *Vinyasa* is practiced in series of 3, 6, 12 and more repetitions with progressive depth of the passes. In each subsequent pass, the pelvis is lowered with incremental depth and the thighs increasingly opened. In the block of strength training, it is practiced within the fixed non-marginal range of thigh mobility.

Photo. 5 **Photo. 6**

4. «Transverse *Vinyasa* on the legs»

Standing in a symmetric pass on straight legs, bend forward and place the palms on the floor. Keep the heels on the floor, exhale, bend both legs and lower the pelvis as low as possible (Photo 7). Inhale in this position and simultaneously move the pelvis to the first side, bending the first leg and fully straightening the other leg, thus, shifting to the transverse pass sitting on the first leg (Photo 8). In this position, draw the thigh of the bent leg as far to the side as possible with the arm. With an inhalation, bend the second leg and shift the pelvis back to the middle position, keeping it as close to the floor as possible (Photo 7). And, with an inhalation, without stopping continue this move, shifting to the second leg, while simultaneously fully straightening the first one and, thus, shifting to the transverse pass sitting on the second leg (Photo 9). In this position, draw the thigh of the bent leg as far to the side as possible with the same side arm. And, with the next inhalation, bend the first leg and again shift the pelvis to the middle position, keeping it as low to the floor level as possible. (Photo 7), etc.

This *Vinyasa* is usually practiced as a warm-up exercise in series of 3, 6, 12 or more shifts to each side with progressive depth of the pass. With each shift the pelvis is kept increasingly lower to the floor level, with the thighs opening progressively wider.

Photo. 9 **Photo. 7** **Photo. 8**

5. «Narrow press with two arms»

Start in the push-up position standing with the palms and the toes of the straignt legs on the floor (easier option: on the knees and toes of the bent legs). At the same time the palms should be positioned on the floor together, level with the solar plexus, with the fingers directed forward (Photo 10 a, b).

Inhal ing through the nose, smoothly bend the arms, direct the elbows backward and press them to the sides of the chest. At the end of this move, the palms should be below the solar plexus (Photo 11 a, b). With a powerful exhalation through the mouth, straighten the arms and raise up to the initial push-up position. (Photo 10 a, b), etc.

Depending on the purpose of the training, such presses with arms are practiced at one of three basic speeds. Fast: in the rhythm of fast and powerful breath. At a medium rate: freely breathing, bend and straighten the arms while counting, for example, complete one press for 3 or 6 counts.

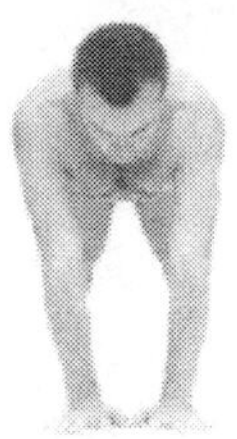

Photo. 10a

Photo. 10b

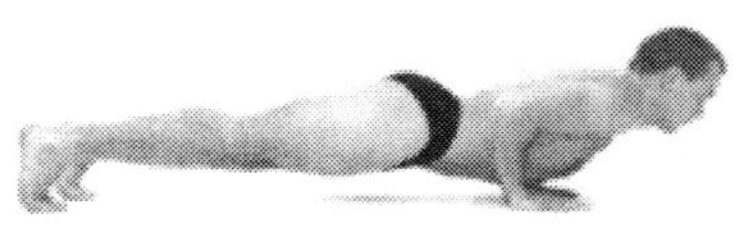

Photo. 11a

Photo. 11b

And at a very slow speed, so as to make the move hardly noticeable, making one complete exercise for 12 or 24 counts. At this rate, the speed at any portion of the movement should be the same.

Presses with arms activate energy flows in the channels that exist in the arms, shoulders, chest and back. The energy is compactly condensed in the joint centers of the arms, and the arm and shoulder muscles are effectively strengthened.

6. «Wide press with two arms»

Start in the push-up position standing with the palms and the toes of the straight legs on the floor (Photo 12 a, b) (easier option: on the knees and toes of the bended legs). At the same time the palms mast be on the

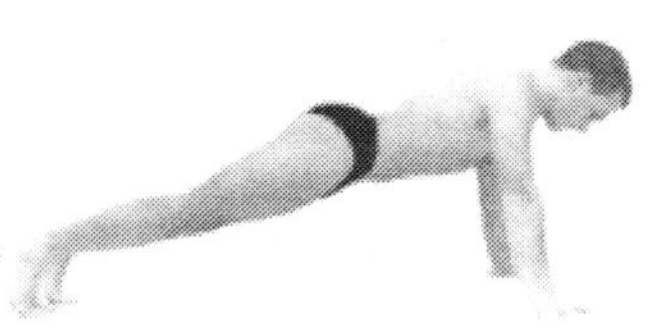

Photo. 12a

Photo. 12b

Photo. 13a

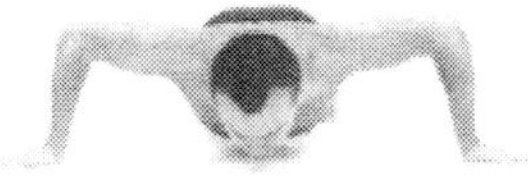

Photo. 13b

floor under the position of the elbows when they are directed to the sides in a transverse line with the shoulders. The fingers should be pointing outward to the sides. Inhaling through the nose, smoothly bend the arms and lower the chest as close to the floor as possible, but without touching it (Photo 13 a, b). Then, with powerful exhalation through the mouth, straighten the arms and raise up to the initial push-up position. (Photo 12 a, b), etc. The arms should be bent in the elbows and held strictly to the sides, in the plane perpendicular to the spine.

7. «Transverse *Vinyasa* in the push-up position»

Start in the push-up position standing with the palms and the toes of the straight legs on the floor (Photo 12 a, b) (easier option: on the knees and toes of the bended legs). At the same time the palms must be on the floor under the position of the elbows when they are directed to the sides in a transverse line with the shoulders. The fingers should be pointing outward to the sides. Inhaling through the nose, direct the elbows strictly to the sides, smoothly bend the arms and lower the chest as much as possible, almost touching the floor (Photo 14). With a powerful exhalation through the mouth, shift the chest, keeping it as low to the floor as possible, towards the first side by bending the first arm and fully straightening the second one (Photo 15). Inhaling through the nose, make a reversed move to return back with the chest in the middle (Photo 14). Then, with the next powerful exhalation through the mouth, shift the chest to the next side still keeping it as low as possible. Now, bend the second arm and fully straighten the first arm (Photo 16). And, inhaling through the nose, again return the chest to the middle position. (Photo 14), etc.

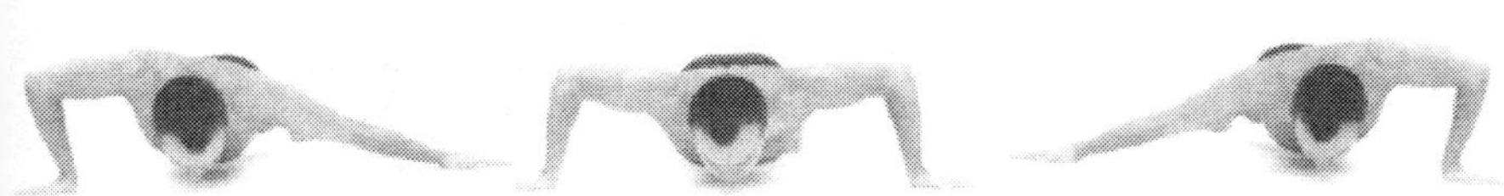

Photo. 16 Photo. 14 Photo. 15

8. «Press with arms and abdominal press from sitting position»

Sitting on the floor with the legs bent (e. g., in Lotus) and the arms held down along the body with the palms touching the floor (Photo 17). Exhale, straighten the arms in the elbows, raise all the parts of the body and the legs off the floor and press the thighs against the abdomen (Photo 18). Inhaling, bend the arms in the elbows and sit on the floor in the initial position (Photo 17), etc.

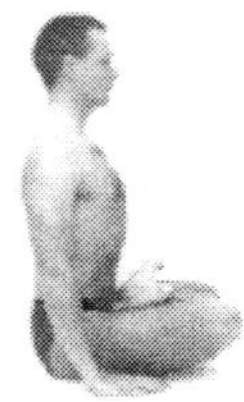

Photo. 17

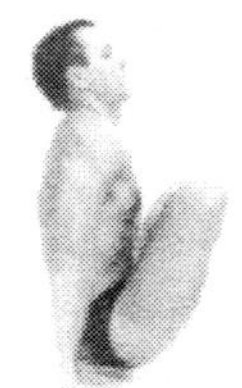

Photo. 18

The arm press in the sitting position may be combined with various positions of the legs. For example, the legs can be stretched in front of you, kept together or apart, in Lotus, or Half-Lotus, etc. It can be practiced in a series of ups and downs in the rhythm of the breath or hanging in the air for 3 through 60 voluntary breath cycles. One should not do more than 60 breath cycles for one raise. If this is passible, more complicated presses at higher levels allow one to achieve the same, or even more powerful energy, results in a shorter time period.

9. «Press with back»

Lieing on the abdomen with the arms straight out in front of you (Photo 19). Simultaneously with an exhalation, strongly contract the muscles of buttocks, back, shoulders and back of the neck to take the legs (knees), chest, head and arms as high as possible from the floor (Photo 20). In this position, inhale and, with another exhalation return to the initial position (Photo 19), etc.

This *Vinyasa* may be performed as a series of short constrictions and relaxation in the rhythm of the breath without any delays or with delays in the upper positions for 3 — 24 breath cycles.

For complete comprehensive strengthening of trapezoids of the back and deltoids of the shoulders, this *Vinyasa* should be practiced in three variants with different positions of the arms. In the first variant, the arms are held behind the back and lifted upward. In the second variant of this

Photo. 19 **Photo. 20**

Vinyasa, they should be raised out to the sides and upwards. And in the third variant, to the front and upwards. When raising up, try to «over-straighten» the elbows as much as you can until you feel a spasm in the biceps.

10. «Press with the lower abdominal muscles»

Sitting on the floor with the legs stretched out in front (Photo 21). Exhale and powerfully constrict the lower muscles of the abdominal press, raise straight legs as high in the air as possible, balance on the buttocks, and lean the body sl ightly back (Photo 22). In the raised position, avoiding hunching the back, draw the body and legs close to each other, trying to «fold» in the vertical plane. With an inhalation, relax the abdominal press muscles and lower the legs to the initial position (Photo 21), etc.

This *Vinyasa* may be practiced as a series of short constrictions and relaxation in the rhythm of the breath without any delays or delaying in the raised position for 3 — 30 breath cycles.

For complete comprehensive strengthening of trapezoids of the back and deltoids of the shoulders, this *Vinyasa* should be practiced in three variants with different positions of the arms. In the first variant, the arms are placed down, behind the back, and pushed upward. In the second variant, they should be held out to the sides and back. And in the third variant, they should be retreated upward and back. In doing this, try to straighten the elbows as much as possible can until you feel a spasm in the triceps.

Photo. 21

Photo. 22

11. «Press with the upper abdominal muscles»

Lying on the floor with the hands locked behind the neck, with the legs bent and feet on the floor at hip width and directed with the knees up (Photo 23). With a powerful exhalation, constrict the muscles of the upper abdominal press as much as possible, rounding as much as possible, lift the arms and shoulders from the floor and «drive the ribs into the abdomen» (Photo 24). In doing this, the waist should be kept on the floor and the elbows should be kept as wide as possible. With an inhalation, relax the abdominal press and lower to the initial position (Photo 23), etc.

This *Vinyasa* may be practiced as a series of short constrictions in the rhythm of the breath without any delays or with delays in the upper position for 3 — 30 breath cycles.

In the raised position, one should try to feel a spasm in the muscles of the upper abdominal press.

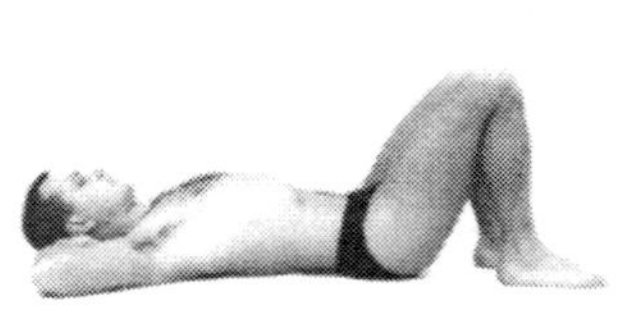

Photo. 23

Photo. 24

12. «Side press with waist muscles»

Lying on the side, resting on one arm (Photo 25). With an exhalation, raise the upper leg in the vertical plane as high as possible (Photo 26). Then with an inhalation, put the raised leg down in the initial position (Photo 25), etc. Decisive in this exercise is the relative position between the pelvis and the thigh of the raised leg. The pelvis should be slightly inclined forward so as to make the buttocks slightly higher than the abdomen. At the same time, the toes should be stretched downward toward the body, so as to make the heel higher than the toes (this position is similar to the extreme position of the leg in a «yoko» kick in karate). Maximum compression should be felt in the side of the waist. The supporting arm should be straight. If the lack of flexibility stops the reaching of the correct position of the pelvis and the thigh with the straight support arm, it is neccesary bend the arm and put the elbow on the floor, but keep the pelvis and the raised leg in the correct position.

This *Vinyasa* may be practiced as a series of short constrictions and relaxation in the rhythm of the breath without any delays or delaying in the raised position for 3 — 24 breath cycles.

Photo. 25

Photo. 26

In the raised position, one should try to feel a spasm of the muscles of the side of the waist.

13. «Press by the front of the neck»

Lie on the floor on the back with straight legs, and the arms stretched along the floor above the head (Photo 27) With an exhalation, powerfully constrict the muscles of the front of the neck, raise the head as high as possible (Photo 28), and try to touch the chest with the chin. Inhaling, lower the head to the floor in the initial position, etc. When raising the head, try to avoid taking the arms off the floor. This *Vinyasa* has an extremely powerful psychic-energy effect. But, due to the high pressure exerted on the carotid artery in the neck when you practice it, pay special attention to how you feel, and avoid overdoing it.

This *Vinyasa* may be practiced as a series of short constrictions and relaxation in the rhythm of the breath without any delays or delaying in the upper position for 3 — 12 breath cycles.

In the raised position, one should try to feel a spasm in the front neck muscles.

Photo. 27

Photo. 28

14. «Press with the back of the neck»

Lie on the abdomen with straight legs, and the arms stretched in front of the body on the floor (Photo 29). Exhaling, powerfully constrict the muscles of the back of the neck, raise the head as high as possible (Photo 30), and try to touch the back with the back of the head. Inhaling, put the head and chin on the floor in the initial position (Photo 29), etc. When raising the head, it is neccesary to try to keep the chest and arms on the floor.

This *Vinyasa* may be practiced as a series of short constrictions and relaxation in the rhythm of the breath without any delays or delaying in the raised position for 3 — 12 breath cycles.

In the raised position you should try to feel a spasm in the back neck muscles.

Photo. 29

Photo. 30

15. «Press with the side of the neck»

Lie on the floor on the side and straighten the lower leg along the line of the body. Then, stretch the lower arm on the floor in front of the body, perpendicular to the direction of the spine. Bend the upper leg and hold the ankle with the upper hand (Photo 31). Exhaling, stretch the upper leg trying to straighten it and use the upper leg to pull the arm and its shoulder to the side of the legs. At the same time, constrict the muscles of the side of the neck, raise the head and try to touch the upper shoulder with the upper ear (Photo 32). Inhaling, put the head back in the initial position (Photo 31), etc. When raising the head, the lower shoulder and arm should be kept on the floor.

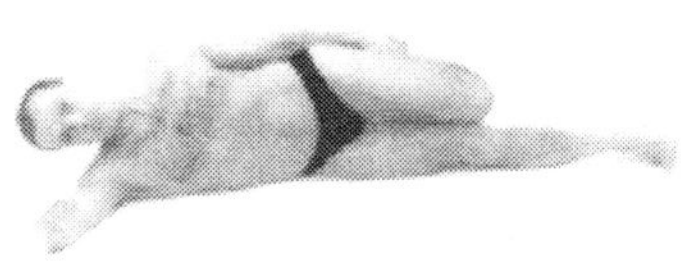

Photo. 31

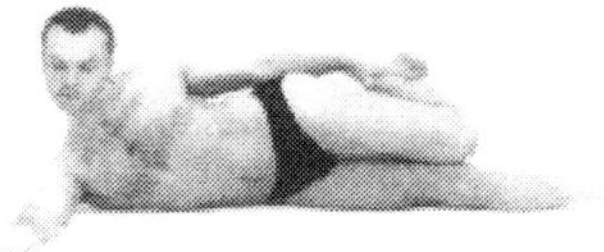

Photo. 32

This *Vinyasa* may be practiced as a series of short constrictions and relaxation in the rhythm of the breath without any delays or delaying in the upper position for 3 — 12 breath cycles. In the raised position, one should try to feel a spasm of the muscles of the side of the neck.

16. «Press with the biceps of the thigh»

Stand in a longitudinal pass and stretch the arms out to the sides level with the shoulders (Photo 33). Exhaling, bend one leg in the knee, constrict the thigh biceps as much as possible and try to press the heel to the buttocks (Photo 34). Inhaling, lower the leg to the initial position (Photo 33), etc. When raising the leg, one should try to feel maximum spasm of the thigh biceps.

This *Vinyasa* should be practiced with the equal number of repetitions with each leg. It can be practiced as a series of short constrictions and relaxation without any delays in the rhythm of the breath or delaying in the raised position for 3 — 24 breath cycles.

Photo. 33

Photo. 34

17. «Press with the biceps of the arms»

Squat on haunches with arms palms up, straight out in front of the body, and resting on the knees. The arms should touch the knees at the end of tricep muscles (right above the elbows). The palms should form a fist with big fingers inside (Photo 35). Exhaling, powerfully constrict the bicep muscles, slowly bend the arms in the elbows, and press the fists against the shoulders (Photo 36). Simultaneously with the contraction of the bicep muscles, it is neccesary to counteract this by contracting the triceps until the arms vibrate. Inhaling, slowly relax the biceps, straighten the arms and lower them to the initial position (Photo 35), etc. In the marginal position of the bent arm one should feel a spasm of the bicep muscles.

This *Vinyasa* may be practiced with both arms simultaneously, or with each arm separately. This can be a series of short constrictions and relaxation without any delays in the rhythm of the breath, or delaying in the raised position for 3 — 24 breath cycles.

Photo. 35

Photo. 36

Attention!

Descriptions of the technique of all preparatory *Vinyasas* are short and consist of the movements in the rhythm of the breath. But, in practice, these are performed with long static fixations in marginal positions in accordance with their basic intent, comprehensive strengthening effect, and secure the ability to practice all the remaining groups of *Vinyasas*.

PRINCIPAL LONGITUDINAL VINYASAS

1. «Head up»

1.1. «Standing on the straight legs»

1.1.1. Standing with the arms down at the sides. With an inhalation radially, raise the arms out to the sides and up above the head (Photo 37). Exhaling, deeply bend back (Photo 38). With the next inhalation raise to the vertical position, keeping the arms up above the head (Photo 37). Then with an exhalation, bend the body forward, at the same time radially (through the sides) lower the arms and put the palms on the floor (Photo 39), etc. With the next inhalation, go back to the initial vertical position, raise the arms radial up and stretching out to the sides and over the head (Photo 37).

If this *Vinyasa* is practiced for several times, thereafter, with an exhale, repeat the back bend, etc. Complete the *Vinyasa* in reverse using the same radial arms motion through the sides to lower the arms down along the body.

1.1.2. Performed similarly to variant 1.1.1, but with a deeper bend backward, until the hands touch the floor (Photo 40).

Photo. 40 **Photo. 38** **Photo. 37**

1.2. «Standing in longitudinal pass»

1.2.1. Standing in a longitudinal pass with the arms dropped down along the body. The angle of the front leg is approximately 90 degrees and the knee of the back leg is resting on the floor. Inhaling, raise the arms radially above the head, keeping them stretched out through the sides (Photo 41). Exhaling, make a back bend, simultaneously lowering the arms on the same wide trajectories through the sides holding them as far back as possible. Bend the back, the palms are on the floor (Photo 42). Inhaling, raise vertically and simultaneously raise the arms above the head on reversed trajectories (Photo 41). Inhaling, fully straighten the front leg and bend forward. Simultaneously, bring the arms forward with a motion derivatived from vertical-spiral to the reversed side (see Chapter «Dance of Shiva», level one), lower the palms and the elbows to the floor on both sides of the front foot (Photo 43). Thereafter, inhale and raise to the initial vertical position, simultaneously raising the arms above the head out to the side (Photo 41), etc.

If this *Vinyasa* is practiced for several times, thereafter, with an exhalation, repeat the back bend, etc. Completing the *Vinyasa*, exhale and lower the arms down along the body by reverse motion out to the sides.

Photo. 42 **Photo. 41** **Photo. 43**

1.2.2. Performed similarly to variant 1.2.1 with the difference that the knee of the back leg is kept straight at all times without touching the floor (Photo 44). The bend forward is practiced with the legs straight as a «Triangular» position (Photo 45).

Photo. 44 Photo. 45

1.2.3. Sitting on the floor in «Hanumanasama» (longitudinal split) (Photo 46). Keep the pelvis perpendicular with respect to the lines of the legs, and the arms down with the palms on the floor at shoulder's width. Exhale and smoothly bend back (Photo 47), so as to keep the line of the spine and the chin in the longitudinal plane running through the coccyx. Inhaling, smoothly raise the body and head on the reversed trajectory back to the initial vertical position (Photo 46). Exhaling, bend forward and stretch the chin towards the floor (Photo 48), so as to keep the line of the spine and the chin in the longitudinal plane running through the coccyx. Inhaling, in the same smooth fashion following the reverse trajectory, raise the body and the head back into the initial vertical position (Photo 46), etc.

Photo. 46

Photo. 47 Photo. 48

1.3. «Sitting with bent legs»

Kneel with the buttocks resting on the heels, and the hands dropped down, resting on the feet (Photo 49). Inhaling, raise the pelvis upward and ahead, make an bend and tip the head back (Photo 50). Exhaling, put the buttocks on the heels, returning to the initial position (Photo 49), and, without stopping, bend forward until the forehead is on the floor (Photo 51). Inhaling, raise the body and the head back to the initial position, i. e., sitting vertically (Photo 49), etc.

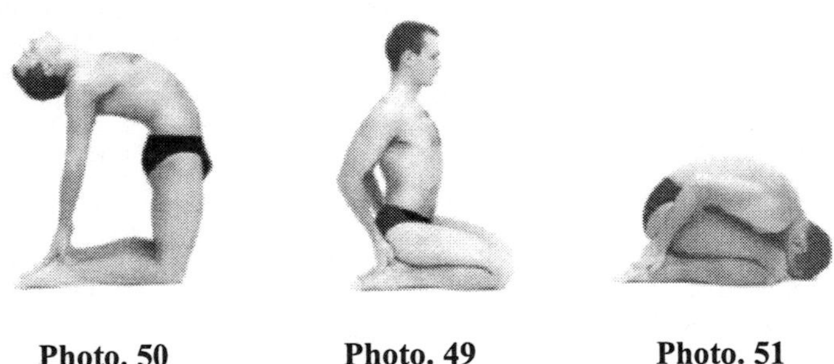

Photo. 50 **Photo. 49** **Photo. 51**

1.4. «Sitting with straight legs»

Sitting on the floor with straight legs, and catch the ankles or toes with the hands (Photo 52). Inhaling, bend the spine and tip the head back (Photo 53). Exhaling, bend the arms and head, and bend forward as far as possible (Photo 54). Inhaling, raise back up to the initial position (Photo 52), etc.

Photo. 53 **Photo. 52** **Photo. 54**

2. «Abdomen down»

2.1. «Standing on the palms, knees and toes»

Standing on the palms (fingers forward), knees and toes (Photo 55). Inhaling, bend the spine and tip the head back (Photo 56). Exhaling, straighten the spine, lower the head, and return to the previous position (Photo 55), then, without stopping, bend the spine in the opposite direction by leaning the head forward and drawing it close to the chest (Photo 57). Inhaling, straighten the spine and raise the head, returning to the initial position (Photo 55), etc.

Photo. 56 **Photo. 55** **Photo. 57**

2.2. «In push up position»

2.2.1. In a «push up position» on the palms of hands, elbows bent, rest on bent knees and toes (Photo 58). Inhaling, make a «diving» motion to straighten the arms and legs, roll forward on the toes and bend the back deeply, going into «Bhujangasana» (Photo 59). Exhaling, reverse the motion by bending the arms, lower the body to the initial position (Photo 58). Then, without stopping, straighten the arms, and, bend the knees, «Roll back» and draw the buttocks close to the heels (Photo 60). Again, without stopping continue the exhalation, straighten the legs and raise the pelvis to make «Adho Mukha Svanasana» (Photo 61). After that, inhaling, make another diving motion, bend the knees, putting them on the floor (Photo 60), then, bending the arms, return to the initial position (Photo 58), etc.

Photo. 59 **Photo. 58**

Photo. 60 **Photo. 61**

2.2.2. Performed similarly to 2.2.1 but without touching the floor with the knees. Initial position: «Chaturanga Dandasana» (lying face down on the palms and the toes) (Photo 62). Inhaling, make a diving motion to straighten the arms, roll forward on the toes and bend the back, changing the position to «Bhujangasana» (Photo 63). Exhaling, make a reverse move by bending the arms and lower the body to the initial position (Photo 62) then, without stopping, roll back, straighten the arms and raise the pelvis, changing the position to «Adho Mukha Svanasana» (Photo 64). Thereafter, inhaling, make another diving motion, bend the arms and return to the initial position «Chaturanga Dandasana» (Photo 62), etc.

Photo. 62

Photo. 63

Photo. 64

3. «Abdomen up»

3.1. Sitting on the floor with legs bent and palms placed on the floor behind the back, slightly raise the pelvis off the floor(Photo 65). Inhaling, powerfully constrict the buttocks, back and the arms, raise the pelvis as high as possible and tip the head back (Photo 66). Exhaling, lower the pelvis, and, without touching the floor (Photo 65) or stopping, continue to move by straightening the legs and pushing the pelvis back and up, between the arms (Photo 67). Powerfully press the muscles of the abdominal press and draw the chest as close to the legs as possible The arms should always be kept straight.

Photo. 66

Photo. 65

Photo. 67

With a subsequent inhalation, bend the knees again, and without touching the floor with the pelvis, push the pelvis forward between the arms and return to the initial position (Photo 65), etc.

3.2. Sit on the floor with straight legs, resting on palms placed on the floor behind the back. Inhaling, powerfully constrict the buttocks, back muscles, and arms to raise the pelvis as high as possible, while keeping the legs straight and the head tipped back (Photo 68). Exhaling, lower the pelvis, and without touching the floor make a powerful contraction of the abdominal press muscles to raise the straight legs in an «angle» as high as possible. Try to draw the legs close the the chest (Photo 69). The arms must always be kept straight and the pelvis must not touch the floor. Thereafter, inhaling, smoothly lower the straight legs to the initial position on the floor, and without touching the floor with the pelvis, raise it as high as possible (Photo 68), etc.

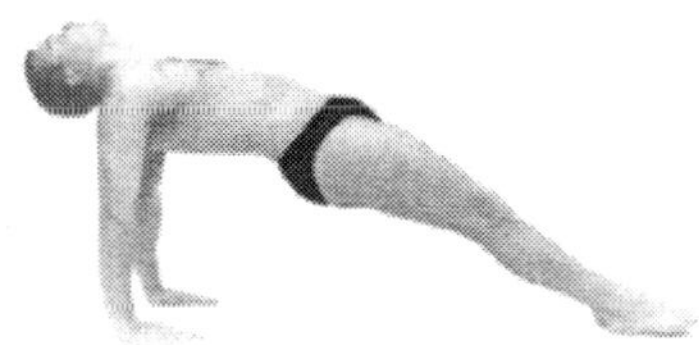

Photo. 68

Photo. 69

4. «On the side»

4.1. Staying in push-up position on the floor on one side, resting on one hand and both feet, so that the foot of the upper leg lies in front of the lower leg (Photo 70). The upper foot should touch the floor with it's internal side and the lower foot with the external side. In this *Vinyasa,* all parts of the body should move strictly in a vertical plane. Inhaling, raise the pelvis as high as possible and, simultaneously, with a circular move raise the free arm above the head. With the palm facing up, use the arm to stretch the upper part of the body. (Photo 71). Exhaling, reverse the move to return to the previous position (Photo 70). Without stopping, continue this motion while lowering the pelvis simultaneously, and position it in front of the body (Photo 72). In the lowest position, the pelvis and the palm of the lowered arm should not touch the floor. Thereafter, inhaling, raise the pelvis and the arm to the initial position (Photo 70), etc.

Photo. 71 **Photo. 70** **Photo. 72**

4.2. Practiced similarly to variant 4.1, but supporting the body with the lower leg only, the upper leg lying on the lower one (Photo 73 — 75).

Photo. 74 **Photo. 73** **Photo. 75**

5. «Head down»

5.1. «On the shoulders»

«Standing» on the shoulders with the legs straight in «Halasana» (Photo 76). Inhal ing, raise straight legs to «Sarvangasana» (Photo 77). Exhaling, simultaneously bend both legs in the knees and lower the feet behind the back in «Setu Bandha Sarvangasana» (Photo 78). With a subsequent inhalation, and with a powerful impulse, constrict the abdominal press and quadriceps to raise both legs symmetrically into the position «Sarvangasana» (Photo 77). Thereafter, with an exhalation, smoothly lower the feet of the straight legs to the floor behind the head in «Halasana» (Photo 76), etc.

Photo. 76 **Photo. 77** **Photo. 78**

5.2. «On the head and hands»

Stand on the head in «Shirshasana» with any foundation on two arms, keeping the body vertical, straight legs lowered in front of the chest and feet placed on the floor (Photo 79). Inhaling, raise the straight legs and change to the vertical position «Shirshasana» (Photo 80). Exhaling, lower the back, bend both legs in the knees and put both feet down on the floor behind the back (Photo 81). On a subsequent inhalation, with a powerful impulse constrict the abdominal press, quadriceps, neck and arm muscles to symmetrically raise both legs into the vertical position (Photo 80). Exhaling, smoothly put the feet on the floor in front of the face in the initial position, keeping the legs straight (Photo 79) etc.

Photo. 79 **Photo. 80** **Photo. 81**

5.3. «On the forearms»

«Stand» on the forearms and hold the straight legs before the chest, toes on the floor (Photo 82). Inhaling, raise straight legs up into the vertical position, «Pincha Majurasana» (Photo 83). Inhaling, bend the back, bend both legs in the knees and change to non-marginal «Vrschikasana» on the forearms (Photo 84), and, without stopping put the feet on the floor behind the back (Photo 85). On a subsequent inhalation, with a powerful impulse, constrict the muscles of the abdominal press, quadriceps, neck and arms to symmetrically raise both legs. First into non-marginal «Vrschikasana» on the forearms (Photo 84), and, without stopping, to the initial vertical position «Pincha Majurasana» (Photo 83). Then exhaling, smoothly lower straight legs and put the feet down on the floor before the chest (Photo 82), etc

Photo. 82 **Photo. 83** **Photo. 84** **Photo. 85**

5.4. «On the palms»

Standing on straight legs, bend forward and place the palms on the floor (Photo 86). Inhaling, straighten the arms and powerfully constrict the shoulder, chest, back and buttock muscles to smoothly raise the legs (Photo 87) changing to «Adho Mukha Vrikshasana» (vertical stand on the hands) (Photo 88). Inhaling, bend the back into non-marginal «Vrshchikasana» on the hands (Photo 89). Smoothly and very slowly (without striking the floor with the feet) lower the feet onto the floor behind the back in «Urdhva Dhanurasana» (Photo 90). Thereafter, slightly bend the legs in the knees, inhale and, then exhaling, with a powerful impulse constrict the abdominal press and quadriceps to raise the legs into the non-marginal «Vrschchikasana» (standing on the hands) (Photo 89). Inhaling, straighten the body and legs and raise them into the vertical stand on the hands «Adho Mukha Vrikshasana» (Photo 88). With an exhalation, lower the straight legs to the (Photo 87). Very smoothly and very slowly (without hitting the floor) put the feet on the floor between the hands, returning to the initial position standing and bending forward (Photo 86), etc. (Attention! Striking the floor with the feet may cause injuries to the disks in the lumbar section of the spine. To avoid this, the legs should be lowered to the floor smoothly and noiselessly both in the back arch and when bending forward).

Photo. 86 **Photo. 87** **Photo. 88**

Photo. 89 **Photo. 90**

PRINCIPAL TRANSVERSE VINYASAS

1. «Head up»

1.1. «Standing on straight legs»

1.1.1. Standing on straight legs with the arms down to the sides. Inhaling, raise the arms up redial above the head in a wide arc to the sides (Photo 91). Exhaling, lower only the second arm, place one hand on the waist and stretch the first side as much as possible by inclining the body towards the lowered arm (Photo 92). All elements of the body should be kept in the transverse vertical plane throughout the movement. Then inhaling, raise the lowered arm up redial above the head in the same wide arc to the side (Photo 91). Exhaling, incline the body to the other side, and make the same motions to the opposite side (Photo 93). Inhaling, again, raise the lowered arms up above the head in the same wide arcs to the side (Photo 91), etc.

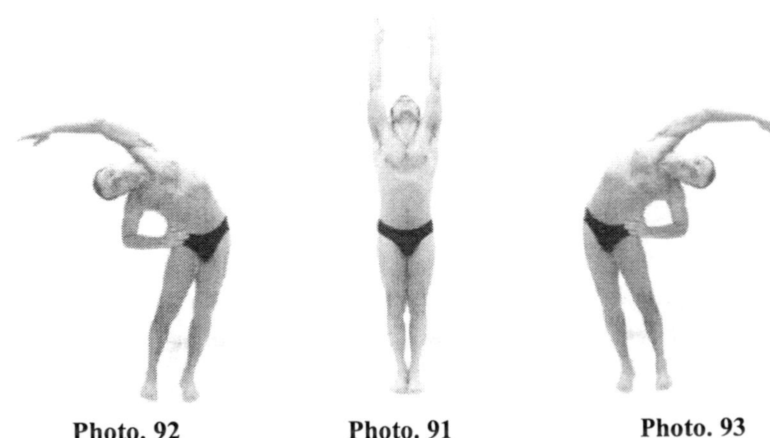

Photo. 92 **Photo. 91** **Photo. 93**

1.1.2. Standing on the straight legs with the arms down to the side. Inhaling, raise the arms up redial above the head from the sides in a wide arc to the sides (Photo 94). Exhaling, grip the wrist of the first hand with the second palm and, stretching the first side of the body as much as possible, incline the body to the other side (Photo 95). Strain the triceps of the lower arm as much as possible and pull the hand of the upper hand to the side with the lower hand so as to stretch the whole side of the body from the knee to the elbow. Simultaneously, try to push the heel of stretched side into the floor. With the subsequent inhalation, raise to the initial vertical position (Photo 94). Change the grip of the hands, and, exhaling, incline the body to the other side, repeating all technical details to the opposite side (Photo 96). With the subsequent inhalation, raise to the vertical position (Photo 94), etc.

Photo. 95 **Photo. 94** **Photo. 96**

1.2. «Standing on the knees»

1.2.1. Kneel, and inhaling, raise the arms radially to the sides up above the head (Photo 97). Exhaling, straighten and extend the second leg strictly to the side. The distance between the knee of supporting leg and the feet should be kept to a minimum, so as to place the knee of the bent leg under the opposite hip. Simultaneously, place the second hand on the waist and stretch the body towards the dropped arm, as much as possible (Photo 98). All elements of the body, except the supporting part of the bent leg

Photo. 98

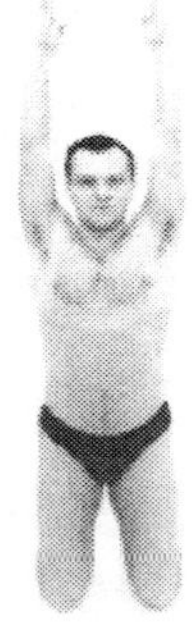

Photo. 97

Photo. 99

should be kept in the vertical plane. With a subsequent inhalation, raise the dropped arm from the side up above the head (Photo 97). And, exhaling, bend the body to the other side, performing all steps described above in the opposite direction (Photo 99). Inhal ing, again, raise the dropped hand up above the head and raise to the vertical position (Photo 97), etc.

1.2.2. Practiced similarly to 1.2.1, the only difference is that when you incl ine the body to the sides, gri p the wrist of the upper hand with the palm of the lower hand in the same fashion as in variant 1.1.2 of the «transverse *Vinyasa* standing on straight legs» (see. Above).

1.3. «Sitting on bent legs for neck stretch»

Sitting vertically on bent legs in «Virasana» (Photo 100), keep the toes together and the knees drawn to the sides, so as to form a triangle with the thighs. Inhal ing, gri p the ankle of the same leg with the first hand, and use the other hand to brace the other side of the head from above. Exhaling, incl ine the body towards the opposite side to the dropped hand, el iminating free motion of the shoulder, then, with the upper hand, stretch the first side of the neck, incl ining the head to the opposite side (Photo 101). Inhal ing, return to the initial position (Photo 100) exhal ing, incl ine the body and the head to the opposite side(Photo 102). Thereafter, with an exhalation, return to the initial position sitting vertically (Photo 100), etc.

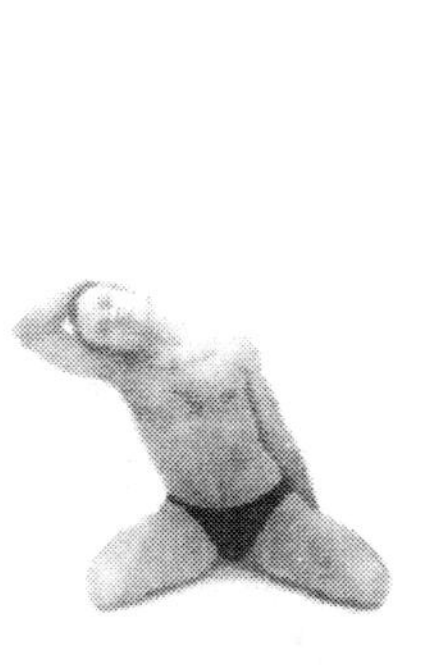

Photo.101

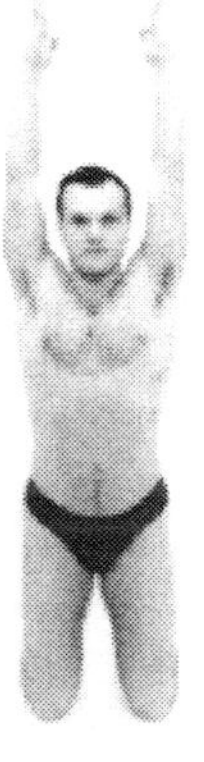

Photo. 100

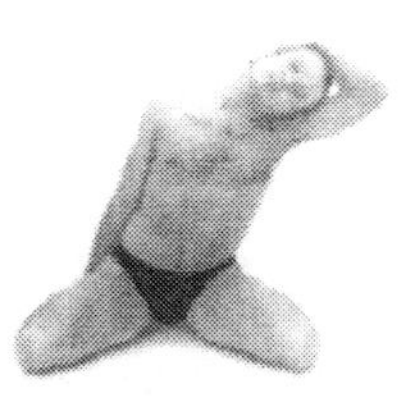

Photo. 102

2. «Abdomen up»

2.1. «Lying on the back for neck stretch»

Lying on the back with bent legs, and the arms to the sides (Photo 103). The knees should be directed up and spread apart, the same width as the hips, with the arms stretched along the side of the body. Inhaling, use the first hand to grip the ankle of the same leg, and use the other hand to brace the opposite side of the head from the above. Exhaling, straighten the gripped hand, eliminate the free motion of the shoulder and, with the upper hand, bend the head to the other side, stretching the first side of the neck (Photo 104). Inhaling, return to the initial position (Photo 103) and, with an exhalation, perform the above part of the exercise to the opposite side, stretching the other side of the neck (Photo 105). Thereafter, with an inhalation, return to the initial position (Photo 103), etc.

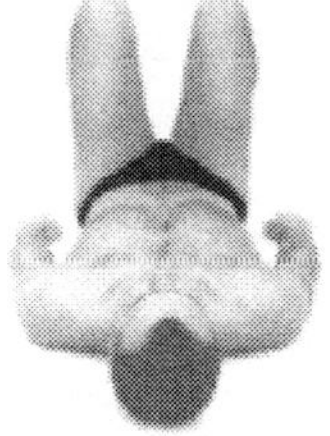

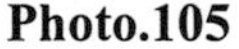

Photo.105 **Photo. 103** **Photo. 104**

3. «Head down»

3.1. «Diagonal on the shoulders»

«Standing» on the shoulders with straight legs in «Salamba Sarvangasana» (Photo 106). Exhaling, smoothly lower straight legs and put the toes on the floor in line with the first shoulder, changing position to «Parshva Halasana» (Photo 107). With an inhalation, raise straight legs up to «Salamba Sarvangasana» (Photo 106). And, exhaling, bend both legs in the knees, bend the waist diagonally back and to the second side and lower the feet to the floor behind the back in «Parshva Setu Bandha Sarvangasana» (Photo 108). On a subsequent inhalation, with a powerful impulse, constrict the abdominal press and quadriceps to symmetrically raise both legs back into the initial vertical position «Salamba Sarvangasana» (Photo 106). Thereafter, repeat the same diagonal cycle to the opposite side, etc.

Photo.107 **Photo. 106** **Photo. 108**

3.2. «Diagonal on the head and palms»

Standing on the head in «Salamba Shirshasana II» with the palms placed on the floor (Photo 109). The points of the head and the palms foundation should form an even-sided triangle. The body should be held in the vertical position with legs straight. Exhaling, keeping the straight legs together, smoothly lower them diagonally down and to the first side and with a powerful effort of the abdominal press lay them as high under the armpit of the first arm as possible (Photo 110). Inhaling, fix this position, smoothly lower the pelvis, free the arms in the elbows and raise the body, head and feet as high as possible, trying to reach vertical posi

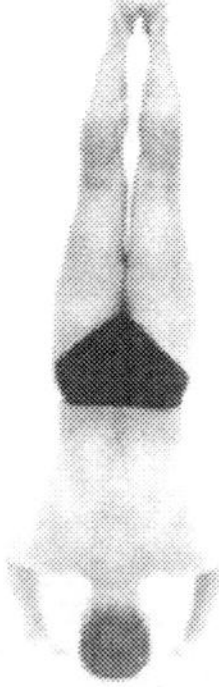

Photo.101 **Photo. 100** **Photo. 102**

tion of the spine in «Dvi Pada Kaundiniasana» (Photo 111). Exhaling, smoothly lower the head on the floor ino the previous position (Photo 110) and, with an inhalation, smoothly raise straight legs into the initial vertical position standing on the head in «Salamba Shirshasana II» (Photo 109). Thereafter, repeat the same diagonal cycle to the other side, etc.

3.3. «Diagonal on the palms»

Standing vertically on the hands in «Adho Mukha Vrikshasana» with straight legs (Photo 112). Exhaling, slowly bend the arms in the elbows, slowly lower straight legs diagonally to the first side, with a powerful effort of the abdominal press lay them as high under the armpit as possible (Photo 113). Inhaling, make no delay and continue the motion by smoothly lowering the pelvis and straightening the arms in the elbows. Raising the body, head and feet as high as possible, try to keep the spine vertical in «Dvi Pada Koundiniasana» (Photo 114). Inhaling, lower the head, body and feet back to the previous position (Photo 113) Then inhaling, straighten the arms in the elbows and smoothly raise straight legs into the initial position of standing vertically on the hands (Photo 112). Thereafter, with an exhalation, repeat the same diagonal cycle to the opposite side, etc.

Photo.112 **Photo. 113** **Photo. 114**

PRINCIPAL TWIST VINYASAS

1. «Head up»

1.1. «Standing on straight legs in transverse pass»

Standing on straight legs in a transverse pass (Photo 115). The feet are placed at a distance equal to the length of the leg, forming an even-sided triangle with the floor. The arms are stretched to the sides, level with the shoulders. Practicing this *Vinyasa,* it is neccesary try to fix the pelvis in a transverse plane, without turning it. Exhaling, use the inertia of the arms to turn the shoulders, arms and head to the first side around a vertical axis (Photo 116). Inhaling, return to the initial position (Photo 115). With the subsequent exhalation, make exactly the same turn to the other side (Photo 117) and, with an inhalation, return to the initial position again (Photo 115), etc.

Photo.117 **Photo. 115** **Photo. 116**

1.2. «Sitting on the thighs»

Sitting on the floor on the thighs, with straight legs widely spread to the sides in «Upavishtha Konasana», and arms stretched to the sides level with the shoulders (Photo 118). Exhaling, turn the shoulders and the head to the first side around a vertical axis, and, lowering the arms, grip the thigh of the second leg with the first hand, and the thigh of the first leg with the second hand (Photo 119). Inhaling, raise the arms on the reversed trajectory, and return to the initial position (Photo 118). With another exhalation, turn to the opposite side in exactly the same fashion (Photo 120). Then, inhaling, return to the initial position again (Photo 118), etc.

Photo. 118

Photo.120

Photo. 119

2. «Abdomen down»

2.1. «Standing in push-up position with arms and legs straight»

Standing in push-up position on four limbs with the arms kept straight in a transverse pass on straight legs (Photo 121). The spine and the head should be on a straight line, close to horizontal. Inhaling, raise the first arm up in a wide bend from the side, and, rotating the shoulders and the head, turn the spine around its horizontal axis (Photo 122). Exhaling, follow the reversed trajectory to return to the initial position (Photo 121). With the next inhalation, turn to the opposite side in exactly the same fashion (Photo 123), and, exhaling, return to the initial position again (Photo 121), etc.

Photo.123 **Photo. 121** **Photo. 122**

2.2. «Standing in push-up position on four limbs with arms straight and legs bent»

Standing in push-up position on four limbs on straight arms and on the knees and toes of bent legs (Photo 124). The spine and the head should be in a straight line, close to horizontal. Inhaling, raise the first arm up in a wide arc from the side, and, rotating the shoulders and the head, turn the spine around its horizontal axis (Photo 125). Inhaling, follow the reversed trajectory to return to the initial position (Photo 124). With the next inhalation, make the same turn to the opposite side (Photo 126) and, exhaling, return to the initial position again (Photo 124), etc.

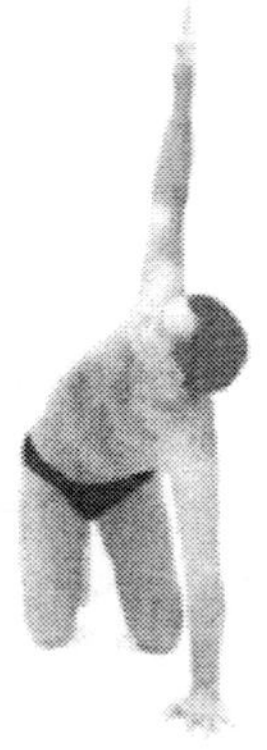

Photo. 126

Photo. 124

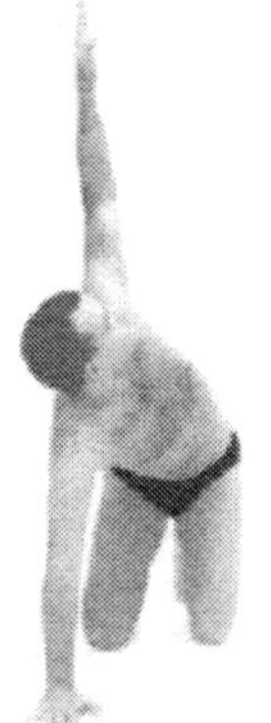

Photo. 125

3. «Abdomen up»

3.1. «Lying on the back»

Lying with the back on the floor with bent legs (Photo 127). The knees should be kept together and directed upward, the arms stretched out along the floor level with the shoulders. Exhaling, turn the spine, lowering the legs onto the floor to the first side (Photo 128). Inhaling, return the legs to the initial position (Photo 127). With the next exhalation, repeat the same turn to the opposite side (Photo 129). Inhaling, return the legs to the initial position (Photo 127), etc.

Practicing this *Vinyasa*, one should fix the shoulders and avoid taking them off the floor.

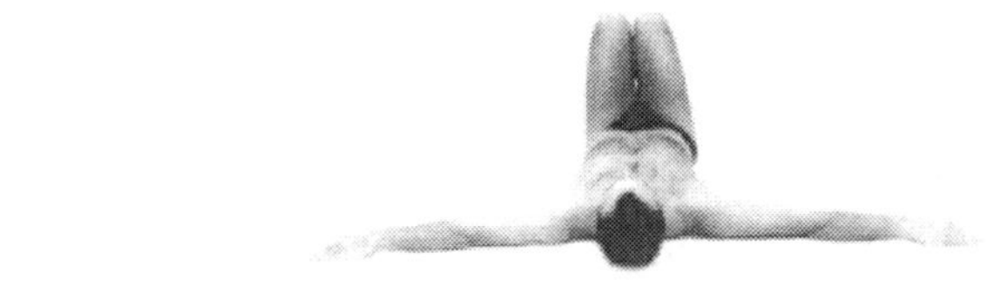

Photo. 127

Photo. 128 **Photo. 129**

3.2. «Diagonal lying on the back»

Lying on the back, arms stretched out on the floor level with the shoulders, and legs kept straight and vertical (Photo 130). With the subsequent exhalation, turn the spine, lowering the legs diagonally towards the first side and slightly towards the line of the arms. Hold the feet in the air, approximately at the height of the feet above the first arm, and simultaneously turning the head to the second side, change the position to «Djathara Parivrtanasana» (Photo 131). Inhaling, follow a reversed trajectory to return the legs and the head to the initial position (Photo 130). With the subsequent exhalation, repeat the same turn to «Djathara Parivrtanasana» to the opposite side (Photo 132). Then, with an inhalation, return the legs and the head to the initial position (Photo 130), etc.

Practicing this *Vinyasa*, it is neccesary fix the shoulders and avoid taking them off the floor.

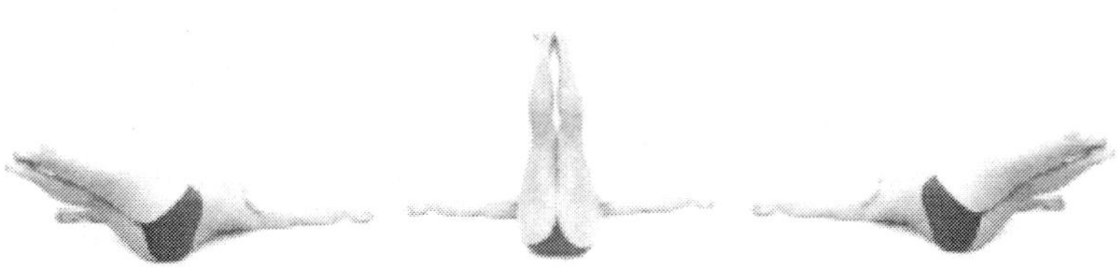

Photo. 132 **Photo. 130** **Photo. 131**

4. «Head down»

4.1. «On the shoulders»

Stand on the shoulders in «Salamba Sarvangasana» (Photo 133) with straight legs stretched wide to the sides. Exhaling, turn the spine, pelvis and legs to the first side in «Parivritta Pada Salamba Sarvangasana» (Photo 134) and, with an inhalation, return them to the initial position «Salamba Sarvangasana» with the legs stretched to the sides (Photo 133). With a subsequent exhalation, make the same turn to «Parivritta Pada Salamba Sarvangasana» (Photo 135) and return to the initial position «Salamba Sarvangasana» with legs stretched to the sides (Photo 133), etc.

Photo.135 **Photo. 133** **Photo. 134**

4.2. «On the head»

Stand on the head in «Sirshasana» with any type of foundation on the arms, legs kept straight and stretched widely to the sides (Photo 136). Exhaling, turn the spine, pelvis and legs to the first side in «Parivritta Pada Salamba Sarvangasana» (Photo 137) and, inhaling, return them to the initial position «Sirshasana» (Photo 136). With the subsequent exhalation, practice the same turn and «Parivritta Pada Salamba Sarvangasana» to the second side (Photo 138), and return to the initial position «Sirshasana» (Photo 136), etc.

Photo.138 **Photo. 136** **Photo. 137**

4.3. «On the palms»

Stand on the hands in «Adho Mukha Vrikshasana» with legs straight and stretched wide to the sides (Photo 139). Exhaling, turn the spine, pelvis and legs to the first side in «Parivritta Pada Adho Jukha Vrikshasana» (Photo 140) and, inhaling follow the reverse trajectory to return them back to the initial position «Adho Mukha Vrikshasana» (Photo 139). With the subsequent exhalation, make the same turn and do «Parivritta Pada Adho Jukha Vrikshasana» to the second side (Photo 141) and return to the initial position «Adho Mukha Vrikshasana» again (Photo 139), etc.

Photo.141 **Photo. 139** **Photo. 140**

SINGLE-LEVEL MULTI-DIRECTIONAL VINYASAS

1. «Abdomen down — on the side»

Face down, support the body on straight arms in the push-up position (Photo 142). Inhale, raise one arm radially in a wide arc to the side, and turn the body from the horizontal to the vertical plane into the position called «lying on the side on one straight arm» (Photo 143). Exhale, put the raised arm back on the floor by simultaneously reversing the turn and return the body and the legs to the initial position lying face down supporting the body on straight arms (Photo 142). Thereafter, with an inhalation and exhalation perform the same movements to the opposite side, etc.

Photo.142 **Photo. 143**

2. «On the side — abdomen up»

Standing in push-up position on the side and supported on the floor on one straight arm (Photo 144). Exhale, lower the raised arm radially in a wide arc up to the side, put the hand on the floor behind the back. Simultaneously, turn the body and legs from the vertical plane to the horizontal, taking the position called «lying on straight legs» «abdomen up» (Photo 145). Thereafter, in the reversed order, from the position «lying on straight legs» «abdomen up», with an inhalation, raise one arm back up in the same wide arc to the side, and return the body and legs to the initial position «lying on the floor on the side on one straight arm». Thereafter, with an exhalation, perform the same movements to the opposite side, etc.

Photo.144 Photo. 145

3. «Head up — abdomen down»

Standing with the arms dropped down, inhale and raise the arms up radially above the head in a wide arc to the sides (Photo 146). Exhale, bend forward, and in the same radially wide arc to the sides, put the hands on the floor at shoulder width. Inhale, bend the spine up and back (Photo

Photo.146  Photo. 147  Photo. 148

Photo.149  Photo. 150

147). Then with an exhalation, shift the weight of the body onto the hands and raise the legs from the floor (Photo 148). Straighten the line of the body and the legs in the air. Simultaneously bend the arms (Photo 149), while smoothly and slowly lowering the body into «Chaturanga Dandasana» (lying down on bent hands) (Photo 150). Inhale in this position and, repeating the previous movements in the reverse order, straighten the arms with an exhalation, toss the pelvis diagonally up and forward (Photo 149), and fix the stand on the hands with straight legs parallel to the floor (Photo 148). Then put the feet on the floor between the hands very smoothly (Photo 147). Thereafter, with an inhalation, raise the body up into the standing position, and simultaneously raise the arms above the head in a wide arc to the sides (Photo 146). Exhaling, again, lower the arms radially in the same wide arc to the sides and let the arms hang down along the body, etc.

4. «Head up — head down»

Standing with the arms dropped down, inhale, and raise the arms radially above the head in a wide arc up the sides (Photo 151). Exhale, bend forward , lower the arms radially in the same wide arc and put the hands on the floor at shoulder's width. Inhale, bend the spine up and back (Photo 152). Inhaling, shift the weight of the body onto the hands while smoothly and slowly raising straight legs into the air (Photo 153). Then without any delay continue the motion by inhaling and raising the body and the legs into «Adho Mukha Vrikshasana» vertical stand on the hands (Photo 154). Thereafter, repeat these motions in the reverse order. Standing vertically on the hands, exhale, smoothly lower the legs towards the abdomen (Photo 153) and very slowly put the feet on the floor between

Photo. 152 **Photo. 153**

the hands (Photo 152). Thereafter, with an inhalation, raise the body up to the standing position, simultaneously raising the arms above the head in a wide arc to the sides (Photo 151). Then, with an exhalation, lower the arms down along the side of the body in the same wide arc, etc.

5. «Abdomen down — head down»

From «Chaturanga Dandasana» (lowered position of the «push up» position) (Photo 155), exhale, straighten the arms and change the position to «Adho Mukha Shvanasana» (Photo 156). In this position inhale, raise the head, ti pping it up and back. Then exhale, pushing off the floor with the legs and jump diagonally up and ahead to the hand stand (Photo 157). With an inhalation, balancing on the hands, powerfully constrict the buttock muscles and the straight spinal muscles to smoothly and slowly raise straight legs, changing to «Adho Mukna Vrikshasana» (Photo 158), or the vertical handstand. In this position, fix the straight line of the body, neck and legs. Then repeat the previous movements in reverse order. With an exhalation, smoothly and without any delay lower straight legs towards the abdomen (Photo 157) and, without hitting the floor, very slowly put the feet on the floor, changing to «Adho Mukha Shvanasana» (Photo 156). Thereafter, bend the arms in the elbows, straighten the line of the leg and the body and return to the initial position «Chaturanga Dandasana» (lying on the floor in the «push up» position) (Photo 155), etc. When you lowering the body from «Adho Mukha Shvanasana» to the position lying

Photo. 155

Photo. 156

Photo. 157

Photo. 158

on the floor, you should make every effort to slow down the motion by using the muscles in the retreating phase, and slightly raise the pelvis up, to compensate for the inertia of the movement downward when you touch the floor.

6. «Abdomen down — abdomen up»

6.1. This *Vinyasa* is a sum of the above described *Vinyasa* movements «abdomen down – on the side» and «on the side — abdomen up», which are performed consecutively.

6.2. From «Chaturanga Dandasana» («push up» position on bent arms) (Photo 159) exhale, straighten the arms, toss the pelvis diagonally up and ahead, powerfully constrict the abdominal press muscles to draw straight legs toward the abdomen and smoothly carry the legs between the arms (Photo 160), thereby changing to the position sitting on the floor with straight legs (Photo 161). Thereafter, with an exhalation, change to any «abdomen up» position, e. g. lie on the back. Thereafter, again, raise the body into the position «sitting on the floor with straight legs». Then inhale, bend the legs, draw the knees to the chest and raise the body and bent legs with the arms (Photo 162). Exhaling, move the body and bent legs backwards between the arms (Photo 163), straightening the legs and smoothly put the toes on the floor in «Chaturanga Dandasana» («push up» position on bent arms) (Photo 164), etc.

Photo. 159 **Photo. 160** **Photo. 161**

Photo. 162 **Photo. 163** **Photo. 164**

7. «Head up — on the side»

This *Vinyasa* is a summary sequence of the above described movements «head up — abdomen down» and «abdomen down — on the side».

8. «Head up — abdomen up»

8.1. This *Vinyasa* is a summary sequence of the elements of *Vinyasas* described above «head up – abdomen down», «abdomen up — on the side» and «on the side — abdomen up».

8.2. Standing with the arms dropped down to the sides, inhale and raise the arms up radially above the head in a wide arc to the sides (Photo 165). Exhaling, bend forward and in the same redial wide arc to the sides put the hands on the floor at shoulder width. In this position inhale, bend the spine backward and up (Photo 166) and, then with an exhalation, shift the weight of the body onto the hands, simultaneously bending the legs in the knees and taking the feet off the ground (Photo 167). Immediately after, smoothly and slowly lower the body, move the legs between the arms (Photo 168) and, with an inhalation, straighten the legs in front of you and sit on the floor (Photo 169). Thereafter, with an exhalation, change the position to any of the «abdomen up», e. g., lying on the back positions. Then repeat the previous movements in reverse order. Lying on the back, again raise the body into the position sitting with straight legs in front of the body. Inhaling, bend the legs, draw the knees to the chest and raise the body and legs off the floor with the arms (Photo 168). Exhaling, smoothly move the weight of the body to the arms, and bend the legs in the knees and lift the feet up from the floor one time (Photo 167). Raise the pelvis higher above the floor, straighten the legs in the knees and smoothly put the feet on the floor between the palms (Photo 166). Inhaling, raise the body to the standing position while simultaneously raising the arms up radially above the head in a wide arc to the sides (Photo 165). Exhaling, in the same radially wide arc to the sides, lower the arms down along the side of the body, etc.

9. «On the side — head down»

This *Vinyasa* is a summary sequence of the above described retreating movements of the «abdomen down — on the side» *Vinyasa* and progressive movements of the «abdomen down — head down» *Vinyasa.*

10. «Abdomen up — head down»

This *Vinyasa* is a summary sequence of the above described retreating movements of the «on the side — abdomen up» and «abdomen down — on the side» *Vinyasas* and progressive movements of the «abdomen down — head down» *Vinyasa.*

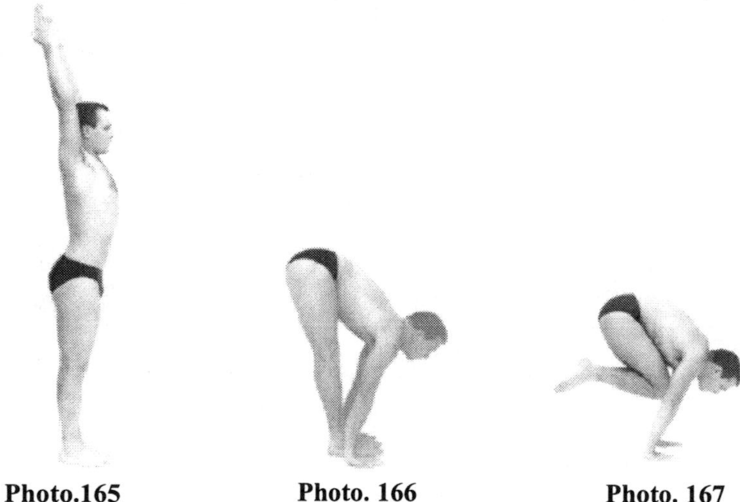

Photo.165 Photo. 166 Photo. 167

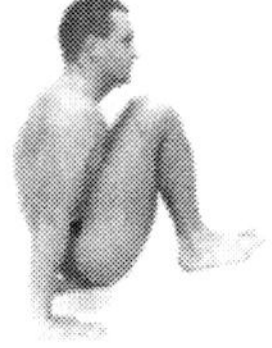

Photo. 168

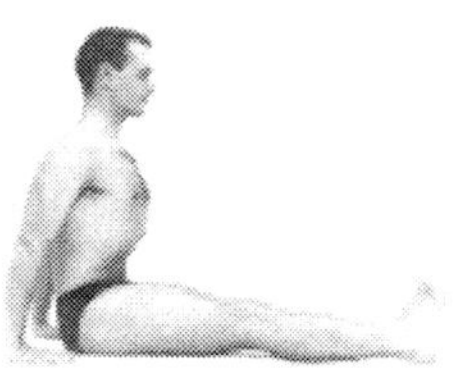

Photo. 169

INTER-LEVEL SINGLE-DIRECTIONAL VINYASAS

1. «Head up»

1.1. «Standing on toes in squatting position — standing on straight legs (press with two legs)»

Standing on straight legs with arms stretched out straight to the sides, level with the shoulders (Photo 170). With an inhalation, bend the legs in the knees, and lower the body, changing the position to standing on the toes in a squatting position (Photo 171). From this position, powerfully exhaling through the mouth, straighten the legs in the knees, returning to the initial position, i. e., standing on straight legs (Photo 170), etc.

Photo. 168 **Photo. 169**

1.2. «Standing on toes in squatting position — standing on the knees»

Standing on the knees, support the body by positioning the palms on the floor at both sides, the toes pointing forward (Photo 172). With an exhalation, roll back over the toes, take the knees off the floor, and, without taking the palms off the floor, smoothly change to the sitting on haunches position (squatting) (Photo 173). Inhaling, place the knees on the floor again, returning to the initial position on the knees and the toes, support

Photo. 168

Photo. 169

ing the body by placing the palms on the floor at the sides (Photo 172), etc.

1.3. «Standing on toes in squatting position — sitting on the floor»

Sitting on the haunches with the arms along the sides of the body (Photo 174). Exhale, and symmetrically shift the center of gravity back, place the palms on the floor, and smoothly place the buttocks on the floor (Photo 175). Inhal ing, symmetrically and smoothly push off the floor with the hands , shift the center of gravity ahead and return to the initial sitting on haunches position (Photo 174), etc.

Photo. 168

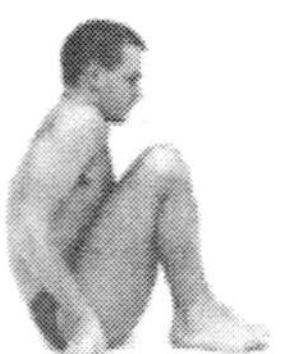
Photo. 169

1.4. «Standing on toes in squatting position on one leg — standing on one straight leg (press with one leg)»

Standing on one straight leg with the second leg stretched as high in front of the body as possible and the arms stretched out to the sides, level with the shoulders (Photo 176). Inhal ing, smoothly bend the supporting leg in the knee, and slowly lower the body and the raised leg. the body and leg should remain in a fixed position while lowering the bent leg to sitting on the «haunches on one leg» (Photo 177). From this position, powerfully exhale through the mouth and straighten the supporting leg in the knee to stand to the initial position, keeping the second leg stretched in the air as

Photo. 176

Photo. 177

high in front of the body as possible, the arms stretched out to the sides, level with the shoulders (Photo 176), etc.

2. «Abdomen down»

2.1. «Push-up on straight arms — Chaturanga Dandasana (press with two arms)»

In a «push-up» position (Photo 178) use the muscles to fix the position of the body, neck and legs in one straight line and thereafter, when you practice this *Vinyasa*, avoid bending them. Inhaling through the nose, smoothly bend both arms in the elbows, and slowly lower the body into «Chaturanga Dandasana» (lying on bent hands) (Photo 179). From this position with a powerful exhalation through the nose, straighten both arms in the elbows and raise the body to the initial «push up» position on straight arms (Photo 178), etc.

Photo. 178

Photo. 179

2.2. «Push-up on one straight arm — lying on one bent arm(press with one arm)»

Face down, supported on the toes, and on one hand, put the palm of the second arm on the thigh of the same leg (Photo 180), fix the position of the body, neck, legs and hand on the hi p with the muscles in a horizontal plane. When performing this *Vinyasa*, do not bend or turn these fixed elements if possible. With the next inhalation through the nose, smoothly bend the supporting arm in the elbow, slowly changing the position to lying on the bent arm (Photo 181). With a powerful exhalation through the mouth, straighten the supporting arm in the elbow, returning to the initial position, face down on one straight hand (Photo 180), etc.

Photo. 180

Photo. 181

3. «On the side»

3.1. «Push-up position on the side on one straight arm — push-up position on the side on one bent arm (press with one arm)»

Staying in push-up position on the side on one straight arm, put the palm of the second hand on the thigh of the same leg (Photo 182). Use the muscles to fix the position of the body, neck, legs and the hand on the hi p in the vertical plane, and when performing this *Vinyasa*, avoid bending or turning. With the next inhalation through the nose, smoothly bend the supporting arm in the elbow and slowly change the position to lying on the side on bent arm (Photo 183). With a powerful exhalation through the mouth, straighten the supporting arm in the elbow and return to the initial position lying on the side on one straight arm (Photo 182), etc.

Photo. 182

Photo. 183

4. «Abdomen up»

4.1. «Lying on the back — staying in push-up position on the straight arms and legs (press with two arms and two legs)»

Lie on the back and put the palms on the floor at shoulder's width, level with the ears. Bend the legs in the knees and place the feet on the floor at hip width as close to the buttocks as possible (Photo 184). With a powerful exhalation through the mouth, raise the body in «Urdhva Dhanurasana» (supporting on the straight arms and legs «abdomen up») (Photo 185) and fully straighten the arms and legs as much as possible. Inhale, smoothly bend the arms and the legs and slowly lower the body back into the initial position lying on the back (Photo 184), etc.

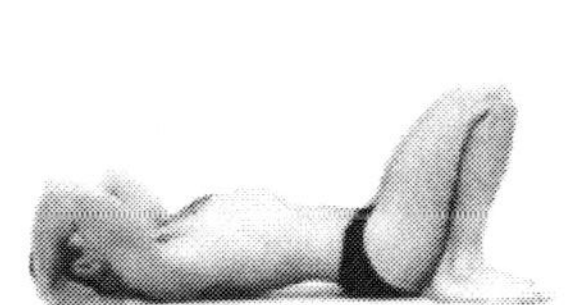

Photo. 184

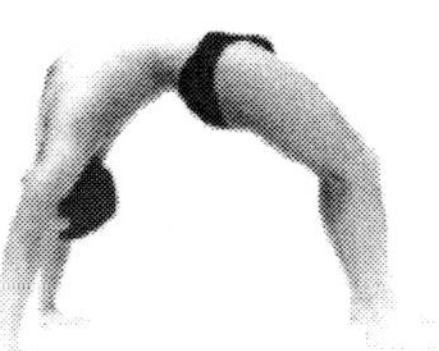

Photo. 185

4.2. «Lying on the back — staying in push-up position on one straight arm and the legs (press with one arm and two legs)»

Lying on the back, put the palm of one hand on the floor above the same shoulder, level with the ear. The second arm is straight and the hand is placed on the thigh of the same leg. The legs are bent in the knees the feet placed on the floor at hip width as close to the buttocks as possible (Photo 186). With a powerful exhalation through the mouth, raise the body in the «Eka Hasta Urdhva Dhanurasana» (Photo 187), fully straightening the supporting arm in the elbow and straightening the legs in the knees as much as possible. With an inhalation, smoothly bend the supporting arm and legs and slowly lower the body back to the initial position lying on the back (Photo 186), etc.

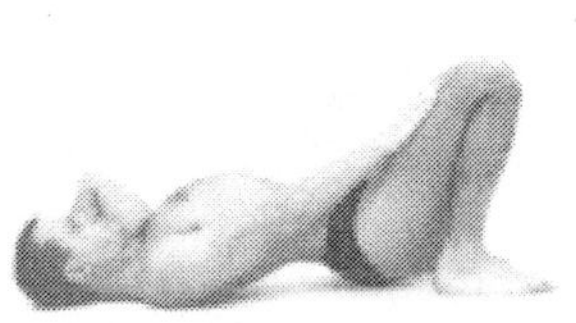

Photo. 186

Photo. 187

5. «Head down»

5.1. «Standing on the shoulders and the back of the head — standing on the top of the head (press with the neck)»

«Standing» on the back of the head and the shoulders in «Salamba Sarvangasana» (Photo 188). Exhale, delay the breath, move the arms behind the head and put the hands on the floor at shoulder width. Then lean the legs and body towards the head to shift the center of gravity in this direction (Photo 189). Simultaneously, powerfully operate the back of the neck, balance with the arms, and push off the floor with the backside of the head. Roll the head backwards and lift the shoulders off the floor, thereby changing position to «Shirshasana» (vertical stand on the top of the head and the palms) (Photo 190). Exhale in this position, inhale and with subsequent exhalation, slightly lean the straight legs towards the face and tip the pelvis backwards to shift the center of gravity. Without stopping, smoothly roll on the surface of the head, lower the shoulders onto the floor (Photo 189). Move the body and legs into a vertical line and return to the initial position, standing on the back of the head and on the shoulders in «Salamba Sarvangasana» (Photo 188), etc.

At the initial level, this *Vinyasa* should be practiced on mats, to avoid causing injuries to the skin of the head.

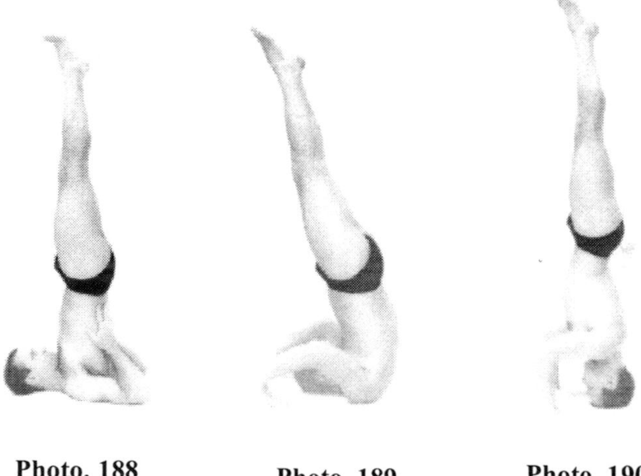

Photo. 188 **Photo. 189** **Photo. 190**

5.2. *«Standing on the top of the head and the forearms — standing on the forearms (press with triceps)»*

Standing on the top of the head and the forearms in «Salamba Shirshasana I» (Photo 191). Exhale, slightly lower the chest to the floor and slighty bend the back. Then without any delay powerfully use the triceps and deltoid muscles of the arms and shoulders to raise the head from the floor, tipping it up and changing position to «Pincha Mayurasana» (stand on the forearms) (Photo 192). Inhaling, smoothly bend the arms in the elbows and slowly lower the head onto the floor returning to the initial position standing on the top of the head and the forearms in «Salamba Shirshasana I» (Photo 191), etc.

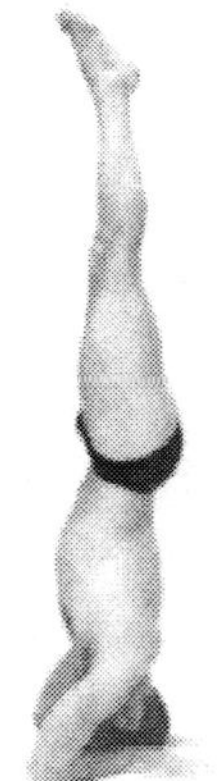

Photo. 191

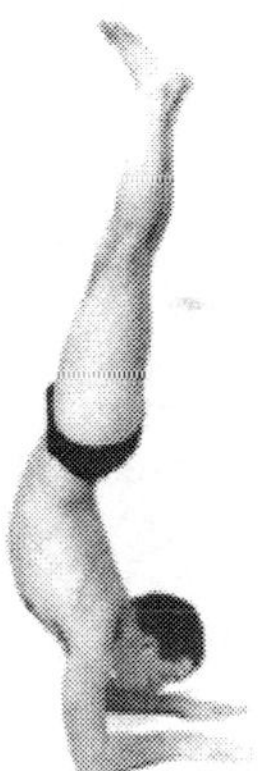

Photo. 192

5.3. *«Standing on the forearms — standing on the elbows»*

Standing vertically on the forearms in «Pincha Majurasana» (Photo 193) and carefully balancing, lift the hands off the floor and put them on the cheeks, changing position to standing on elbows only in «Shajanasana» (Photo 194). Thereafter, lower the hands back to the floor and return to the initial position standing on the forearms in «Pincha Majurasana» (Photo 193), etc.

Photo. 193 Photo. 194

5.4. «Standing on the chin and forearms — standing on the forearms (press with forearms)»

Stand on the chin and forearms (Photo 195). Exhale and powerfully use the triceps and shoulders, to raise the head in the air changing position to «Pincha Majurasana» (stand on the forearms) (Photo 196). Inhal ing, smoothly bend the arms in the elbows and slowly put the chin on the floor, returning to the initial position standing on the chin and forearms (Photo 195), etc.

Photo. 195

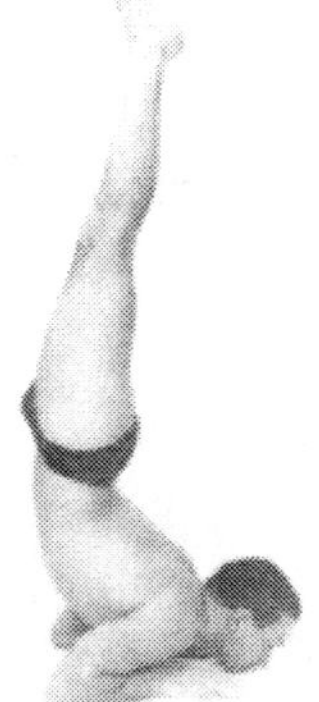

Photo. 196

5.5. «Standing on the forearms — standing on the palms (press with the arms)»

Stand in «Pincha Mayurasana» (stand on the forearms) (Photo 197). Exhaling, slightly bend the elbows and slightly lower the shoulders and chest closer to the floor. Still exhaling, bend the back to shift the center of gravity slightly ahead, and powerfully constrict thc triceps to raise the elbows from the floor. Fully straightening the arms, raise the body in «Adho Mukha Vrikshasana» (vertical stand on the palms) (Photo 198). Inhaling, smoothly bend the arms, slowly lower the elbows onto the floor and return to the initial position «Pincha Mayurasana» (stand on the forearms) (Photo 198). Inhaling, smoothly bend the arms and slowly lower the elbows back onto the floor, returning to the initial position «Pincha Majurasana» (stand on the forearms) (Photo 197), etc.

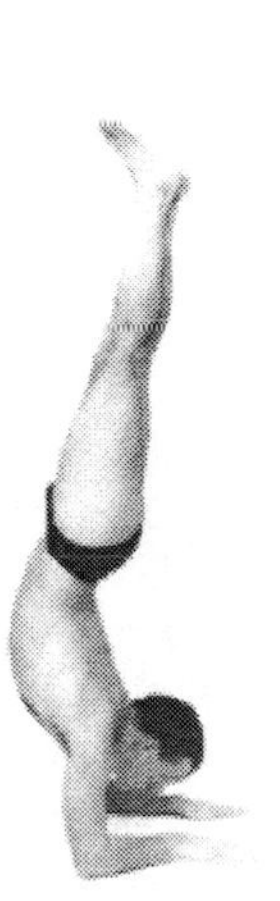

Photo. 197

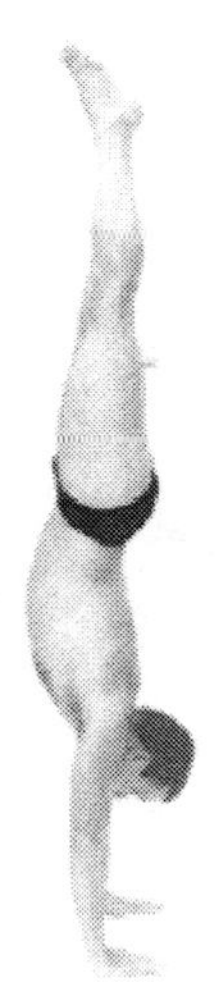

Photo. 198

5.6. «Standing on the chin and the palms — standing on the palms (press with the hands)»

Standing vertically in non-marginal «Ganda Bherundasana» (on the chin and the palms) (Photo 199). Exhaling, slightly tip the legs towards the head, bend the back slightly to shift the center of gravity ahead. Then, take the chin off the floor by powerfully straightening the arms and raising into «Adho Jukha Vrikshasana» (vertical stand on the palms) (Photo 200). Inhaling, smoothly bend the arms and slowly lower the chin back to the floor, returning to the initial non-marginal «Ganda Bherundasana» (stand on the chin and the palms) (Photo 199), etc.

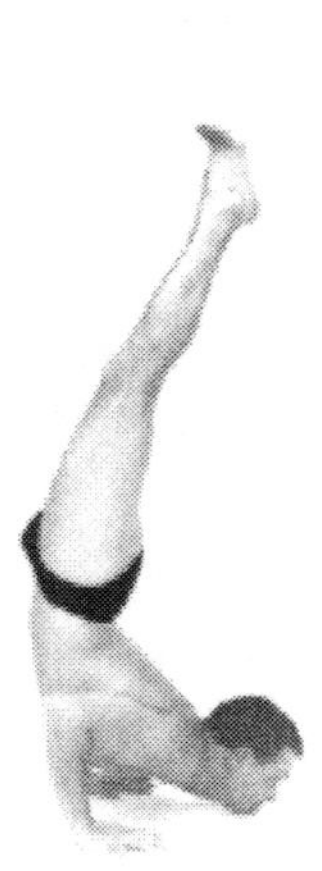

Photo. 199

Photo. 200

5.7. «Standing on the top of the head — standing on the palms (press with the arms)»

Standing vertically in «Salamba Shirshasana II» (on the top of the head and the palms (Photo 201). Exhaling, shift the legs slightly towards the back, lower the elbows and chest closer to the floor, creating a slight bend in the back. Then take the top of the head off the floor, stretch the chin forward and powerfully straighten the arms fully and raise into «Adho Mukha Vrikshasana» (vertical stand on the palms) (Photo 202). Inhaling, smoothly bend the arms and slowly put the top of the head on the floor, returning to the initial «Salamba Shirshasana II» (Photo 201), etc.

5.8. «Standing on the shoulders and the back of the head — standing on the palms (press with the arms)»

Standing vertically in «Salamba Sarvangasana» (on the shoulders and the back of the head) (Photo 203). Inhale and delay the breath, put the hands on the floor at shoulder width, as far behind the head as possible. Then, lean the legs and body towards the head to shift the center of gravity in this direction (Photo 204). Powerfully operating the muscles of the back of the neck and the arms, push off the floor with the back of the head and the arms and simultaneously tip the head forward thereby changing position to «Adho Mukha Vrikshasana» (vertical stand on the palms) (Pho

Photo. 201 **Photo. 202**

to 205). Exhaling, smoothly bend the arms, simultaneously slightly lean the legs and body towards the head to shift the center of gravity in this direction. While in the air, press the chin against the chest, slowly put the head on the floor. Then roll slightly ahead and put the shoulders on the floor (Photo 204). Without stopping put the palms on the back, changing

Photo. 203 **Photo. 204** **Photo. 205**

position to the initial «Salamba Sarvangasana» (stand on the shoulders and the back of the head) (Photo 203), etc.

5.9. «Standing on both hands (palms) — standing on one hand (palm)»

Standing in «Adho Mukha Vrikshasana» (vertical stand on the palms with straight legs spread wide) (Photo 206). Exhaling, carefully and precisely balance the torso. Then shift the center of gravity onto one arm, raise the second arm upward, thereby changing position to «Eka Hasta Adho Mukha Vrikshasana» (stand on one palm) (Photo 207). With an inhalation, lower the raised hand onto the floor returning to the initial «Adho Mukha Vrikshasana» (vertical stand on the palms) (Photo 206). Thereafter, repeat the same procedure raising another arm, etc.

Photo. 206 **Photo. 207**

5.10. «Standing on the top of the head and the palms — standing on the head (top of the head) without hands»

Standing vertically in «Salamba Shirshasana II» (on the head and the palms) (Photo 208). Exhale, carefully and accurately balance the body, raise both arms in the air and press them against the sides of the body changing position to «Niralamba Shirshasana» (stand on the head without hands) (Photo 209). Inhaling, lower the arms onto the floor into the initial position, returning to «Salamba Shirshasana II» (vertical stand on the head and the palms) (Photo 208), etc.

To avoid causing injuries to the skin of the head when practicing this *Vinyasa*, it is better to use a special pad in the form of a hat made of tough material (for example, of polyurethane resin or the material used for tatami mats used in judo). One side of this hat should form to the head the

Photo. 208

Photo. 209

other, the floor-side, should be flat.These pads should be placed the flat side on the floor and with the head on the formed side.

INTER-LEVEL MULTI-DIRECTIONAL VINYASAS

1. «Head up — abdomen down»

1.1. «Standing on the knees and the toes — standing in push-up position on bent arms, knees and toes»

«Standing» on the knees and the toes, raise straight arms and stretch them in front of the body at shoulder width (Photo 210). The wrists should be bent, so as to make the palms face forward with the fingers pointing upward. Constricting all the muscles of the legs, torso and neck simultaneously, firmly fix this position of the body. With an inhalation, shift the center of gravity center ahead and fall forward onto the palms as smoothly as possible. Bend the arms, after touching the floor with the palms, and use the arm muscles to control the fall as much as possible, thereby changing the position to lying face down on bent arms, knees and toes (Photo 211). Inhale in this position, and, with an exhalation, use a powerful impulse to straighten the arms and push off the floor. Raise the fixed body upwards, and balancing, stop in the initial position standing on the knees and toes, straight arms stretched in front of you at the shoulder width (Photo 210).

Photo. 210 **Photo. 211**

1.2. «Standing on straight legs — standing in push-up position on bent arms»

Stand on straight legs, raise straight arms and stretch them in front of the body at shoulder width (Photo 212). The wrists should be bent, so as to make the palms face forward, fingers pointed upwards. Constricting all the muscles of the legs, arms, torso and neck firmly fix this position of the body. With an inhalation, shift the fixed body's center of gravity so as to fall forward onto the palms as smoothly as possible. Bend the arms after the palms touch the floor, and use the arm muscles to control the fall as much as possible, thereby changing position to «Chaturanga Dandasana» (lying face down on bent hands) (Photo 213). Inhale in this position and, with an exhalation, push off the floor with an extremely powerful impulse, and toss the straight body in the air. When reaching the balancing point, stop in the initial position, standing on straight legs with the arms stretched in front of you at shoulder width (Photo 212).

Photo. 212 **Photo. 213**

2. «Head up — on the side»

2.1. «Standing on the knees and toes of bent legs — standing in push-up position on one bent arm, one knee and one toe»

Standing on the knees and toes of bent legs with the arms dropped down to the sides, raise one straight arm and stretch it to the side level with the shoulder (Photo 214). The wrist of this hand should be bent so as to make the palm face away from the body, the fingers pointed upwards. Straining all the muscles of the legs, arms, torso and neck, firmly fix this position of the body. With an inhalation, shift the center of gravity center of the fixed body to the side of the raised arm and fall towards this side onto the palm as smooth as possible. Bend the arm after the palm touches the floor, and use the muscles of the arm to control the fall as much as possible, thereby changing the position to lying face down on the side on one bent arm, one knee and one toe (Photo 215). Inhale in this position, and, with an exhalation, use a powerful impulse to push off the floor with the supporting arm. Toss the straight body in the air, catch the balancing point and stop in the initial position standing on the knees and toes with one arm stretched to the side level with the shoulders (Photo 214).

Thereafter, change the position of the arms, make the same fall and push off to the other side.

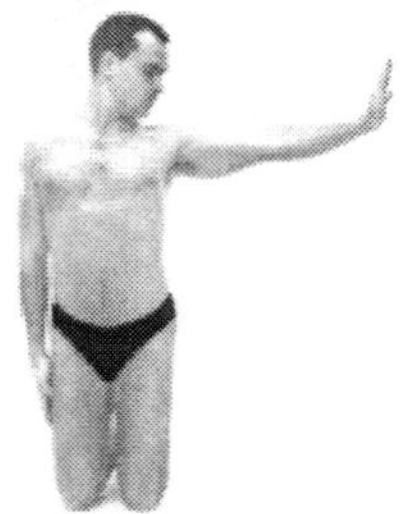

Photo. 214

Photo. 215

2.2. «Standing on straight legs — standing in push-up position on the side on one bent arm»

Standing on straight legs with the arms dropped down along the side of the body, raise one straight arm and stretch it to the side, level with the shoulders (Photo 216). The wrist of this hand should be bent so as to make the palm face to the side, the fingers pointed upwards. Straining all muscles of the legs, arms, torso and neck, firmly fix this position of the body. Inhaling, shift the fixed body's center of gravity towards the raised arm and fall to that side onto the palm as smoothly as you can. Bend the arm after the palm touches the floor, and use the muscles of the arm to control the fall as much as possible, thereby changing the position to lying on the side on one bent arm (Photo 217). Inhale in this position, and, with an exhalation, use a powerful impulse to push off the floor with the supporting arm. Toss the straight body in the air, catch the balancing point and

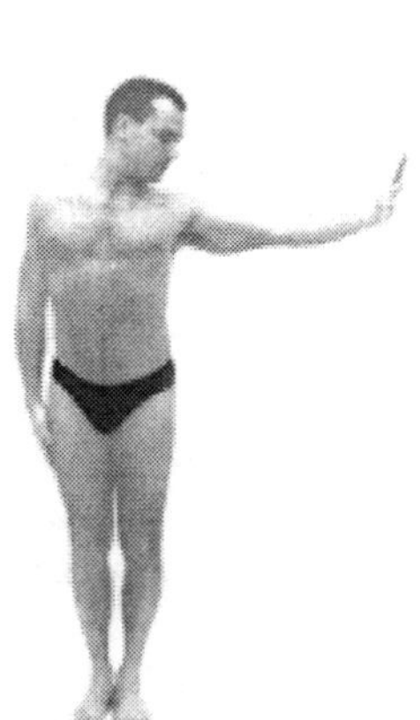

Photo. 216

Photo. 217

stop in the initial position standing on straight legs with one hand stretched to the side level with the shoulders (Photo 216).

Thereafter, change the position of the arms, make the same fall and push off to the other side.

3. «Head down — abdomen down»

3.1. «Standing on the head and the hands — staying in push-up position on the bent arms and toes»

Standing vertically on the head with any type of foundation with the hands, in «Shirshasana» for example. Resting on the palms, fingers facing forward (Photo 218), strain the muscles of the legs, torso and neck simultaneously and firmly fix this position of the body. With an exhalation, slightly slant the torso and straight legs to the side of the chest and shift the fixed body's center of gravity to the same side. With this shift take the head off the floor and using the arms to brake the fall (Photo 219), smoothly and as slowly as possible, lower the toes to the floor, thereby changing the position to «Chaturanga Dandasana» (Photo 220). When the down motion is complete the toes should point forward, and the pelvis should be slightly higher than the line of the legs and the body. This compensates for the inertia of the downward motion of the pelvis when touching the floor with the toes.

If for the initial position a variant of «Shirshasana» is used, where the hands are in a different position than described above, at the end of the down motion of the legs quickly shift the hands from the initial supporting position and place them on the floor at shoulder width, as used on the position described as «lying face down».

Photo. 218 Photo. 219 Photo. 220

3.2. «Standing on the forearms — staying in push-up position on bent arms and toes»

Standing vertically on the forearms in «Pincha Majurasana» (Photo 221), simultaneously strain all the muscles of the legs, torso and neck and firmly fix this position of the body. With an exhalation, slightly lean the straight legs towards the chest and shift the fixed body's center of gravity towards the chest. Using the arms to brake the downward motion (Photo 222), change the position to «Chaturanga Dandasana» (lying face down on the bent arms and toes) (Photo 223) as smoothly and slowly as possible can. At the end of the downward motion, quickly change the position of the arms from the initial one on the forearms, and place the palms on the floor at shoulder width, as in the «push-up position». When the toes touch the floor, they should face forward, and the pelvis should be slightly higher than the line of the legs and the body in order to compensate for the downward inertia of the pelvis.

Photo. 221 **Photo. 222** **Photo. 223**

3.3. «Standing on the palms — standing in push-up position on bent arms and toes»

Standing vertically on the palms with fingers facing forward in «Adho Mukha Vridshasana» (Photo 224), strain all the muscles of the legs, torso and neck and firmly fix this position of the body. Exhaling, slightly lean the straight legs towards the chest and shift the fixed body's center of gravity center towards the chest. Simultaneously, slowly bend the arms in the elbows (Photo 225) and change the position to «Chaturanga Dandasana» (lying face down on the bent arms and toes) (Photo 226) as smoothly and slowly as possible. When the toes touch the floor, they should face for ward, and the pelvis should be sl ightly higher than the line of the legs and the body in order to compensate for the downward inertia down of the pelvis when the toes touch the floor.

Photo. 224 **Photo. 225** **Photo. 226**

3.4. «Standing on the palms with fingers facing forward — standing in push-up position on the palms with fingers facing forward»

Standing vertically on the palms with fingers facing forward in «Adho Mukha Vridshasana» (Photo 227). Exhale, lean the legs back and the pelvis towards the chest, thereby creating a sl ightly bend back. Then strain all the muscles of the legs, torso and neck to firmly fixing this position of the body. Bend the arms in the elbows (Photo 228), and without touching the floor with the legs or head, lower the body to the horizontal position as smoothly and slowly as possible, thereby changing the position to «Hamasana» (Photo 229).

Photo. 227 **Photo. 228** **Photo. 229**

3.5. «Standing on the palms with fingers facing backward — standing in push-up position on the palms with fingers facing backward»

Standing vertically on the palms with fingers facing backward in «Adho Mukha Vridshasana» (Photo 230). Exhale, lean the legs back and the pelvis towards the chest, thereby creating a slightly bent back. Strain all the muscles of the legs, torso and neck and firmly fix this position of the body. Then bend the arms in the elbows (Photo 231) and lower the fixed body to the horizontal position as smoothly and slowly as possible, thereby changing the position to «Majurasana» (Photo 232).

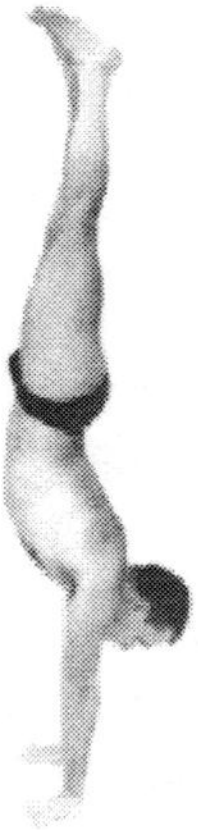

Photo. 230  **Photo. 231** 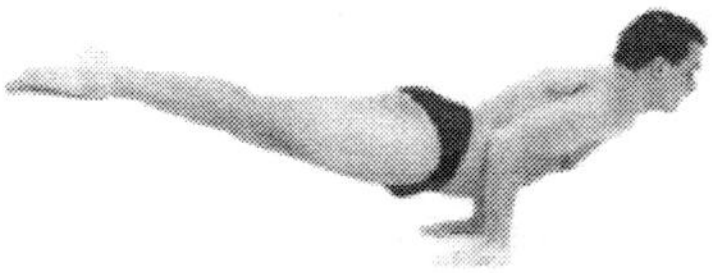 **Photo. 232**

4. «Head down — head up»

4.1. «Standing on the head and the hands (palms) in Shirshasana — standing on the palms on Bakasana»

Standing vertically on the head and the palms in «Salamba Shirshasana II» (Photo 233). Exhale, bend the legs in the knees, lower them to the side of the chest and support the knees under the armpits. Then without the legs touching the floor, lift the head off the floor, and straighten the arms in the elbows as much as possible, thereby changing the position to «Bakasana» (Photo 234). Inhale in this position, and, with an exhalation, bend the arms in the elbows, put the head back on the floor in front of you. With an inhalation, use the muscles of the shoulders, back and legs to take the knees off the arms. Straighten the body and legs upward into a vertical line and return to the initial vertical position, standing in «Salamba Shirshasana II» (Photo 233).

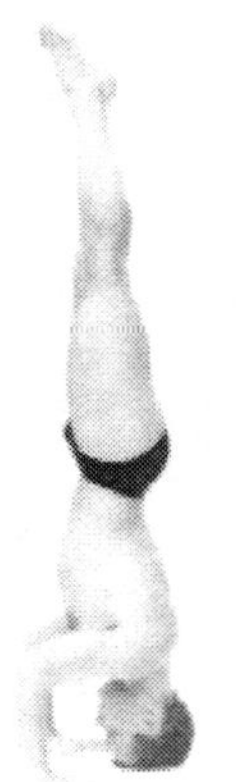

Photo. 233

Photo. 234

4.2. «Standing on the palms in Adho Mukha Vrikshasana — standing on the palms in Bakasana»

From «Adho Mukha Vrikshasana» (vertical stand on the palms) (Photo 235) exhale, bend the legs in the knees (Photo 236), lower the thighs to the chest (Photo 237) and put the knees on the arms under the armpits, thereby changing the position to «Bakasana» (Photo 238). Inhale in this position, and, standing and balancing on the hands, powerfully use the muscles of the shoulders and back to take the knees off the arms (Photo 237). Lift the body and bent legs to a vertical line (Photo 236). Exhaling, use the buttock muscles to straighten the legs upward and return to the initial position «Adho Jukha Vrikshasana» (Photo 235).

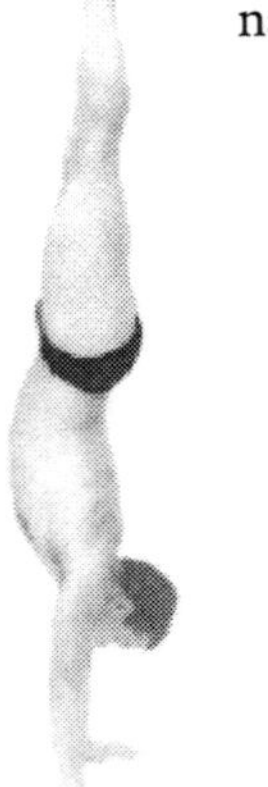

Photo. 235

Photo. 236

Photo. 237

Photo. 238

4.3. «Standing on the palms with Lotus in Adho Mukha Padma Vrikshasana — standing on the palms with Lotus in Kykkytasana»

From «Adho Mukha Padma Vrikshasana» (vertical stand on the palms with Lotus) (Photo 239). Exhaling without any delay, lower the Lotus toward the abdomen (Photo 240) and press the knees, folded in Lotus, against the armpits. Then lower the pelvis as low as possible (without touching the floor). At the same time, raise the head as high as possible and fully straighten the arms, thereby changing the position to «Kukkutasana» (standing on hands with Lotus under the armpits) (Photo 241). Standing in this position, with an inhalation, powerfully use the muscles of the shoulders and back to lift the knees off the arms, straighten the body to a vertical line (Photo 240) and raise Lotus to the initial vertical position, «Adho Mukha Padma Vrikshasana» (Photo 239).

Photo. 239 **Photo. 240** **Photo. 241**

4.4. «Standing on the palms — sitting on bent knees and feet»

"Standing" vertically on the hands in «Adho Mukha Padma Vrikshasana» (Photo 242). Exhale, smoothly lower the body while bending the legs in the knees (Photo 243) and sit on the floor on the knees in «Virasana» (Photo 244). Inhale in this position, shift the center of gravity onto the arms and powerfully use the muscles of the shoulders and the back to lift the bent legs off the floor (Photo 243). With an exhalation, use the buttock muscles to raise the legs back up and straighten them in the knees, returning to the initial vertical position, «Adho Mukha Padma Vrikshasana» (Photo 242).

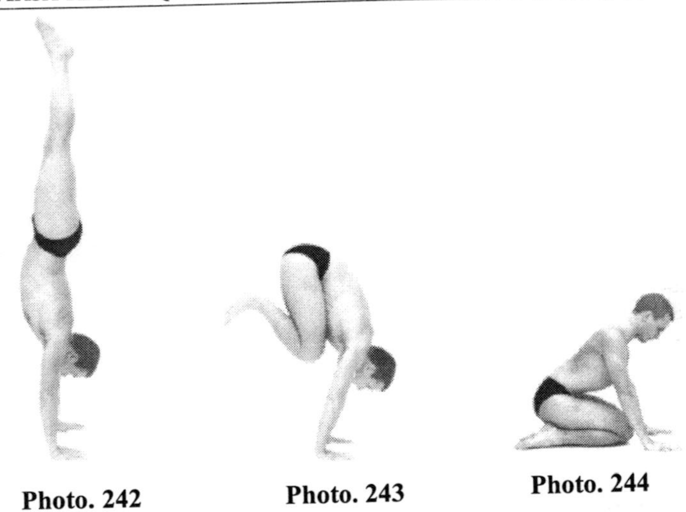

Photo. 242 **Photo. 243** **Photo. 244**

4.5. «Standing on the palms — sitting on the thighs in longitudinal split»

Standing vertically on the hands in «Adho Mukha Padma Vrikshasana» (Photo 245). Exhale, smoothly lower one, and then the other leg towards the chest. Both legs should be kept straight (Photo 246). Without touching the floor, slowly move the first leg between the arms, and then lower the pelvis onto the floor, thereby changing position to «Hanumasa

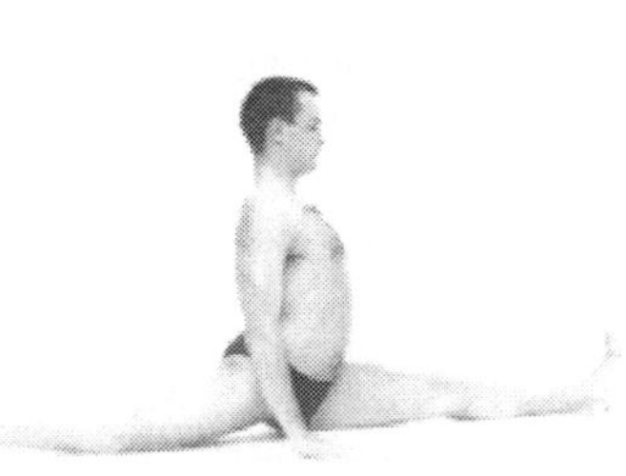

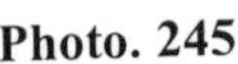

Photo. 245 **Photo. 246** **Photo. 247**

Photo. 248 **Photo. 249** **Photo. 250**

na» (longitudinal split) (Photo 247). Inhale in this position, and, with an exhalation, lift the pelvis off the floor, draw the feet on the floor towards each other, reducing distance between them (Photo 248). Without stopping, move the center of gravity onto the arms and lift the straight legs off the floor smoothly joining them as they move upward (Photo 249). With an exhalation, raise the legs to the initial position, standing vertically in «Adho Mukha Padma Vrikshasana» (Photo 250).

4.6. «Standing on the palms — sitting on the thighs in transverse split»

«Standing» vertically on the hands in «Adho Mukha Padma Vrikshasana» with straight legs spread wide apart (Photo 251). Exhaling, slowly lower the spread legs down towards the chest (Photo 252) and smoothly place the feet on the floor (Photo 253). Then spread them as wide apart as possible, thereby changing position to «Sama Konasana» (transverse split) (Photo 254). Inhale in this position, lift the pelvis off the floor, simultaneously drawing straight legs on the floor towards each other (Photo 253). Without any delay, shift the center of gravity onto the arms and take the toes off the floor (Photo 252). With an exhalation, powerfully use the straight muscles of the back and the buttock muscles to smoothly raise the straight legs. Keeping them wide apart, return to the initial position, standing vertically on the hands in «Adho Mukha Padma Vrikshasana» (Photo 251).

Photo. 251 Photo. 252

Photo. 253 Photo. 254

4.7. «Standing on the palms — standing on hands with straight legs on the shoulders»

Standing vertically on the hands in «Adho Mukha Padma Vrikshasana» with straight legs drawn wide apart (Photo 255). Exhaling, smoothly lower the legs towards the chest (Photo 256) and slowly place them under the shoulders. Turn the spine to the vertical position, keep the pelvis as low as possible without letting it touch the floor. The head and feet should be raised as high as possible, thereby changing the position to «Tittibhasana» (Photo 257). Inhale in this position, turn the spine again, and simultaneously, without touching the floor, lean the head, chest and feet forward. Now lift the pelvis upward. Then, without any delay, powerfully use the straight muscles of the back and the buttock muscles to push the thighs off of the shoulders (Photo

Photo. 255 Photo. 256 Photo. 257

256) and, with an exhalation, smoothly raise the straight legs upward, returning to the initial position, standing vertically on the hands in «Adho Mukha Padma Vrikshasana» (Photo 255).

4.8. «Sitting on the floor in Lotus — standing on the forearms in Lotus»

Sitting on the floor, fold the legs in Lotus. Then breathing naturally, place the hands on the floor in front of you. Shift the center of gravity forward, lift the buttocks off the floor and raise Lotus into the vertical position, resting on the knees. Bend forward and place the hands and forearms on the floor at the shoulder width (Photo 258). In this position, with an exhalation, shift the center of gravity onto the arms, powerfully use the muscles of the shoulders and the abdominal press to lift the knees off the floor and draw them under the armpits moving them along the arms, while standing on the forearms (Photo 259). Inhaling, powerfully use the straight muscles of the back and the muscles of the buttocks to lift the knees off the arms. Then with an exhalaation, raise the Lotus upward, changing position to «Padma Pincha Majurasana», i. e., standing on the forearms with Lotus (Photo 260). Inhale in this position, and, with an exhalation, lower the knees until they are under the armpits (Photo 259). Without any delays, smoothly return to the initial position, standing on the forearms and the knees with Lotus kept vertical (Photo 258).

Photo. 258 **Photo. 259** **Photo. 260**

4.9. «Sitting on the floor in Lotus — standing on the palms in Lotus»

Sitting on the floor with legs kept straight, fold the legs in Lotus. Breathing freely, put the hands on the floor in front of you at shoulder width, shift the center of gravity ahead, lift the buttocks off the floor and raise up on the knees (Photo 261). Inhaling, shift the center of gravity

Photo. 261 Photo. 262 Photo. 263

onto the arms, and at the same time powerfully use the abdominal press and shoulder muscles to lift the knees off the floor. Balancing on the hands, raise the body to vertical and stabilize the balance (Photo 262). Without any delay, exhale and powerfully use the straight muscles of the back and the buttock muscles to raise Lotus upward, thereby changing position to «Padma Adho Mukha Vrikshasana» (stand on the palms with Lotus kept vertical) (Photo 263). From this position, exhaling, smoothly and slowly lower Lotus towards the abdomen (Photo 262). Without any delay, smoothly put the knees on the floor, thereby changing position to the initial one, i. e., standing on the palms and the knees with legs folded in Lotus on the floor (Photo 261). After that, sit on the floor, release the legs and straighten them out in front of you.

5. «Head down — on the side»

5.1. «Standing on the hands — standing on one hand and one foot»

From «Adho Mukha Vrikshasana», standing vertically on the palms with legs kept straight and spread wide apart (Photo 264), exhale, lower one and the another straight leg to the first side and change the position to «Ardha Chandrasana», (lying on the side on one straight arm and one straight leg) (Photo 265). Inhale in this position, and then, with an exhalation, swing the raised leg, lowering it down to the floor (Photo 266), and, with an inhalation, strongly swing this leg upward in the vertical plane, using the inertia of its motion to take the supporting leg off the floor and change the position to the initial «Adho Mukha Vrikshasana», (standing vertically on the palms with legs kept straight and spread wide apart) (Photo 267).

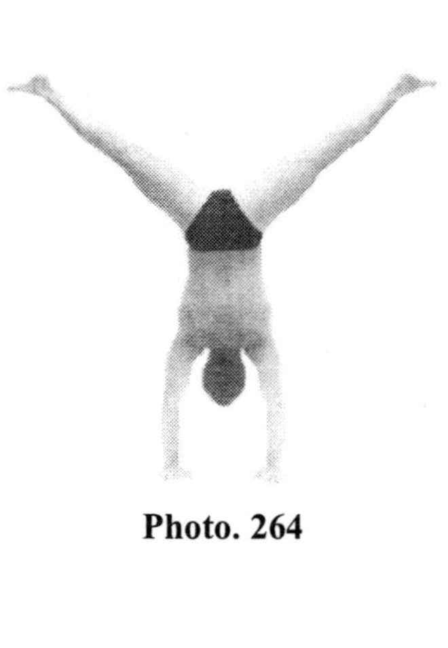

Photo. 264

Photo. 265

Photo. 266

Photo. 267

SPECIALIZED NON-MARGINAL VINYASAS

1. «Head up»

1.1. «Standing on straight legs kept together — standing on longitudinal pass»

1.1.1. Standing on straight legs (Photo 268). With an exhalation, step backward with the second leg to make a longitudinal pass, simultaneously bending the knee of the front leg at approximately 90 degrees (Photo 269). Then, with an inhalation, make a reverse step and bring the back leg forward, moving it into the initial position, standing on straight legs (Photo 268).

1.1.2. Standing on straight legs (Photo 268). With an exhalation, step forward with the first leg to make a longitudinal pass, simultaneously bending the knee of the front leg at approximately 90 degrees (Photo 269). Then, with an inhalation, make a reverse step with the front leg backward, moving it into the initial position, standing on straight legs (Photo 268).

Photo. 268

Photo. 269

1.2. «Standing on straight legs kept together — standing in transverse pass»

Standing on straight legs with arms straight out to the side at shoulder width(Photo 270). With an exhalation, step to the side with the first leg making a transverse pass (Photo 271). Then, with an inhalation, make a reverse step and draw the same leg inward, returning to the initial position, standing on straight legs with arms extended(Photo 270). After that,

Photo. 270 **Photo. 271**

make the same step to the other side with the second leg, and return to the initial position.

1.3. «Standing in a longitudinal pass on straight legs — standing in transverse pass on straight legs»

Standing on straight legs in a longitudinal pass with first leg forward (Photo 272). With an exhalation, turn 90 degrees to the second side, thereby changing the position to a transverse pass with straight legs (Photo 273). With an inhalation, turn 90 degrees to the reverse side, returning to the initial position, i. e., standing on straight legs in a longitudinal pass (Pho to 272). Thereafter, make the same turn to the second side, and return to the initial position.

Photo. 272 **Photo. 273**

Photo. 274 **Photo. 275**

1.4. «Standing in longitudinal pass with one leg bent — standing in transverse pass with one leg bent»

Standing in a longitudinal pass with the first leg forward and bent at approximately 90 degrees (Photo 274). With an exhalation, turn 90 degrees to the second side, changing the position to a transverse pass on the first leg (Photo 275). Then inhale,and turn 90 degrees to the other side, returning to the initial position, standing in a longitudinal pass, the first leg ahead and bent at approximately 90 degrees (Photo 274). After that, perform the same movements on the other side, with the other leg bent, and return to the initial position.

2. «Head down»

2.1. «Standing on the shoulders and the back of the head»

«Standing» vertically on the shoulders with palms on the back in «Salamba Sarvangasana I» (Photo 276). With an exhalation, straighten both arms and lower them to the floor behind the back at shoulder width, thereby changing position to «Salamba Sarvangasana II» (Photo 277). With an inhalation, radially, in the plane of the same shoulder, raise one straight arm up along the body. Then, with an exhalation, put it on the floor behind the head (Photo 278). Thereafter, with an inhalation, on the reverse trajectory raise the same arm along the body, and, with an exhalation, return it to the floor behind the back in «Salamba Sarvangasana II» Photo 277). Thereafter, repeat the same movements with the other arm. After that, in the plane of the same-side shoulders, with an inhalation simultaneously raise both straight arms to the sides of the body, thereby changing position to «Niralamba Sarvangasana II» (Photo 279). Then, with an exhalation, put the arms on the floor behind the head at shoulder width, thereby changing the position to «Niralamba Sarvangasana I» (Photo 280). Then, with an inhalation, following reversed trajectory, raise both arms upward along the body in «Niralamba Sarvangasana II» (Photo 277). Af ter that, with an exhalation, radially through the sides lower both straight arms to the floor at the sides, level with the shoulders in «Niralamba Sarvangasana III» (Photo 281), and, with an exhalation, continuing this motion, place the hands behind the back and fix them on the floor at shoulder width in «Salamba Sarvangasana II» (Photo 277). From this position, bend the arms in the elbows, place the palms behind the back, returning to the initial position standing in «Salamba Sarvangasana I» (Photo 276).

Photo. 276 Photo. 277 Photo. 278

Photo. 279 Photo. 280 Photo. 281

2.2. «Standing on the head»

Standing vertically on the head and the shoulders in «Baddha Hasta Shirshasana I» with the fingers of both hands locked (Photo 282). Precisely balance the body and inhale. With the exhalation, quickly and symmetrically change the position of the hands by unlocking the fingers, and turning the arms, palms down with fingers pointing forward, thereby changing the position to «Baddha Hasta Shirshasana II» (Photo 283). In this position, precisely balance the body, inhale, and, with an exhalation, quickly and symmetrically change the position of the hands, keeping the elbows on the floor, take the hands off the floor, and symmetrically change the position of the hands, keeping the elbows on the floor, take the arms off the floor, make the fist of the fingers and position them so that the ends of the fingers touch the same-side shoulders in «Baddha Hasta Shirshasana III» (Photo 284). In this position, accurately balance the body, and inhale, then, with an exhalation, quickly and symmetrically shift the hands to the next position, placing the forearms on the floor in front of the face, with the arms of the crossed hands gri pping the opposite elbows, thereby changing position to «Baddha Hasta Shirshasana IV» (Photo 285). In this position precisely balance the body, inhale, and, with an exhalation, release the gri p of the hands, quickly and symmetrically put the forearms on the floor so as to make the elbows touch the floor at shoulders' width, with the back sides of the arms touching each other, and the palms pointing in different directions in «Mukta Hasta Shirshasana I» (Photo 286). In this position precisely balance the body, inhale, and, with an exhalation quickly and symmertically turn the arms, bend the elbows at 90 degrees and put the palms on the floor on the side of the chest placing them at shoulders' width, fingers pointing toward the face, thereby changing the position to «Mukta Hasta Shirshasana II» (Photo 287). In this position precisely bal

Photo. 282 **Photo. 283** **Photo. 284** **Photo. 285** **Photo. 286**

Photo. 287 **Photo. 288** **Photo. 289** **Photo. 290** **Photo. 291**

ance the body, inhale, and, with an exhalation, turn the palms on the floor, directing the fingers away from the face, thereby changing position to «Mukta Hasta Shirshasana III» (Photo 288). In this position, precisely balance the body, inhale, and, with an exhalation, quickly and symmetrically, fully straighten the arms in the elbows, turn the palms upwards, and place the back sides of the arms on the floor on the side of the face at the shoulders' width, thereby changing the position to «Mukta Hasta Shirshasana IV» (Photo 289). In this position precisely balance the body, inhale, and with an exhalation, turn the arms, palms down and, symmetrically, move the straight hands to the side, and place them in one line with the shoulders in «Mukta Hasta Shirshasana V» (Photo 290). In this position precisely balance the body, inhale, and, with the exhalation, (very carefully, to avoid injuring the head or neck), move the arms backward so as to place the palms behind the back, at shoulders' width in «Mukta Hasta Shirshasana IV» (Photo 291). In this position balance the body, inhale, and, with an exhalation, bend the arms and place the forearms on the floor on both sides of the head, returning to the initial position standing in «Baddha Hasta Shirshasana I» (Photo 282).

After one has mastered the movements of this *Vinyasa*, and it can be practiced without any mistakes, it is possible to move on to learning the movements connecting the options of «Shirshasana» described above in other combinations.

SPECIALIZED MARGINAL VINYASAS

1. «Trikonasana — Hanumanasana»

Standing on straight legs in «Trikonasana» or a longitudinal triangle, bend forward and place the hands on the floor on the sides of the front leg at the shoulder width (Photo 292). Exhaling, spread the feet as wide as possible, and keep them back as far as possible. Simultaneously, relax the thigh biceps of the front leg. Then, draw the thigh of the back leg backward, thereby changing position to «Hanumanasana» (longitudinal split) (Photo 293). In this case the thighs are lowered to the floor without any pressure from above, but as a result of spreading the legs forward and backward. After this, in reversed order, exhale, pressing the hands against the floor, draw the legs together and raise the pelvis. This returns one to the initial position standing on straight legs in «Trikonasana» (Photo 292).

Photo. 292

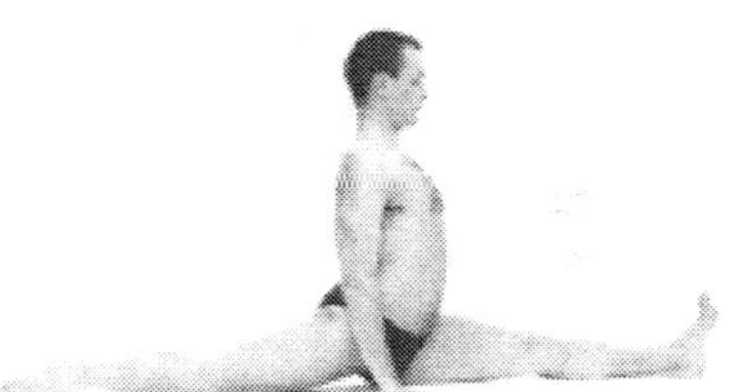

Photo. 293

2. «Prasarita Padasana — Sama Konasana»

Standing on straight legs that are spread wide in «Prasarita Padasana» or a transverse triangle. Exhale, bend forward and place the hands on the floor in front of the body at the shoulder width (Photo 294). Inhale in this position, and, with an exhalation, relax the thighs as much as possible and spread the legs as wide apart as possible, changing position to «Sama Konasana» (transverse split) (Photo 295). The thighs should be lowered and put on the floor without any pressure from above, but as a result of spreading the legs apart. After that, in the reversed order, with an exhalation, press the hands against the floor to raise the pelvis up. Draw the legs together and return to the initial position standing on straight legs in «Prasarita Padasana» (Photo 294).

Photo. 294

Photo. 295

3. «Initial pass — Vademasana»

Sitting on the floor in the initial pass of «Vademasana», grip the feet with the same-side hands (Photo 296). Exhaling, powerfully use the muscles of the arms to bring the feet together while relaxing the muscles of the legs, and join the feet in «Vademasana» (Photo 297). Inhaling, relax the arms and lower the feet into the initial position, i. e., «Vademasana» pass (Photo 296).

Photo. 296

Photo. 297

4. «Halasana — Super Halasana»

«Standing» on the shoulders with the legs kept straight and lowered onto the floor behind the back. Keep the body vertical and the palms on the back in non-marginal «Halasana» (Photo 298). Exhaling, straighten the arms on the floor, and form a fist with palms facing upward. Then lean the body towards the head as low as possible, and simultaneously, move the legs on the floor as far behind the back as possible in marginal «Halasana» (Photo 299). Inhale in this position, and when exhaling, bend the legs and place the knees on the floor as far behind the head as possible, thereby changing the position to marginal bend forward or «Super Halasana» (Photo 300). Here it is necessary to relax and deeply stretch the back of the neck and chest. Try to lower the pelvis and draw it as close to the head as possible. Inhaling, reduce the bend forward and straighten the legs (Photo 299). Without any delay, draw the legs closer to the head and

Photo. 298

Photo. 299

Photo. 300

return the body to the vertical position with palms placed on the back in the initial non-marginal «Halasana» (Photo 298).

5. «Initial stand on the chin, shoulders and palms — Viparita Salabhasana»

Lying abdomen down on the floor, arms along the torso and palms on the floor near the hips. Powerfully use the muscles of the back and the shoulders to raise to the initial stand, head down, supported by the chin, shoulders and the palms with non-marginal back bend (Photo 301). In this position, with an exhalation, fully straighten the arms and press them to the floor. Relax the front side of the neck and body and lower the feet to the floor. Straighten the legs in the knees as much as posible, and move the feet on the floor as far to the front of the face as is possible, thereby changing the position to marginal back bend in «Viparita Salabhasana» (Photo 302). Inhaling, reduce the depth of the bend, draw the hands closer to the chest and take the legs off the floor. Raise them into the non-marginal vertical stand with head down supported by the chin (Photo 301). With an exhalation, lower the body and legs into the initial position lying on the abdomen on the floor.

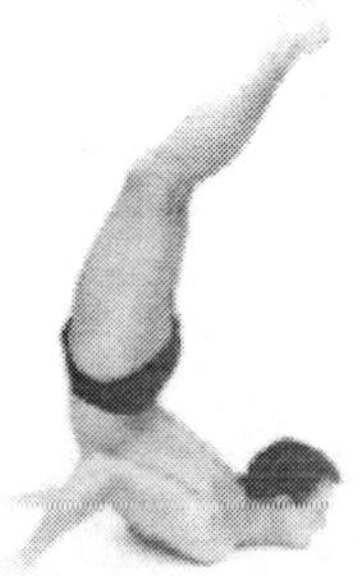

Photo. 301

Photo. 302

CIRCULAR SINGLE-LEVEL VINYASAS

1. «Chakrasana in Grivasana»

Sitting on the floor in «Virasana», with the knees spread so as to make an even-sided triangle by the thighs, arms dropped down along the body and hands gripping the ankles (Photo 303). In this position it is possible to do a couple of circular motions of the head to one side and then to the other as slowly as is possible. When doing this exercise, it is necessary to strain all the muscles of the neck simultaneously and create enough resistance between the neck muscles to make the neck vibrate from the strain.

The first of these circular movements with self-resistance begins with an inhalation. Smoothly tip the head back, bend the arms and pull the ankles with the hands so as to lower the shoulders as much as possible (Photo 303). Exhaling, slowly turn the head into the first position with the head bent to the side (Photo 304), and then to the position with the head bent forward (Photo 305). Inhaling, without any delay, continue a slow circular motion, moving the head to the position with the head bent to the second side (Photo 306) and then to the position with the head bent back (Photo 303). After that, with the next exhalation, and inhalation, make the same slow circular motion of the head to the other side in reverse sequence.

Try to make these circular movements with maximum inclination of the head, without any haste, and without «cutting» the radius of the circle.

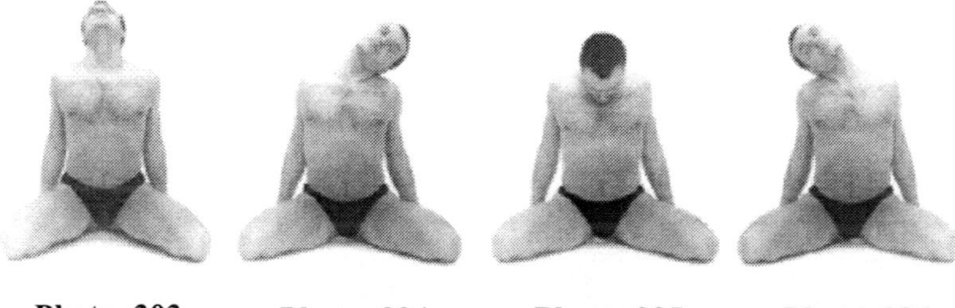

Photo. 303 **Photo. 304** **Photo. 305** **Photo. 306**

2. «Chakrasana in Tadasana»

Standing on straight legs in «Tadasana». Place the feet on the floor parallel to each other at hip width, raise straight arms up above the head and lock the arms. In this position fix the position of the body, arms and head to make a straight line. Then very slowly and smoothly make a radial movement with the arms around the hips. To begin this movement, first bend forward in the hips (Photo 307) and, with an inhalation, smoothly move the body to one side (Photo 308). Then move into the position of the back bend (Photo 309). Thereafter, without any delay, with an exhalation, continue this radial motion. Move the body to the position of bending to the other side (Photo 310) and return to the initial position of bending forward (Photo 307). With the subsequent inhalation and exhalation, make the same complete slow radial motion to the opposite side.

Try to make such circular movements with maximum inclination of the body, without any haste and without cutting the radius of the circle. Precisely control the inclination of the pelvis towards the side opposite to the inclination of the arms, and try to move smoothly and evenly.

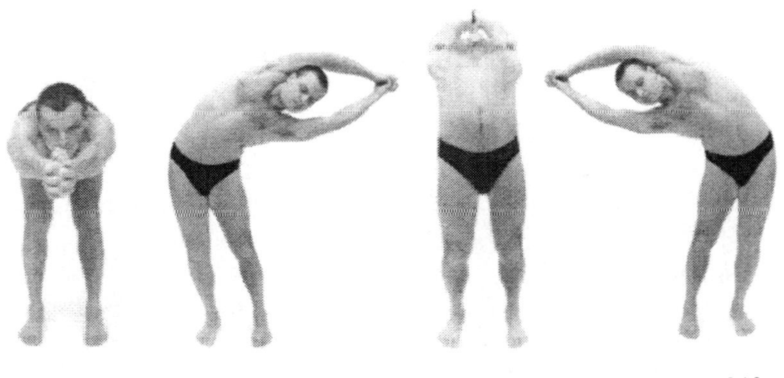

Photo. 307 **Photo. 308** **Photo. 309** **Photo. 310**

3. «Makarasana — Parshva Makarasana — Viparita Makarasana — Parshva Makarasana — Makarasana»

Lying face down with the arms stretched on the floor in front of the body in «Makarasana» (Photo 311). Push off the floor with the knee of one leg and turn the body on the side in «Parshva Makarasana» (Photo 312). After that, without any delay, continue to roll to the side and turn onto the back in «Viparita Makarasana», with the arms stretched on the floor above the head (Photo 313). Without any delay, continue to roll to the same side, push off the floor with the other leg and turn to «Parshva Makarasana» on the other side (Photo 314). Without any delay, continue to roll to the same side, turn on the abdomen in the initial position lying in «Makarasana» on the abdomen with arms stretched on the floor in front

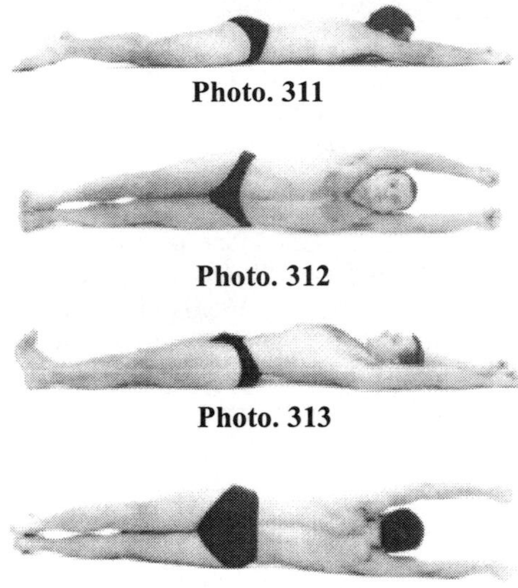

Photo. 311

Photo. 312

Photo. 313

Photo. 314

of the body (Photo 311). After that, without any delay, make the same series of turns to the other side.

4. «Complete somersault»

Sitting in a squat on the toes with the palms placed on the floor in front of the body at shoulder width (Photo 315). Exhale, shift the center of gravity ahead, lean the body forward and put the top of the head on the floor (Photo 316). Without any delay, move the gravity center further ahead until the body is supported by the hands. Push off the floor with both hands and use the inertia of this push to roll over the head and forward onto the shoulders (Photo 317). Then roll further onto the back, buttocks and toes (Photo 318). Stop the motion with the hands by putting them on the floor in front of the body, returning to the initial position (Photo 315). Inhale in this position, and, with an exhalation, push off the floor with the hands, move the gravity center backward, roll over the buttocks (Photo 318) onto the back, and shoulders. Tip the legs behind the head, and put the palms on both sides of the head at shoulder width. Then tip the legs behind the back, press the floor with the hands to raise the shoulders above the floor (Photo 317). Roll over the head (Photo 316) and return to the initial position, squatting on toes (Photo 315).

Photo. 315 Photo. 316 Photo. 317 Photo. 318

5. «Halasana — Ubhaja Pandagushtasana — Paschimottanasana»

«Standing» on the shoulders and the back of the head. With straight legs behind the back, gri p the toes with the hands and breath naturally in «Halasana» (Photo 319). Bend the knees, shift the center of gravity back and powerfully push off with the legs to roll forward. Without touching the floor with the legs, balance in «Ubhaja Pandagushtasana» (Photo 320). Thereafter, shift the gravity center further ahead and as smoothly as possible lower straight legs onto the floor, changing position to sitting with toes gri pped with the hands in «Paschimottanasana» (Photo 321).

Photo. 319 Photo. 320 Photo. 321

6. «Supta Konasana — Ubhaja Pandagushtasana — Upavishtha Konasana»

«Standing» on the shoulders and the back of the head with legs kept straight and spread wide apart, gri p the toes with the hands and breath naturally in «Supta Konasana» (Photo 322). Bend the knees, shift the center of gravity backward and powerfully push off with the legs to roll over. Without touching the floor with the legs, balance in «Ubhaja Pandagushtasana» (Photo 323). Thereafter, shifting the gravity center ahead, lower straight legs onto the floor, sitting in «Upavishtha Konasana» gri pping the toes with the hands (Photo 324). In this position, shift the center of gravity ahead, bend the arms in the elbows and the legs in the knees while bending forward. Then with a powerful push, raise the body, straighten the legs, pull on the feet and lift the legs off the floor, finally balancing on the buttocks in «Ubhaja Pandagushtasana» (Photo 323). Thereafter, shifting the gravity center further backward, roll over onto the shoulders and lower straight legs onto the floor in «Supta Konasana» gripping the toes with the hands (Photo 322).

Photo. 322 **Photo. 323** **Photo. 324**

7. «Paschimottanasana — Parshva Paschimottanasana — Viparita Paschimottanasana — Parshva Paschimottanasana — Paschimottanasana»

Sitting on the floor with legs kept straight, grip the outer sides of the feet with the hands and deeply bend forward in «Paschimottanasana» (Photo 325). Breathing naturally, push off the floor with the first leg. Trying not to change this posture, roll onto the side, in «Parshva Paschimottanasana» (Photo 326). Thereafter, without any delays, continue to roll to the same side trying not to change this posture and roll onto the back in «Viparita Paschimottanasana» (Photo 327). Thereafter, continue to roll to the same side, roll over onto the opposite side, in «Parshva Paschimottanasana» (Photo 328). Then continue to roll to the same side, trying not to change this posture, to the initial position, sitting on the floor in «Paschimottanasana» (Photo 325). After that, make the same series of turns to the other side.

Photo. 325

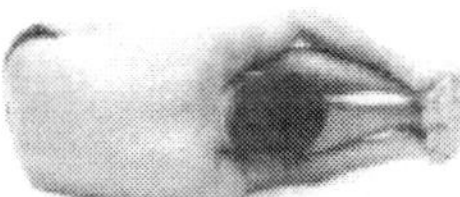

Photo. 326

Photo. 327

Photo. 328

8. «Adho Mukha Shvanasana — Urdhva Dhanurasana»

Stand on straight arms and legs in «Adho Mukha Shvanasana» (Photo 329). Breathing freely, raise the first straight leg upward and bend it at the top towards the second leg. At the same time, push the first hand off the floor and turn to the second side, lowering the raised arm and leg on the floor to change position to «Urdhva Dhanurasana» (Photo 330). Standing in this position, raise the first straight leg again, bend it at the top towards the second leg, take the first hand off the floor, turn to the other side, lowering the raised arm and leg onto the floor and returning to the initial «Adho Mukha Shvanasana» (Photo 329). After that, make similar movements to the other side.

Photo. 329

Photo. 330

9. «Ushtrasana — Dhanurasana — Parshva Dhanurasana — Dhanurasana — Ushtrasana»

From «Ushtrasana» (Photo 331), exhale, shift the center of gravity ahead and roll forward through the hi ps onto the abdomen in «Dhanurasana» (Photo 332). Inhale in this position, and with an exhalation, shift the center of gravity to the first side and turn on the side in «Parshva Dhanurasana» (Photo 333). Inhale in this position, and with an exhalation, turn onto the back (Photo 334). Inhale in this position, and with an exhalation, raise the pelvis as high as it is possible and press the chest against the chin, thereby changing position to a «bend» standing on the shoulders (Photo 335). Inhale in this position, and with an exhalation, lower the pelvis back onto the floor in the previous position (Photo 334). Inhale in this position, and with an exhalation, turn onto the side in «Parshva Dhanurasana» (Photo 333). Pushing off the floor with the lower shoulder and the leg, return to the initial «Dhanurasana» (Photo 332). Thereafter, repeat the same series of movements to the other side from «Parshva Dhanurasana» (Photo 333) to the «bend», standing on the shoulders (Photo 335) and again return to «Dhanurasana» (Photo 332). In this position, breathing naturally and roll ing forward on the chest and backward on the

Photo. 331 Photo. 332 Photo. 333

Photo. 334 Photo. 335

hips, create enough momentum to return the knees back to the initial «Ushtrasana» (Photo 331).

It is better to do this exercise on a special gymnastics mat to avoid injuring knee-caps.

10. «Chakra Bandhasana — Kapotasana — Pandagushtha Dhanurasana — Parshva Pandagushtha Dhanurasana — Ganda Bherundasana — Chakra Bandhasana»

Standing on the head, forearms and toes, grip the feet with the hands in «Chakra Bandhasana» (Photo 336). Exhaling, shift the center of gravity ahead, roll forward through the toes and lower the knees onto the floor, changing position to non-marginal «Kapotasana» (Photo 337). Inhale in this position, and with an exhalation, straighten the arms and shift the center of gravity to roll forward through the knees and hips onto the abdomen in non-marginal «Pandagushtha Dhanurasana» (Photo 338). Inhale in this position, and with an exhalation, shift the center of gravity to the first side and lay on the side in non-marginal «Parshva Pandagushtha Dhanurasana» (Photo 339). Inhale in this position, and with an exhalation, push off the floor with the lower shoulder and the leg to return to the previous «Pandagushtha Dhanurasana» (Photo 338). Then make the same motion to the second side and return to «Pandagushtha Dhanurasana». In this position, with an inhalation, lean the legs, arms and body backwards. Then with an exhalation, powerfully push off with the hip to roll forward

Photo. 336 Photo. 337 Photo. 338

Photo. 339 Photo. 340

onto the chest and chin, drawing the elbows aside in non-marginal «Ganda Bherundasana» (Photo 340). Inhale in this position, and with an exhalation, firmly place the legs on the floor. Then increase the back arch and shift the center of gravity onto the legs. Symmetrically draw in the elbows until they are at the shoulder width and lift the chest off the floor, changing position to initial «Chakra Bandhasana» (Photo 336).

If there is a reserve of flexibility that is substantially greater than that required to practice intermediary postures of this *Vinyasa*, it is possible to do the series of the motions in the reversed order.

11. «Chakrasana in Sarvangasana» or «Halasana — Parshva Halasana — Parshva Setu Bandha Sarvangasana — Setu Bandha Sarvangasana — Parshva Setu Bandha Sarvangasana — Parshva Halasana — Halasana»

Standing on the shoulders and the back of the head, with straight legs behind the head and hands placed on the back, breath freely in «Halasana» (Photo 341). Without stopping, use the feet to move in a circle around the body from one position to another in the following sequence: «Halasana» (Photo 341) — «Parshva Halasana» (Photo 342) — «Parshva Setu Bandha Sarvangasana» (Photo 343) — «Setu Bandha Sarvangasana» (Photo 344) — «Parshva Setu Bandha Sarvangasana» (Photo 345) — «Parshva Halasana» (Photo 346) — «Halasana» (Photo 341). And then in reverse order.

Photo. 341 **Photo. 342** **Photo. 343**

Photo. 344 **Photo. 345** **Photo. 346**

12. «Chakrasana in Shirshasana» or «Shirshasana — Parshva Shirshasana — Parshva Setu Bandha Shirshasana — Setu Bandha Shirshasana — Parshva Setu Bandha Shirshasana — Parshva Shirshasana — Shirshasana»

Standing on the head and forearms with straight legs touching the floor and the toes in front of the face, breath freely in «Shirshasana» (Photo 347). Without any stopping, use the feet to move in a circle around the body from one position to another in the following sequence: «Shirshasana» (Photo 347) — «Parshva Shirshasana» (Photo 348) — «Parshva Setu Bandha Shirshasana» (Photo 349) — «Setu Bandha Shirshasana» (Photo 350) — «Parshva Setu Bandha Shirshasana» (Photo 351) — «Parshva Shirshasana» (Photo 352) — «Shirshasana» (Photo 347). And then in reverse order.

Photo. 347 **Photo. 348** **Photo. 349**

Photo. 350 **Photo. 351** **Photo. 352**

CIRCULAR INTER-LEVEL VINYASAS

1. «Standing on the top of the head and on the palms — lying on the back»

Standing vertically on the top of the head, palms in «Mukta Hasta Shirshasana» (Photo 353). Exhale, lean the legs towards the head, shift the pelvis, smoothly bend the neck and lower the shoulders onto the floor (Photo 354). Then lower the back and straight legs (Photo 355). Swing the arms over the head and lay them on the floor along the body, lying in «Shavasana» (Photo 356). Inhale in this position, and with an exhalation, put the palms on the floor at the shoulder width, as far behind the head as possible (Photo 355). Raise the legs straight up (Photo 354) and powerfully contract the muscles of the neck to make a fragment of a back somersault. Then balancing with the arms, return to the initial position «Mukta Hasha Shirshasana» (Photo 353).

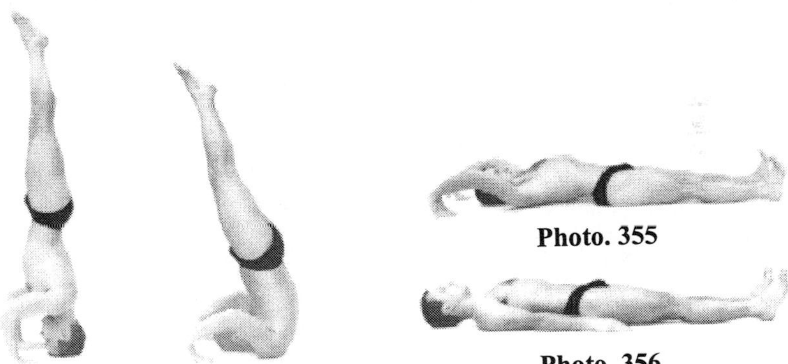

Photo. 353 **Photo. 354** **Photo. 355** **Photo. 356**

2. «Standing on the palms — sitting on haunches and palms»

Standing vertically on the hands in «Adho Mukta Vrikshasana» (Photo 357). Exhale, slowly bend the arms in the elbows, in the air tuck the chin into the chest and slowly put the back of the head on the floor (Photo 358), continue a incomplete frontal somersault motion onto the floor by gradually roll ing onto the back, buttocks and toes. Stop this motion with the hands in a squatting with palms on the floor (Photo 359). Inhale in this position, and with an exhalation, make a fragment of the back somersault by pushing off the floor with the hands and shifting the center of gravity backward. Gradually roll backwards and raise the legs, quickly placing the hands on the floor far behind the head at shoulder width (Photo

Photo. 357 **Photo. 358** **Photo. 359**

358). Without any delay, using a powerful gradual constriction of the muscles of the neck and then arms, lift the head off the floor, returning to the initial position standing vertically on the palms in «Adho Mukha Vrikshasana» (Photo 357).

3. «Vrschikasana — Ganda Bherundasana — Bhujangasana»

Standing on straight hands, bend the spine backwards in non-marginal «Vrschikasana» (Photo 360). Exhaling, slowly bend the arms in the elbows, simultaneously begin to turn the body backward in the air, and gradually put the chest, abdomen, hips, thighs, and feet on the floor. Fully straighten the arms in the elbows, thereby changing position to «Bhujangasana» (Photo 361). Inhale in this position, and with an exhalation, preserving the bent back, bend the arms in the elbows and bend the legs in the knees to roll over the abdomen, and chest. Then powerfully use the muscles of the back to fully lift the thighs off the floor. Without any delay, powerfully use the muscles of the chest and shoulders to press the hands against the floor and lift the body off the floor. Simultaneously, continue to turn the body in the air, thereby returning to the initial position, standing on straight hands (palms) in non-marginal «Vrschikasana» (Photo 360).

Photo. 360

Photo. 361

4. «*Standing on straight legs — standing on the palms*» *or* «*cartwheel*»

When starting to learn this *Vinyasa*, the initial position should be standing on straight legs (Photo 362). With an exhalation, begin to make a cartwheel to the first side using the arms and one leg (Photo 363). Then with a quick radial move, bend the body to the first side, put the first hand on the floor with a quick upward wave of the second leg through the side (Photo 364). Without any delay, change the position to «Adho Mukha Vrikshasana» (vertical stand on the palms) with straight legs spread wide apart (Photo 365). Continue rolling on the floor to the same side, shift the gravity center, lower the second leg onto the floor and take the first hand off the floor (Photo 364). Using the inertia of the side motion, return to the initial position standing on straight legs (Photo 362).

Thereafter, this *Vinyasa* is performed to the other side.

At the advanced level this *Vinyasa* begins and ends with the position standing on the hands in «Adho Mukha Vrikshasana» (Photo 365). At the advanced level of practicing it, it is possible to start with any position, but the *Vinyasa* should be practiced «in parts», with delays in all of its intermediate positions, i. e., standing on the legs, standing on the hands, standing on one hand.

Photo. 362

Photo. 363

Photo. 364

Photo. 365

ATTACHMENTS

ATTACHMENT 1

A SHORT DESCRIPTION OF GRAPHIC FORMS, GIVEN IN TABLE 1.

The first digit of the numbering below corresponds to the row order number in Table 1. The second digit of the numbering below, after a dot, corresponds to one of the four complexity levels.

1.1. The inability to touch the legs with the head sitting with legs straight. Practicing preparatory exercises, developing the depth of the forward bend in the loin, for example, incomplete «Paschimottanasana».

1.2. The ability to bend deeply forward, with any type of foundation, ability to place both legs behind the head, e.g., practice «Yoga Nidrasana», i. e., two legs behind the head lying on the back, hands hugging the thighs and the loin.

1.3. The ability to bend deeply forward, with any type of foundation, ability to place both feet under the armpits with the palms gripping the same-side knees, e. g., «Utthita Kandasana».

1.4. The ability to bend forward very deeply, the ability to reach the buttocks with the chin, e. g., in «Tittibhasana II» (turned skull and arm lock).

2.1. The inability to practice «Urdhva Dhanurasana» (gymnastic arch). Practicing preparatory exercises, developing the depth of the bend forward in the loin, for example, incomplete «Bhujangasana» — lying arms straight supporting the body with straight arms.

2.2. The ability to practice «Urdhva Dhanurasana» (gymnastic arch), with a rather deep back bend, arms straight and the distance between feet and hands not exceeding three lengths of the foot.

2.3. The ability to practice «Tiriang Mukhottanasana» (gymnastic back arch), deep back arch in the loin while gripping the ankle joints with the same-side hands.

2.4. In an extra-deep back arch, the ability to place the head on the buttocks and catch the shoulders with the feet, e.g., practicing «Vrschikasana», a «Scorpion» posture in the handstand.

3.1. Little ability to lean the body strictly to the side at the waist (without turning the chest down to the floor!), e. g., in «Parighasana» or doing a side bend when standing on the knees and gripping the wrist of the upper arm with the hand of the lower arm.

3.2. The ability to do a rather deep bend in the waist strictly to the side, e. g., standing on straight legs and gripping the wrist of the upper arm with the hand of the lower arm. The central line of the head and the arm lock reaches a horizontal line.

3.3. The ability to deeply bend the body at the waist strictly to the side when standing on straight legs and gripping the wrist of the upper arm with the hand of the lower arm. The central line of the head and the arm lock crosses the horizontal line and is inclined towards the floor.

3.4. The ability to extra deeply bend the body at the waist strictly to the side, e. g., standing on straight legs gripping the wrist of the upper arm with the hand of the lower arm. The arm lock almost reaches the floor.

4.1. The ability to do a simple twist of the spine at the waist, e. g., sitting on the floor with legs bent in the knees, holding one of the thighs under the armpit of the other arm.

4.2. The ability to do a rather deep twist of the spine at the waist, e. g., practicing «Marichyasana IV» or sit on the floor with one leg in half-lotus, the other leg, bent in the knee facing up. The thigh is kept under the armpit of the opposite arm, the hands are locked behind the back.

4.3. The ability to deeply twist the spine at the waist, e. g., practicing «Ardha Matsiendrasana III» or sit on the floor legs folded in Lotus, one thigh lying on the floor the other one raised in the vertical plane, hugged with the opposite arm, the hands locked behind the back.

4.4. The ability to extra deeply twist the spine at the waist, e. g., practicing «Nari purna Matsiendrasana». Or to sit on the floor legs folded in Lotus, one thigh lying on the floor the other one raised in the vertical plane, pressed against the back of the twisted body and hugged with the opposite arm, both hands gripping the toe of the raised leg.

5.1. Slight mobility of the dorsal section of the spine. Practicing preparatory exercises, developing the depth of the forward bend, e. g., «Halasana» or stand on the shoulders and the back of the head with straight legs kept behind the head.

5.2. The ability to rather deeply bend the dorsal section of the spine forward, e. g., practicing «Halasana» or the stand on the shoulders and the back of the neck with the toes and the knees touching the floor behind the head.

5.3. The ability to deeply bend the dorsal section of the spine forward, e. g., practicing «Halasana» or the stand on the shoulders and the back of the neck, the legs folded in Lotus and knees placed on the floor behind the head.

5.4. The ability to extra deeply bend the dorsal section of the spine forward, e. g., practicing «Halasana» or the stand on the shoulders and the back of the neck, the legs folded in Lotus, knees placed on the floor behind the head and thighs lowered to almost touching the head.

6.1. Slight back mobility of the dorsal section of the spine. Inability to practice simplest variations of «Ganda Bherundasana» («Scorpion» posture variety). Practicing preparatory back arches, developing the depth of the back bend in the dorsal section, e. g., standing on the floor on the chin, palms, knees and feet so as to keep the thighs in the vertical plane

6.2. The ability to rather deeply bend the dorsal section of the spine backwards, e. g., practicing «Ganda Bherundasana» («Scorpion» posture variety) standing on the floor on the chin, palms, knees and feet, keeping the thighs in the vertical plane and placing the feet on the floor in front of the face.

6.3. The ability to deeply bend the dorsal section of the spine back, e. g., practicing «Viparita Shalabhasana» («Scorpion» posture variety) by standing on the floor on the chin, palms, knees and feet, keeping the thighs in the vertical plane, and placing the feet on the floor in front of the face as far as possible.

6.4. The ability to extra deeply bend the dorsal section of the spine back, e. g., practicing «Chakra Bandhasana» standing on the knees, feet and chest, arms gripping the same-side knees, buttocks placed on the head.

7.1. Slight ability to bend the dorsal section of the body strictly to the side (without turning the chest down towards the floor!), e. g., in «Parighasana» or doing side bends while standing on the knees with the hand of the lower arm gripping the wrist the upper arm.

7.2. The ability to rather deeply bend the dorsal section of the body strictly to the side, e.g., standing on straight legs with the hand of the lower arm gripping the wrist the upper arm. The central line of the head and the hand lock reaches a horizontal line.

7.3. The ability to deeply bend the dorsal section of the body strictly to the side, e.g., standing on straight legs with the hand of the lower arm gripping the wrist the upper arm. The central line of the head and the hand lock crosses the horizontal line and is inclined towards the floor.

7.4. The ability to extra deeply bend the dorsal section of the body strictly to the side, e.g., standing on straight legs with the hand of the lower arm gripping the wrist the upper arm. The hand lock almost touches the floor.

8.1. The ability to practice the simplest twists of the spine at the waist, e. g., sitting on the floor with legs bent in the knees, one of the thighs kept under the armpit of the opposite arm.

8.2. The ability to rather deeply twist the spine at the waist, e. g., practicing «Marichyasana IV» or sit on the floor with one leg in half-lotus and the second leg bent in the knee, facing up. The thigh kept under the armpit of the opposite arm and the hands locked behind the back.

8.3. The ability to deeply twist the spine at the waist, e. g., practicing «Ardha Matsiendrasana III» or sit on the floor legs folded in Lotus, one thigh lying on the floor and the other one raised in the vertical plane, hugged with the opposite arm. The hands are locked behind the back.

8.4. The ability to extra deeply twist the spine at the waist, e. g., practicing «Naripurna Matsiendrasana» or sit on the floor legs folded in Lotus, one thigh lying on the floor. The other one raised in the vertical plane, pressed against the back of the twisted body and hugged with the opposite arm. Both hands grip the toe of the raised leg.

9.1. Inability to deeply bend the cervical section of the spine forward. Practicing preparatory developing exercises, e. g., «Sarvangasana» (shoulder stand) in its incomplete form, with the body and the legs kept vertical.

9.2. The ability to rather deeply bend the cervical section of the spine forward, e. g., practicing complete «Sarvangasana» (shoulder stand) in its complete form, with the body and the legs kept vertical, the chin firmly pressed against the chest.

9.3. The ability to deeply bend the cervical section of the spine forward, e. g., practicing complete «Halasana» or standing on the shoulders and the back of the head. The legs are folded in Lotus, knees placed on the floor behind the head.

9.4. The ability to extra deeply bend the cervical section of the spine forward, e. g., practicing complete «Halasana» or standing on the shoulders and the back of the head. The legs are folded in Lotus, knees placed on the floor behind the head, the thighs lowered and almost touching the head.

10.1. Slight back mobility in the cervical section of the spine with a backward bend. Practice preparatory exercises, developing this type of mobility, e. g., incomplete «Setu Bandhasana» or standing on the head, palms of the bent arms and the feet, legs bent.

10.2. Rather deep back- bend in the cervical section of the spine. The ability to practice complete «Setu Bandhasana» standing on the forehead, palms and feet, with the arms and legs kept straight.

10.3. The ability to deeply bend the cervical section of the spine back, e. g., practicing «Viparita Shalabhasana» or back arch lying on the floor on the chin, shoulders and straight arms, feet placed on the floor in front of the face.

10.4. The ability to extra deeply bend the cervical section of the spine back, e. g., practicing «Viparita Shalabhasana» or back arch lying on the floor on the chin, shoulders and straight arms, feet placed on the floor in front of the face, back firmly pressed against the back of the neck.

11.1. Slight ability to bend the head (neck) strictly to the side (without turning the face up or down!), e. g., sitting in «Virasana» the toes touching each other and the knees spread.

11.2. The ability to rather deeply bend the head (neck) strictly to the side, e. g., sitting in Lotus posture, one hand gripping the toe of the opposite leg behind the back, the other hand gripping the head over the top above the ear.

11.3. The ability to deeply bend the head (neck) strictly to the side, e. g., sitting in Lotus posture, both hands gripping the toes of opposite legs behind the back. Using only the muscles of the neck, bend the head to the side so that the ear almost touches the same-side shoulder which is lowered by pulling down the arm as low as possible.

11.4. The ability to extra deeply bend the head (neck) strictly to the side, e. g., sitting in Lotus posture both hands gripping the toes of opposite legs behind the back. Using only the muscles of the neck, bend the head to the side so that the ear firmly presses against the same-side shoulder which is lowered by pulling down the arm as low as possible.

12.1. The ability to practice simple twists of the cervical section of the spine, e. g., lying on the abdomen on the floor, elbows of both arms on the floor. One cheekbone is placed on the palm of the opposite hand and the second hand is gripping the back of the head near the opposite ear.

12.2. The ability to rather deeply twist the cervical section of the spine, e. g., lying on the abdomen on the floor with legs folded in Lotus, elbows of both arms pressed against the floor. One cheekbone is placed on the palm of the opposite hand and the second hand is gripping the back of the head near the opposite ear.

12.3. The ability to deeply twist the cervical section of the spine, e. g., lying on the abdomen on the floor with legs folded in Lotus, elbows of both arms pressed against the floor. One cheekbone placed on the palm of the opposite hand the second hand gripping the back of the head near the opposite ear. The chin is turned 45 degrees over the shoulder line behind the back.

12.4. The ability to extra deeply twist the cervical section of the spine, e. g., lying on the abdomen on the floor with legs folded in Lotus, elbows of both arms pressed against the floor. One cheekbone placed on the palm of the opposite hand the second hand gripping the back of the head near the opposite ear. The chin is turned 90 degrees over the shoulder line behind the back (i. e., face is turned 180 degrees with respect to its natural direction).

13.1. Inability to practice «Hanumasana» (longitudinal split). Practicing preparatory exercises developing mobility in the hip joints, e. g., varieties of «Trikonasana» (longitudinal tiriangles), «Virabhandrasana» (longitudinal pass), or an incomplete «Hanumasaana» (longitudinal split).

13.2. The ability to practice complete «Hanumasana» (longitudinal split).

13.3. The ability to practice «Hanumasana» (longitudinal split) with negative angle, i.e., deeper than the straight line of the legs, sitting hips on the floor, the foot of the front leg placed on a stand.

13.4. The ability to practice «Utthita Trivikramasana» standing on one leg with the other one raised higher than the vertical line and drawn behind the shoulder of the same arm in the longitudinal split with negative angle.

14.1. Inability to practice «Hanumasana» (longitudinal split). Practicing preparatory exercises developing mobility in the hip joints, e. g., varieties of «Trikonasana» (longitudinal tiriangles), «Virabhandrasana» (longitudinal pass), or an incomplete «Hanumasaana» (longitudinal split).

14.2. The ability to practice complete «Hanumasana» (longitudinal split) with the pelvis inclined backward.

14.3. The ability to practice «Hanumasana» (longitudinal split) the pelvis inclined deeply backward, i.e., in the back- arch both hands gripping the ankle joint of the back leg.

14.4. The ability to practice «Eka Pada Tiriang Mukhottanasana» standing on one leg bending backward, both hands gripping the ankle joint of the supporting leg. The other leg is raised vertically in a longitudinal split, and the pelvis deeply inclined backward.

15.1. Inability to practice «Sama Konasana» (transverse split). Practice preparatory exercises developing mobility in the hip joints, e. g., varieties of «Prasarita Danasana» (transverse split), transverse pass on one or on both legs or incomplete «Sama Konasana» (transverse split).

15.2. The ability to practice complete «Sama Konasana» (transverse split).

15.3. The ability to practice complete «Sama Konasana» (transverse split) with negative angle, i. e., deeper than the straight line of the legs, the feet placed on stands and sitting thighs pressed against the floor.

15.4. The ability to practice «Utthita Sama Konasana» (transverse split) with negative angle standing on one leg.

16.1. The ability to slightly cross the thighs, e. g., standing on straight legs.

16.2. The ability to rather deeply cross the thighs, e. g., practicing the element of «Garudasana» posture with the legs, sitting on the floor.

16.3. The ability to deeply cross the thighs, e. g., practicing the element of «Garudasana» posture with the legs, sitting on the floor and simultaneously, braiding one arm and both legs.

16.4. The ability to extra deeply cross the thighs, e. g., practicing the element of «Gomuchasana» posture, sitting on the floor thighs crossed extra deeply.

17.1. Inability to practice «Ardha Padmasana» or Half-Lotus. Practice preparatory exercises, developing mobility in hip joints, e. g., sitting on the floor one leg straight and the other leg bent in the knee as in «Janu Sirsasana». Also incom plete «Ardha Padmasana» or «Baddha Konasana» sitting on the floor legs bent, feet together and the thighs drawn wide apart until they touch the floor.

17.2. The ability to rather deeply turn the thighs, e. g., practicing «Ardha Padmaana» or Semi-Lotus, sitting on the floor with one leg straight and the other bent in the knee, pressed against the floor. The ankle-joint is placed on the knee of the other leg, and the knee is bent at approximately 90 degrees.

17.3. The ability to deeply turn the thigh, e. g., practicing the initial pass of «Vamadevasana» keeping the front leg bent for 90 degrees in front of you with the thighs firmly pressed against the floor.

17.4. The ability to deeply turn the thigh, e. g., practicing initial pass of «Vamadevasana» keeping the front leg bent for 90 degrees in front of the body with its ankle joint placed on a stand, its knee touching the floor and both thighs firmly pressed against the floor.

18.1. Inability to practice complete «Virasana». Practice preparatory exercises, developing mobility in hip joints, e. g., «Tiriang Mukha Eka Pada Paschimottanasana» or sitting with buttocks on the floor, one leg straight and the other one bent, knees together, and angling the ankle, or incomplete «Virasana» or sitting on the heels of bent legs.

18.2. The ability to rather deeply turn the hips, e. g., practicing complete «Virasana I» or sitting with buttocks on the floor between the feet with the knees firmly pressed against each other.

18.3. The ability to deeply turn the hips, e. g., practicing complete «Virasana II» or sitting with buttocks on the floor with legs bent at 90 degrees, feet pointing to the sides and the knees firmly pressed against each other.

18.4. The ability to extra deeply turn the thighs, e. g., practicing complete «Virasana II» or sitting with buttocks on the floor with legs bent at 90 degrees, feet placed on stands and pointing to the sides and the knees firmly pressed against each other.

19.1. Inability to completely straighten the leg in the knee. Practice preparatory exercises developing mobility in knee joints, e. g., standing in a longitudinal pass on the heel of the front leg and the foot of the back leg, pressing the knee of the front leg with the hands, above and below the knee-cap.

19.2. The ability to completely straighten the leg in the knee, e. g., standing in a longitudinal pass on the heel of the front leg and the foot of the back leg, pressing the knee of the front leg with the hands, above and below the knee-cap.

19.3. The ability to over-straighten the leg in the knee, e. g., standing in a longitudinal pass on the heel of the front leg and the foot of the back leg, pressing the knee of the front leg with the hands, above and below the knee-cap.

19.4. The ability to over-straighten the leg in the knee, e. g., standing in longitudinal pass on the heel of the front leg and the foot of the back leg without using the hands, operating the muscles of the front leg only.

20.1. Inability to completely practice the element of «Vamadevasana» with the back leg. Practice preparatory exercises developing mobility in the knee joints, e. g., «Tiriang Mukna Eka Pada Paschimottanasana». Also sitting with buttocks on the floor, one leg straight and the other leg bent so as to bring the knees together, or practicing incomplete «Virasana» or sitting on the floor on the heels of bent legs.

20.2. The ability to completely practice the element of «Vamadevasana», e.

g., standing in a longitudinal pass on the foot of the bent front leg and the knee of the bent back leg, grip the back leg with the hand of the same side arm and press the ankle joint down against the side of the thigh.

20.3. The ability to completely practice the element of «Vamadevasana», e. g., standing in a longitudinal pass on the foot of the bent front leg and the knee of the bent back leg, hold the foot of the back leg with the same side of the waist without using the hands.

20.4. The ability to completely practice the element of «Vamadevasana», e. g., standing in a longitudinal pass on the foot of the bent front leg and the knee of the bent back leg, holding the back leg with the toes from the outside under the same thigh without using the hands.

21.1. Inability to practice complete «Padmasana» or Lotus. Practice preparatory exercises developing mobility in knee joints, e. g., sitting on the floor one leg straight the other one bent in «Jana Sirsasana» or incomplete «Ardha Padmasana».

21.2. The ability to completely practice «Padmasana» or sitting on the floor with the legs folded in Lotus and using the hands to close the knees up to the hip width.

21.3. The ability to fold the legs in «Padmasana» (Lotus) without the use of the hands in any position and to practice «Kandasana» («Namaste» with the legs) sitting on the floor.

21.4. The ability to practice «Kandasana» («Namaste» with the legs) sitting on the floor and using the hands to close the knees up to hip width.

22.1. Inability to place the heels of straight legs on the floor in «Adho Mukha Shvanasana». Use preparatory exercises to develop mobility in the ankle joints, e. g., practicing incomplete «Adho Mukha Shvanasana» with the feet strictly parallel at the hip width, and the heels lowered down to the floor as much as possible.

22.2. The ability to place the heels of the straight legs on the floor in complete «Adho Mukta Shvanasana».

22.3. The ability to place the heel of straightened back leg on the floor in «Trikonasana (even-sided tiriangle formed by the legs) while strictly keeping the parallel position of the feet.

22.4. The ability to place the heel of a straightened back leg on the floor in «Virabhandasana» (deep longitudinal pass of the legs with the back leg straight and the front leg bent in the knee at 90 degrees).

23.1. The inability to practice complete «Virasana» sitting on the floor with the toes directed strictly backward. Practice preparatory exercises to develop mobility in ankle joints, e. g., «Tiriang Mukha Eka Pada Paschimottanasana» or sitting with buttocks on the floor, one leg straight the other one bent so as to join the knees together. Also practicing incomplete «Virasana», sitting on the heels of bent legs.

23.2. The ability to practice complete «Virasana» with the toes directed strictly backward, shifting the center of gravity backward and raising the knees.

23.3. The ability to stand on the feet with the toes turned strictly backward.

23.4. The ability to stand on the tiptoes with a negative angle in the ankles with toes facing strictly backward.

24.1. The ability to stand in «Prasarita Padottanasana» (transverse triangle) without taking the outer sides of the feet off the floor, legs spread and the pelvis raised above the floor not more than the length of the torso.

24.2. The ability to stand in «Prasarita Padottanasana» (transverse triangle) without taking the outer sides of the feet off the floor, legs spread widely apart and the pelvis raised above the floor not more than shoulder height.

24.3. The ability to stand in «Prasarita Padottanasana» (transverse triangle) without taking the outer sides of the feet off the floor, legs spread wide apart and the pelvis raising above the floor not more than at the arm's height.

24.4. The ability to stand in «Sama Konasana» (transverse split) without taking the outer sides of the feet off the floor.

25.1. The ability to stand on straight legs with thighs and legs crossed and spread wider than shoulder width, without taking the internal sides of the feet off the floor.

25.2. The ability to stand on straight legs with thighs and legs crossed and spread apart twice the shoulder width, without taking the internal sides of the feet off the floor.

25.3. The ability to lie on the side of the lower leg with the supporting arm kept straight, without taking the internal side of the foot of the supporting leg off the floor.

25.4. The ability to lie on the side of the lower leg straight with the supporting arm bent in the elbow, without taking the internal side of the foot of the supporting leg off the floor.

26.1. Inability to practice «Virasana» sitting with buttocks on the floor between the heels, knees drawn together, feet turned and toes pointed to the sides perpendicular to the thighs. Practice preparatory exercises to develop mobility in ankle joints, e. g., «Tiriang Mukha Eka Pada Paschimottanasana» or sitting with buttocks on the floor, one leg straight the other one bent, both knees kept together and the foot of the bent leg facing to the side perpendicular to the thighs. Also, incomplete «Virasana» sitting on the heels of bent legs with feet turned and toes pointed strictly perpendicular with respect to the thighs.

26.2. The ability to practice «Virasana» sitting with buttocks on the floor between the heels, knees drawn together, feet turned and toes pointed strictly perpendicular to the thighs.

26.3. The ability to practice «Mula Bandhasana» sitting on the feet with soles pressed together, and to rotate the ankles, toes turned backward and heels turned forward.

26.4. The ability to practice «Mula Bandhasana» sitting on the feet with soles pressed together, and to rotate the ankles, toes turned backward and heels turned forward, with the pelvis inclined backward in the hips and supporting the body by the elbows placed on the floor behind the back.

27.1. Inability to practice «Baddha Konasana» sitting with buttocks on the soles of the feet connected together (the throne posture). Practice preparatory exercises to develop mobility in the ankle joints, e. i., initial position in «Janu Sirsasana», sitting on the floor with one leg straight and the other one bent, use the hands to turn the foot of the bent leg towards the abdomen. Also, «Bandha Konasana» sitting on the floor on the buttocks, legs bent, soles drawn together and knees spread as wide apart as possible, grip the toes with the hands and inclining the body ahead.

27.2. The ability to practice «Baddha Konasana» sitting with buttocks on the feet soles firmly pressed together (the throne posture).

27.3. The ability to practice «Baddha Konasana» sitting with buttocks on the feet soles firmly pressed together, the body deeply inclined forward.

27.4. The ability to practice «Baddha Konasana» sitting with buttocks on the floor in front of the feet, soles firmly pressed together, the body deeply inclined forward.

28.1. Inability to place the chin on the floor between straight arms stretched along the floor in front of the body at shoulder width while standing on the knees with thighs kept in the vertical plane.

28.2. The ability to place the chin on the floor between straight arms stretched along the floor in front the body at shoulder width while standing on the knees with thighs kept in vertical plane.

28.3. The ability to practice «Mukta Hasha Sirsasana VI» (see. «Vinyasa Technique» chapter, «Head Down» subsection, «Standing on the Head «Vinyasa», p. 356) standing on the head supporting the body by placing the palms of straight arms in front of the head at shoulder width.

28.4. The ability to practice «Mukta Hasha Sirsasana VI» standing on the head supporting the body by placing the palms of straight arms in front of the head at the shoulder width and the body deeply inclined towards the arms in a back arch.

29.1. Inability to draw the arms back in the shoulders when sitting on the floor with palms placed on the floor behind the body at shoulder width, and lowering the arms towards the floor for the distance equal to the length of one of the feet.

29.2. The ability to draw the arms back in the shoulders when sitting on the floor, palms placed on the floor behind the body at shoulder width where the arms are lowered towards the floor to the distance equal to the length of one of the feet.

29.3. The ability to draw the arms back in the shoulders when sitting on the floor, palms placed on the floor behind the body at shoulder width where the arms are lowered towards the floor to the distance equal to half the length of one foot.

29.4. The ability to draw the arms back in the shoulders when sitting on the floor, palms placed on the floor behind the body at shoulder width where the arms are lowered on the floor and firmly touching it.

30.1. Lying on the floor on the abdomen with the arms stretched out to the sides from the shoulders, being unable to turn the body abdomen up using the feet of the bent legs on the floor while gripping the hands behind the back. Doing this one must keep the arms strictly perpendicular to the line of the spine and avoid taking the shoulder of the lower arm off the floor. Practicing preparatory exercises developing mobility of the shoulder joints, e. g., the above described exercise without the grip of the hands and supporting the body by placing the palm of the upper arm on the floor in front of the chest.

30.2. Lying on the floor on the abdomen with the arms stretched out to the sides from the shoulders, the ability to turn the body abdomen up using the feet of the bent legs on the floor and gripping the hands together behind the back.

Doing this it is important to keep the arms strictly perpendicular to the line of the spine and avoid taking the shoulder of the lower arm off the floor.

30.3. Lying on the floor on the abdomen with the arms stretched out to the sides from the shoulders, ability to turn the body abdomen up the feet of the bent legs on the floor, gripping the hands behind the back. Bend the upper arm and firmly press its elbow against the lower arm, simultaneously further turning the body around the lower shoulder by drawing the leg closest to the upper arm, towards the hands. Doing this it is important to keep the arms strictly perpendicular to the line of the spine and avoid taking the shoulder of the lower arm off the floor.

30.4. Lying on the floor on the abdomen with the arms stretched out to the sides from the shoulders, the ability to turn the body abdomen up using the feet of the bent legs on the floor and lie back on the lower arm. The arm should be strictly perpendicular with respect to the line of the spine and its shoulder should not be taken off the floor.

31.1. Lying on the floor on the back with arms stretched to the sides from the shoulders, being unable to turn the body abdomen down so as to place the lower arm below the throat with the chin facing the floor. The knees of the bent legs are pressed against the floor, the pelvis is raised up and the upper shoulder lowered towards the floor to a height smaller than the length of the foot. Doing this one must keep the arms strictly perpendicular with respect to the spine and avoid taking the shoulder of the lower arm off the floor. Practicing preparatory exercises developing mobility of the shoulder, e. g., doing the above exercise supporting the body by placing the hand of the upper arm on the floor near the chest.

31.2. Lying on the floor on the back with arms stretched to the sides from the shoulders, the ability to turn the body abdomen down so as to place the lower arm below the throat with its shoulder lying on the floor, the chin facing the floor. The knees of the bent legs pressed against the floor and the pelvis raised up, and locking the arms behind the back, where the upper arm is lowered, elbow down towards the floor.

31.3. Lying on the abdomen on the floor firmly cross straight arms under the throat perpendicular to the spine, the ability to raise the pelvis upward and ahead, supporting the body by placing the knees of the bent legs on the floor and reach the floor with the forehead.

31.4. The ability while lying on the floor on the abdomen to firmly cross straight arms under the throat strictly perpendicular with respect to the spine and simultaneously place the chin and the chest on the floor.

32.1. The inability to lie with the chest on the floor, without taking the shoulders off the floor when the pelvis is raised above the floor, and the body is supported on the knees of the bent legs. Being unable to firmly press the elbow of one arm against the floor with the knee of the same side leg. The arm dropped down along the body and bent in the elbow under 90 degrees so as to make its forearm facing to the outside strictly perpendicular with respect to the line of the spine. Develop mobility of the shoulder joint practicing this exercise in its incomplete form.

32.2. Lying with the chest on the floor without taking the shoulders off the floor, pelvis raised above the floor and supporting the body on the knees of the bent legs. The ability to firmly press the elbow of one arm against the floor with the knee of the same side leg. The arm dropped down along the body and bent in the elbow under 90 degrees so as to make its forearm facing to the outside strictly perpendicular with respect to the line of the spine.

32.3. Lying with the chest on the floor without taking the shoulders off the floor, pelvis raised above the floor and supporting the body on the knees of the bent legs. The ability to firmly press the elbows of both arms against the floor with the same side knees. The arms dropped down along the body and bent in the elbow under 90 degrees so as to make their forearms face to the outside strictly perpendicular with respect to the line of the spine.

32.4. Lying with the chest on the floor without taking the shoulders off the floor, the arms dropped down along the body and bent in the elbows under 90 degrees so as to make their forearms face to the sides, strictly perpendicular to the line of the spine, wrists placed on stands, the ability to firmly press the elbows to the floor without assistance of the legs.

33.1. Slight mobility in shoulder joints. Practicing preparatory exercise developing this type of mobility, e. g., sitting on the floor with the legs bent and kept together, knees facing up. Pull the elbow of one arm (bent under 90 degrees) with the hand of the other arm towards the middle, placing its wrist on the same side knee.

33.2. Sitting on the floor with the arms bent in the elbow and fixed. With the backsides of the wrists under the armpits, the ability to press the hands against the sides of the ribcage, and join the elbows with the knees of the bent legs.

33.3. The ability, in any position, e. g., sitting on the floor with the legs folded in Lotus, to fix the backsides of the wrists under the armpits, press the hands against the sides of the ribcage, and join the elbows with the effort of the chest and shoulder muscles.

33.4 Lying on the abdomen on the floor the ability to fix the backside of the wrist of the first hand under the armpit. With the hand firmly pressed against the side of the ribcage, put the shoulder of this arm on the floor, its elbow lying under the opposite shoulder. Then without taking the shoulder of the first arm off the floor, put the shoulder of the second (free) arm on the elbow of the first (bent) arm.

34.1. Inability to fully straighten the arms in the elbow joints. Practice preparatory exercises developing this type of mobility, e. g., sitting on the toes with palms placed on the floor the fingers facing strictly backward, place the knees at the beginning of the triceps muscles. Apply pressure with the knees to unbend the arms in the elbows as much as possible.

34.2. The ability to fully straighten the arms in the elbow joints when sitting on the toes, palms placed on the floor with the fingers facing strictly backward. Place the knees at the beginning of the triceps muscles above the elbows and apply pressure of the knees, unbending the arms in the elbows as much as possible.

34.3. The ability to over-straighten the arms in the elbow joints when sitting on the toes, palms placed on the floor with the fingers facing strictly backward. Place the knees at the beginning of the triceps muscles above the elbows and apply pressure of the knees to unbend the arms in the elbows for 5 — 25 degrees deeper than the straight line.

34.4. The ability to over-straighten the arms in the elbow joints 10 — 30 degrees deeper that the straight line with the effort of the triceps muscles only (without any assistance of the knees), e. g., standing vertically.

35.1. Inability to lock the arms behind the back as in «Gomukhasana» due to the lack of mobility in the shoulder joint of the upper arm. Practice preparatory exercises developing mobility in the shoulder joints, e. g., sitting on the floor with the legs bent and the knees facing upward. Bend the elbow of the first arm and placc it on the same side knee, and use the other hand and the chin to draw the wrist of the first hand as close towards the outer side of the shoulder as possible.

35.2.Sitting on the floor with the legs bent and the knees looking upward. The ability to bend the elbow of the first arm and place it on the same side knee, and use the other hand and the chin to press the wrist of the first hand to the outer sides of the shoulder.

35.3. Sitting on the floor with the legs bent and the knees looking upward. The ability to bend the elbow of the first arm and place it on the same side knee and use the second hand from under the shoulder of the of the first arm to draw the wrist of the first hand deeply backward, at the side of its shoulder.

35.4. In any position, e. g., sitting on the floor the legs folded in Lotus with the arms gripped behind the back as in «Gomukhasana». Lower the elbow of the upper arm forward, and, without unlocking the arms, slip the arm of the upper hand at the side of its same side shoulder and deeply lower it at the side of the shoulder using the lower hand.

36.1. Inability to grip the arm lock as in «Gomukhasana» due to the lack of mobility in the elbow joint of the lower arm. Practice preparatory exercises developing mobility in the elbow joints, e. g., sitting on the floor with the legs bent and the knees facing upward. Bend the elbow of the first arm and press it against the internal side of the same side knee, and use the second hand to firmly press the wrist of the first hand to the internal side of the homonymous shoulder, i. e., to its armpit.

36.2. Sitting on the floor with the legs bent and the knees looking upward. The ability to bend both arms in the elbows, place the back sides of the wrists on the sides of the ribcage as high under the armpits as possible and pressing the back sides of the elbows with the internal sides of the knees, join the elbows together.

36.3. In any position, e. g., sitting on the floor the legs folded in Lotus , the ability to bend both arms in the elbows, drawing the outer sides of the wrist to the ribcage as high under the armpits as possible. Then using the effort of the chest and shoulder muscles alone, join the elbows to make them touch.

36.4. Lying on the floor on the abdomen, e. g., with the legs folded in Lotus. The ability to bend the first arm in the elbow, drawing its wrist on the closest side of the ribcage as high under the armpit as possible, putting its shoulder in the floor to place its elbow under the shoulder of the second arm. Then without taking the first knee off the floor, firmly press the second shoulder to the elbow of the first arm.

37.1. Sitting on the floor legs kept straight and the palms of the straight arms placed on the floor fingers facing forward. Without bending the elbows and without taking the lower palms off the floor, the ability to do a forward bend with the torso and arms of 75 degrees with respect to the floor line.

37.2. In a «Spider» posture, supporting the body by placing the palms of straight arms on the floor, the toes placed on the floor and the legs against on the same side shoulders. With the fingers facing forward, the ability to shift the gravity center ahead, without bending the arms in the elbows and without taking the palms off the floor, incline the arms forward to make the angle of 60 degrees with respect to the floor line.

37.3. In a «Spider» posture, supporting the body by placing the palms of straight arms on the floor, the toes placed on the floor and the legs against the same side shoulders. With the fingers facing forward, fully straighten the legs simultaneously raising the pelvis. Without bending the arms in the elbows and without taking the palms off the floor , the ability to incline the arms forward to make the angle of 45 degrees with respect to the floor line.

37.4.In any position, e. g., sitting on the floor legs folded in Lotus, the ability to stretch the arms to the sides along the horizontal shoulder line, with the palms facing to the side and fingers pointing upward. With the effort of the forearm muscles only, pull the internal sides of the arms towards the body to make the palm planes cross the vertical line and drop inside.

38.1. Standing on all fours in the «Cat» posture and placing the back sides of the hands on the floor so as to make the fingers face backward, without bending the elbows and without taking the hands off the floor, the ability to shift the gravity center and incline straight arms backward to make an angle of at least 90 degrees with respect to the floor line.

38.2. Standing in «Chaturanga Dandasana» on straight arms and supporting the body by placing the backsides of the hands on the floor with fingers pointing strictly backward. Without bending the arms in the elbows and without taking the wrists off the floor, the ability to lean the arms backward to make an angle of at least 75 degrees with respect to the floor line.

38.3.Standing in «Adho Mukha Shvanasana» supporting the body by placing the backside of the hands on the floor with the fingers pointing strictly backward. Without bending the arms in the elbows and without taking the wrists off the floor, the ability to lean the arms backward to make an angle of at least 45 degrees with respect to the floor line.

38.4.In any position, e. g., sitting on the floor with the legs folded in Lotus, the ability to stretch the arms to the side along the horizontal shoulder line with the palms directed inward and the fingers pointing vertically downward. Using the effort of the forearm muscles, pull the inward sides of the arms towards the body to make the palm planes cross the vertical line and incline inside.

39.1. In any position, e. g., standing on the floor with the legs kept straight, the ability to stretch the first hand horizontally in front of the body, fix straight fingers and the palm in the vertical plane so as to make the palm face inside. Then grip the wrist of the first hand with the hand of the second arm and incline it down so as to make its central line form the angle of 25 degrees with respect to the horizontal line. The palm of the first hand should always be kept in the vertical plane.

39.2. Same as 39.1., but inclining the central line of the wrist of the first hand down to form the angle of 45 degrees with respect to the horizontal line.

39.3. In any position, e. g., sitting on the floor in «Virasana», same as 39.1., but inclining the central line of the wrist of the first hand down to make the angle of 60 degrees with respect to the horizontal line.

39.4. In any position, e. g., sitting on the floor in «Padmasama», the ability to stretch the arms horizontally in front of the body with straight fingers and the palm fixed in the vertical plane so as to make the palm face inside. Using the effort of the forearm muscles only, incline the wrists downward so as to make the central lines of the palms at an angle of 90 degrees with respect to the horizontal line. The palm of the first hand should always be kept in the vertical plane.

40.1. In any position, e. g., standing on the floor with the legs kept straight, the ability to stretch the first arm horizontally in front of the body, fix straight fingers and the palm in the vertical plane making the palm face inside. Grip the wrist of the first hand with the second hand and raise it upward so its central line forms an angle of 5 degrees with respect to the horizontal line. The palm of the first hand should always be kept in the vertical plane.

40.2. Same as 40.1, but raising the central line of the wrist of the first hand upward to form an angle of 25 degrees with respect to the horizontal line.

40.3. In any position, e. g., sitting on the floor in «Virasana», same as 40.1, but raising the central line of the wrist of the first hand upward to make the angle of 45 degrees with respect to the horizontal line.

40.4. In any position, e. g., sitting on the floor in «Padmasana», stretch both arms horizontally in front of the body, fix straight fingers and the palms in the vertical plane making the palms face inside. Using the forearm muscles alone raise the wrists upward, their central line forming an angle of over 50 degrees with respect to the horizontal line. The palm of the first hand should always be kept in the vertical plane.

41.1.In any position, e. g., standing on straight legs, the ability to fully straighten and stretch the first arm horizontally in front of the body with the palm down. Use the second hand to grip the first and turn the first arm outward to move the palm of the first hand into the horizontal plane facing upward.

41.2. In any position, e. g., sitting on the floor in «Virasana», the ability to stretch straight arms in front of the body and turn them palms facing outward. Cross the forearms to place one arm above the other one and grip one palm on the other. Then twist the hands, bend the arms in the elbows, and without any delay, lower the hand lock down, turn it towards the abdomen, raise it upward between the arms and straighten the arms in the elbows. Now twist the hand-lock forward, thereby turning the wrist with the hand of the lower arm outward so as to place the palm of the upper hand in the vertical plane facing outward.

41.3., The same as 41.2, but with a deeper rotation of the wrist of the upper hand with the wrist of the lower hand outward and down so as to make the palm of the upper hand reach the horizontal plane facing downward.

41.4. In any position, e. g., sitting on the floor in «Padmasana» the ability to stretch straight arms horizontally in front of the body and turn the wrists outward and down with the effort of the forearm muscles alone to make their palms reach horizontal plane facing downward.

42.1. In any position, e. g., standing on straight legs, the ability to fully straighten and stretch the first arm horizontally in front of the body and turn its hand inward with the second hand to place the palm of the first hand in the vertical plane facing outward.

42.2. In any position, e. g., sitting on the floor in «Virasana», the ability to stretch straight hands in front of the body and turn the palms facing outward. Cross the forearms to place the first arm under the second arm and grip one palm with the other one. Twist the hands in the arm lock, and without unlocking the fingers and keeping the palms together, turn the wrist of the first hand with the arm of the second hand deeper inward to place the palm of the lower hand in the horizontal plane facing upward.

42.3. Same as 42.2, but with a deeper rotation of the wrist of the lower hand with the wrist of the upper hand, placing the palm of the lower hand in the vertical plane facing inward.

42.4. In any position, e. g., sitting on the floor in «Padmasana», the ability to stretch straight arms horizontally in front of the body and turn their wrists inward and upward with the effort of the forearm muscles alone to make the palms reach the horizontal plane facing upward.

ATTACHMENT 2

SHORT DESCRIPTION OF GRAPHIC FORMS GIVEN IN TABLE 2

The first digit of this numbering corresponds to the column number in Table 2.

The second and the third (dash-separated) digits of this numbering, after a dot, correspond to a particular complexity level of such forms. The majority of the forms given in Table 2 have been described in detail in B.K.S. Iyengar's «Light on Yoga», which is wide spread and known to the majority of the practitioners. Therefore given below are only the names of the forms depicted in Table 2, in accordance with their names given in that book and with short technical descriptions thereof.

1.1-2. «Utthita Hasta Padangusthasana» — standing vertically on one leg, gripping the second (raised) leg with the same side straight arm holding the leg by the foot.

1.2.-3. «Utthita Hasta Padangusthasana» — standing vertically on one leg, gripping the second (raised) leg with the same side bent arm holding the leg by the foot.

1.3-4. «Utthita Hasta Trivikramasana» — standing vertically on one leg in a longitudinal split, gripping the second (raised) leg with the same side bent arm holding the leg by the foot.

2.1-2. «Supta Padangusthasana» — lying on the back, gripping the raised leg with the same side straight arm.

2.2-3. «Supta Padangusthasana» — lying on the back, gripping the raised leg with the same side bent arm.

2.3-4. «Supta Trivikramasana» — lying on the back in longitudinal split, gripping the raised leg with the same side bent arm.

3.1-2. «Eka Pada Sarvangasana» — standing vertically on the shoulders, one leg lowered on the floor in front of the chest.

3.2-3. «Eka Pada Sirsasana» — standing vertically on the head, one leg lowered on the floor in front of the chest.

3.3-4. «Eka Pada Vrksasana» — standing vertically on the hands, one leg lowered in front of the chest in longitudinal pass.

4.1-2. «Urdhva Prasarita Ekapadasana» — standing on one leg and bent arms, the other leg raised above the horizontal line.

4.2-3. «Urdhva Prasarita Ekapadasana» — standing on one leg and bent arms, the other leg raised 75 degrees above the horizontal line.

4.3-4. «Viparita Trivikramasana» standing on one leg and bent arms in a longitudinal split, the other leg raised vertically.

5.1-2. «Urdhva Prasarita Ekapadasana» — standing on one leg, gripping the other leg and raising it above the horizontal line with the same side hand.

5.2-3. «Urdhva Prasarita Ekapadasana» — standing on one leg, gripping the other leg and raising it 75 degrees above the horizontal line with the same side hand.

5.3-4. «Viparita Trivikramasana» — standing on one leg in longitudinal split, gripping the other (raised) leg on the foot with the same side hand.

6.1-2. «Utthita Hasta Padangusthasana» — standing on one leg, gripping the other leg and raising it to the side above the horizontal line with the same side hand.

6.2-3. «Utthita Hasta Padangusthasana» — standing on one leg, gripping the other leg and raising it to the side over 75 degrees above the horizontal line with the same side hand.

6.3-4. «Utthita Hasta Trivikramasana» — Utthita Hasta Trivikramasana» — standing on one leg in a longitudinal split, gripping the other leg and raising it to the side with the opposite side hand.

7.1-2. «Supta Padangusthasana» — lying on the back, gripping the foot of the leg raised to the side with the same side hand with the arm straight.

7.2-3. «Supta Padangusthasana» — lying on the back, gripping the foot of the leg raised to the side with the same side hand of a bent arm.

7.3-4 «Supta Trivikramasana» — lying on the back in longitudinal split, gripping the foot of the leg raised to the side with the opposite side hand.

8.1-2. «Parsva Eka Pada Sarvangasana» — standing vertically on the shoulders, one leg lowered to the side on the floor.

8.2-3. «Parsva Eka Pada Salamba Sirsasana II» — standing vertically on the head, one leg lowered to the side on the floor.

8.3-4. «Parsva Eka Pada Vriksasana» — standing vertically on the shoulders, one leg lowered to the side towards the floor.

9.1-2. «Vasisthasana» — lying on one hand and one leg, gripping the foot of the leg raised upward and to the side, with the hand of a free straight arm.

9.2-3. «Vasisthasana» — lying on one hand and one leg, gripping the foot of the leg raised upward and to the side, with the hand of a free bent arm.

9.3-4. Vasisthasana» — lying on one hand and one leg, holding the upper leg, raised to the side and upward, with the upper shoulder.

10.1-2. «Padangusthasana» — lying on the abdomen, gripping the toes of the same side leg with straight arms and drawing it to the side and forward, with the straight arm.

10.2-3. «Padangusthasana» — lying on the abdomen, gripping the toes of the same side leg with bent arms and drawing it to the side and forward.

10.3-4. «Trivikramasana» — lying on the abdomen in longitudinal split, one leg stretched to the side and forward, gripped with the hand of the opposite bent arm on the toes.

11.1-2. «Utthita Trikonasana» — standing on straight legs in longitudinal pass, bend the body towards the front leg, the palm of the same side straight arm near its foot, and the pelvis and the chest turned so as to be placed in the vertical plane.

11.2-3. «Hanumanasana» — sitting on the floor in transverse split, gripping one foot with bent arms and the body inclined towards this foot 45 degrees with respect to vertical line.

11.3-4. «Hanumanasana» — sitting on the floor in transverse split, gripping one foot with bent arms and the body inclined to the side so as to put the body on this leg.

12.1-2. «Hanumanasana» — sitting vertically on the floor in incomplete transverse split.

12.2-3. «Hanumanasana» — sitting vertically on the floor in complete transverse split.

12.3-4. «Hanumanasana» — sitting vertically on the floor in complete transverse split, the front leg placed on a stand.

13.1-2. «Parsvottanasana» — standing on straight legs in longitudinal pass with the body inclined towards the front leg.

13.2-3. «Hanumanasana» — sitting on the floor in longitudinal pass with the body inclined towards the front leg.

13.3-4. «Hanymanasana» — sitting on the floor in longitudinal split with the negative angle, the front leg placed on a stand and the body inclined towards the front leg.

14.1-2. «Eka Pada Sirsasana» — sitting vertically on the floor with one leg kept straight, the other leg drawn behind the same side shoulder, this leg's foot gripped with the opposite hand.

14.2-3. «Eka Pada Sirsasana» — sitting vertically on the floor with one leg behind the head.

14.3-4. «Buddhasana» — sitting vertically on the floor, one leg behind the back and the feet under the armpit of the opposite arm.

15.1-2. «Durvasana» — standing vertically on one leg with the other leg drawn behind the same side shoulder and gripped on the foot with the opposite side hand.

15.2-3. «Durvasana» — standing vertically on one leg with the other leg behind the head.

15.3-4. «Buddha Durvasana» — standing vertically on one leg with the other leg behind the back, its foot under the armpit of the opposite arm.

16.1-2. «Visvamitrasana» — lying on the first hand and second leg, the first leg, drawn behind the shoulder of the supporting arm.

16.2-3. «Kala Bhairavasana» — lying on the first hand and second leg with the first leg behind the head.

16.3-4. «Buddha Kala Bhairavasana» — lying on the first hand and second leg with the first leg behind the back, its foot under the armpit of the second arm.

17.1-2. «Utthita Ekapadasana» — standing on one leg, the other leg kept straight and raised in front of the face without using the hands. Make the angle at least 90 degrees with respect to the vertical line.

17.2-3. «Utthita Ekapadasana» — standing on one leg, the other leg kept straight and raised in front of the face without using the hands. Make the angle at least 135 degrees with respect to the vertical line.

17.3-4. «Utthita Ekapadasana» — standing on one leg in longitudinal split, the other leg kept straight and raised in front of the face without using the hands to make a vertical line.

18.1-2. «Vishvamitrasana» — lying on straight arms and one leg, the other straight leg on the shoulder.

18.2-3. «Kaka Bhairavasana» — lying on straight arms and one leg, the other leg behind the head.

18.3-4. «Kala Bhairavasana» — lying on straight arms and one leg, the other leg behind the back, its foot under the armpit of the opposite arm.

19.1-2. «Prasarita Padottanasana» — standing on straight legs, spread to form a transverse even-sided tiriangle.

19.2-3. «Sama Konasana» — sitting on the floor in transverse split.

19.3-4. «Sama Konasana» — sitting on the floor in transverse split with the negative angle, the feet placed on stands.

20.1-2. «Ardha Chandrasana» — lying on the side on one straight leg and the same side straight arm.

20.2-3. «Utthita Sama Konasana» — standing on one leg, the other leg raised to the side in an incomplete transverse split.

20.3-4. «Utthita Sama Konasana» — standing on one leg with the other leg raised to the side in a complete transverse split.

21.1-2. «Prasarita Padottana Salamba Sarvangasana I» — standing on the shoulders, legs straight, spread to form a transverse even-sided tiriangle.

21.2-3. «Prasarita Padottana Salamba Sirsasana II» — standing on the head, legs straight, spread in an incomplete transverse split.

21.3-4. «Prasarita Padottana Adho Mukha Vriksasana» — standing on the hands with straight legs spread in a complete transverse split.

22.1-2. «Upavistha Konasana» — sitting on the floor legs straight, drawn to the side in an even-sided tiriangle, the body inclined forward.

22.2-3. «Sama Konasana» — lying on the abdomen on the floor in transverse split.

22.3-4. «Sama Konasana» - lying on the abdomen on the floor in transverse split, with negative angle, feet placed on stands.

23.1-2. «Urdhva Mukha Prasarita Padottanasana» — lying on the back with straight legs spread to form an even-sided tiriangle.

23.2-3. «Urdhva Mukha Prasarita Padottanasana» — lying on the back with straight legs spread in an incomplete transverse split.

23.3-4. «Urdhva Mukha Sama Konasana — lying on the back with straight legs spread in a complete transverse split.

24.1-2. «Tittibhasana I» — standing on the hands, the spine kept vertical and straight legs placed on the same side shoulders.

24.2-3. «Utthita Kurmasana» — standing on the hands, the spine kept vertical and both legs behind the head.

24.2-3. «Utthita Kandasana» — standing on the hands, the spine kept vertical and both legs under the armpits of the same side arms.

25.1-2. «Tittibhasana I» — standing on the hands, the spine kept vertical and straight legs placed on the same side shoulders.

25.2-3. «Utthita Kurmasana» — standing on the hands, the spine kept vertical and both legs behind the head.

25.3-4. «Utthita Kandasana» — standing on the hands, the spine kept vertical and both legs under the armpits of same side arms.

26.1-2. «Uttanasana» standing on straight legs and deeply bending the body forward.

26.2-3. «Tittibhasana II» standing on straight legs, deeply bending the body forward to draw in between the legs, hugging the thighs and the loin with the arms.

26.3-4. «Tittibhasana III» standing on straight legs, deeply bending the body forward to draw in between the legs, hugging the thighs and the loin with the arms with the head almost touching the buttocks.

27.1-2. «Paschimottanasana» — sitting on the floor with legs kept straight, the body deeply bent forward.

27.2-3. «Supta Kurmasana» — lying on the abdomen, both legs behind the head, hugging the thighs and the loin with the arms.

27.3-4. «Supta Kandasana» — lying on the abdomen with both feet under the armpits of the same side arms.

28.1-2. «Ubhaya Padangusthasana» — balance sitting on the buttocks, the legs kept straight and the body deeply inclined forward and folded in the vertical plane.

28.2-3. «Utthita Kurmasana» — standing on the hands, the spine kept vertical and both legs behind the head.

28.3-4. «Utthita Kandasana» — standing on the hands, the spine kept vertical and both feet under the armpits of same side arms.

29.1-2. «Urdhva Mukha Paschimottanasana» — lying on the back, the legs kept straight and pressed against the chest.

29.2-3. «Yoga Nidrasana» — lying on the back with both legs behind the head, the arms hugging the thighs and the loin.

29.3-4. «Supta Kandasana» — lying on the back with both feet under the armpits of the same side arms, the palms gripping the knees.

30.1-2. «Dhanurasana» — back arch lying on the abdomen, the same side ankles gripped by the hands and drawn down and backward.

30.2-3. «Padangustha Dhanurasana» — back arch lying on the abdomen, the same side ankles gripped by the hands and drawn upward and backward.

30.3-4. «Padangustha Dhanurasana» — back arch lying on the abdomen, the toes gripping the chin and the arms drawn to the sides.

31.1-2. «Ustrasana» — back arch standing on the knees and the feet, gripping the same side ankles with the hands to draw down and backward.

31.2-3. «Kapotasana» — back arch standing on the knees and the feet, the same side ankles gripped with the hands to draw upward and backward to make the head lay on the feet.

31.3-4. «Laghuvajrasana» — back arch standing on the knees and feet, the palms gripping the same side knees and the head raised to the buttocks.

32.1-2. «Viparita Dhanurasana» — back arch standing on the shoulders, back of the head and feet. The arms are gripping the same side ankles.

32.2-3. «Chakra Bandhasana I» — back arch standing on the forearms and the feet. The arms are gripping the same side knees and the head is raised to the buttocks.

32.3-4. «Chakra Bandhasana II» — back arch standing on the shoulders, elbows, and feet. The arms are gripping the same side knees and the head is raised to the buttocks.

33.1-2. «Ganda Bherundasana I» — back arch standing on the chin, shoulders and palms.

33.2-3. «Ganda Bherundasana II» — back arch standing on the chin, shoulders and feet. The hands of bent arms are gripping the same side feet.

33.3-4. «Padma Ganda Bherundasana» — back arch standing on the chin, shoulders and knees with legs folded in Lotus. Grip the same side knees with the hands of bent arms.

34.1-2. «Bhujangasana» — back arch lying on straight legs supporting the body on straight arms.

34.2-3. «Raja Kapotanasana I» — back arch lying on the thighs of bent legs with the feet placed on the head. The body is supported on straight arms.

34.3-4. «Raja Kapotanasana II» — back arch lying on the thighs of bent legs with the feet placed on the back between the shoulder blades. The body is supported on straight arms.

35.1-2. «Urdhva Dhamurasana» — back arch standing on the legs, the hands drawn down and backward gripping the same side knees.

35.2-3. «Tiriang Mukhottanasana I» — back arch standing on the legs, the hands drawn upward and back gripping the same side ankles.

35.3-4. «Tiriang Mukhottanasana II» — back arch standing on the legs, the hands drawn down and back gripping the same side knees. Place the neck between the legs and the head in front of the thighs.

36.1-2. «Dhanurasana» — back arch lying on the thighs, the hands drawn down and back gripping same side knees.

36.2-3. «Bhujangasana» — back bend lying on straight legs, the same side knees gripped with the hands drawn down and backward.

36.3-4. «Bhuja Tiriang Mukhottanasana» — back arch lying on straight legs, the hands, drawn up and back, gripping the same side ankles.

37.1-2. «Eka Pada Raja Kapotasana II» — back arch standing in longitudinal pass on the foot of the front leg and the knee of the back leg. The foot of the back leg is gripped with the hands drawn down and back.

37.2-3. «Eka Pada Raja Kapotasana II» — back arch standing in longitudinal pass on the foot of the front leg and the knee of the back leg. The foot of the back leg is gripped with the hands drawn up and back and the foot placed on the head.

37.3-4. «Eka Pada Raja Kapotasana II» — back arch standing in longitudinal pass on the foot of the front leg and the knee of the back leg. The foot of the back leg placed on the back between the shoulder blades, the arms dropped down and the palms placed on the floor.

38.1-2. «Eka Pada Raja Kapotasana IV» — back arch standing in an incomplete longitudinal split on the heel of the front leg and the knee of the bent leg. The arms dropped down and the palms placed on the floor.

38.2-3. «Eka Pada Raja Kapotasana IV» — back arch sitting in a complete longitudinal split. The foot of the back leg is gripped with the hands, drawn up and back, and the foot placed on the head.

38.3-4. «Eka Pada Raja Kapotasana IV» — back arch sitting in a complete longitudinal split. The foot of the back leg is placed on the back between the shoulder blades, the arms dropped down and the palms placed on the floor.

39.1-2. «Natarajasana I» — back arch standing on one leg. The ankle of the second leg, drawn back and up, is gripped by both hands, drawn down and back.

39.2-3. «Natarajasana II» — back arch standing on one leg. The foot of the second leg, drawn back and up, is gripped by both hands, drawn up and back, the foot placed on the head.

39.3-4. «Natarajasana III» — back arch standing on one leg, the knee of the second leg, drawn back and up, is gripped by both hands, drawn up and back.

40.1-2. «Eka Pada Viparita Dhanurasana» — back arch standing on the shoulders, back of the head and the foot of one leg. The ankle of this leg is gripped with the hands of both arms. The second straight leg is raised vertically.

40.2-3. «Eka Pada Urdhva Dhanurasana» — back arch standing on the palms of straight arms and the foot of one leg. The other leg is straight and raised vertically.

40.3-4. «Eka Pada Tiriang Mukhottanasana» — back arch standing on the foot of one leg. The ankle of this leg is gripped with the hands of both arms. The second leg is kept straight and raised vertically in a longitudinal split.

Presently Andrew Lappa is a president of the Kyiv Yoga Federation (Ukraine) (www: yoga.com.ua and yoga.com.ua/lappa). He conducts regular practical classes at his privat training centers, located at the following addresses:

1. Ukrane, Kyiv, metro station «Arsenalna», 22 Sichnevoho povstania St. tel.: (380-044) 290-85-10

2. Ukrane, Kyiv, metro station «Klovskaya», 13-A Pechersky spusk St. tel.: (044) 290-81-86

Forms of lessons: individual and group training.

Complexity levels: beginners, advanced and intensive.

He also conducts regular seminars and intensive training classes (3 — 14 days) in Kyiv, Moskaw, Crimea and other cities and resort areas of the CIS, in nature places, etc.

Video materials on the theory and practice of Yoga:

- Training and methodology materials and demonstration tapes of standard sequences of Yoga and Dance of Shiva;
- Practice in the free flow mode;
- Demonstration performances by Masters;
- Video records of lessons, seminars and lectures.

Training and methodology publication

by Andrew LAPPA
YOGA: TRADITION OF UNIFICATION

Russian editor:
A. Kostenko

Engtlish editor:
M. Pollard

Engtlish corrector:
A. McAlen

Typeset:
V. Virich

Photo:
A. Lappa

Submitted for typesetting: 10.05.2000.
Format: 84x108/32. Offset paper. Circulation 1000.